DEVON AND CORNWALL RECORD SOCIETY

New Series

Volume 66

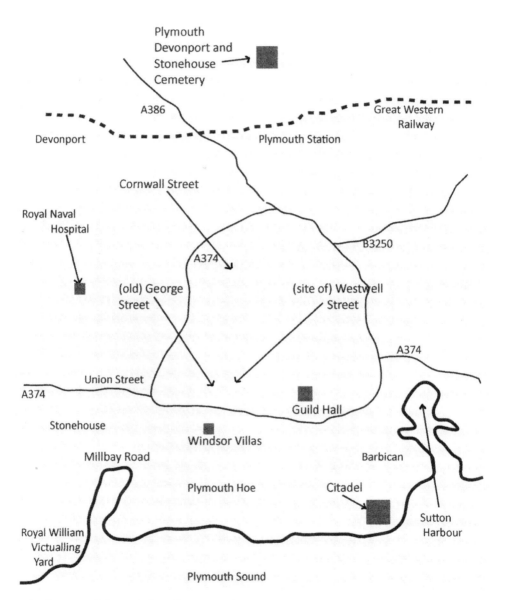

Plymouth Devonport and Stonehouse Cemetery

A386

Great Western Railway

Devonport

Plymouth Station

Cornwall Street

Royal Naval Hospital

B3250

A374

(old) George Street

(site of) Westwell Street

A374

Union Street

A374

Guild Hall

Stonehouse

Windsor Villas

Barbican

Millbay Road

Plymouth Hoe

Citadel

Royal William Victualling Yard

Sutton Harbour

Plymouth Sound

Indicative map of Plymouth (Dee Tracey, 2023).

THE MEMOIR OF JOHN BUTTER

Surgeon, Militiaman, Sportsman and Founder
of the Plymouth Royal Eye Infirmary

Edited by
Dee and Mike Tracey

DEVON AND CORNWALL RECORD SOCIETY

THE BOYDELL PRESS

First published 2023

A publication of the
Devon and Cornwall Record Society
published by The Boydell Press
an imprint of Boydell & Brewer Ltd
PO Box 9, Woodbridge, Suffolk IP12 3DF, UK
and of Boydell & Brewer Inc.
668 Mt Hope Avenue, Rochester, NY 14620–2731, USA
website: www.boydellandbrewer.com

ISBN   978 0 90185 317 2

Series information is printed at the back of this volume

A CIP catalogue record for this book is available
from the British Library

The publisher has no responsibility for the continued existence or accuracy
of URLs for external or third-party internet websites referred to in this book,
and does not guarantee that any content on such websites is,
or will remain, accurate or appropriate

This publication is printed on acid-free paper

The Devon and Cornwall Record Society is very grateful to the following people, who donated generously towards the publication costs of this book.

Patrons
Jonathan Barry
Richard Batten
Murray Burring
Judith Cannell
Peter Cowell
Sheila Harding
Richard Moyse
Dee and Mike Tracey
Dr Stuart A. Windsor
One other patron has chosen to remain anonymous.

Supporters
John Allan
Gillian Badcock
Christine and Rab Barnard
Ann and Roger Claxton
David Dance
Paul Graham
Tom Greeves
John Maddicott
Elizabeth Parkinson
John Pitts
Margaret A. Rice
Brendon Sparks
Mark Stoyle
Jill Strobridge
John Wade
Tess Walker
W. J. Yeoman
One other supporter has chosen to remain anonymous.

Contents

List of Illustrations   viii

Acknowledgements   ix

List of Abbreviations   x

Editorial Method   xi

Introduction   I
  General Introduction   I
  John Butter   4
  Butter and Early Nineteenth-Century Medicine   10
  South Devon Militia   22
  Butter's Plymouth   27
  The Plymouth Royal Eye Infirmary   34

The Memoir   47

Appendices
  1. List of Names   201
  2. Medical Glossary   212

Bibliography   216

Index   221

ILLUSTRATIONS

Frontispiece: Indicative map of Plymouth (Dee Tracey, 2023).

1.   Front cover of volume one of the Memoir (Dee Tracey, 2023).   xii

2.   Inside of the front cover of volume one of the Memoir (Dee Tracey, 2023).   2

3.   An example of the two different styles of handwriting employed in the Memoir (Dee Tracey, 2023).   3

4.   Higher Venmore, Woodbury, East Devon (Dee Tracey, 2023).   5

5.   The Butter/Ashford family tree (Dee Tracey, 2023).   6

6.   7 Windsor Villas, Plymouth (Sheila Harding, date unknown).   9

7.   The Butter family vault in Ford Park Cemetery, Plymouth (Dee Tracey, 2022).   10

8.   John Abernethy, c.1820 (mezzotint after Sir Thomas Lawrence). Reproduced by kind permission of the Wellcome Collection.   12

9.   René Laénnec, 1826, from R. T. H. Laénnec, *Traité de l'auscultation médiate et des maladies des poumons et du coeur* (Paris, 1826). Reproduced by kind permission of the Wellcome Collection.   16

10.   One of Laénnec's early stethoscopes, c.1820. Reproduced by kind permission of The Science Museum Group, London.   17

Acknowledgements

We are very grateful to Sheila Harding, Butter's great-great-great-niece, who first made us aware of the existence of the Memoir and then allowed us to utilise it for an extended period. We are grateful also to her late father, Christopher Ashford (Coroner for Exeter and East Devon) and two friends of his, Kenneth Rowe (Pro-Chancellor of Exeter University and Mayor of Exeter) and Patrick Russell (a consultant obstetrician and gynaecologist), who first transcribed the Memoir many years ago, and whose work formed the basis of the digitisation exercise undertaken by Dee Tracey. Sheila also helped us considerably in compiling the family tree.

The staff of the Devon Heritage Centre were extremely helpful, as were Claire Skinner at The Box in Plymouth, and Graham Naylor and his colleagues at Plymouth Central Library.

Roger Hamling worked wonders improving the quality of some of the illustrations, and he and his wife Liz were endlessly patient in resolving IT and other problems.

Jonathan Barry read the entire text and gave us much valuable assistance, particularly in the realm of medical history.

Our editor, Professor Catherine Rider, provided helpful advice along the way and invaluable assistance with the production process. We are very grateful to her and to the D&CRS trustees for agreeing to publish the Memoir, which would not otherwise be in the public domain.

ABBREVIATIONS

DHC	Devon Heritage Centre
FLS	Fellow of the Linnean Society
FRS	Fellow of the Royal Society
FRCS	Fellow of the Royal College of Surgeons
L&NW	London and North Western (railway)
MD	Doctor of medicine
MRCS	Member of the Royal College of Surgeons
NHS	National Health Service
ODNB	Oxford Dictionary of National Biography
OED	The Shorter Oxford English Dictionary
P&O	Peninsular and Oriental Steam Navigation Company
RM	Royal Marine
SDM	South Devon Militia
SD Railway	South Devon Railway

EDITORIAL METHOD

The first part of the Memoir is written in the third person, which is at times confusing, although, for no obvious reason, it changes to the first person near the beginning of volume five. For the sake of clarity, transcription is in the first person throughout. Legibility is relatively good, but there are instances, particularly with names and medical terms, where the meaning is not absolutely clear, and these are indicated where appropriate. Some year-headings are included in the original, and the missing ones have been added.

The original text contains few paragraphs, no quotation marks and very little punctuation. For ease of reading, the first have been added generally, the second wherever required, and the third as often as needed to clarify meaning and/or to facilitate reading. Where punctuation does appear in the original, it has been retained unless clearly inappropriate. Similarly, the original spellings have been retained without comment, except where they could be misleading. A few instances of obvious repetition have been omitted, as have occasional sections of rambling discourse that add little to the narrative flow; the gaps have been indicated in the text.

Asterisks* have been used to denote appearances in the List of Names. Every appearance of a particular name has been so indicated, other than where it has already appeared in the same paragraph.

Terms appearing in the Medical Glossary have been denoted thus,+ again on every occasion other than a second appearance in the same paragraph. Terms that are explained in the text have not been included.

Square brackets [1838] have been used throughout the text to indicate the date of quotations taken from the Memoir.

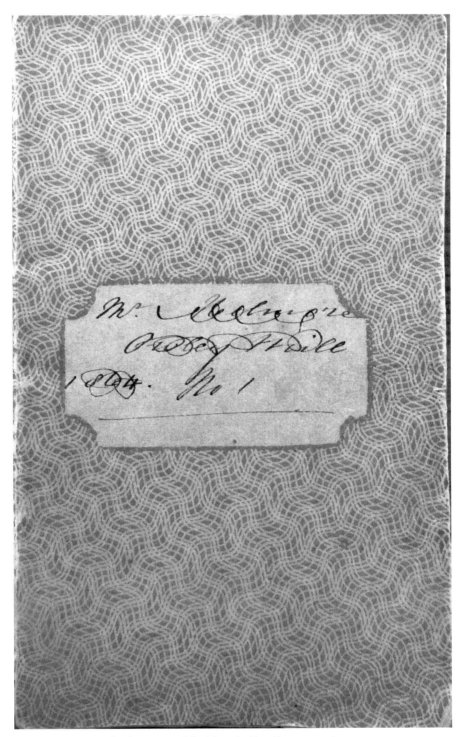

Fig. 1. Front cover of volume one of the Memoir (Dee Tracey, 2023).

INTRODUCTION

General Introduction

The Memoir is essentially John Butter's life story, from his birth in Woodbury, Devon, in 1791, to the middle of 1853, shortly before he went blind. He died in Plymouth in 1877. Why he wrote, and for whom, is not clear, although, in describing a device for removing fishhooks from the throats of careless anglers [1820], he does write that 'this notice may be useful to others', and there are several other apparent indicators of an intention to publish. Apart from fishhook removal, he gives many valuable insights into

- the history of medicine and of medical education, in pursuit of which he spent time in London, on the continent, and in Edinburgh, where he was responsible for the introduction of the stethoscope to Scotland;
- the foundation and growth of the Plymouth Royal Eye Infirmary;
- his experiences with the South Devon Militia, particularly during its acquaintance with the Luddites;
- his life as a physician and a surgeon;
- his travelling, both at home and on the continent;
- his love of hunting and game-shooting;
- his social life in and beyond Plymouth; and
- his ventures into the property market.

The Memoir is written in nineteen notebooks, 3¾ x 6¼ inches in size. They are virtually identical, except that volumes one to three have pale orange covers (and, on the front, somebody else's illegible name crossed-through), volume five is blue and the rest green. All except volume five, which is blank, have a calendar for 1854 inside the back cover, and an almanack for the same year inside the front. So far, so good, but the very first entry is an apparently arbitrary and isolated date, '12 December 1865'. The situation is further confused by the fact that volumes one and two have the date 1864 inscribed on their front covers as, presumably, the time at which they were written. Volume three is dated 1864/5, volumes five to seven 1866, and all the others are undated. What happened? Did Butter suddenly come across a cache of ten-year-old books? Had he bought them in order to write his life story, and then not got around to it before he went blind? Why does the first of the 1864 books start with a date right at the end of 1865? When were the undated volumes written?

What we do know is that the books are written in ink, in two distinctly different hands, and completely filled from first page to last. The last instalment ends abruptly, and it seems probable that there was originally a twentieth, and presumably final, volume. Some of the outer covers have become loose and have separated, but all the books remain in otherwise good condition. They have been passed down through the Ashford family (Butter's sister Catherine married James Ashford) to their present owner Mrs Sheila Harding, great-great-great-niece of John Butter.

Butter dictated the Memoir when he was blind, relatively late in life, and this complicates matters. The overall accuracy of the narrative seems to be pretty good,

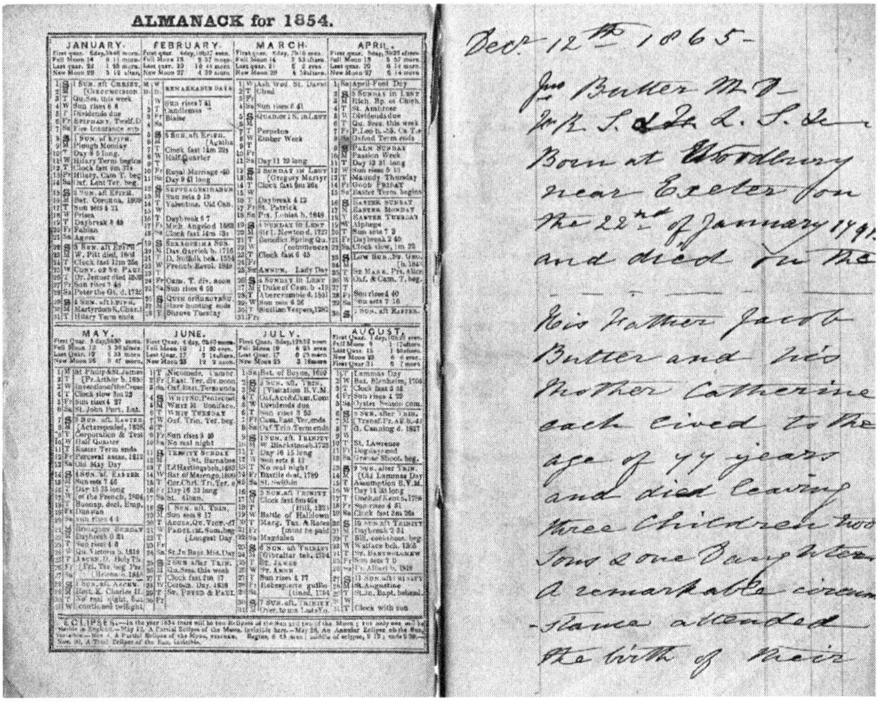

Fig. 2. Inside of the front cover of volume one of the Memoir (Dee Tracey, 2023).

but there are a number of apparent mistakes, which have been indicated in the transcription. Where did they come from? Did the scribes mishear what he said, or did Butter's memory fail him? He twice makes mention of a journal that he had kept, but for how long and how comprehensively is not known. Given the fine detail of dates that appears in many places, it seems probable that it was a lifelong affair and that he used it as an aide-memoire, although, if so, the years 1827–31 were presumably lost, as the Memoir entries for that period are vanishingly short. The journal was presumably read to him in order to jog his memory, but whether or not the resultant text was then read back to him for confirmation and approval is another matter. One might have expected him to pick up on a number of what are clearly transcription errors, but the only notable amendments to the text are in 1817 and 1835, when, in each case, a sheet of paper containing further information has been inserted into the relevant volume, and in 1847, when a newspaper cutting has been added. It is just possible that the volumes we now have constitute a fair copy, completed after any amendments had been made, but the considerable extra work involved would hardly have been justified. It is not known who were the scribes, and it could not have been easy work. What little punctuation they did use was decidedly arbitrary, they were inconsistent spellers, and it seems highly unlikely that they were medical men. They did, however, write as legibly as one could reasonably hope, and that in itself is something for which to be grateful.

Trying to analyse Butter's character is not easy, given that he was writing with the benefit of hindsight and was, doubtless, conscious of how he was portraying himself.

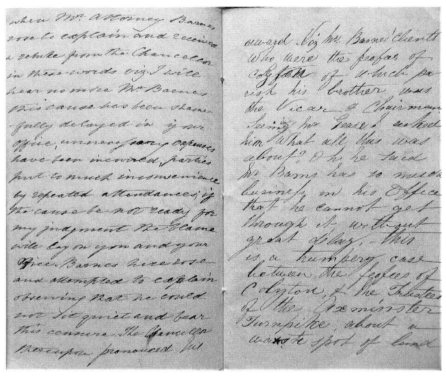

Fig. 3. An example of the two different styles of handwriting employed in the Memoir (Dee Tracey, 2023).

It is clear that he had plenty of confidence in his own ability, and he was rarely slow to point out where he had succeeded after others had failed. He did, however, report a number of his own failures, and his tone could not be described as unduly boastful. He certainly made every effort to maximise his medical education, both at home and abroad, and he does seem to have been a skilful and adaptable surgeon, very receptive to new ideas and with a markedly greater success rate than many of his contemporaries. He was devoted to blood-letting, as were all surgeons at the time (other, seemingly, than those domiciled in Bath [1822 et al.]), but not slavishly so, and neither was he hidebound by tradition, as indicated by, for instance, his enthusiasm for the long splint and his denunciation of the use of mercury to combat syphilis. He did rather abandon the stethoscope, but he was nearing the end of the hospital phase of his career before he brought it into the country, so he lacked the opportunity to develop any knowledge and appreciation of its true capabilities.

On a personal basis, he does seem to have had a clear idea of his social status, although he did not go out of his way to trumpet it – his reference to having been in correspondence with the Queen's physician about a wet-nurse for the Prince of Wales, for instance, is very casual [2.11.1841]. That said, his equally passing reference to Joseph Paxton's achievements at the Great Exhibition is decidedly patronising [14.7.1851]. He was also not above letting a social equal get away with rape [17.7.1845], albeit making quite clear his disgust, but in general he does seem to have had a social conscience, as well as a marked sense of duty, together with the determination, skill and vision required to put them into effect. He probably treated more of the poor and humble than many of his fellow-practitioners, although it must be said that a large proportion of them were while he was with, and being paid by, the South Devon Militia (SDM). There were quite a few other instances, such as the Ougier family [8.3.1852], but the practicalities of business dictated that his patients should normally be able to pay their way. Much charitable work was, of course, done by the Eye Infirmary, and, although it had its own surgeons, Butter almost certainly did operations there, and he must have given a great deal of time and expertise in his role as Physician, quite apart from the endless hours devoted to the running of the organisation. If he had never done anything else, the Infirmary alone would constitute a legacy to be proud of.

John Butter

Butter's private life does not form so integral a part of his Memoir as might be expected. Apart from late nights with the SDM, and a lifelong passion for field sports, he tells us relatively little about the things and people closest to him. We hear more about his affection for his great-aunt in Bath than we do about his feelings for his wife – their marriage was childless, but there is no indication that it was anything other than happy, and in all probability he just wanted to keep private things private. It is, nevertheless, possible to fill in quite a bit of background.

John Butter was born at Cooks Venmore Farm, later known as Higher Venmore, in Woodbury, East Devon, on 22 January 1791. His parents were Jacob Butter (1760–1838) and Catherine Farr (1760–1837). Catherine is easily identifiable: she was baptised on 4 July 1760 in East Budleigh, the only child of Samuel Farr and Joyce, née Turnock. Jacob's origins, however, are less clear and are not helped by his son's somewhat cavalier attitude to his forebears. On the first page of the Memoir, John clearly conflates two generations, claiming to have 'had seven grandfathers and grandmothers all living at my birth'. On the same page, however, he refers to his father's 'grandfather Langdon', who was the father of John's paternal grandmother, and this provides the necessary clarification. The Butter and Langdon families had been connected for a very long time: in 1611, Philip Butter had married Agnes Langdon in the Exmoor village of Wootton Courtenay, and the connection was still strong in 1801, when John's uncle James married Mary Langdon at Milton Abbas, in Dorset.

We know that Jacob's father was also named Jacob, and that a Jacob Butter married Mary Langdon (thus providing the required 'paternal grandmother Langdon') in Tolpuddle, Dorset, on 6 November 1759. There was a significant Langdon presence in the area, but there were no Mary Langdons born there between 1720 and 1745, nor, for that matter, any Jacob Butters, so both parties to the marriage must have been incomers. Jacob junior was baptised in Tolpuddle on 15 December 1760,[1] so there can be little doubt that we have the correct family, although why two people with established roots in Woodbury should have married in Tolpuddle must remain a mystery.

Mary Langdon had been baptised in Woodbury on 18 October 1732, probably by her grandfather Gilbert, who was the Vicar. Mary's father, also a Gilbert, had, at the

---

[1] www.familysearch.org

Fig. 4. Higher Venmore, Woodbury, East Devon (Dee Tracey, 2023).

age of fourteen, been apprenticed to a cheirosurgeon[2] in Bovey Tracey, which cost Gilbert senior a fee of £21. Gilbert junior served his apprenticeship, married Mary Holwill, the cousin of a distinguished Exeter doctor, and practised in Woodbury until his death in 1791. Jacob senior and the former Mary Langdon eventually settled at Higher Venmore Farm, where it is reasonable to assume that Jacob made his living as a farmer. Jacob junior, however, was apprenticed to his grandfather Gilbert, whose practice he eventually took over, using the farm as his base; there is reputedly still a 'surgery' sign over one of the doors there. The farm and, indeed, a large proportion of the parish was part of the Rolle estate; Lord Rolle* was one of Jacob's patients and was, in due course, responsible for John's appointment to the SDM.

Jacob and Catherine had six children, of whom John was the eldest. John's younger brother Jacobus, born in 1793, also became a doctor and initially practised in Lympstone, before taking over in Woodbury after his father died in 1838, when he might have felt a little hurt that a newspaper obituary recorded Jacob specifically as 'the father of Dr Butter, of Plymouth'. It went on to say that 'he practised the medical profession for nearly 60 years, with great credit to himself and satisfaction to the public. He was respected by the rich, and beloved by the poor for kindness and attention in sickness, and for the relief he afforded to their wants and afflictions.'[3] Jacobus did not marry, and his tenure at Woodbury lasted only eight years, as he died of dropsy[+] in May 1846, after which the practice passed out of the family.

---

[2] There is no very satisfactory definition of a cheirosurgeon, but it is probably a corruption of 'chirurgeon', a variant of the French word for 'surgeon' (*chirurgien*), which was commonly used in this country.

[3] *Western Times*, 16.6.1838.

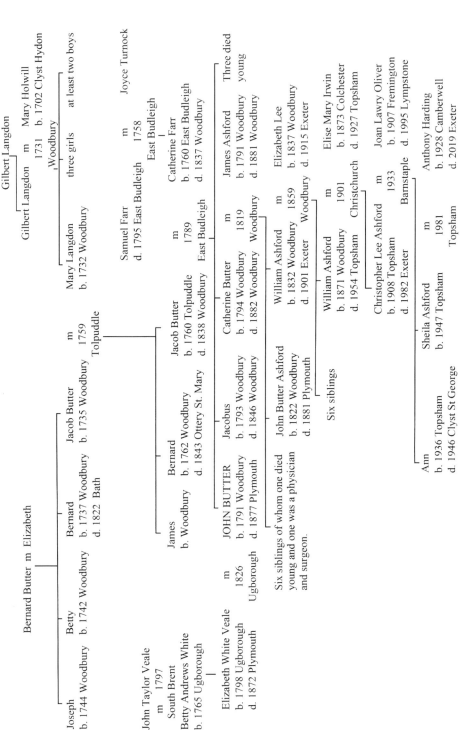

Fig. 5. The Butter/Ashford family tree (Dee Tracey, 2023).

Catherine, the third child of Jacob and Catherine, was the last to survive, the three subsequent children all dying at a young age. She married James Ashford in October 1819. James was a yeoman farmer living at Venmore Farm, next door to Higher Venmore, which Catherine inherited when her brother died. She and James had eight children, one of whom died young, but three continued in the medical profession. The oldest, John Butter Ashford, born in May 1822, was apprenticed to his uncle John and was living at, and inherited, 7 Windsor Villas, Plymouth, when Butter died in 1877. He himself died there barely four years later, aged fifty-eight, on 18 March 1881.

John and Jacobus received a classical education at Exeter Grammar School under the Rev. Bartholomew [1808].[4] John left when he was sixteen, although in later life he became a Steward (governor) and was elected their Chairman in 1826. He had a large number of acquaintances and belonged to more than twenty different societies. Around half were medical in one way or another, including two Royal Colleges (Surgeons in London and Physicians in Edinburgh), and he was also a Fellow of the Royal Society.[5] His interests were wide-ranging, including natural history, which led to his becoming one of the longest-standing members of the Linnean Society, and he was also a member of the Wernerian Society, to whom he twice talked on 'the change of plumage exhibited by many species of female birds, at an advanced period of life …'[6] In addition to this, he 'gave two lectures on Natural History, and one on Comparative Anatomy at the Plymouth Athenaeum' [1816], he was a patron of the Royal Western Yacht Club,[7] and in 1863 he was treasurer of the West of England Institution for the Deaf and Dumb. His standing in the local community was further demonstrated by his becoming a magistrate [1822], and by his election as a Freeman of the City of Plymouth in 1832.

Butter's loss of sight, which dominated his later life, is mentioned only once in the Memoir, as early as 1817: 'I never dreamt myself of becoming blind. The Almighty however decreed otherwise, in my 64th year', which was some thirty-seven years later. There is no other suggestion that his sight had been failing, and he had continued to treat patients until at least May 1853, when the Memoir ends. Thereafter, he worked as a consultant at the Eye Infirmary until just before he died in 1877. He does not mention how everyday life must have been affected, although neither of his great passions, hunting and shooting, is referred to after 1847 – possibly by then his eyesight was too bad for him to be able to safely enjoy potentially dangerous sports.

Apart from the early years of studying and travelling, when he was generally fairly hard-up, Butter's standard of living was rarely less than comfortable. In due course, he became very wealthy, helped by a couple of generous legacies. In 1826, his great-aunt (his great-uncle Bernard's widow[8]) left him £8,900 net of duty. Twelve

---

[4] What is now Exeter School was founded in 1633 as the Exeter Free Grammar School and installed in the medieval buildings of St John's Hospital, with funding from Exeter's wealthy merchants. Rev. Bartholomew became master in 1793 when there were, on average, forty day boys and fifty boarders (www.exeterschool.org.uk).
[5] *Medical Times & Gazette*, 10.3.1887, p. 275.
[6] *Memoirs of the Wernerian Natural History Society: Vol. 3, for the Years 1817–18–19–20* (Edinburgh: Archibald Constable & Co., 1821), pp. 183–206.
[7] *Exeter and Plymouth Gazette*, 1.11.1836.
[8] Her name was Elizabeth, but it is never mentioned in the text. Her husband and son were both Bernard, but they are referred to throughout as Barnard.

years later, his father died, and he and his two siblings were each left £1,000, whilst Butter inherited substantial estates in Axmouth, Musbury and Colyton, as well as property in Woodbury. The 1826 windfall was particularly welcome, as in May of that year, in the course of what he described as 'the most important ... year of my life', Butter married Elizabeth White Veale, who was born in 1798 and seems to have been the only child of John and Betty Veale. This meant that she inherited land in Ugborough when her father died, to add to that she had already inherited from her grandfather. Butter bought more land in the area, so that by 1839 he owned 858 acres in South Brent and Ugborough, occupying seventy-five acres of this himself and having tenants on the rest. He was also joint owner of a further forty acres. By 1873, his holdings in the South Brent area had reached 984 acres with an estimated gross rental of £1,064 5s. Nor was it just land: at the Brent Fair of 1869, he sold 'Fat Cattle ... viz: 6 prime fat steers, 6 fat heifers, 17 fat wethers, 17 ewes, 6 lambs also a handsome brown colt, rising three years old, calculated for a Hunter Sale.'[9] He talks in the Memoir [1832] about 'my farm', but it seems very unlikely that he did any hands-on farming.

In 1820, Butter bought his first home, in what was then fashionable George Street, Plymouth, where Lord St Vincent (First Lord of the Admiralty and instigator of the Plymouth Breakwater) had an official residence. He foresaw 'that George Street would become a great thoroughfare on the completion of the Union Road to Stonehouse dock'. He was perhaps happiest, however, at the rather remote Owley Cottage, a two-up, two-down moorland cottage near Wrangaton in the parish of South Brent. The Memoir entries about Owley are somewhat confusing, as he asserts that he first slept there in 1833, but that Elizabeth did not do so until 1841. In 1842, however, he reveals that they owned more than one cottage in the area, renting out the others, so they had presumably moved their second home from one to another. They had certainly been making annual excursions to the moor ever since 1832, when, suffering from rheumatic fever, Butter was desperate to get away, 'so loathsome was the contaminated air of Plymouth'. Ever afterwards, he justified their trips on the basis that 'health was always preferable to wealth' [1832]. That did not, however, prevent his final move, in 1842, to 7 Windsor Villas in Lockyer Street, designed by John Foulston. The building lies within the Hoe Conservation Area and is now Grade II listed. The Memoir records that the property cost him the sizeable sum of £2,213 7s 3d, albeit including £200 for a new stable. It records also that his reason for moving was to avoid having 'to give up Society', indicating the major part that the social scene undoubtedly played in his life.

Butter does seem to have been occasionally a little naive. In 1836, as executor of George Hunt's will, he endured such a nightmare that he swore never to get so involved again, but he did – several times! His other problem was with politics, of which he generally steered well clear. His one notable, and potentially disastrous, involvement came in the 1852 Parliamentary election. Somewhat unwisely, he allowed himself to be cajoled into chairing the campaign of Charles John Mare,* a wealthy Londoner. Mare campaigned as a Protestant and a shipowner with a desire to correct the 'lamentable neglect' of the port facilities. To general surprise, he was elected at the head of the poll but never took his seat as he was found guilty of substantial bribery. Butter seems to have had no inkling of this and was not

---

9 *Western Times*, 24.7.1869.

Fig. 6. 7 Windsor Villas, Plymouth (Sheila Harding, date unknown).

summoned to the House of Commons hearing into the matter. Indeed, 'the leading barrister complimented me on my speech at the [hustings] meetings and said he had no complaint to make against me bar my vituperation of lawyers'. It is, however, rather strange that in the evening after the hearing Butter drank with Mare at his house and the next day was his guest at 'the launch of the most magnificent ship in the world'[10] [1853] and at the subsequent excessively ostentatious banquet. Butter was quite open about this, and clearly saw no wrong in it, but it does, nevertheless, constitute a strange little footnote to his story.

He died at home in Windsor Villas on 13 January 1877, a little more than four years after Elizabeth. In accordance with his wishes, he was buried in his wife's vault at the Plymouth Devonport and Stonehouse Cemetery,[11] and his name was added to her tombstone. The terms of his will initially named Elizabeth as sole executrix and divided his estate between her and his nephews and nieces, with a small number of other bequests, including Elizabeth's right to pew number seventy-seven in the Episcopal church of St Andrew in Plymouth. Subsequent codicils do not specifically mention Elizabeth's death, but in 1874 John's nephew, James Ashford, was

[10] The *Himalaya* at Mare's Blackwell site on the Thames. Weighing 3,438 tons, she was built for P&O and was said at the time to have been the biggest ship ever constructed.

[11] Now Ford Park Cemetery.

Fig. 7. The Butter family vault in Ford Park Cemetery, Plymouth (Dee Tracey, 2022).

appointed sole executor, with a further and final codicil appointing Charles Edwin Ashford and William Ashford as joint executors should James die before John. The total value of the estate was a very substantial £53,691 13s 10d.

Butter and Early Nineteenth-Century Medicine

It was perhaps inevitable that both John and his brother Jacobus should have followed their father into the medical profession. John seems to have shown promise at an early age, when his father, unable to gain any other relief, allowed him to carry out his first 'operation' – a tooth extraction: 'necessity obliged him to instruct a Schoolboy in the art of using a German Key[+] ... so much to his ease and comfort that it induced him to present me with my first fee'. At the age of sixteen, Butter treated a local village lad suffering from ringworm [1807], and within two years he was undertaking six months' residential medical training at the Devon and Exeter Hospital,[12] although he does not mention to whom, or even if, he was apprenticed.

---

[12] The Devon and Exeter Hospital was built on a former tilt-yard in Southernhay and opened to the public in 1743. Within five years, it had a hundred beds, with patients looked after by eight nurses, six physicians, five surgeons and an apothecary. The regime was relaxed – until the 1830s, patients were allowed to come and go as they pleased during the day, so long as they did not return drunk and they helped with the domestic chores: feeding the pigs, pumping

Whilst still very young, although not unusually so for medical students at the time, he gained experience in treating the injuries and illnesses, including typhus and dysentery, of soldiers returning from the battle of Corunna[13] [1809].

Despite not being a graduate of Cambridge or Oxford, the normal means of becoming a pupil at one of the London hospitals, Butter was fortunate to have a letter of introduction from one of his father's patients and, on leaving Exeter, was accepted as a 'perpetual [i.e. full-time] pupil' of John Abernethy* at St Bartholomew's.[14] As a prerequisite to medical study, students were expected to be of good character and to have had a 'strong' education. Subjects studied had to include Latin (which was used extensively during lectures, for examinations and in medical papers), logic, physics and chemistry; others, such as Greek, German, mathematics, zoology and botany, were 'useful'.[15] St Bartholomew's is one of the two medical hospitals in the country that survived the Reformation (the other was St Thomas's, while a third 'hospital', Bethlem, was an asylum for the insane), and although many more were added from the 1700s onwards, it maintained a high status and reputation. Shortly after Butter left, the Apothecaries Act of 1815 required compulsory licensing and education for those who were, in effect, the GPs of their day, so that by 1841 Bart's had three hundred pupils.[16] There were many fewer when Butter was there, and when he was at Guy's, although there is a complete dearth of information about his time at the latter establishment.

Medical training involved very little practical work and was undertaken principally in the lecture theatre, by observing the surgeon on his ward rounds and by reading books and periodicals. The timetable of lectures at Bart's listed medicine, chemistry and materia medica[+] early in the morning; midwifery in mid-morning or late afternoon, anatomy at 1 or 2 p.m. and surgery at 7 or 8 p.m.[17] Butter's experience of ward rounds was more useful than that of most of his colleagues because Abernethy,* recognising his great promise, appointed him a dresser. Dressers were unqualified apprentices, but the post was granted only to outstanding pupils, who 'gained much sought-after experience by performing minor surgical tasks and seconding surgeons'.[18] The appointment was normally held for one year and usually had to be paid for by the student. Abernethy's regard for Butter is clear, not only

water and serving meals. Robert Dingwall et al., *An Introduction to the Social History of Nursing* (Abingdon: Routledge, 2002), p. 2.

[13] The battle of Corunna, which took place on 16 January 1809, was a rearguard action to hold off the French while British troops boarded ships for a seaborne evacuation. The evacuation succeeded, but only at the cost of French control of northern Spain.

[14] Founded in 1123, St Bartholomew's hospital has provided continuous patient care on the same site for longer than any other hospital in England. It began a major re-build in 1730 that was finally completed in 1769. The Governors approved the construction of a new lecture theatre in 1791, primarily to accommodate the popularity of the lectures given by John Abernethy.* Keir Waddington, *Medical Education at St. Bartholomew's Hospital, 1123–1995* (Woodbridge: The Boydell Press, 2002).

[15] Thomas Neville Bonner, *Becoming a Physician: Medical Education in Britain, France, Germany and the United States 1750–1845* (Baltimore and London: The Johns Hopkins University Press, 1995), p. 71.

[16] Roy Porter, *The Greatest Benefit to Mankind* (London: W. W. Norton & Company, 1997), pp. 298, 316–17.

[17] Florent Palluault, 'Medical Students in England and France 1815–1858, a Comparative Study' (Unpublished D.Phil Thesis, University of Oxford, 2003), p. 76.

[18] Ibid., p. 123.

Fig. 8. John Abernethy, c.1820 (mezzotint after Sir Thomas Lawrence). Reproduced by kind permission of the Wellcome Collection.

by virtue of this appointment, but by his remark when Butter applied to become a member of the Royal College of Surgeons:[19] 'If I was called upon to select any one pupil out of my class more likely than another to pass the examinations at Surgeon's Hall you are the person I would fix on' [1811].

Somewhere in a full day of lectures and ward rounds, time had to be found for the written word. Between 1794 and 1817, around 150 guidebooks for medical study were published in France, Germany and Great Britain.[20] There were also many papers written on a wide variety of subjects, published mostly in the monthly or annual transactions of a number of medical societies. Butter himself later produced several articles, including, for the *Edinburgh Medical and Surgical Journal* alone: 'Practical Observations on the Compression of Cancerous Breasts',[21] 'On the Poisonous Effects of Nitre'[22] and 'Observations upon the Action of Mercury in the Cure of Venereal Disease'. This last paper described the remedy as 'worse than the disease itself, having seen sailors who had been salivated times over and left with loss of teeth, rotten bones and ruined constitution' [1819].[23] He wrote also what he refers to as his 'Thesis de Ophthalmia' [1820], a forty-seven-page essay in Latin.[24]

The growth of medical libraries was important, not only to students but also to practising doctors. Hospitals had their own, but in 1818 Butter became a member of the Plymouth Medical Society, which had been founded in 1794 and whose library contained about four hundred volumes, having been the first to be set up in the region, and probably the first outside London; that at Exeter, for instance, was not formed until 1814.[25] Butter eventually went one stage further and, having started by purchasing a skeleton and books from his fellow-student Baker, built up a collection with which he later created his own small medical museum at his house in George Street.

Butter's training at Bart's continued during his early days as assistant surgeon to the SDM, thanks to Major Seale,* his Commanding Officer, who either granted him specific leave of absence or simply required him to muster only twice a month. His expertise in all manner of ailments became renowned both in the Militia and within the wider population wherever the Militia was based. He was obliged to set aside three days a week for the locals 'in order to prevent crowds of people from inter-rupting me from performing my medical duties at the Regimental Hospital' [1812]. Butter's treatment was free of charge, which inevitably meant that local doctors lost both patients and income, but their complaints went unheeded.

---

[19] Originally formed in 1540 as the College of Barber-Surgeons in the City of London. The surgeons moved away from the barbers by an Act of Parliament in 1745 and were granted their own charter as the Royal College of Surgeons in London in 1800. This was extended to cover the whole country in 1843 and the name changed to The Royal College of Surgeons of England, https://www.rcseng.ac.uk/about-the-rcs/history-of-the-rcs/

[20] Bonner, *Becoming a Physician,* p. 71.

[21] *Edinburgh Medical and Surgical Journal: Vol. 14* (October 1818), pp. 498–507.

[22] *Edinburgh Medical and Surgical Journal: Vol. 14* (January 1818), pp. 34–9.

[23] *Edinburgh Medical and Surgical Journal: Vol. 15* (April 1819), pp. 195–212.

[24] John Butter, *Disputatio Medica inauguralis, quaedam de ophthalmia complectens* (Edinburgh: P. Neill, 1820).

[25] Margaret Ivy Lattimore, 'The History of Libraries in Plymouth to 1914' (Unpublished PhD thesis, University of Plymouth, 1982), pp. 443, 445.

Having returned to Plymouth, the SDM was disembodied (stood down) in 1816, and Butter, no longer required for active service, soon tired of the town's decline and decided to undertake a tour of the continent. The Memoir does not specify that this was to study medicine, but it does record that at every opportunity he sought a medical environment, naming some of the hospitals he visited and the eminent doctors and other professional people he met.

The Paris School of Medicine's reputation for excellence encouraged the attendance of a large number of students from different countries, many of whom had no knowledge of the French language, making life difficult for all concerned. Butter, however, was well received – he had taught himself French before leaving England, although he needed practice in speaking it, and was fortunate to have friends who were able to be of assistance. A Mr Eastlake, for instance, helped him obtain an invitation to visit the Military Hospital from Baron Larrey,* the Chirurgien en Chef (chief surgeon) of the French army. A Monsieur Blainville[26] introduced him as a visitor to the National Institute of France, where he saw many of the most learned and distinguished men in the country. Butter was also able to attend Hôtel Dieu[27] in Paris, the oldest and, at that time, the most famous hospital in Europe. There he witnessed his first tonsillectomy, performed by the celebrated Professor Dupuytren.*

In Paris, Butter found a heavily regulated and unified structure very unlike the laissez-faire system operating at home.[28] Cadavers were used for dissection and medical education and were, in the early nineteenth century, considerably more plentiful in France than in England, where the price for legally acquired bodies was always very high. This made it difficult for many English students to afford one, and Butter was by no means unusual in being obliged, with two colleagues, to share the body purchased by their wealthier friend, Josias Baker. As only bodies of criminals were officially available, the shortage engendered a rise in the 'trade' of body-snatching – a gruesome but lucrative business. In 1825, for example, the going rate for a corpse in good condition was £9 11s 0d.[29] It was not until the Anatomy Act of 1832 that physicians, surgeons and medical students were given extended access to bodies, specifically of those who had died in hospital, in prison, in the workhouse, or who were donated by a next of kin in exchange for burial at the expense of the anatomy school.

On leaving Paris, Butter visited Italy, where he arranged to meet Professor Scarpa* and was also able to inspect

[26] Possibly Henri Marie Ducrotay de Blainville (1777–1850), a zoologist and anatomist and an associate of Georges Cuvier.*

[27] Founded by St Landry in 651 AD, initially to shelter the poor and homeless as well as the sick. From 1580, the hospital regulations specified that doctors and surgeons were to visit patients twice a week. During this period, it often housed more than 3,500 patients at any one time. Damaged by fire in 1772, it was not fully re-built until Napoleon's time. During the French revolution and the wars that followed, the huge number of wounded led to changes in medical practice. In 1785, the hospital established a formal training procedure, including both demonstrations and hands-on experience, and by 1795, as in England, hospitals were regarded as the principal institutions of medical training.

[28] Palluault, 'Medical Students', p. 19.

[29] Julia Bess Frank, 'Body Snatching: A Grave Medical Problem', *Yale Journal of Biology and Medicine* 49 (1976), p. 402.

the Florentine galleries of pictures, and cabinets of wax-works exhibiting the human body ... If I had never dissected a human body I might have learnt human anatomy here and not destroyed my health and risked my life as I had done ... at the foul dissecting room at St Bartholomew's Hospital. [1817]

The dissecting room at Bart's was indeed foul, and a veritable breeding ground for disease, in which respect, unfortunately, it differed only in degree from the rest of the hospital.

Butter returned to Paris on his way home and 'from 6 o'clock in the morning [hospital rounds commenced then during the summer, and at 7 a.m. in the winter] until midnight during these five days my time was fully occupied with study or pleasure' [1817].

Soon after his return from Europe, and no doubt inspired by the innovative medical procedures he had witnessed, Butter was, in 1817, eager to enrol at the renowned Edinburgh University medical school. The prospect of the long, arduous journey from Devon to Scotland was apparently no deterrent. The University had been founded in 1583, but the Faculty of Medicine did not gain formal recognition until 1726 and was based in temporary accommodation until 1741, when the purpose-built Royal Infirmary of Edinburgh was erected. By 1764, the number of medical students was so great that it became necessary to build a new two hundred-seat anatomy theatre, and throughout the nineteenth century the University maintained its place as one of the most prestigious in the medical world.[30] A long list of alumni includes Sir Arthur Conan Doyle (1859–1930), who devoted rather more of his time to writing than to medicine; Joseph Lister* (1827–1912), a pioneer of antiseptic surgery; James Young Simpson* (1811–70), the first physician to demonstrate the anaesthetic properties of chloroform; and Charles Darwin (1809–82), who found the lectures intolerably dull![31]

Butter brought back from his continental journey not only knowledge but a number of new procedures and inventions, one of which was the stethoscope.[32] It is known that in November 1817 he showed it to Andrew Duncan junior,* editor of the *Edinburgh Medical and Surgical Journal*,[33] which is one of only two records of

---

[30] Guenter B. Risse, *Hospital Life in Enlightenment Scotland: Care and Teaching at the Royal Infirmary of Edinburgh* (Cambridge: Cambridge University Press, 2010).

[31] Charles Darwin, *The Autobiography of Charles Darwin, 1809–1882*, ed. Nora Barlow (London: Collins, 1958), pp. 46–8.

[32] Invented in February 1816 by René Théophile Hyacinthe Laénnec*: 'I was consulted by a young woman labouring under general symptoms of diseased heart and in whose case percussion and the application of the hand were of little avail on account of the great degree of fatness ... I rolled a quire of paper into a kind of cylinder ... and was not a little surprised and pleased to find that I could thereby perceive the action of the heart in a manner much more clear and distinct than I had ever been able to do by the immediate application of the ear.' René Laénnec, *A Treatise on the Diseases of the Chest and on Mediate Auscultation – Translated, with Notes, Biography and Bibliography by Sir John Forbes* (New York: Samuel S. and William Wood, 1838), p. 6. The first stethoscopes were about 25 cm long and 3.5 cm in diameter. They were in two pieces that screwed together and had a detachable chest piece and earpiece. Some were made of brass, but Laénnec preferred wood, paper or Indian cane.

[33] Founded by Andrew Duncan senior,* *The Medical and Physical Philosophical Commentaries* was first published in 1773 as a quarterly journal of medicine – the first medical review journal to be published regularly in Great Britain. By 1775, it was being translated into German, and by the end of the decade it printed news from medical societies throughout Great Britain, France,

Fig. 9. René Laénnec, 1826, from R. T. H. Laénnec,
*Traité de l'auscultation médiate et des maladies des
poumons et du coeur* (Paris, 1826). Reproduced by kind
permission of the Wellcome Collection.

the stethoscope in Britain at that time. The other relates to Augustus B. Granville, who was present at the Necker Hospital on 13 September 1816 when René Laénnec* demonstrated his invention. It is possible that Laénnec, who was said to be 'remarkable for his great kindness and courtesy to foreigners, particularly the English',[34] presented each of them with an instrument, which they then took back to Britain almost simultaneously. The two men knew each other, and Butter records that they met in Paris 'for the last time' just before he returned home, implying that Granville was still in France when Butter became the first person to bring a stethoscope into England, although there seems little doubt that Granville was the first to use it here. Perhaps we could conclude that, in practical terms, Granville introduced it to England and Butter to Scotland. Whatever the exact sequence of events, it was a groundbreaking development, although few recognised it as such at the time.

The invention of a new medical instrument inevitably threw up the challenge of how best to apply it. Learning how to use the stethoscope to diagnose diseases of the chest had initially to be carried out in large hospitals where the number of patients made it easier to assess and compare the different sounds heard. This excluded many provincial surgeons and physicians, so that its use spread slowly in England, and many physicians viewed it with suspicion. Granville related that he used his stethoscope in his practice at Saville Row, but that most of his contemporaries to whom he exhibited and explained it 'made themselves merry at the credulity of French doctors

---

Denmark, Russia and America. In 1775, the name was changed to *Annals of Medicine*, and in 1804 it was discontinued in favour of the *Edinburgh Medical and Surgical Journal* edited by Andrew Duncan junior.*

[34] Laénnec, *A Treatise on the Diseases of the Chest and on Mediate Auscultation*, pp. xxvii–xxviii.

Fig. 10. One of Laénnec's early stethoscopes, c.1820. Reproduced by kind permission of The Science Museum Group, London.

and my own'.[35] Even John Forbes, its greatest English advocate, could understand the problems:

> I am ready and willing to concede that this difficulty of attaining a complete practical knowledge of Auscultation is one of the greatest drawbacks to its value; as it will ever prevent the indolent and careless from making themselves master of it. But I will venture to add, that no one who has once mastered its difficulties, and who cultivates his profession in that spirit which its high importance and dignity demand, will ever regret the pains taken to overcome them, or willingly forego the great advantages which he has thereby acquired.[36]

So far as can be established, the first published notice in Great Britain of Laénnec's* invention was based on Butter's instrument, when, in the *Edinburgh Medical and Surgical Journal* of November 1818, Dr Duncan* explained the basic facts of auscultation, albeit without using the word 'stethoscope'. Laénnec described the stethoscope's use as 'mediate auscultation', that is, listening with a tool interacting between the patient's body and the physician's ear. The second known notice, recorded in August 1819, and again using 'auscultation' rather than 'stethoscope', was in the *London Medical Repository*, which reported on Laénnec's memoir to

[35] P. J. Bishop, 'Reception of the Stethoscope and Laénnec's Book', *Thorax* 36 (1981), p. 487.
[36] Laénnec, *A Treatise on the Diseases of the Chest and on Mediate Auscultation*, p. x.

the Académie des Sciences, where he briefly described the instrument and its use.[37] Butter made no further reference to either auscultation or the stethoscope, so it seems unlikely that he ever used it, and he might well not have fully appreciated its diagnostic value.

Before the advent of anaesthetics, surgery was always the last option for patients, and it was still sufficiently primitive that operations needed to be carried out with as much speed and accuracy as possible in order to lessen the agony for the patient and improve the chances of a successful outcome. Being confident and quick was far better than being slow and careful, so speed and physical ability were highly valued. However, despite the high reputation of medical treatment in Paris, Butter's Memoir records that he was not entirely happy with some of the methods of surgery seen there – especially the operating technique of Baron Larrey* at the Military Hospital:

> another poor soldier had a lumber abscess to be opened; for this work the Baron thrust [a] heated iron into the abscess, the aperture was enlarged from the size of a sixpence to that of a crown piece, and so this poor fellow was left with dry cloths put over the wound to absorb the remaining quantities of matter. [1817]

Robert Liston,* one of the most renowned surgeons of his time, was not much gentler than Larrey,* his patients suffering very rough treatment, as indicated by Butter's observation of an operation carried out in 1819 at University College, London:

> an incision was made … into which the fore finger of the left hand, not the smallest in the room, was forced into the bladder, tearing and not cutting the parts for a sufficient aperture to extract the stones which came out with a flush of water on the floor.

Liston was, however, the first surgeon in England to use an anaesthetic, when, in December 1846, two days after he had witnessed the use of ether in a dental extraction, he performed a successful amputation.[38] Liston's operation was witnessed by both James Young Simpson* and Joseph Lister.*

The use of a gas to help alleviate pain dated back to the thirteenth century, when di-ethyl ether was originally synthesised. In 1772, Joseph Priestley discovered that nitrous oxide had anaesthetic powers, and in 1799 Humphrey Davy suggested that it should be inhaled during surgical operations. These discoveries were never used clinically, and Michael Faraday's later experiments with ether helped to show why – at that time, it was just too difficult to quantify and control their effects. The eventual use of ether and chloroform came quite late in Butter's career. He witnessed an early use of chloroform in one of Liston's* last operations, where the patient was 'narcotized' by Dr Snow,* but, according to the Memoir, Butter only once attempted to use it himself: 'he [an eye patient] wished to try the effects of chloroform which he attempted to inhale, but it produced such frightful effects on his nervous system as to oblige us to desist from a further trial'. This is recorded as having taken place

---

[37] Mr. Gray, 'New French Mode of Discovering Ulcers in the Lungs', *London Medical Repository* 12 (1819), pp. 150–1.

[38] *Case Notes on Frederick …*, published as *Centenary of the First Public Operation under an Anæsthetic in Europe Carried Out at University College Hospital by Robert Liston on 21st December 1846* (London: University College Hospital, 1946), p. 7.

in 1847, but chloroform was recognised and accepted as an anaesthetic only towards the end of that year, and the operation almost certainly occurred some time later. Chloroform had been known about since 1831 but was not trialled as an anaesthetic until Simpson* was trying to relieve the pain of childbirth.[39] This was a year after ether was first used – in Boston, Massachusetts – where a neck tumour was removed without any sign of patient distress. Both gases gave immediate relief to patients and far better medical results from surgery, though neither was ideal, and there was no fund of knowledge and experience to guide safe practice. Fortunately, John Snow developed a method of controlling the amounts to be used: in 1853 and 1857, he administered chloroform to Queen Victoria in childbirth, and this royal patronage silenced the last remaining objections to anaesthesia.

The primary cause of deaths associated with surgery was the lack of appreciation of the deadly nature of infections, both during the operation and afterwards during recuperation. This was not fully recognised until the middle of the nineteenth century. Liston,* who could amputate a limb in two-and-a-half minutes, believed in keeping wounds clean, used clean bandages and frequently changed the dressings. He washed his hands before operating and wore a clean apron (although he did not change it during the day, and it was for his own protection rather than for the benefit of the patient). In the five years between 1835 and 1840, Liston conducted amputations on sixty-six patients at Bart's, of whom ten died; other surgeons 'were sending 1 in 4 patients to the mortuary'.[40]

Butter, even early in his career, was a comparatively quick and successful operator: 'a question [was] put to me by a Surgeon present, as to the time it would take to tie the femoral artery.[+] The answer was – not 5 minutes. A bet was offered that I, the Dr, would not do it in the time but I performed it in two minutes' [1812].

Confidence in Butter's surgical abilities was shown in 1820 by a patient who, at a time when breast removal, like all surgery, was brutal, specifically requested that he should perform her mastectomy. The patient not only recovered but kept in touch and, in later years, introduced Butter to his future wife. Seven years earlier, Butter had carried out his first mastectomy whilst serving with the SDM in Huddersfield, having concluded that the alternative treatment, known as compression of the breast, was not successful and that surgery had better results. Without anaesthetic, a patient had to endure the operation graphically described by Fanny Burney in a letter to her sister. This operation, performed in 1812 by one of the most experienced French surgeons, took over fifteen minutes, and she suffered excruciating pain, having been given only a wine cordial, most probably laced with laudanum, before it began. Her recovery was long and painful, but she lived for another twenty-nine years.[41]

The strain of working as a surgeon must have been immense, and individuals had different ways of approaching it – Liston's* rather gung-ho approach contrasts with that of Abernethy,* who, particularly towards the end of his career, described

[39] Porter, *The Greatest Benefit to Mankind,* p. 367.
[40] Richard Hollingham, *Blood and Guts: A History of Surgery* (London: BBC Books, 2008), p. 38.
[41] Helle Mathiasen, 'Mastectomy without Anaesthesia: The Case of Abigail Adams Smith and Fanny Burney', *American Journal of Medicine, Medical Humanities Perspective* 124 (May 2011), p. 474.

walking into the operating theatre as like 'going to a hanging' and was sometimes known to shed tears and vomit after a particularly gruesome procedure.[42]

In 1821, Butter finally gave himself a formal business setting with his name over the door of premises in George Street, and thus confirmed his position in a system of medical provision that was 'small-scale, disaggregated, restricted and piecemeal in its operations'.[43] Doctors were self-employed, and the market could be both competitive and insecure, although Butter was buoyed to a considerable extent by his social and SDM connections. He also had the advantage of being both a physician and a surgeon, which was by no means so unusual as it had once been, although the difference between them was still the subject of much snobbery: 'many of my old patients now wished to know in what light they were to regard me, as a Physician or as a Surgeon' [1820]. The original Hippocratic oath had forbidden any cutting and regarded surgery as an inferior trade because it was done with the hands, not the head. Butter, and many of his contemporaries, seem to have been quite happy to mix and match, but there was no doubt that many physicians were still aloof. 'Gentleman physicians' had wielded considerable power and influence over the medical community for centuries[44] and could practise anywhere in the country or abroad. With his MD from Edinburgh, Butter was entitled to be called a physician, and he was, indeed, a Fellow of the Royal College of Physicians in Edinburgh. He could not become a Fellow of the London College without giving up his diploma in surgery, which he was not prepared to do. Surgeons gained far more practical experience than physicians, working on hospital wards and in the local community, and covering a wide range of conditions, diseases and accidents. Despite this, physicians were still considered, and certainly considered themselves, the elite of the profession. Butter's attitude is perhaps best summed up by his comment that 'the year 1821 proved more than usually prosperous … but I could not do without surgery which enabled me to get many large fees which I should otherwise have lost by acting as the mere physician'.

How much of a businessman Butter was is not clear: there is no indication that he kept either case notes for his patients or any records of his income and expenditure. He probably earned rather more than the average annual income for medical professionals, which seems to have hovered somewhere just above £200 for pretty much the whole of his career,[45] even though he claimed to have 'too often forgotten … the motto which was early instilled into my mind … accipe dum dolet – take a fee when people are sick, or when offered' [1852].

Butter does seem to have had rather more knowledge of joint and limb disorders than most medical practitioners of his day. He had seen how much more advanced and successful the treatment of fractures was in Paris than in England, and the Memoir records his introducing Nasdom's+ long splint to the west country: in 1820, he presented one to the Devon and Exeter Hospital, and he took another to use in

[42] Harold Ellis, 'John Abernethy, Surgeon: A Founder of the Medical School at St Bartholomew's Hospital', *Hospital Medicine* 75, no. 3 (March 2014), p. 174.

[43] Porter, *The Greatest Benefit to Mankind*, p. 628.

[44] Lindsey Fitzharris, *The Butchering Art* (London: Penguin Random House, 2017), p. 8.

[45] Anne Digby, *Making a Medical Living: Doctors and Patients in the English Market for Medicine, 1720–1911* (Cambridge: Cambridge University Press, 2002); Irvine Loudon, *Medical Care and the General Practitioner, 1750–1850* (Oxford: Oxford University Press, 1986).

his own practice. That very year, he used it on a coachman whose thigh-bone was fractured in several places. For a severe limb injury, amputation was the only hope, and Butter carried out a number of such operations including, relatively early in his career, whilst in Huddersfield with the SDM: 'I amputated the little boy's thigh who afterwards recovered most rapidly his health and strength and grew fat' [1813].

As with all medicine, a great deal of Butter's work must have been routine, although most of the procedures mentioned in the Memoir are relatively complicated and were doubtless included because of their interest. They show Butter's commitment – he rarely gave up hope of saving or curing a patient, even, at times, leaving his own sickbed to attend someone in need. It is noticeable that he was often called in when local doctors lacked either the capability or the confidence to do what was required. He was receptive to, and knowledgeable about, new methods of treatment, which seem often to have been very successful. In the light of this, it is perhaps surprising that he retained a strong faith in blood-letting, although it must be said that he seemed often to get good results from it, and many patients clearly believed in it as fervently as he did.

A great deal of Butter's work took place away from Plymouth, requiring many miles in the saddle; to visit a patient in Teignmouth, for example, was a return journey of between forty and fifty miles. His horse would have had to carry not only its rider, but two large saddle bags containing instruments, ointments, lotions and bandages, occasionally his 'amputation kit', and a change of clothes – it was, at times, necessary for him to stay overnight or longer. An amputation kit, most probably housed in a leather box, usually contained two trephines,[46] a variety of knives, one pair of nippers, a tourniquet, tweezers, scissors and a hey saw.[47]

In 1825 he wrote his most widely recorded publication: *Remarks on Irritative Fever, Commonly Called the Plymouth Dockyard Disease, with Mr Dryden's Detailed Account of the Fatal Cases.*[48] Butter felt that it was medically important to publicise the disease. At the time of an outbreak in 1824, he was travelling in Wales, and Dryden, then the Assistant Surgeon at the dockyard, was on duty. Butter had no official connection with the dockyard, but Dryden 'communicated to me the most authentic information respecting the disease which they thought was either Lock-Jaw, a modified species of Plague or a malady altogether anomalous and new in its character'. Butter describes a number of cases, and explains where and how the infection entered the body, the symptoms and how long they lasted, the methods of attempting a cure and whether or not the patient died. A review in the *London Medical Repository* includes letters from Astley Cooper* and John Abernethy* that agree with Butter's assessment, although the reviewer cannot resist a gentle dig at his style of writing.[49]

Butter himself suffered from a number of illnesses, particularly quinsy.+ He was, however, still willing to attend patients with even the most infectious diseases, including cholera, which erupted out of India in the early nineteenth century. Seaports were particularly vulnerable, and Plymouth was second only to London for

---

[46] A hole saw used in surgery to remove a circle of tissue or bone.

[47] A skull saw – named after William Hey.*

[48] Published by Underwoods, London; Black, Edinburgh; and Macarthur, Dublin (1825), p. 302.

[49] *The London Medical Repository: Vol. 1, Jun–Dec 1825* (London: Thomas & George Underwood, 1825), p. 500.

the severity of the outbreak that reached the city in June 1832. A wooden hospital was hastily erected at Five Fields, but 1,031 Plymothians died.[50] Cholera returned in 1849, when there were 1,894 victims, although the worst year nationally was 1854, when 23,000 people died in Great Britain. John Snow* mapped the epidemic to a contaminated public well pump in Broad Street, Soho, and after he removed the handle, thereby closing the pump, the instances of infection dropped almost immediately. Butter had already recognised that cholera was affected by sanitary conditions, but, like everybody else, he was not aware that it is a waterborne disease: 'cholera was reported in Stonehouse Lane and other places about Plymouth, also many at Brent, and other places where there was filth and good enough for this loathsome disease to feed on' [1850]. Cholera apart, he recognised that once the ill-tended and overflowing graveyard at St Andrews Chapelry was closed in 1853, 'that low tone of health usually complained of by residents in this neighbourhood is now wholly removed' [1847].

This was, regrettably, only too typical of urban living at the time, with narrow crowded streets and high pollution rates taking a heavy toll. Hospitals were to be avoided unless absolutely necessary, being dirty and overcrowded, whilst medical intervention was still risky and largely ineffectual. On 26 April 1832, the *Exeter Flying Post* wryly observed that 'the inhabitants of the Island of Sark may be said to live in an Utopian region, being neither killed by doctors nor troubled by lawyers'. If intended seriously, this judgement was a little unfair. Butter was by no means alone in seeking to raise the quality of medical care, and in recognising both the importance of hygiene and the dangers posed by pollution:

> Let us suppose that poor persons who feed themselves with food convenient for their bodies and breathe pure air, not contaminated with the taint of towns or mid-night revels, take their rest of night and enjoy 'sweet sleep the lot of the labouring man', and thus does their blood keep more healthful and fit to repair damages done to different parts of the body. [1844]

Given that healthy lifestyles were an impossibility for most urban families, it is perhaps not surprising that life expectancy at the age of ten in England in 1800 was between thirty and forty years, and by 1850 had risen only to forty-eight years. Further gradual rises were seen as the nineteenth century progressed, in which major advances in medical practice undoubtedly played their part, but it would need a marked improvement in living conditions before the full value of these developments could be felt across all sectors of the population.

South Devon Militia[51]

The militia was a part-time semi-voluntary force that could be mobilised in the event of a national emergency or called out to help keep the peace during events such as the Luddite disturbances of 1811–13. As a constitutional force, it had a continuous

---

[50] Felicity Goodall, *Lost Plymouth* (Edinburgh: Birlinn, 2009), p. 265.

[51] There seems to be a marked scarcity of published work on the SDM, the exception being held in the DHC, ref:s356.11/DEV/ANN: Col. Fisk et al., *Annals of the Militia: Being the Records of the South Devon Regiment, Prefaced by An Historical Account of Militia Organization* (Plymouth: Wm. Brendon & Son, 1975).

history from the Saxon era until the early twentieth century, although the militia of Butter's time derived from Pitt's Militia Act of 1757, a somewhat belated response to the inefficiencies of the then force that had become apparent during the Jacobite rebellion. The Defence Act of 1803 further improved matters, enabling more men to be enrolled to meet the threat of a French invasion.

The militia was organised by county, the Lords Lieutenant being empowered to appoint officers to raise the relevant quota, which, for Devon in 1758, was 1,600 men. At that time, there were four regiments, but in 1763 this was reduced to three, based in Exeter, Plymouth and Bideford/Barnstaple.

When Butter joined the SDM in 1810, its colonel was Lord Rolle.* He was, so far as can be established, the longest serving of any militia colonels, having joined as an ensign and, once appointed Colonel in 1788, remaining in post until he died in 1842. In practical terms, however, the regiment was run by the commanding officer: when Butter enlisted, this was Major Seale,* who eventually replaced Lord Rolle as Colonel, and was himself replaced by the second Lord Morley,* the last colonel under whom Butter served. Among the officers were an adjutant, who had responsibility for the recruitment, discipline, equipment and efficiency of the men, as well as a quartermaster, a surgeon, an assistant surgeon, a sergeant major and a drum major. There was also a paymaster – Captain John Hawkins served in the role from 1790 until 1820, and became, in due course, a patron of the Plymouth Eye Infirmary. The regimental rank and file were local farmers, tradesmen and labourers, aged between eighteen and fifty, conscripted by ballot from their own communities. Butter was responsible for 'passing' recruits, presumably following a medical examination: '21st [August 1852] I passed 17 recruits for the Militia, on the 25th 12 more recruits', and 'at Morley, on the 27th I examined 74 and passed 69'.

The regimental uniform was, in 1773, red with dark green facings: in 1800, the facings were yellow, and by 1814 they were white. The regimental badge from about 1800 was a lion rampant (derived from the coat of arms of the early Earls of Devon), with a garter inscribed with the regimental title. Men were conscripted to serve for three years, later increased to five, unless they could produce a substitute. When the regiment was disembodied, they were paid for a further two months but were free to pursue their civilian lives. Training, which took place over a period of several weeks every year, was thought not necessary after the end of the wars with France and America and was dispensed with by Act of Parliament in 1817. The SDM, however, although disembodied on 8 February 1816, had training sessions in 1820, 1821, 1825 and 1831, but then not again until 1852. The session in May 1821 took place in the Longroom Barracks, Stonehouse, and lasted for three weeks, ending with a review on the Hoe where 'Major General Sir D Pack testified his entire approbation of the evolution, steadiness and soldier-like appearance of the men.'[52]

The South Devons were based at the Citadel in Plymouth, where the officers' mess was in the Governor's house. Officers were expected to attend the mess during training and were charged for dinner whether or not they were present. Guests, paid for by the officer, could be invited on Tuesdays and Thursdays – the mess had to be informed by 10 a.m. and the guests' names entered in a book kept for that purpose. The minutes of the mess committee meeting held at 'Dr Butter's' on 30 August 1853 show that the regiment owned its own mess equipment, as it was 'resolved that the

---

[52] *Star (London)*, 30.6.1821.

Plate, Crockery, Furniture, Glass etc belonging to the officers of the South Devon Militia may be loaned to Mr Hapny during the months training of the Regiment commencing on the 14th September'.[53] In October, it was resolved 'that the plate be deposited in the names of the Mess Committee at the Naval Bank, any removal to be authorised by two signatures from the Mess Committee'.[54]

The regiment was temporarily in Exeter when Butter was summoned by Lord Rolle* to be its Assistant Surgeon, taking over from Robert White, and, within a year, to become Surgeon, taking over from James Colby. His maintenance of that role from 1811, when he was just twenty years old, until he resigned in 1854, to be succeeded by John Tucker, was the longest of any serving surgeon in the South Devons and quite possibly in the country. The first South Devon surgeon had been appointed in 1780, and Butter was the tenth. He claims to have taken over the role from another John Tucker, who had resigned to get married. The marriage certainly took place exactly as Butter recorded it, but, according to the regimental history, John Tucker had served as surgeon for only a few months in 1803, well before Butter's time. It is possible that he had remained involved with the South Devons in some other capacity, and that Butter had confused the issue, but the accuracy of the wedding details does suggest that, in this particular instance, the regimental history is more at fault than Butter's memory.

When the regiment was away from Plymouth, the men were given a lodging allowance and were housed either in local barracks, such as those described by Butter at Shorncliffe[55] in Kent, or, if there were no such barracks, in local inns and hostelries, as at Huddersfield and Sheffield during the Luddite riots. So far as it is possible to ascertain, the officers rented private rooms. In Sheffield, Butter 'engaged an empty house for an Hospital and private apartments for my own accommodation' [1812].

Regimental life on the move was tough, particularly for the ordinary foot soldier, and wagons, heavy with equipment, had to be manhandled through rough, often muddy terrain. It was not all bad, however: 'much merriment was excited on this long march [to Rochester to face the French invasion threats], [with] the singing, riding, duck hunting and whist playing' [1810]. This was Butter's first march with the regiment, and he obviously enjoyed himself, although he did have the considerable advantage of being seated on a horse.

Once settled into their accommodation, and when not on duty, regimental life for the officers allowed time for a variety of activities. At Chatham, they set up a whist club that seems to have played all evening, every evening. Perhaps more significantly, the minutes of a meeting held in October 1853[56] record that the daily allowance of port and sherry was then one pint of each per officer, and it would seem that something similar had long been the case. Butter recorded that in 1811

> a bottle of port for dinner was commonly allowed, and sometimes two and three were drank. None were allowed to escape a bumper toast without a doctor's certificate, and in order to avoid inevitable drunkenness a Militia Captain with a

---

[53] *South Devon Militia Mess Minutes Book, 1853–1907* [DHC: 6855L/1/6/5].
[54] Ibid.
[55] Shorncliffe barracks were established in 1794.
[56] *SDM Mess Minutes Book.*

softer head than his comrades quietly and unobserved drew his bumper glass of wine off the table and poured it into his jackboots.

The Kentish Gazette (27.9.1811) reported on another form of diversion. This was a

well contested foot-race … between a private of the South Devon Militia and a Mr Bryce of Lynstrad for 20 guineas. The distance was one mile and so well were they matched that they ran abreast till within about the last 200 yards when Bryce left the soldier and came in a few yards before him.

There was some serious work to be done: 'Chatham Jan 29th, on Saturday 300 prisoners marched from hence to Norman Cross under the charge of the South Devon Militia',[57] but after the regiment had moved from Chatham to Shorncliffe there was more recreation, this time shooting, coursing and fox hunting.

Perhaps the most difficult deployment for the regiment during Butter's time was when it was sent north to help quell the Luddite riots. It is interesting to note that it was considered necessary for Butter to purchase additional medical equipment in preparation for the anticipated troubles. One wonders why he was not already adequately equipped, or were the Luddites perhaps expected to cause more mayhem than a French invasionary force? Whether they were or not, the SDM set out to make a positive impression, and the troops doubtless looked splendid marching into town in full uniform with their band playing.

Unfortunately, the band did not always prove beneficial in lifting people's spirits – in 1812, it was reported that on

Sunday night as Mr S Kirby of Bridge Hill near Sheffield was returning from Chapel in his gig, accompanied by his son, the horse took fright at the noise of the drums of the South Devon Militia (which were beating for their evening parade) – both were thrown out near the bridge. Mr Kirby was killed and his son was 'much hurt'.[58]

A member of that band was John Henry Distin, who, whilst in the north, was considered good enough to play principal trumpet in the Sheffield Festival Orchestra, and is one of the most important people in brass band history. The Distin Family brass ensemble, led by John Henry, and the various projects it undertook, are considered the main reason why brass bands of today are established in their current format.[59] The SDM band played even when the militia was disembodied: the *Star* of 21 July 1827 reported that 'the Duchess of Clarence [on arriving] at Laira Bridge was met by the Mayor and Corporation of Plymouth with the bands of the Royal Marines and the South Devon Militia'. By October 1853, however, things had changed, and the Mess Book records a resolution that 'four days pay to be paid to Capt. Fisk* for keeping up a good Corps of Drummers and Pipes'[60] and that the old musical instruments should be sold and the proceeds allocated to the Corps.

[57] *The Kentish Weekly Post or Canterbury Journal*, 1.2.1811.

[58] *Star (London)*, 23.11.1812.

[59] Ray Farr, *The Distin Legacy: The Rise of the Brass Band in 19th Century Britain* (Cambridge: Cambridge Scholars Publishing, 2013), p. 24.

[60] *SDM Mess Minutes Book*.

Back in 1813, having successfully completed its deployment in the north, the regiment was ready to return home: 'I am happy to inform you all is now quiet here and that the military are withdrawing ... the South Devon Militia expect daily orders to move.'[61] They duly marched south, reaching Dartmoor prison in August, where they stayed for two months guarding the French. The prison had been founded in 1803 to house the huge numbers captured in the Napoleonic wars, although no prisoners actually reached its gates until 1809. By the end of that year, the prison was full, and conditions got considerably worse in 1813 when prisoners from the American war with Great Britain began to arrive. When the conflicts finally ceased, all the prisoners were repatriated, and the prison closed in 1816, not to re-open as a penal establishment until 1850.

In March 1814, 'the regiment embarked on board the prison ships in the harbour [Hamoaze] to do duty in the room of the Monaghan Militia' – an Irish regiment stationed in England from 1812 to 1814.[62] By July 1815, 'the regiment was quartered in George's Square Barracks but the regimental hospital was fixed at Frankfort Barracks, Plymouth'. George's Square barracks, where Butter had the use of a stable for his horse and dogs, was a single-storied building erected in 1757 and named in honour of George II.

Other than his being involved with training and recruitment, Butter records little about the work of the South Devons following their return to Plymouth. The regiment was disembodied in 1816, and he was eager to leave Plymouth and travel on the continent. The SDM fell into a degree of neglect,[63] and the permanent staff was reduced: 'Lord Rolle,* on the late reduction at Plymouth of the staff of the South Devon Militia ... direct[ed] the Adjutant to present each discharged non-commissioned officer with a sovereign on his Lordship's account.'[64]

New barracks were built at Mutley, on the edge of Plymouth, in 1840,[65] and, regardless of minimal staffing, the SDM managed to continue functioning on a social level: 'the staff of the South Devon Militia, with their families, were regaled on Thursday last, at Ryall's Prince of Wales Inn, with a substantial dinner of good old English fare – the gift of their respected Lt Col. Sir John Yarde Buller,* Bart.' One of the toasts was to 'Dr Butter [who] honoured the happy party with a visit' and, in turn, 'expatiated largely on the merits of Lieut.-Colonel Buller'.[66]

By 1852, there was growing international tension with France and Russia, and a new Militia Act was passed. In November, the SDM undertook twenty-one days' training in Plymouth: 406 volunteers answered to their names, and eight were reported absent[67] (there was scope for conscription if volunteer numbers were inadequate). The regiment was then embodied for 'home defence at Devonport in 1854, following the outbreak of war with Russia'.[68]

[61] *Morning Post*, 22.3.1813.
[62] *Morning Post*, 3.3.1814.
[63] Fisk et al., *Annals of the Militia*, p. 52.
[64] *The Morning Advertiser*, 9.7.1829.
[65] Crispin Gill, *Plymouth: A New History*, vol. 2 (Newton Abbot: David and Charles, 1979), p. 119.
[66] *Western Courier, West of England Conservative, Plymouth and Devonport Advertiser*, 15.9.1847.
[67] Fisk et al., *Annals of the Militia*, p. 78.
[68] Ibid., p. 80.

The 1852 Act fixed the Devon Militia at two regiments of infantry and one of artillery. The SDM retained its infantry role (North Devon got the artillery) but lost its traditional name and became simply the 2nd Devon Militia. It was embodied as such during the Crimean War and the Indian Mutiny, after which it carried out an annual training programme. In 1855, control passed definitively to the War Office – previously, responsibility for the militia as a whole had lain with the Home Office, with the War Office taking over only at times of embodiment. The Lord Lieutenant was still expected to oversee the general provision of the militia on a county basis, but the whole concept was very much on its last legs.[69] In 1881, the former SDM became the 3rd battalion (2nd Devon Militia) Devonshire Regiment, and then slowly declined until the militia was finally abolished under the terms of the 1907 Territorial and Reserve Forces Act, which created what became, in 1921, the Territorial Army.

Butter's Plymouth

The Plymouth that Butter found when he arrived with the SDM in 1814 was not the Plymouth of today. It was just one of three towns – Plymouth, Plymouth Dock and Stonehouse – which did not merge until 1914, when they became the single county borough of Plymouth.[70] The town of Plymouth had been formally incorporated in 1439,[71] but as early as 1296 Edward I had assembled a large fleet in the harbour,[72] establishing a process that by 1377 had played a major part in making Plymouth the fourth-largest settlement in the kingdom.[73] Succeeding centuries saw substantial maritime activity, both naval and commercial, with on-shore developments to match. The most significant of these started in 1690, with the building of the dockyard at what is now Devonport. Only eight years later, Celia Fiennes thought it 'one of the best in England, a great many good shipps built there, and the great depth of water … shelters the shipps'.[74] Two docks were constructed, with three more following during the first half of the eighteenth century,[75] by which time it was firmly established as the largest employer of labour in the area, and by far the most significant force in the local economy.

Nine years after work had started on the dockyard, the first Eddystone light was erected. This, together with an open seaway, made the approach to Plymouth as safe as it could be, although the outer harbour in particular remained very vulnerable to storms.

In 1760, the Royal Naval Hospital was opened in Stonehouse. It was superbly designed, with detached buildings, each dealing with different diseases and complaints, arranged around a substantial courtyard, thus largely eliminating

[69] R. J. Stoneman, 'The Reformed British Militia, c. 1852–1908' (Unpublished PhD thesis, University of Kentucky, 2014), p. 34.
[70] For the purposes of this chapter, all references to Plymouth are to the three towns together, unless otherwise specified.
[71] W. G. Hoskins, *Devon* (Chichester: Phillimore & Co., 1954, re-published 2003), p. 455.
[72] Goodall, *Lost Plymouth*, p. 21.
[73] Richard Nicholls Worth, *A History of Devonshire* (London: Elliot Stock, 1886), p. 205.
[74] Christopher Morris (ed.), *The Illustrated Journeys of Celia Fiennes 1685–c.1712* (London: Macdonald & Co., 1982), p. 201.
[75] C. W. Bracken, 'Historical Notes on the City of Plymouth', in *The Book of Plymouth* (Plymouth: British Medical Association, 1938), p. 72.

the risk of cross-contamination and infection. The prison reformer John Howard did not think much of the local prisons, but he wanted to see the Royal Naval Hospital principles (and its metal beds) incorporated into prison design everywhere. Somewhat ironically, in view of what was to follow, 'French doctors who visited in 1787 were so impressed that their notes and observations became the blueprint for French hospital planning until the twentieth century.'[76] In 1797, the army followed suit, and the similarly designed military hospital was built by prisoners-of-war on the north side of Stonehouse Creek. The Royal Marines' contribution was slightly different: a splendid new barracks, built in Stonehouse in 1782–3.

Non-military infrastructure was also developing. The first bank came in 1772, whilst the Stonehouse bridge eased one major transport and communication difficulty in 1773, and the Torpoint ferry another in 1791. In 1802, the Devonport Leat started to bring fresh water from twenty-seven miles away on Dartmoor – the existing Drakes Leat (to Plymouth) and Stonehouse Leat both dated from the sixteenth century.

Culturally, this was the beginning of possibly Plymouth's finest hour. Sir Joshua Reynolds (1723–92), born in Plympton, is undoubtedly the area's best-known artist, and was the founding President of the Royal Academy, but at least four other local artists exhibited there.[77] Samuel Hart (1806–81) became the Academy Librarian, while Charles Lock Eastlake* (1793–1865), a friend of Butter, arguably outdid them all, becoming the first man to be both President of the Academy and Director of the National Gallery. The first theatre in Plymouth was built in 1762, and in the early years of the following century came the Proprietary Library and the Plymouth Institution, later to become the Athenaeum, of which Butter was a member. Nor was the spiritual side of things completely overlooked: in 1796, 'The Household of Faith' became the first purpose-built Sunday school anywhere in the country.[78] All these developments provide a modest counterpoint to the view of at least one observer that turn-of-the-century Plymouth was 'an ill-built, disagreeable place, infested with all the filthiness so frequently seen in sea-ports'.[79] This was nothing new: two centuries earlier, Plymouth had been (in the words of W. G. Hoskins) 'stinking, sprawling, and full of poverty-stricken fishermen'[80] and simply scraping a living was always hard for the vast majority of the population, whilst even the well-to-do frequently found that death and disease were not far away.

With the coming of the French Revolutionary Wars, the press-gangs were out in force, and hundreds of ships filled the harbour. It was not only ships – supplies and accommodation had to be found on land, both for transient soldiers and sailors and for the many wives who followed their husbands to war. Nor was all the traffic outward-bound. Many combatants returned needing hospital treatment, or for a variety of other reasons, and there were large numbers of prisoners of war. The most notable prisoner was, of course, Napoleon, and large crowds strained for a view of him from the land, while up to one thousand small boats sailed out to the *Bellerophon*, anchored in the Sound.

[76] Goodall, *Lost Plymouth*, pp. 58–9.
[77] The others were James Northcote (1746–1831) and Benjamin Haydon (1786–1846).
[78] Goodall, *Lost Plymouth*, p. 217.
[79] W. G. Maton, 'Observations on the Western Counties of England', in R. Pearse Chope (ed.), *Early Tours in Devon and Cornwall* (Newton Abbot: David & Charles, 1967), p. 269.
[80] Hoskins, *Devon*, p. 456.

During and after the war, Plymouth acquired 'buildings which had no rival in the south-west peninsula',[81] largely as a result of the efforts of John Foulston, a distinguished architect who 'made Plymouth one of the handsomest towns in England'.[82] He could, and did, design anything from small Regency terraces to monumental neoclassical structures, including a new civic centre, and the huge edifice, 268 feet in frontage, which incorporated the Theatre Royal in its west wing and the Royal Hotel in its east. A substantial marketplace was erected in 1809, and in 1813 came both the Exchange building and the creation of the Port of Plymouth Chamber of Commerce, one of the earliest in the country. In 1809, there was a faltering start to the provision of free education for poor children, when local Quakers were instrumental in setting-up the Plymouth Public Free School, although it is noticeable that the prospectus gave greater emphasis to 'improvement of morals' than it did to education per se. An adult school followed some time later.[83] The Dock Public School for Boys also opened in 1809.

As the war drew to a close, thought was being given to the problems of the outer harbour. The solution was the mile-long breakwater, designed by John Rennie, which was started in 1812 and finally completed by his son, also John, in 1847.[84] It is a magnificent construction, the value of which was amply demonstrated a few years ago, when forty-ton blocks of concrete were deposited to reinforce the seaward side of the defences. After a particularly severe storm, one of the blocks was found on the landward side![85] Butter took an interest in the construction of the breakwater and visited the limestone quarry at Oreston, source of the four-and-a-half million tons of stone required to complete the project.

The war had produced great wealth for Plymouth, with around a thousand captured ships brought into port in the first ten years alone, and over a hundred registered prize stores set up around Sutton Harbour.[86] This helped to pay for Foulston's grand buildings, but it directly benefitted relatively few of the local population. For the lucky ones, as well as for the still poverty-stricken masses, the coming of peace was not an unmixed blessing, marking, in the view of one Devon-based historian, 'the opening of one of the grimmest periods in modern British history'.[87] These were the years of the Peterloo Massacre, the Cato Street Conspiracy and the suspension of habeas corpus, but to the average Plymothian it was probably of more significance that thousands of dockyard workers were laid off, and that the town was gripped by a severe economic recession that did not lift for several years. There was an established factory area in Millbay, with an iron foundry, lime kilns, soap and glass factories and a gas company, amongst others,[88] but both it and the various other sources of non-dock employment were also suffering and could do little to offset

[81] Goodall, *Lost Plymouth*, p. 195.
[82] W. G. Hoskins, *The Making of the English Landscape* (London: Penguin, 1985), p. 143.
[83] Martin Wyatt, 'The Quaker Contribution to Education in Plymouth', *Transactions of the Devonshire Association* 152 (Exeter: D. A., 2020), pp. 207–14.
[84] Walter Minchinton, *Devon's Industrial Past: A Guide* (Dartington: Dartington Centre for Education and Research, 1986), p. 13.
[85] Nigel Overton, talk to Exmouth Historical & Archaeological Society, 1.9.2014.
[86] https://plymouthlawsociety.co.uk/about/history/
[87] C. P. Hill, *British Economic and Social History, 1700–1939* (London: Edward Arnold, 1967), p. 114.
[88] Gill, *Plymouth: A New History*, vol. 2, p. 213.

the jobs that had been lost. Things were not helped by the fact that Mt Tambora had erupted in Indonesia, creating a volcanic cloud that made 1816 'the year without a summer'. Butter was by then 'heartily sick of … [the] doleful dismal deserted town of Plymouth', and the following year he decided to visit the continent to get away from it all. When he returned, he found little improvement, although by 1819 things were slowly getting better. It is a sad fact, though, that he never really warmed to the place 'where I was doomed to live half a century and upwards' [1820].

A new Custom House, designed by David Laing, was built in 1820, but the most significant construction event of that year, and arguably of the whole period, was the completion of Foulston's design for Union Street, which finally joined the three towns together along one road. Union Street made it not only easier to travel, but also a lot safer. The old roads had been dominated by marshes, which 'were very desolate and dreary at night … it was once the custom for those who had to go from one town to the other after sunset to wait until a little party had collected sufficiently strong to repel attack before commencing to traverse'.[89]

Some years prior to this, Butter had become personally involved with Foulston in the provision of Plymouth's first public baths and had 'a letter published in the Plymouth Newspaper … urging the establishment of baths under the Hoe' [1817]. This was quite a letter. The norm was two, or at the most three short paragraphs: Butter's took up nearly one-and-a-half columns. The baths were not to provide ablution facilities for the great unwashed, but to capitalise on 'the advantages which Plymouth possesses for a watering-place or town of fashionable resort for bathers'.[90] Unfortunately, a huge gale in 1824 did so much damage that it put an end to any idea of using the designated part of the Hoe, and it was not until 1830 that the Royal Union Baths were finally opened, although they had to be demolished in 1847 because the land was needed for the South Devon Railway Company's station at Millbay.[91] By the time the West Hoe Baths opened in 1859, any hope of Plymouth ever becoming a fashionable resort had long gone.

In 1823, the Prince Regent offered tracts of land on Dartmoor to help find employment for some of the poor people living in the three towns, and Sir Thomas Tyrwhitt paid for the building of the Plymouth and Dartmoor Railway. Horse-drawn carriages ran on a 4'6" gauge iron track, taking granite to Plymouth and coal, timber, sea-sand, lime and general supplies on the return trip, with which Tyrwhitt hoped, in vain, to 'improve the economy of moorlands around Princetown'.[92]

On 1 January 1824, when Dock's population was around thirty-three thousand against Plymouth's twenty-one thousand, making it the largest town in Devon and Cornwall, it finally got recognition as Devonport: its inhabitants clearly resented what they regarded as the belittling name of Plymouth Dock. The re-naming was celebrated with the erection of the Column, 124-feet tall and designed by Foulston in the Doric style to sit alongside Devonport Guildhall, built a couple of years earlier. In 1837, Devonport was formally incorporated as a borough.

[89] Richard Nicholls Worth, *The History of Plymouth from the Earliest Period to the Present Time* (Plymouth: Brendon & Son, 1871), p. 225.
[90] *Plymouth and Plymouth Dock Weekly Journal*, 1.7.1824.
[91] https://www.oldplymouth.uk/Royal%20Union%20Baths.htm
[92] Worth, *The History of Plymouth*, p. 346.

It was also in 1824 that the two Rennies began another magnificent construction, the Royal William Victualling Yard. Thirteen acres of top-quality buildings were sited around a square shipping basin on the edge of Stonehouse Creek, a task that took eleven years. The Yard was built to provide a central point for provisioning the navy; there had been a victualling yard in Plymouth since 1654, but the process had been essentially a piecemeal one and a byword for corruption and scandal. It would be so no longer.

Transport facilities were improving steadily, and the Laira Bridge, designed by James Meadows Rendel and completed in 1827, was the second-longest iron bridge in Britain. It was made of cast iron produced in Coalbrookdale, which gave it a nice link to the first-ever iron bridge.[93] The local turnpike trusts also did their bit, and by 1830 there were eleven major coaches a day leaving the three towns for London, Bath, Bristol, Portsmouth and Falmouth. There were similar improvements in both water and rail transport. Butter occasionally used the Torpoint passage and was doubtless pleased when James Rendel designed a steam-powered floating bridge (chain ferry), which came into use in 1834 and could accommodate coaches without the need for passengers to disembark.[94] In 1849, the South Devon Railway at last reached central Plymouth: it was a single-track broad-gauge line, essentially an extension of the Great Western from Exeter. By 1854, Brunel had taken it across the Tamar, via the magnificent Royal Albert bridge. Travel within the towns also began to develop: horse-drawn buses were running by 1832, and in the same year gas-powered street lighting was introduced.[95]

Whatever was happening in other spheres of life, maritime issues continued to be of supreme importance. The civilian waterfront was more than long enough to accommodate berthing, cargo-handling, warehousing and the facilities required for the coming of the railway. This provided the impetus for Brunel to develop the Great Western docks complex, which played a vital part in maintaining Plymouth's importance as a commercial port. Different areas specialised in different services – Sutton Harbour dealt with fishing vessels for instance, while most of the heavy, dirty trade went to the Cattewater wharves.[96] Plymouth came to dominate Devon's seaborne trade, both overseas and coastal: its share of the county's totals grew from less than half in 1800 to 90 per cent and 75 per cent respectively by 1900.[97] There was also a flourishing travel industry: ocean liners took advantage of the new pier built especially for them at Millbay, and the coming of mail contracts in the 1850s saw the trade really take off.[98] The fishing industry also developed significantly during the first half of the nineteenth century, with trawlers from Brixham and Plymouth dominating the Devon trade. Virtually all the Plymouth trawlers were built locally,[99]

---

[93] www.olddevonport.uk

[94] www.oldplymouth.uk

[95] Gill, *Plymouth: A New History*, vol. 2, p. 122.

[96] David J. Starkey, 'The Ports, Seaborne Trade and Shipping Industry of South Devon, 1786–1914', in Michael Duffy et al. (eds), *The New Maritime History of Devon*, vol. 2 (London: Conway Maritime Press, 1994), p. 35.

[97] Starkey, 'The Ports, Seaborne Trade and Shipping Industry', p. 37.

[98] Crispin Gill, 'Ocean Liners at Plymouth', in Duffy et al., *The New Maritime History of Devon*, vol. 2, p. 227.

[99] Anthony Northway, 'The Devon Fishing Industry in the Eighteenth and Nineteenth Centuries', in Duffy et al., *The New Maritime History of Devon*, vol. 2, p. 130.

and although shipbuilding had died to negligible proportions by 1900, in Butter's day it was still a significant industry, particularly in Stonehouse but also at Cattedown, Mutton Cove and Cremyll. Production varied, but around eleven ships were produced annually, at an average of something less than one hundred tons apiece. Dartmouth was producing at roughly the same level, but nowhere else came close.[100]

On the naval front, there was some post-war modernisation of the dock facilities, but it was low-key and finished by 1822. In 1840, there was a disastrous fire in the North Dock, which required extensive repairs, but the main emphasis was turning to two new developments, steam and iron. In 1846, work began on the Keyham Steamyard, designed to be capable of dealing with the largest steamships in the navy, and to enable them to be docked at any stage of the tide (Butter was present at the laying of the foundation stone). Even then, further dredging and extensions were required in the 1860s to accommodate still larger vessels. In the year 1869–70, Devonport Dockyard worked on thirty-seven ironclads and 132 other vessels, which was not far short of the total numbers handled by all eleven of the navy's overseas yards.[101]

The nineteenth century, particularly after the accession of Victoria, was a period when Devon was declining in relation to England as a whole, and only Plymouth developed on a scale similar to that experienced elsewhere. From about mid-century onwards, there were around eleven or twelve thousand members of the armed services in the three towns, and whilst the docks continued to be the biggest employer of civilians, the numbers of fishermen and merchants deriving their living from the sea was not far behind. Nor were the building trades – Rennie's breakwater alone employed 765 men at its peak. Diversity was further enhanced when the railway enabled Plymouth to become the wholesale centre for the region, with a concomitant increase in the town's retail trade.

All this was very welcome, but it threatened to be overwhelmed by the fact that the population of the three towns more than doubled from the forty-five thousand of the 1801 census to 103,000 by 1851, and much of the housing stock deteriorated under the pressure. In Plymouth alone, where the population rose by thirty-six thousand, the number of houses increased by just 3,396, and many of those were created by infilling within existing courts that were already overcrowded, dark, ill-ventilated and lacking the most basic of facilities – it was not unknown for entire courts to share one standpipe, which was switched on for only one hour a day. In 1846, there were ninety-one people recorded as living in one house in New Street, and the average occupancy across the town was over nine (in London and Liverpool, it was seven, and in Manchester six).[102] Despite considerable local publicity, nothing much changed until the advent of Local Boards of Health. Plymouth got one in 1854, but Devonport had to wait until 1866, and Stonehouse operated as a 'Sanitary District'. The Boards were active: roads were paved, water supplies were extended, courts

[100] David J. Starkey, 'Devon's Shipbuilding Industry, 1786–1970', in Duffy et al., *The New Maritime History of Devon*, vol. 2, p. 81.
[101] Peter Hilditch, 'Devon and Naval Strategy since 1815', in Duffy et al., *The New Maritime History of Devon*, vol. 2, p. 156.
[102] W. J. Odgers, *Report on the Sanitary Condition of Plymouth* (Plymouth: Health of Towns Association, 1847), quoted in Ann Bond, 'Working Class Housing in Victorian Plymouth: From Slum to Council House, Part 1; Slums and Artisans' Dwellings', *The Devon Historian* 81 (Exeter: Devon History Society, 2012), pp. 18–19.

were opened up to light and ventilation, and a comprehensive sewerage scheme was completed. Unfortunately, the effect was marginal at best, because in order to achieve it many houses had to be demolished, insufficient new ones were built, and the displaced residents had no alternative but to crowd even more heavily into those that were left.[103]

Overcrowding and poor-quality accommodation were just as much a problem in the local cemeteries, which were appallingly maintained and overflowing with decomposing corpses, which were a major contributor to the ill health of anyone unfortunate enough to live anywhere near them. It was 1849 before the Plymouth Stonehouse and Devonport Cemetery Company's new facility was opened at Ford Park, a mile or so from the town centre.

All this had considerable ramifications for public health, with disease and poverty living hand-in-hand. Indeed, disease of one sort or another was pretty well endemic. The first Medical Officer of Health was not appointed until 1874, although there had been other medical organisations before this. The Plymouth Medical Society, one of the oldest in the country, was set up in 1794, followed by the Public Dispensaries (Plymouth in 1798 and Devonport in 1815), where an annual subscription of one guinea entitled the subscriber to recommend four patients for free treatment. In May 1840, the area's first hospital, the South Devon and East Cornwall, opened its doors, albeit with only twelve beds, although by 1863 this had increased to fifty-five. It was 'neatly built and forms in philanthropic character, and in external appearance, an object of credit to the town'.[104] In 1863, Devonport got the comprehensively named Royal Albert Hospital and Eye Infirmary for Devonport, Stonehouse, Cornwall and West Devon.[105]

By the mid-nineteenth century, across the three towns, there were twenty-four physicians and fifty-one surgeons, including one with the unfortunate name of Butcher. There were even thirteen dentists, against Butter's claim of thirty or so years earlier that there had then been none [1822].[106] All this was, of course, in addition to the care provided at the various naval and military establishments.

Butter lived through a period of enormous change in Plymouth, although in some ways the problems at the end were much as they had been at the beginning. There was too much reliance on the navy, whose requirements were dictated largely by external considerations, and the doubling of the population brought severe pressures. There were enormous improvements in housing, sanitation, transport and medical provision, but these were often negated by sheer numbers. There were some magnificent buildings to be proud of, and an undoubted element of prosperity for many, but for the great majority of working Plymothians the benefits were often no better than marginal, and much remained to be done.

[103] Bond, 'Working Class Housing', pp. 19–20.

[104] G. Flintoff, *Flintoff's Directory and Guide Book to Plymouth, Devonport, Stonehouse and Their Vicinities* (Plymouth: G. Flintoff, 1844), p. 35.

[105] J. Elliot Square, 'Medical History of Plymouth, with Anecdotes and Reminiscences', in *The Book of Plymouth*, pp. 89–112.

[106] F. Brendon, *A Directory of Plymouth, Stonehouse, Devonport, Stoke and Moricetown* (Plymouth: F. Brendon, 1852), pp. 110, 160, 248.

The Plymouth Royal Eye Infirmary

Early eye surgery was very much limited to the treatment of cataracts, which goes back to the sixth century BC when an operation known as couching was performed. The cataract remained in the eye but was dislodged from the line of sight with a needle. This produced instantaneous improvement in vision, but the retention of the cataract and the prevailing lack of hygiene frequently resulted in blindness shortly thereafter. Couching, which is still used in many of the less-developed parts of the world, remained the only available option until what is generally accepted as the first true cataract extraction, performed in 1747 by the French surgeon Jacques Daviel (interestingly, Butter, although well aware of Daviel's breakthrough, describes himself as performing a number of couching operations, albeit apparently success-fully, even as late as 1840). The new process undoubtedly represented great progress, with an overall success rate of around 50 per cent, but post-operative complications were still considerable. Despite the risks, Daviel's procedure (known as ECCE – extracapsular cataract extraction) remained the basis of the accepted approach for over a century, until intracapsular cataract extraction (ICCE) became, for a time, the preferred method, despite still high failure rates. By the 1970s, improvements in operative methods and surgical tools had made ECCE again the preferred approach.

Within these broad trends, there seems to have been room for personal variation. John Hill,* a Barnstaple surgeon who had trained at Guy's and St Thomas' hospitals,[107] noticing that

> wounds accidentally inflicted upon the Lens ... had a happy result, endeavoured to imitate the process by introducing a needle through the corner and breaking up the Lens without dislocating it, and was rewarded with a success which far exceeded his expectations, and thus the anterior operation in a few years ob-tained a general preference.[108]

This was a method he would doubtless have taught his apprentices, who included John Cunningham Saunders* and William Adams;* indeed, Butter refers to Saunders using precisely this technique in his Memoir entry for 1814. Hill clearly had less success with one of his more established colleagues:

> occasionally he rode over to Exeter for the purpose of relating his successful exploits with the needle to his friend Mr Sheldon who felt a deep interest in Ophthalmic Operations, but uninfluenced by Mr Hill's suggestions he clave to extractions with a pertinacity not altogether praiseworthy, for I saw him myself operate five times following without the slightest success.[109]

Few doctors at this time took the bold step of specialising solely in ophthal-mology. Amongst those who did was Baron de Wenzel (1724–90), who came to Britain from Germany and travelled around the country extracting cataracts, 'which he did with great skill and success – not however, until he had spoiled a hat full of

[107] Sir William Adams, *A Reply to a Recent Publication against Him* (London: Baldwin, Craddock and Joy, 1818), p. 27.
[108] James Billet, *Brief History of Ophthalmic Surgery in Great Britain during the Present Century* (Taunton: A. Pile, 1866), p. 4.
[109] Ibid., pp. 4–5.

eyes (in his words) in acquiring the right mode to do it'.[110] He improved on Daviel's treatment with so much success that he became oculist to George III, who himself suffered from cataracts. Other doctors who began to take ophthalmics seriously were Guillaume Dupuytren* (in France) and Antonio Scarpa* (in Italy), both of whom Butter met on his travels. In England, William Porterfield made his name with *A Treatise on the Eye: The Manner and Phenomena of Vision*, published in two volumes in 1759, but 'there is no evidence that Porterfield ever actually practised clinical ophthalmology, or even studied its pathology'.[111] Another early 'specialist' was Thomas Young (1773–1829), who published, amongst other things, *Observations on Vision*, which was read to the Royal Society in May 1793.[112]

Despite the writings of these two gentlemen, the appearance of a number of articles on diseases of the eye in various medical journals, and the expertise of a handful of renowned practitioners, specialising in ophthalmology at the beginning of the nineteenth century was regarded by some with contempt. There was a long-held belief that all specialisation was an inferior form of medical and/or surgical activity, and the restriction of practice to diseases of the eye and/or ear had especially low prestige.[113] William Lawrence (1783–1867) wrote that it had been the province of 'quacks, mountebanks, and itinerant practitioners, but that knowledge of diseases of the eye was now (1834) indispensable to medical practitioners'. He went on to describe in great detail the diseases and their treatment.[114] Ophthalmics eventually became a respectable sphere of practice when the huge numbers of soldiers afflicted with trachoma+ after serving in Egypt in the Napoleonic wars caused serious manpower problems in both the French and English armies, and specialist knowledge suddenly became critical. Even so, it was not until 1803 that the first formal course in ophthalmology was taught in Europe, at the medical school of the University of Gottingen,[115] and not until 1817 that lectures on diseases of the eye were delivered in England.

Saunders* became the first surgeon trained in Britain to devote himself entirely to diseases of the eye and ear,[116] and it was the devastating effects of trachoma+ that encouraged him, in conjunction with John Richard Farre, to found a charitable institution – 'The Dispensary for Curing Diseases of the Eye and Ear' – which opened at 40 Charterhouse Square, London, in March 1805. He served as its first surgeon, and it soon ceased to deal with ears and became the first hospital in the world devoted entirely to the treatment of eyes. The Dispensary, renamed the London Ophthalmic Infirmary, subsequently moved to new buildings in Lower Moorfields, near Liverpool Street Station, and is today the world-renowned Moorfields Eye hospital.

---

[110] Billet, *Brief History of Ophthalmic Surgery*, p. 3.
[111] D. Doyle, 'Notable Fellows: William Porterfield (1696–1771)', *Journal of the Royal College of Physicians of Edinburgh* 40, no. 2 (2010), p. 188.
[112] G. Peacock, *Miscellaneous Works of the Late Thomas Young*, vol. 1 (London: John Murray, 1855), p. 1.
[113] Porter, *The Greatest Benefit to Mankind*, p. 367.
[114] William Lawrence, *A Treatise on the Diseases of the Eye* (Washington: Duff Green, 1834), p. 7.
[115] Porter, *The Greatest Benefit to Mankind*, p. 385.
[116] Harold E. Henkes, *History of Ophthalmology* 5 (London: Kluwer Academic Publishers, 1993), pp. 43–51.

The second establishment in the United Kingdom to be dedicated solely to diseases of the eye was the Exeter Eye Infirmary,[117] which was founded by William Adams* just three years after the Dispensary in London. Adams, though an apprentice of Hill,* was taught how to operate on cataracts by Saunders,* who 'instructed Mr Adams, in the most disinterested manner, in the diseases of the eye, and in the operation for the cataract'.[118] Adams had obtained the Prince Regent's patronage before proposing the foundation of the Infirmary, which was initially based in Holloway Street: 'against this Institution the four Physicians and four Surgeons of the [Devon and Exeter] hospital raised their most decided objections and declared such an Institution to be an unnecessary inroad upon the Hospital' [1809]. This was nothing new – Butter records a similar reaction when the London Dispensary was proposed: 'great opposition was raised by the faculty in London against Mr. Sander's proposal. So great were his exertions and so anxious his studies in getting subscriptions to defray the expenses of an ophthalmic institution that his health broke down and an attack of apoplexy[+] deprived him of life' [1814].

One wonders how these doubting physicians and surgeons reacted when the need for such an Infirmary at Exeter was amply demonstrated by its first annual report in November 1809. This indicated that 815 patients had been treated, including a child of seventeen months, five children aged between two and seven years and eight between seven and twenty years. At the other end of the scale, there were four patients between fifty and seventy and six aged between seventy and eighty. They had all undergone cataract operations, mostly with success, although a complete cure often took time.[119]

Butter's interest in diseases of the eye is evident throughout his Memoir: at the age of only seventeen, 'an acquaintance … enabled me to witness his Uncle's operations and treatment of Ophthalmic patients, and he invited me to attend the operations at the Hospital. Thus began my first lesson in Ophthalmic Surgery' [1809]. By the time he was twenty-one, and serving with the SDM in Huddersfield, he was already so successful 'as to induce many patients afflicted with complaints in the eye to come to our Regimental Hospital for relief' [1812]. He was also successful where others had failed: 'I … succeeded by one operation in restoring vision after the failure of 13 previous operations' [1812].

The first tentative thoughts about the establishment of an eye infirmary in Plymouth occurred in 1814: 'Mr Tottan … proposed and would have assisted in the formation of an Ophthalmic Institution in Plymouth if I would attend to it, but I could not then promise to do so whilst I remained Surgeon of the SDM, which regiment might be

[117] It initially had seven beds that were 'attended' by a matron, a nurse and a servant. A rapid growth in the number of patients necessitated a move to larger premises, and a three-storey house was found in Magdalen Street, which opened as a hospital in 1813. It was run as a charity for people unable to afford treatment, who were recommended by the 'officiating minister' of their parish; patients able to pay were asked for an 'annual subscription of one guinea or a benefactor of 10 guineas or upwards'. Outpatients received advice and medicines that were 'applied gratuitously'; the majority of inpatients required an operation for cataract. *The Literary Panorama and Annual Register: vol. 9* (Holborn: C. Taylor, 1811), p. 381.

[118] *A Treatise on Some Practical Points Relating to the Diseases of the Eye by the Late John Cunningham Saunders, with Additions by J R Farre* (London: Longman, Hurst, Rees, Orme and Brown, 1811), p. xviii.

[119] W. Adams, *Practical Observations on Ectropium or Eversion of the Eye-Lids* (London: J. Callow, 1812), p. 112.

ordered to Ireland at any time.' This followed a successful operation on both eyes for a Mrs Symons, observed by Mr Tottan, who was her son-in-law and clearly had a keen interest in ophthalmic surgery: 'many curious cases were hunted up by Mr. Tottan, one was the first case of hydro ophthalmy[+]' [1814].

The Plymouth Public Dispensary had been established in 1798, after a group of eminent local people met to discuss provision of medical care for the poor, and the Dock and Stonehouse Public Dispensary was established in Chapel Street, Devonport, in 1815. There were no hospitals in the city specifically devoted to diseases of the eye, and although the Dispensaries did dedicate one day a week for the treatment of ophthalmic patients, it seems that few attended.[120] Butter 'had long meditated in Edinburgh and in Plymouth ... to attempt the establishment of an Asylum for Lunatics of whom there were many, or an Eye Infirmary', and in 1821, having chosen the latter, he and his friend Edward Moore met at Moore's house to formulate some proposals. They then wrote a circular letter explaining their ideas and soliciting subscriptions, and distributed it around the town, particularly to medical people. By the time the subsequent public meeting was held at the Guildhall on 6 December, they already had a large number of people willing to subscribe. At the meeting, Butter outlined the need for the Infirmary, drawing attention to the size of the local population in relation to other places that already had one. The meeting formally agreed that the Infirmary should be set up with Butter as Physician and Edward Moore as Surgeon. There followed a lengthy and heated discussion about the position of a second surgeon, the principal candidates being Mr Luscombe and Mr Fuge.[121] Fuge was clearly a stalking-horse for the local medical establishment and claimed that there were already sufficient numbers of surgeons in Plymouth, Dock and Stonehouse. The discussion became very heated, with a certain amount of hissing from the floor (possibly pre-arranged) and a threat from Butter to resign if Fuge was elected; Luscombe won by a majority of twenty votes. Samuel Barnes,* surgeon to the Exeter Eye Infirmary, was elected as a consultant.[122]

The Plymouth Eye Dispensary opened in a suite of rooms at 16 Cornwall Street on 25 December 1821. Sergeant Major John Elliott from the SDM was employed as Dispenser (of medicine) and his wife Eliza as Matron. The need for the institution was emphasised when the first half-yearly meeting was held at the Dispensary on 2 July 1822, chaired by the Mayor, Edmund Lockyer,* with Sir M M Lopes* MP as President. The report showed that in the seven months since the inception of the Eye Dispensary a staggering 442 patients had 'already been placed on the Books':[123] 259 had been discharged, of whom 239 were cured, thirteen 'had benefit', and seven were 'not relieved', whilst 183 remained 'under the care of the Charity'. Subscribers included the Duke of Bedford, who gave £10 10s 0d, and Thomas H. Jones from as far away as Jersey, who gave 10s 6d. An address by Edmund Lockyer praised the huge success of the Dispensary in Plymouth and pointed out that it had 'also been the means of relieving many persons, afflicted with complaints of the eyes, residing in distant parts of Devon and Cornwall'. The Committee hoped to be able

---

[120] *Plymouth and Plymouth Dock Weekly Journal*, 13.12.1821.
[121] The newspaper clearly identifies Fuge, but Butter calls him John Hele [1821]. He was, in fact, John Hele Fuge (1781–1871), who was created MRCS in 1802 and FRCS in 1844.
[122] *Plymouth and Plymouth Dock Weekly Journal*, 13.12.1821.
[123] *Exeter Flying Post*, 11.7.1822.

'to convert the Eye Dispensary into an Eye Infirmary, and to establish a few Beds for the reception of the more urgent and dangerous cases; as it has been experienced that the salvation or restoration of sight often depends upon the immediate control and domestic management of Patients'.[124]

The first annual meeting was held at Plymouth Guildhall on 11 January 1823. Lord Rolle* was elected President, and it was duly decided that the Dispensary should now be converted to an Infirmary. The Treasurer's report showed a balance of £67, and the number of patients 'admitted' during the year had been 715, of whom 521 were cured. The *Exeter Flying Post* recorded that

> after the reports had been read, a large group of poor objects who had been cured of their complaints, some of them after 20 years, entered the hall, and by their declarations and gratitude and thanks, produced a very sensible affect on the gentlemen assembled. The proceedings having been closed, about 30 of the company adjourned to the Royal Hotel, where a sumptuous dinner was served up, and several appropriate toasts and speeches delivered on the occasion; and the party broke up highly satisfied with the beneficial results of the charity possessing the strongest claims to their recommendation and support.[125]

Every year, the Infirmary published its annual and quarterly reports, although the published extracts only rarely included secondary statements beyond the bare facts and statistics. They showed the number of patients admitted, the number that were successfully treated, those continuing in treatment and those unable to be helped. They also recorded specific procedures carried out, such as cataract operations, and ended with a list of subscribers for the period and the amounts of money given. These reports appeared in Plymouth-based newspapers, and occasionally in those further afield, such as the *North Devon Journal* (8.10.1824), which commented: 'the progress of the Plymouth Eye Infirmary presents numerous cheering instances of the great benefit arising to society from such Institutions'.

The Infirmary was established at 16 Cornwall Street, but all the reports from December 1826[126] to October 1828[127] give the address as 1 Cornwall Street – no explanation has been found for the change of venue, and the move is curious. Number 1 was, however, a property Butter knew well – it had been his lodgings above a 'mixed business' of druggist and grocer, where his landlord was Mr Rowe. Perhaps Butter did not initially want to set up the Infirmary at no. 1 because of a scandal caused by a court case brought against Edward and William Rowe by Mr and Mrs Jewell in 1821, for putting 'poisonous ingredients into a cake eaten by their daughter and her friends when they were invited by Anne Rowe to take cake and Ale at her House'.[128] Presumably the scandal had been forgotten by 1826. Cornwall Street was home to a wide diversity of shops and businesses; one of the gates into the Pannier Market opened from it, and John Foulston designed and built the first Plymouth Public Library there. Most of the street is now incorporated into Drake Circus. Unfortunately, 'our corner house in Cornwall St. did not suit well our purposes on

---

[124] *Exeter Flying Post*, 11.7.1822.
[125] *Exeter Flying Post*, 16.1.1823.
[126] *Plymouth Herald*, 30.12.1826.
[127] *Exeter & Plymouth Gazette*, 4.10.1828.
[128] The Box: Plymouth Borough Records, ref: 1/702/100.

account of the noises during market days and times of the fairs. We thence removed our Institution into Westwell St' [1822].

The move to 8 Westwell Street did not actually take place until some time between November 1828 and April 1829. Westwell Street led to Plymouth Hoe and in 1765 was known as Love Lane, reputed to be a favourite resort of courting couples. The west well, in a field alongside the path to the Hoe, was filled in during 1810, and properties were built along the road, which was first recorded as Westwell Street in 1812. The Civic Centre now covers the original site. After a long settled period, the Infirmary was forced to move again, for the last time in Butter's lifetime, in December 1844: 'we might have longer remained had not the Committee been blind or perverse in allowing the premises to be bought over our heads' [1822].

Butter encountered considerable difficulties in finding new accommodation: 'what was agreed upon at one meeting was annulled at the next, one division was for buying, the other for building and so we vacillated to and fro for years' [1822]. After a particularly acrimonious falling-out over a property in Princess Square, Butter took matters into his own hands and bought Buckland House, in Millbay Road. He gave the committee a choice: '"I will transfer to Trustees for the uses and benefit of the Plymouth Eye Infirmary, or I will keep it as private property for myself ... Shall it be taken for the Institution or not?" The Committee then agreed to accept of my offer' [1822].

The Infirmary was funded by subscriptions and donations, generally varying between ten shillings and ten guineas, although there were occasional payments of significantly larger amounts. For example, in October 1850 there was £50 from 'the Earl of Mount Edgcumbe and other Trustees of Hele's Charity, per Deeble Boger Esq' (this charity donated a number of times – Deeble Boger was a lawyer in the family firm based in Plympton). Sir Thomas Dyke Acland* donated £10 10s 0d annually for a number of years. Charles Mare* donated £10 10s 0d in 1852, no doubt hoping to reinforce Butter's support for his cause in the forthcoming parliamentary election. Legacies could be quite substantial: £100 was received from the Executors of Miss Cordelia Bewes (whose brother had entered into a partnership with Deeble Boger's firm in 1843),[129] £200 from the estate of Charles Anthony of Longcause House, Totnes, who had himself been a 'successful practitioner in medicine',[130] and £300 from Captain Thomas Grove in 1827.[131]

Despite the donation income and the generosity of subscribers, the Infirmary went through various difficult times financially, particularly in the late 1840s and early 1850s when a number of its original subscribers died or otherwise ended their support. In January 1854, for instance:

Your committee respectfully draw the attention of the subscribers to the increase of expenditure during the last year, owing to the dearth of provisions, the high prices of drugs, the rise in blankets, sheeting, coals etc and express regret that the annual income has been inadequate to meet their demands without leaving a balance against the charity of £24.15s.

[129] *Exeter and Plymouth Gazette*, 10.10.1840.
[130] *Western Daily Mercury*, 1.12.1864.
[131] *North Devon Journal*, 15.11.1827.

The most detailed breakdown of expenditure came in 1861: 'insurance £1.16s, diet and sundries £162.18.2d., drugs and leeches £82.9.9d., instruments and glasses £19.0.7d., printing, advertising and stationery £24.4.5d., tradesmen's bills £67.1.4d., gas company £4.13.8d, salary of the dispenser [Mr Bayntun] £84.'[132]

Finances improved somewhat, but the situation was rarely comfortable – in 1864, the annual report stated that 'the institution has ample sums for carrying out all its objects', although this sits oddly with 'the treasurers report which showed that the balance in hand was £121.2s.4d. against £199.2.7d. bills due and unpaid'. Perhaps this was because 'the repairs to the house, both external and internal, so long required and postponed for want of funds have now been completed'. Mr Bayntun was given a gratuity of £10 and a pay rise, but there were clearly issues with the need for much fuller funding of patients:

> Mr Eccles* said it would be very desirable if there could be a further extension of the charity, or rather that some of the restrictions they at present had should be removed, so that patients might be induced to remain a longer time under their care and that others who were afflicted with eye disease might be inclined to go to them, and undergo those operations which would in many instances preserve their sight. Dr Rendle [Edmund Rendle, surgeon at the Infirmary since 1833[133]] said that in the early part of the spring a man had received an injury to one of his eyes. It was a case that required prompt attention, but the man had no money and they could not take him in. They accordingly sent him to the union with a letter to the guardians stating that if he were not attended to, his sight would be lost. He afterwards came back to them but the opportunity for effecting a cure was gone … the consequence was he is now a charge upon the parish. Mr Mennie would not be for excluding paupers but he thought the parishes to which those paupers belonged ought to be called on to reimburse them.[134]

Many parishes already did, although possibly not to the full extent of the costs involved. It is recorded that at least as early as 1835 'various parishes in the town and neighbourhood' were paying 6d per day for the treatment of pauper in-patients.[135] The system remained in force, in one guise or another, and doubtless at differing rates, until the advent of the NHS.

It was not long after the 1864 report that 'building' funds were obtained for two wards by 'generous donations' – a list of donors and the sums they donated appeared in the *Western Morning News* (7.1.1867). A concert to raise funds for furniture was given by the Plymouth Vocal Association and was so successful that Mr Cottman, the conductor, 'intimated' that he would give an annual concert for the charity.[136] By January 1871,

> the state of the house was in excellent order, and the advantages of the addition to the original building were daily felt and appreciated, but the amount of annual subscriptions did not permit the full development of the benefits as to the free

---

[132] *Western Morning News*, 15.1.1861.
[133] *Western Times*, 26.1.1833.
[134] *Western Daily Mercury*, 1.12.1864.
[135] Square, 'Medical History of Plymouth, with Anecdotes and Reminiscences', p. III.
[136] *Western Morning News*, 12.1.1869.

admission of patients and the reduction of diet charges which some desired to see carried out. The balance in hand was £61 2s 5d and there was still a small balance once all the bills were paid.[137]

The high esteem in which the Infirmary was held was evident from a very early stage of its development, and Butter's reputation resulted in a significant number of influential people becoming patrons, the first being Sir Ralph Lopes.* In 1828, the Duke of Clarence joined their number, and the Infirmary consequently became the Plymouth Royal Eye Infirmary. When the Duke became King William IV, in June 1830, 'THE KING' was proudly added to the annual reports. William had long had connections with Plymouth, both personally and through his naval career. Butter's close association with Lord Rolle* perhaps helped him to attract such an important figure. William was followed in due course by Prince Augustus Frederick, the Duke of Sussex, who died in 1842, Prince Albert (also Lord High Steward of Plymouth), who died in 1861, and the Prince of Wales, the future Edward VII, who became a patron in 1864. Amongst other patrons were the Earl of Mount Edgcumbe; Thomas James Agar-Robartes of Lanhydrock, who along with Lady Robartes, as a patroness, was proposed by Butter at the annual meeting in 1870; William Gordon Cornwallis Eliot, Earl of St Germans (the St Germans Board of Guardians were regular donors to the Infirmary[138]); and Sir Thomas Dyke Acland.* As well as Lady Robartes, the Infirmary had two other patronesses – Louisa Trefusis, Lady Rolle and Frances Talbot, the Countess of Morley, who was the daughter of a surgeon. Both ladies were supporting the Infirmary by 1828, if not earlier.

The quarterly reports show that John Butter was always designated 'Physician', and that Edward Moore and William Joseph Square* were both named as 'Surgeons'. Square was also a surgeon at the South Devon and East Cornwall Hospital in Princess Place, Plymouth, as well as being a licensed apothecary. He retired in 1869 after thirty years of service and was replaced by his son,[139] another William.[140] Sergeant Major Elliott and his wife were the first people to be employed at the Infirmary, undoubtedly because Butter knew their capabilities from their time with the SDM. Mrs Elliott died in 1841 at the age of seventy-one, but her husband remained there until shortly before his own death in 1848. George Bayntun took over the role as resident Dispenser in 1847, and his wife Eliza became Matron.

George and Eliza Bayntun were initially paid £33 a year with an extra £7 allowed for a nurse. In 1854, they had the help of a general servant, with six in-patients under their care – four males (a labourer and three copper-miners) and two females (a labourer's daughter, aged twelve, and a copper-miner's daughter, aged thirteen). In that year's annual report, Butter noted that 'while the number of patients treated was very great, it would be remembered that persons belonging to the East of Cornwall, where mining operations were extensively carried on, formed a numerous class of patients'.[141] There is, however, no explanation as to why miners should have been particularly vulnerable.

---

[137] *Western Morning News*, 10.1.1871.
[138] *Western Daily Mercury*, 7.2.1862.
[139] *Western Morning News*, 11.1.1870.
[140] 1871 census.
[141] *Western Courier*, 18.1.1854.

It has not been possible to identify an entry for the Eye Infirmary in the 1861 census (it seems to be in the 5 to 10 per cent of entries known to have been lost), but the Bayntuns were still living there when the annual report for 1870 was produced: 'it was satisfactory to state that the building was in good condition, and that domestic arrangements, under the care of Mr & Mrs Bayntun, were all that could be desired'.[142] They were to remain working at the Infirmary for many more years – the annual report for January 1881 noted:

> nor did he [Mr Moore, the Secretary] think persons could ever be more attached
> to a master and mistress than the patients were to Mr & Mrs Bayntun ... they [the
> committee] had at last persuaded Mr & Mrs Bayntun to take a little holiday –
> the first for 32 years – for the benefit of their health.[143]

The 1871 census does not give the occupations of the in-patients but does give their birthplaces, all of which were in Devon and Cornwall. Once again, there were four males, this time with three females. As well as Eliza and George, there were a cook, a parlour-maid and a house-maid, the last two aged eighteen and fifteen respectively.

The Eye Infirmary's reliance on subscriptions and donations meant there was a limit to the number of patients that could be accommodated at any one time, and a ticket system was used to obtain treatment: it seems that subscribers and benefactors were given preference and could nominate patients, whilst others, too poor to subscribe, had to rely on either the overseers of the poor, or clergy from their parish to arrange the funding of a ticket. The system clearly had its problems:

> as a great number of patients come from a distance for relief at the Eye Infir-
> mary, without tickets or friends, it would be kind of those subscribers who still
> retain their old tickets to sign and send them back to the Infirmary, where they
> could be filled out for patients who would otherwise find great trouble in pro-
> curing them.[144]

Perhaps the most successful treatment given was for cataracts, and these operations were performed on patients of all ages, from very young children to a seventy-two-year-old.[145] News of one operation was reported in a number of English papers and even in the Irish press: 'at the Plymouth Eye Infirmary a child of fourteen months old who was born blind has been restored to its anxious parents possessed of the invaluable blessing of sight and three other persons have had their vision restored'.[146] The quarterly report for March 1832 announced that 'a child of 9 months old, born blind, has been cured by operations on both eyes'.[147] In October 1845, it was reported that 'five patients blinded from cataracts have been operated on during the quarter, two of whom are infants blind from birth, one two months old, the other five months',[148]

---

[142] *Western Morning News*, 11.1.1870.
[143] *Western Morning News*, 11.1.1881.
[144] *Exeter and Plymouth Gazette*, 7.7.1849.
[145] *Exeter and Plymouth Gazette*, 4.7.1829.
[146] *Sander's Newsletter*, 23.10.1827.
[147] *Royal Devonport Telegraph & Plymouth Chronicle*, 31.3.1832.
[148] *Exeter & Plymouth Gazette*, 25.10.1845.

and an eight-month-old child was operated on in September 1839.[149] Other treatments included those for tumours of 'divers' kinds, 'simphloma' (syphiloma[+]), ectropion,[+] ptosis,[+] trichiasis[+] and a small number of 'artificial pupils'.[150] Rather more alarmingly, the Infirmary's quarterly report of 2 October 1848 stated that two patients were admitted 'with gun-shot wounds of the eye-ball'.[151] An earlier report had noted a successful operation on one eye after an explosion in a quarry, although the other eye had been lost.[152]

Squinting was another affliction cured by the Infirmary – in 1841, Butter gave a paper to the annual meeting of the British Association for the Advancement of Science: 'General Observations on the Pathology and Cure of Squinting', which lists the different kinds of squinting, their causes and treatment. It was reported that

> there was no remedy known to the close of the year 1839. The year 1840 shed a new light on this subject. A cure now is almost certain from an operation. The author considered that during the last year (1840) some thousands of squinters were cured perfectly in the United Kingdom, and many hundreds in the three towns of Plymouth, Stonehouse and Devonport, of whom a great number have been operated on at the Plymouth Royal Eye Infirmary. He considered the operation simple, safe and successful in skilled hands and had never known an untoward result or loss of vision from it in his own practice, which appeared, from the living instances of patients cured and shown at the meeting, to have been considerable.[153]

The Infirmary reports from July 1823 onwards included the number of in-house patients (described as 'dieted') for the relevant quarter. It had been

> agreed to take into the house such patients as may be affected with urgent or dangerous diseases and for the present to limit the number to three at any one time. This accommodation, now so happily attained through public munificence, as being heretofore much wanted, [is] considered extremely desirable for poor patients who have come from distant parts of the country with the hope of finding a cure at the Plymouth Eye Infirmary.[154]

There were four beds in Westwell Street in 1835,[155] but the move to Millbay Road and the subsequent extension of Buckland House meant a substantial increase in availability. The first report detailing the number of in-patients appeared in 1839: 'above 10,000 patients have been relieved since the formation of the Institution, of whom

[149] *Western Times*, 5.10.1839.
[150] *Plymouth and Plymouth Dock Weekly Journal*, 3.7.1823.
[151] *Western Times*, 7.10.1848.
[152] *Western Times*, 5.4.1834.
[153] Review of: John Butter, 'General Observations on the Pathology and Cure of Squinting' in *Notices and Abstracts of Communications to the British Association for the Advancement of Science at the Plymouth Meeting, August 1841*, p. 79, an addendum to *Report of the Eleventh Meeting of the British Association for the Advancement of Science; Held at Plymouth in July 1841* (London: John Murray, 1842).
[154] *Plymouth and Plymouth Dock Weekly Journal*, 3.7.1823.
[155] Square, 'Medical History of Plymouth, with Anecdotes and Reminiscences', p. 111.

433 have been dieted and lodged in the house'.[156] Patients remained in the Infirmary because surgeons did not yet know how to use stitches to hold the incision in the eye together and therefore stop the cataract returning, and patients would have to lie quietly in a darkened room for weeks after the operation. The quarterly number of in-patients was usually between twenty and forty. By 1870, the 'total number of house patients since the commencement of the charity had reached 3,112'.[157]

In-patients were never more than a small proportion of the total numbers treated annually, which had reached well over a thousand by 1844 at the latest.[158] The number of patients described as 'incurable' was always remarkably low, and as the years went by the number of available treatments increased significantly. During 1860, for instance, 772 patients had been cured and 271 had received benefit, ninety-nine as in-patients. Cataracts and obstructed lachrymal[+] passages were operated on, and there were several iridectomies.[+] These arose from the purchase of 'a new apparatus called the ophthalmoscope ... and a number of diseased eyes examined by it for exploring the morbid internal changes in the delicate tissues within the eye ball, constituting diseases never before seen or explained'.[159] To complement this,

> the committee have acceded to the recommendation of your medical directors in fitting up a new operating room with superior light and also in ventilating, painting and colouring the interior walls which may now vie with any in the Kingdom, though limited means have not enabled them to carry out other requisite alterations nor the repair of the exterior.[160]

Use of the ophthalmoscope revolutionised the depth and efficiency of examinations, which had, until then, been carried out by visual examination, perhaps with the aid of a magnifying glass. The machine had been invented in 1851 by Hermann von Helmholtz and 'much improved by Dr Graefe of Berlin',[161] but was not in common use until 1854. 'Dr Graefe was ... [also] the author of a treatise on Glaucoma produced by intra-ocular pressure, to which he has given a new name and applied a new remedy, which last consists of opening the eyeball, letting out the aqueous humour[+] and excising a portion of the iris.' Such operations were soon being practised at the Plymouth Eye Infirmary: 'since the operation for Squinting ... [was] first practised at your institution in 1840 ... no new operation on the eye has been received with such general interest as iridectomy[+] for the cure of diseases once deemed hopeless'.[162]

Butter's failing sight must have been becoming increasingly serious early in the 1850s, and it was obvious that he would soon have to retire. It was probably because of this, as well as of his enormous contribution to the success of the Eye Infirmary, that, after the official business of the annual meeting held on 10 January 1853,

[156] *Western Times*, 5.10.1839.
[157] *Western Morning News*, 10.1.1871.
[158] *Exeter and Plymouth Gazette*, 4.1.1845.
[159] *Western Morning News*, 15.1.1861.
[160] Ibid.
[161] *Western Morning News*, 15.1.1861.
[162] Ibid.

Dr William, the Rev. John Hatchard and other gentlemen spoke in the highest terms of his skill, benevolence, the zeal and labour on behalf of the Royal Eye Infirmary, which had distinguished Dr Butter's long connection with the Institution. It was decided to obtain a portrait of the learned Doctor, the cost of which it was thought would not exceed £100, and then appropriate the balance to the purchase of a piece of plate to be presented to Dr Butter, as a further testimony of the high estimation in which his services were held.[163]

Only twelve days later, the *Exeter and Plymouth Gazette* reported that 'the final list [of subscribers] contained over 450 names and the amount raised was about £200'. The portrait was painted by John Lucas* and presented on 16 January 1854. Unable to be at the presentation because of illness, Butter wrote a letter, read by Captain Fisk,* thanking the testimonial committee and

testifying to the artist's great anxiety and patience, deep study and careful revision bestowed on the subject. He has rendered the irksome and tedious task of sitting both easy and agreeable. He has treated the subject historically by the introduction of suitable accessories borrowing a hint of the portrait of John Hunter by Joshua Reynolds and of Dr Jenner by Northcote.[164]

The accessories show Butter with a scroll in his hands with the words 'Address delivered 1821.' Another scroll on the table shows the Infirmary's thirty-second annual report, which had just been published, and there are two books, one his 1825 treatise on the Dockyard Disease, and the other comprising 'sundry memoirs published in various journals'. There is also an open book, one side of the page showing a translated motto from Celsus[165] 'our eyes are subject to grievous and various diseases and ought to be preserved with the utmost care', the other showing five different specimens of diseased eyes. Butter thanked the committee for the silver salver that bore an inscription that associated his name with the cure or relief of twenty-four thousand patients, and thanked everyone who had been involved with the Infirmary, including especially William Square and George Bayntun for their many years of service, and Dr Edward Moore who had been with him for all thirty-two years.

Butter's sight finally failed, and a special meeting was held on 11 February 1856 to elect replacements for him and Dr Moore. It was proposed

that John Butter be elected as consulting physician … The Doctor in returning thanks said that while the affliction with which it had pleased Almighty God to visit him rendered him unable to continue those active services he had hitherto given, he still should have much pleasure in rendering any assistance he could in the position they had been pleased to elect him to.

---

[163] *Western Courier*, 12.1.1853.
[164] *Western Courier*, 25.1.1854.
[165] A second-century Greek philosopher, noted for his opposition to Christianity.

Dr Moore was elected physician and William Joseph Square was elected senior surgeon in place of Dr Moore,[166] with John Henry Eccles* as his assistant.[167] Butter remained a consultant to the Infirmary for another twenty years.

The secretary's report to the annual meeting of 1876 revealed that Butter's health was failing: 'our respected friend Dr Butter still feels himself identified with, and is anxious for the prosperity of his favourite institution, though from his own failing health and from the ability of the rest of the medical staff, his services had not been practically called for'.[168] It also announced that since the inception of the Infirmary, 50,221 patients had been treated, 49,103 had been cured or relieved and only 824 were pronounced incurable. The following year's report 'regretted that age and infirmity prevented Dr Butter from giving them advice'.[169] Butter died that very day.

The Eye Infirmary continued to successfully treat more and more patients and grew too large for Buckland House, despite adaptation and expansion. In 1897, a new hospital was conceived, and building started in Apsley Road, near Mutley station. This was completed in 1901 and remained in use until the Infirmary was transferred to Derriford Hospital, initially retaining its name in full, although it has now been abbreviated to REI. It was formally opened by the Countess of Wessex on 23 April 2013. The Apsley Road building, which is Grade II listed, has since been converted into luxury flats.

A generous grant from the Eye Infirmary's League of Friends enabled Butter's portrait to be professionally restored before being moved to its present home in the foyer of the main entrance to the REI, a worthy memorial to his many years of wisdom, tenacity and skill in the service of the Infirmary.

[166] *Exeter and Plymouth Gazette*, 16.2.1856.
[167] *Western Times*, 16.2.1856.
[168] *Western Morning News*, 15.1.1876.
[169] *Western Morning News*, 13.1.1877.

THE MEMOIR

JOHN BUTTER

Decr. 12th 1865.

Jno. Butter M.D. M.B. S & L.S.

I was Born at Woodbury near Exeter on the 22nd of January 1791 and died on the …
My Father Jacob Butter and my Mother Catherine each lived to the age of 77 years
and died leaving three children – two sons and one daughter.

A remarkable circumstance attended my birth and the subject of this narrative. I
had seven grandfathers and grandmothers all living at my birth and had I been born
3 months earlier I might have had eight. Another remarkable circumstance is that my
father and mother were not married until they had passed their thirtieth year of age
and that I was not born for 15 months after their marriage. At my Christening another
remarkable circumstance occurred: two of my great-grandmothers, both above 90
years of age, rode on a horse with side-saddle pillion two miles forward and two
miles backward and the united ages of the three, including the horse, amounted [to]
206 years.

My father practised the Medical Profession at Woodbury and the surrounding
parishes above half a century and succeeded his grandfather Langdon in that parish.
I and my brother Jacobus both received a classical education at the Exeter Grammar
School under the Revd Mr Bartholomew. We both chose the medical profession.

1807

On leaving school at 16 I performed my first surgical operation by a tooth for
my own Father whose sufferings prompted him to ride to Exmouth and Budleigh
without success for the purpose of getting this Tooth extracted. Necessity obliged
him to instruct a Schoolboy in the art of using a German Key+ with which I extracted
my Father's Tooth so much to his ease and comfort that it induced him to present
me with my first fee. I then undertook the treatment of a poor boy in the village who
had long been afflicted with scald head alias Tincea Capita.+ This patient had bid
defiance to my Father's skill and had baffled the treatment received at the Devon &
Exeter Hospital. He was cured by taking a Plesner's pill every night and a purging
powder twice a week, and externally by the application of Tar Ointment to the head
every night, covered with a silk cap and washed off every morning with a lather of
yellow soap.

1809

At the age of 18 I became a resident pupil in the Devon & Exeter Hospital for 6
months; whilst there many opportunities were afforded me for improvement during
the year 1809.

In 1808 the West of England Eye Infirmary was established by Mr afterwards Sir Wm Adams* aided by the strenuous exertions of Samuel Milford Esqre a most active County Magistrate. Against this Institution the four Physicians and four Surgeons of the [Devon and Exeter] hospital raised their most decided objections and declared such an Institution to be an unnecessary inroad upon the Hospital. They were consequently excluded from witnessing the new operations at the Eye Infirmary.

An acquaintance with Mr Adams' nephew Hocking enabled me to witness his Uncle's operations and treatment of Ophthalmic patients and he invited me to attend the operations at the Hospital. Thus began my first lesson in Ophthalmic Surgery. During my Hospital term Sir Jno Moore's defeat at Corunna took place with the British Army and the surviving troops returned to Plymouth where sufficient accommodation could not be found for the sick, of whom numbers were forwarded by Waggons and Vehicles to the Horse Barracks at Exeter where they were inspected by a Staff Surgeon Grant and attended by Mr Miller and Mr Luscombe, who were glad enough to get young men to prepare medicines for the sick soldiers labouring under Typhus Fever and other maladies. With two others my services were accepted so that I saw these many diseases incidental to a soldier's life.

Another rare opportunity offered of my studying Veterinary Art and Comparative Anatomy under Mr James White then the ablest practitioner in the west of England. His practical works on Veterinary Science can be read with advantage even at the present time.[1]

From Sept. 1809 my father sent me to London with £50 in my pocket in order to attend the lectures there but without any plan advice or guide as to which lectures I should attend. An officious patient of my father's pompously proposed to assist me by an introductory letter to his nephew a House Surgeon at St Bartholomew's Hospital. The nephew's advice was after reading his Uncle's letter that I should enter my name as a perpetual pupil to Mr Abernethy* and other Lecturers involving an immediate deposit of £45, leaving me only with a pound or two to subsist on. After paying my coach fare and travelling expenses from 5 o'clock on a Friday morning to Saturday evening I had next to search for lodgings, having been billeted for a few nights in the house of a carpenter where everything was unclean and uncomfortable. I was then almost adrift having no friend or adviser at hand and very little money in my pocket.

One day in passing through Smithfield bars I observed lodgings to be let at a Hairdresser's shop, and on enquiring was induced to rent a single bedroom at 7d per week. Here I quartered myself during the winter of 1809 but visited no-one and was almost ashamed to tell any one where I resided.

My constant attendance on Abernethy's* lectures Anatomical and Surgical enabled me to form the acquaintance of an Devonshire youth from Newton, Josias Baker who possessed a great advantage over me as his senior in having an abundant supply of money which enabled him to purchase the most splendid works published in Italy Germany and England. Baker had another superior advantage of residing in the house of Wm. Lawrence* then Demonstrator of Anatomy at St. Bartholomew's Hospital. Baker and I became intimate friends. We dissected together and compared notes afterwards, being joined by two others Webb of Bath and Brown. These four

---

[1] His *Treatise on Veterinary Medicine* was originally published in two volumes in 1808 and was up to four volumes by 1815: James White, *A Treatise on Veterinary Medicine*, 4 vols. (London: Longman, 1807–15).

joined in dissecting the body of a man named Antonio Cordoza, a fine Spaniard above 6 feet, hung at Newgate for the murder of a comrade on board a ship in the Thames. Baker was the monied man and purser to pay for this magnificent subject of which we each dissected a quarter and paid accordingly as he could raise his share. The bones of this subject Baker had masserated and made into a skeleton of which he became the possessor. This skeleton with many of Baker's books and valuable prints and instruments came into my possession by purchase sometime afterwards when Baker resigned the Medical Profession and became a Wine Merchant by marrying the daughter of a man dealing in Sicilian and Italian Wines. They were subsequently brought to Plymouth, where a small museum was built for their reception, after being dragged about the country for years with the South Devon Militia. One day Mr Bird, a Barrister on the Western Circuit living at Plymouth came into this Museum and remarked on this fine skeleton the history of which had been given to him [and] said 'that was the first prisoner I ever defended at the Old Bailey'.

1810

As the spring of 1810 drew on my father had previously prepared me for the receipt of a letter from Lord Rolle* as Colonel of the SD Militia offering me the Assistant Surgeonry then vacant in his regiment. This offer was declined principally on my mother's account as she strongly objected to her son becoming a soldier. In April 1810 I was surprised by the receipt of a second letter from Lord Rolle stating that my commission dated the 5th April was ordered and that I must join the regiment at Exeter at my earliest convenience. In May 1810 I left London and reached Exeter late on a Saturday night, slept at the London Inn, breakfasted [and] proceeded down Fore Street soon after the Cathedral bells had chimed for morning service. At the corner of Castle Street I met an officer in uniform who I guessed might belong to the SD Militia.

On reaching the Mess Room I learnt that Lord Rolle* would dine at the Officers' Mess at 5 o'clock which I was requested to attend. I accordingly presented myself and Lord Rolle graciously introduced me to the Officers then present. Leave of absence was then granted me to visit my parents in Woodbury until my presence was required. Not many days elapsed before a route had arrived from the War Office dated 10th May ordering the SD Militia to march in two divisions from Exeter to the Eastward, the 1st division on the 21st May to Honiton where they were to be followed by the Staff and the 2nd division on the next day. I had not been at Woodbury with my parents many days when an order reached me from Col Lord Rolle to join the 1st division at Honiton. Accordingly I started on horseback and sent my baggage by another conveyance. My nearest way from Woodbury was over Woodbury Aylesbeare and Ottery Commons. I rode a long-striding shilly-legged mare much to be admired in figure but unsafe in her action. At a very stoney part of the road whilst going at a slow pace between a walk and a trot she stumbled all at once on her knees and head and fell on her side, casting me forward on the stoney road which marked my chin and face and hands and knees and tore my clothes. Both horse and rider were dismal figures to look at. Fortunately I had a relation living near Ottery to whom I presented myself, leaving the mare with him and taking his horse to ride from Ottery to Honiton. Arriving there without any change of raiment I had to dine at the Mess in my riding clothes and to get well laughed-at by the Colonel and Officers present.

On the following days the 1st division continued their march through Somerton, Langport, Shaftesbury, Salisbury, Petworth, Petersfield, Seven Oaks, Maidstone and Rochester. The original route was made out for Bristol but its destination altered at different places. Much merriment was excited on this long march with singing, riding, duck hunting and whist playing. At Rochester the SDM remained in quarters until some of the Chatham Barracks could be vacated for their reception on the 24th of June.

On my joining the regiment at Exeter the Surgeon was called Tucker[2] and the Assistant Surgeon White. In their march through Stockland, Dorsetshire, Assistant Surgeon White visited a wealthy cousin in his regimentals, became attached to her, married and resigned his commission. The Medical Staff then consisted of John Tucker and John Butter who were quartered with the SDM in Chatham Barracks with the North Yorks and Denbigh Militias.

The sports of the year were Racket and Horse Racing by day and Whist playing at night. After the summer months passed away Surgeon Tucker applied for leave of absence to visit his family and friends living in Lyme in Dorsetshire and Chard in Somersetshire. Whilst on this tour he proposed an offer of marriage to a wealthy cousin, an engagement followed. On his return from this tour to Chatham Barracks he in confidence informed me of his engagement and said it was not his intention to marry until the beginning of the year 1811. Mr Tucker kindly put me in possession of his plans thinking and wishing that I might be able to prepare myself for succeeding him in the Surgeonry of the Regiment. I had therefore to follow up the course of lectures delivered in London during the winter session of 1810. For this purpose I obtained leave of absence of the Commanding Officer with the understanding that I should be present and mustered at Headquarters twice a month, on the 10th and 24th with intermediate leave. Chatham being only 30 miles from London, I could easily run down by coach in the afternoon and return by the Dover Mail early on the following morning.

This plan I pursued for three or four months. There was a Regimental Whist Club at this time called the Flip Club because the beverage drink was that mixture which was made with egg, beer, spirit and spices. The Club met nightly after Mess at the different officer's rooms and played till bedtime. I studied Hoyle's[3] games and proved myself very successful at the Whist Table, generally on the winning side, and although the stakes were small, 1d per point at Long Whist, I contrived to win enough in this way to pay my expenses from London to Chatham twice a month.

1811

When Surgeon Tucker gave notice of his approaching nuptials in the spring of 1811 I thought it right to try my luck at Surgeon's Hall and therefore applied to Mr Abernethy* and other Professors for their certificates of my attendance on the proper

---

[2] This is at variance with the regimental history: see the section on the SDM in the Introduction.

[3] Edmond Hoyle (1672–1769) was a writer, best known for his works on the rules and playing of card games.

lectures. This application was made before the expiration of the Session when the following dialogue then occurred:

Mr A 'Why do you ask for my certificate before the end of the season?'

A 'Because I wish to pass my examination at the College of Surgeons.'

Mr A 'Why so? What is the hurry?'

A 'I will tell you Sir my position. I am an Assistant Surgeon in the SD Militia. The Regimental Surgeon has given me notice in confidence of his early intention to resign the Surgeonry in order to get married and settle in private practice. I cannot succeed him in the Surgeonry without a Diploma from the College which I wish to obtain.'

Mr A 'Well and what is to hinder you?'

A 'I don't know that I can comply with your rules altogether and I may not be able to produce all the certificates required.'

Mr A 'What will be wanting?'

A 'I may as well tell you the truth Sir at once. I am not 22 years of age and therefore cannot furnish that deficiency.'

Mr A 'Stand up' – he said:

'What height do you call yourself?'

A 'Above 6 feet' – I replied.

Mr A 'Keep your own counsel. Who the devil would think of asking a fellow 6 feet high whether or not he was of age. Answer their questions and fear not. If I was called upon to select any one pupil out of my class more likely than another to pass the examinations at Surgeon's Hall you are the person I would fix on.'

A A humble bow of course expressed my thanks for the compliment.

Mr A shook hands and wished me success.

1811 April 15th

I presented myself before the President and Court of Examiners at the College of Surgeons and deposited the necessary certificates. I was the last of eleven that went in and the first out. Sir Charles Blicke* the Chairman rose and enquired my name and then gave a paper to Mr Cline* for examination.

The following dialogue then occurred:

Mr C 'Your name is John Butter?'

A 'Yes Sir.'

Mr C 'Where have you studied?'

A 'At the Devon & Exeter Hospital, at St Bartholomew's & Guy's in London.'

Mr C 'What is a hernia?'

A 'A protrusion of any viscus from the proper cavity.'

Mr C 'How many different kinds of hernia are there?'

A   'Several. The femoral, inquinal, ventral and others.'

Mr C   'How would you treat a strangulated hernia?'

A   'I would first try the taxis or steady pressure. Failing this I would per-
        haps bleed from the arm, apply ice to the part, put the patient into a
        warm bath, order injections common followed by a tobacco glyster⁺;
        these failing I would resort to the operation for hernia.'

Mr C   'Would you do this yourself?'

A   'Certainly Sir.'

Mr C   'And what would you expect to find?'

A   'A sack of the peretoneum⁺ containing fluid and the portion of the intes-
        tine confined by a stricture, which I would divide, enlarge the aperture
        and return the bowel.'

Mr C   'Would you do this yourself?'

A   'I would Sir.'

Mr C   'What is a fistula lackrymalis?'

A   'An obstruction in the nasal duct conveying the tears from the eyes into
        the nose.'

Mr C   'How would you overcome this obstruction?'

A   'By syringing the punctum⁺ often with warm water and passing gold
        probes down to the lacrimal sack⁺ and nasal duct.'

Mr C   'Suppose you could not overcome the obstruction. What would you do
        in the event of an abscess forming?'

A   'I would open the abscess and pass a silver style⁺ down through the
        obstructed duct.'

Mr C   'Would you do this yourself?'

A   'Certainly Sir.'

Mr C   Taking a pen and writing thus on the paper – 'Satisfied, HC.' Edmond
        Balfour the Secretary then rose and said: 'Mr John Butter 22 [sic] if you
        please for your diploma which shall be ready signed & sealed on this day
        week, if you will send to the College for it.'

I then bowed and left the room. I might then have left St. Bartholomew's Hospital
satisfied with my success but having a quarter part of a subject for dissection I
was unwilling to leave London before my anatomical researches were complete.
Imprudently, by dissecting this putrid subject before breakfast I brought on an attack
of cholera,⁴ vomiting purging fever which nearly cost me my life and obliged me
to hurry down to Chatham where my brother officers thought I would have died
and Surgeon Tucker calculated on never finding me his successor. I was wasted to
a skeleton and the purging and cramp never left me until my mother and brother
arrived at Chatham and insisted on my return with them into Devonshire where,

⁴ The cholera outbreak of 1832 was the first time the disease reached this country, but the
term cholera was used before then to describe acute intestinal diseases (Jonathan Barry,
personal communication).

at Woodbury, with pure air and a milk diet consisting of junkets, syllabubs, blanc mange and Devonshire cream the abrasion of my bowels were healed and my health rapidly restored in the course of two months.

On resuming my military duties at Chatham the officers were astonished to see my unexpected recovery. Mr Tucker the Surgeon resigned and settled at Lyme in Dorsetshire after marrying his cousin Miss [Mary Ann] Follett. A more worthy or honorable man never existed.

Another John Tucker, not related to the former, was then appointed Assistant Surgeon in the SDM. so that I steered between two John Tuckers, a predecessor and a successor.[5]

The SD Militia continued at the Chatham barracks until October 20th 1811 when they were ordered to Shorncliffe and arrived on the 25th and 26th between Hythe and Folkestone. My Assistant Surgeon Tucker had gone into Devonshire on leave about this time, so that the medical charge of the regiment devolved wholly on myself during the wet and trying March which laid up many soldiers with sickness and rendered frequent venesection+ necessary to subdue pulmonary+ disease. Soon after their arrival at Shorncliffe I was called up at night to visit Lieut. Black of the Royal Veteran battalion who was occupying a Barrack room in one of the Martello Towers so numerous on the coast of Kent. The Adjutant's family occupied another room in the same barrack. The groans of the poor man disturbed their rest and I was sent for. On my arrival I found rather a stout and burly man labouring under ventral hernia+ of many days duration during which he had suffered greatly and vomited much without any relief from his bowels. I told the patient that nothing but an operation could save his life but he said 'who is there to do it? A consultation of Staff Surgeons has been held on my case this day and declared me too far gone for an operation.' One of the Staff Officers resided at Dover, another at Hythe and the third as Assistant Surgeon resided within the same port. Him they called up and from him I learnt the truth of this statement. Still the operation afforded the only hope, which the sick man embraced and desired it might be performed. I therefore undertook it in the presence of the hospital sergeant orderly and the Assistant Surgeon who seemed himself half dead from the dropsy,+ asthma and enlargement of the spleen and liver. On cutting into the hernia sack a quantity of bloody water escaped which disposed the poor broken down Assistant at first to believe that the gut itself had been opened and the contents discharged. The strangulated bowels were of the darkest chocolate colour and agglutinated together in such a manner as to leave little hope of recovery. After division of the stricture the bowels were easily returned into their proper cavity, the belly bandaged up and some opening medicine given which in a few hours completely unloaded the bowels of their contents so long pent up. Recovery was more rapid than could have been expected in a patient labouring under [these] diseases. In a short time he was walking round the ramparts telling the tale of his wonderful recovery from expected death and sounding the praises of the SDM Doctor whom Providence had placed before him.

At this time I was not the Surgeon of the Regiment only the senior assistant, the junior being absent. I had not applied for the vacant appointment; I was dissuaded from so doing by the advice of older officers whom I considered my friends. After

[5] See introductory article about SDM.

the fame now acquired I determined to wait no longer without ascertaining Col. Lord Rolle's* decision about the vacant Surgeonry of the regiment.

I then addressed the following official letter to his Lordship:

Shorncliffe Barracks
Novr. 1811

My Lord,

So long a time having elapsed since the resignation of Mr Tucker as Surgeon of the SD Militia I beg as senior assistant Surgeon to ask your Lordship's decision as to the appointment of his successor.

I have the honor to be
My Lord
your Lordship's
obedient and humble servant
Jno Butter
Assistant Surgeon
SD Militia

The following gracious reply was quickly returned:

Bicton Novr. 1811

Dear Sir,

I have long waited for an application from you for the vacant Surgeonry of the SD Militia and have refused many other candidates.

By this post I have written to the Lord Lieutenant for your commission as Surgeon and have requested that it may be antedated 1 month.

Wishing you success,
I remain
Dear Sir, Faithfully Yours
Rolle
SDM

This letter I shewed to Major Seale* the Commanding Officer and to paymaster Mr John Hawkins two sincere friends and advisers. Both were startled at his Lordship's favourable answer as they had advised me again and again not to apply for the appointment but to wait until it was offered.

At Shorncliffe Barracks we spent our time most pleasantly from the 26th day of October 1811 to the 9th of Feb. 1812. The 95th Rifle Brigade occupied a portion of the Barracks and exercised often on the same ground as the S Devons; shooting, coursing and foxhunting with Mr Brookman's Hounds constituted the field sports. Situated between Hythe, Sandgate and Dover excursions were made on foot or horseback to these places. Farmer Jeffery lived near and occupied the government ground with a large flock of sheep. This man had been a smuggler in his day and still carried on traffic with Frenchmen. Six spade guineas[6] were sold to this old smuggler for 28s each and were supposed to be sent to France where Bonaparte was greatly in need of gold. The Emperor's camp at Boulogne could be seen on fine days with a powerful telescope, likewise the Pillar.[7] This French camp was intended to be the French Army for invading England, and preventives were taken by the English nation against these threats by the erection of Forts and Martello Towers along the coast from Dover to Portsmouth. These forts were garrisoned by Veteran Soldiers from different Regiments who had returned in a disabled state from the army of the Netherlands, commanded by Lord Chatham during their retreat from the French army.

The Walcheren fever[+] as it was called destroyed half of the British forces and wasted 20 millions sterling and so punished the survivors who had lived and returned to England with ague, diseased livers, enlarged spleens and general dropsy[+] as to render them unfit for any active military service. At Shorncliffe Hospital several of their cases came under my immediate treatment. One dropsical veteran who had been twice tapped for Ascites[+] was afterwards cured by the following draught taken at night viz: 20 drops of Spirit of Turpentine and 30 of Laudanum, Hydrastic purge[+] twice a week, and a drink called Imperial and composed of Cream of Tartar, lemon juice and sugar. The spleen by them was called the Ague Cake. It was much enlarged in Lieutenant Black who was the nephew, I ought to have stated, of the celebrated Dr Black, Professor of Chemistry in Edinburgh. The General Officer Commanding the Kentish District was Sir Jno Murray the celebrated hero acting under Wellington in driving the French back across the Douro River in Portugal. Sir Jno Murray dined with the SDM at Chatham and therefore was well known to Major Seale* and the other officers. On the General's retiring from the Kentish Command a public dinner was given to him and his staff at Hythe by officers of the different regiments. Col. Cutliffe of the 23rd Light Dragoons, a distinguished cavalry officer under Wellington, had also returned from Portugal and taken a part in this public dinner. There were present officers of the 95th Rifles, the Tipperary Militia under Col. Bagalle, Col. Lang of the SD and others making up in number nearly 60 persons. These were drinking days in many regiments, a bottle of port for dinner was commonly allowed and sometimes two and three were drank. None were allowed to escape a bumper toast without a doctor's certificate and in order to avoid inevitable drunkenness a Militia Captain with a softer head than his comrades quietly and unobserved drew his bumper glass of wine off the table and poured it into his jackboots, then worn high up to the knee with knee breeches before Wellington boots and trousers were introduced into the Army. At this military dinner commencing at 6 o'clock on a winter's evening and not terminated at 7 o'clock on the following morning drunkenness was the prevailing evidence of the banquet. Many persons dropped off their seats, others fell on going out of the room without assistance. The Tipperary boys were vociferous and full of obscene and indecent toasts and the General himself thrice appeared so drunk as to fall asleep and intimate to the party that it was time to break up and retire. Whilst the General was in one of those slumbers the President of

---

[6] The spade, produced 1787 to 1799, was the last gold guinea to be issued in Britain.

[7] The 'Pillar' is the Column de la Grande Armée at Boulogne, started in 1804 to commemorate a successful invasion of England that never took place. By 1811, it had reached only twenty of its planned fifty metres, and Butter must have struggled to see it. Work then ceased, and the column was not completed until 1843.

the day gave the following toast: 'to the Immortal Memory of the lamented Sir John Moore, to be drank in silence'. Whether the word silence or a jog of the General's elbow roused him from this somnolency is not clear. He soon attempted to rise from his chair and began to say: 'Mr President I rise', but instead of rising fell on his knees and then continued: 'Mr President, this is a toast I always drink kneeling.' Tremendous applause followed from everyone present who was sober enough to witness this drama, which was repeated twice afterwards when the company had become select and few in number. Only the Col. and Captain of Grenadiers of the SDM besides myself remained out of 20 officers who had dined there. Thrice had I risen to return to Shorncliffe from Hythe and had been importuned to stay yet longer, but when the clock struck seven I started, soon after me the Col. and then came the Captain all separately and neither two together. Remnants of this extraordinary banquet remained until breakfast time when the General washed himself, had his boots cleaned, appeared on parade at 10 o'clock apparently 'sober' and put an officer under arrest as a joke for drunkenness, but soon released him. So ended this remarkable banquet.

Herrings and smuggled spirits were common enough at Shorncliffe. At Mess it was an object to get a second herring fried with onions, so delicious were they. One day at Mess the subject of a bet was brought up which I had made some months before at Chatham with Captain Toll of the Light Brigade company, who thought a great deal more of himself than others thought of him. Capt. T betted 10 guineas to one that Tom Crib* had made himself champion of England by beating John Gully. I answered that those two men had never fought a public battle and was answered with a question: 'what do you know, Sir, of these men? Don't I attend the fives court and witness the pugilistic performances?' I replied: 'you may do so', and repeated my remark [that] those two men were like brothers and had never fought a battle with each other. 'Will you back your remark with a bet?' was the rejoinder. 'No' I said 'I never bet but always refuse.' 'Then Sir your opinion is worth nothing unless you will back it up.' A good deal of joking and chaffing then went the round of the Mess table and the offer of the bet was frequently repeated. I said at last: 'well Captain T my rule for the first time will be broken if I accept your bet but if on reflection you confess your mistake your bet may be withdrawn'. 'Hoorah' was the cry at the table, 'the Doctor is taken in at last, a bet, a bet, let it be recorded' and so the bet held good. All but one seemed to be against me but the wild officer first seen with his dogs at Exeter always backed me. So stood this unsettled bet for months. Meanwhile I had written letters of enquiry to Tom Crib,* the Champion of England, and to John Gully who had also been a Champion and afterwards MP for Pontefract and one of the wealthiest men on the Turf. Their answers would have been curiosities in these literary days of penmanship, orthography etc. Their literary composition was about equal and ran thus:

> 1811 – copy –
> 'Sir,
> I certifie that I never did fight John Gully in public nor in private, Tom Crib,
> Champion.'

John Gully's answer was laconic but worded to the same effect. These answers were obtained and kept secret and known only to a few until one day by arrangement at the Mess table the question was asked of the President if that bet made at Chatham months ago between Captain T and the Doctor had ever been settled. Answered in the negative, the President first appealed to Captain T who equivocated at first and said he could not prove his position, but still he should not pay the debt without certificates from Gully or Crib. Whereupon certificates were handed up and read by the President. Captain T then said to his mess mate on the opposite side: 'there Sir, take your paltry sum' an expression resented by all present.

Shorncliffe Barracks are temporary wings, each wing comprising officers apartments sub-divided into four barrack rooms, two below, two above with servants apartments in the rear and a covered entrance porch in the front. These were occupied by four officers; I had one room and three noisy officers the other three. These three inmates nightly returned in a boisterous state after smoking and drinking smuggled spirits. They frequently disturbed my rest by knocking and rattling my locked door. One night they were more than usually clamorous and called me up from my bed after midnight to bleed Captain E for his cough. I accordingly bled him from the arm and intentionally left him bleeding and went below stairs until he fainted and fell on the floor; his faintness produced the sensation of death amongst his drunken companions who loudly called for me to stop the bleeding. On my return and tying up the arm of the fainting man who quickly recovered after dashing some cold water in his face, when a stout Grenadier Captain then advanced bearded like a [?] and fiercely accosted me: 'Sir, you will have to answer at the bar for killing my poor deceased friend Jim, he is all but dead Sir.' A Lieutenant weeping then said: 'how could you think of killing my best friend?' Another Captain then spoke whilst staring wildly and taking a pinch of snuff, said: 'this is a bad job, murder, for which you will be tried and we three shall be witnesses against you'. I only laughed at these drunken expressions of unnecessary alarm for the fainted officer soon recovered after the use of cold water to his face and some to his mouth flavoured with blue ruin alias gin. After this scene I was never disturbed in my rest by this midnight party.

My commission as Surgeon of the SDM dated the 22nd Nov. 1811 reached Headquarters at Shorncliffe in due course on the [blank] day of Decr. 1811 and produced for the new surgeon the congratulations of the officers and men belonging to the regiment. The Commission had been antedated to the 22nd of Nov. but no additional allowance made for my sole care of the sick from the preceding May to that period. Fees to the Lord Lieutenant's Clerk for stamps and engrossing were settled by the paymaster who had the pleasure afterwards to pay me 11/4 per diem instead of 7/- per diem and also extra allowances of 2/- a day for a horse. A beautiful little grey Arab horse from Lord Heathfield's Stud at Nutwell near Limpstone was entrusted to the care of a private soldier to ride up from Devonshire to Shorncliffe, a distance of 200 miles and upwards, and the little animal on his arrival appeared like a skeleton.

England about this period was in a most critical state, threatened by invasion from France (with the Army visible on the other side of the Straits of Dover) and disturbed within with inflammatory speeches and harangues, public meetings and concealed intrigues. Sir Francis Burdett[8] had been committed to the Tower and Major Cartwright[9] had succeeded in stirring up dissentions and riots in the manufac-

[8] A reformist politician briefly imprisoned for breach of privilege of the House of Commons after questioning the House's right to imprison a fellow-reformer.
[9] A gentleman of some means, John Cartwright was a political agitator who (contrary to Butter's opinion) eschewed violence and believed strongly in the need for parliamentary

turing districts where the rioters had commenced their acts of violence in breaking the machinery at different manufactories under the mistakened notion that the use of machinery would superceed hand labour and deprive the manufacturing labourers of their work.

The Government found it necessary to remove Militia Regiments from their own manufacturing counties in which they had been raised to Garrisons in distant parts, and to place other Regiments in disturbed districts. Intimation was given that the South Devon might be removed from Kent to the inland counties on the first emergency. I was therefore called upon by my Commanding Officer to prepare myself with all necessary instruments and bandages likely to be required in the event of a conflict with the rioters. Leave of absence was granted for a few days to go to London for this purpose and leave my address with the paymaster and adjutant who would write to me in the event of a route. I proceeded to London accordingly and purchased some beautiful instruments from Sevigny* and others and returned from London by the Mail to Dover, where I slept and the next day visited the public buildings and harbours of the Town of Dover. I then started for Shorncliffe on foot by way of Folkestone and Sandgate[10] intending to reach my destination in time for the Mess Dinner at 5 o'clock. On reaching the table land I was soon struck with the unusual silence and total absence of every living being. I could not account for such an unexpected change until I reached my own barracks which was empty and the furniture gone, the doors locked and windows shut, the mess room closed likewise. No person being visible to answer an enquiry, I entered the fort and called upon my old patient Lieut. Black of the 7th Royal Veteran Battalion who appeared quite hearty and recovered from the effects of his operation. 'Where are the South Devon gone?' I asked 'and when did they leave?' The Lieut. answered: 'the last division left early this morning and the first division yesterday for Canterbury, soon after the receipt of their route for Chatham. It is thought that their destination will be fixed for the disturbed districts.' I then said that I had walked all the way from Dover in time, as I thought, for the Mess Dinner, but the poor veteran replied that he could offer me nothing but a bit of bread and cheese and a glass of wine which was not accepted. Darkness coming on, the sooner I retreated my steps back to Dover the better. The veteran asked me how it was that I had not received the Paymaster's Adjutant's letters directed to my London address, and the answer was because I left by the Dover Mail at 8 o'clock overnight. Farewell was the word and off I started, reaching Dover after dark and returning to the comfortable Inn where I had slept and left my luggage to be forwarded by the carrier. A good dinner and a comfortable bed prepared me for an early start next morning by an early coach for Canterbury where I found the last division of the SDM drawn up in marching order in the street and where I left the coach to join them. Inquiries of course from the officers were made as to my missing the letters, about which satisfactory answers were given.

The march was then resumed through Sitenbourne [Sittingbourne] to Chatham where a new route ordered the Regiment to march to Gravesend and there to cross the Thames to Tilbury fort, thence to Romford in Essex, onwards to Bedford and Leicester where they rested for some days. The march was called a forced one and the orders to march as far as possible every day. The rains had now set in heavily

---

reform.

[10] Around eleven miles.

and the roads and lowlands were like mud pits every day. We were wet through and through and the poor women and children riding on baggage waggons were well washed.

Coughs and colds and other sickness had set in and obliged me to leave patients under the care of medical practitioners at different places. On reaching Leicester one of the Sergeants[11] died and the sick list had increased considerably.

Leicester being tolerably quiet, the Regiment was ordered forward to Nottingham where great riots had taken place amongst the lace manufacturers, much machinery broken and many buildings damaged by the rioters. In marching through Market Harborough I had much pleasure in finding there my former companion and fellow-lodger in London called Abbey, whose father was a great Northamptonshire grazier. I left under his medical charge two sick soldiers who soon recovered.

At Nottingham the gallant SDM soon restored peace and order amongst the disaffected rioters. The lace mills were guarded by sentinels, a close watch kept over the lace frame breakers and punishment awarded accordingly. The Bedford Militia were also stationed at Nottingham and a squadron of the 15th Light Dragoons. There was also a division of another Militia Regiment – a curious circumstance occurred here to a private soldier who had fallen over some stairs whilst drunk [and had] injured his hip which had confined him to the Regimental Hospital so long as to induce the Surgeon to form an opinion that his lameness was simulated and not real and that therefore he ought to be forced to do his duty. The Commanding Officer prudently advised the Surgeon to invite a consultation of other Regimental Surgeons then in Nottingham. This was done and while the case appeared obscure to the majority, I immediately saw and pronounced dislocation of the head of the right thigh bone backwards upon the ilium.[+] The limb was shortened, the toes turned inwards and the only wonder was that the accident had not sooner been detected. Pulleys were obtained and the dislocation reduced to the great comfort of the suffering soldier to my satisfaction and to the wisdom of the Commanding Officer who had ordered this consultation preparatory to a court martial.

Nottingham is the centre of the manufacturing business. There was a good country hospital well conducted by Messrs Wright, Surgeons. I witnessed an amputation of a leg there for elefantiasis[+] and brought away by permission a piece of skin over the shinbone from two to three inches thick which is still preserved in spirits.

The market place there is spacious and convenient and suited for the exercise of officers' horses on days not fixed for market. One day an officer riding a beautiful horse could not get the animal to pass the boundary where he was usually turned. After various trials the officer was riding back to the market much displeased with his restive horse and while he stopped to speak to some of the SD officers looking on, the paymaster asked if he would allow me to try the horse. The officer readily assented and dismounted for that purpose. I mounted with a good stick in my hand and rode to the market boundary where the horse attempted to turn on the right and was well hit a rap from the stick on the nose. The animal plunged a bit and reared and tried to turn on the other side and was met with another rap on that side. Upon this he started off on a full gallop up the street and onto the Nottingham Racecourse which was about a mile off, having thrown two shoes in this skirmish and got

[11] Richard Braginton, Lord Rolle's quarter-sergeant, buried with full military honours: *Nottingham Mercury*, 22.2.1812.

himself into a good sweat and was in no position to gallop further although forced once around the racecourse. The horse was then walked quietly back with the shine taken off his polished coat and with the gentleness of a lamb, not refusing to pass and repass any place where his former objection had been disputed. The officer then was much pressed to sell the horse which he refused to do.

Lord Rolle* joined his Regiment at Nottingham and added much to their pleasures during his stay. I was President at the Mess table one day at dinner which was very good of its kind and, after all had partaken bountifully of Tarts and Puddings, to the surprise of the party a roasted turkey poult[12] was put down which many saw with regret that their appetites had been previously satisfied. But as it was supposed to be a compliment to the noble Col. his Lordship begged to have a taste of the bird, and knowing his good appetite a fair share of the breast and wing was placed before him. The President also having a good twist of his own backed his noble Col. Then came the epicure of the regiment who must from politeness support his Col. and with the aid of some sauces, particularly sauce piquant, contrived to render substantial help in demolishing this dainty bird. A standing joke ever after was that the Col. and the Doctor had cleared the turkey poult after a good dinner.

After so many days passed at Nottingham in restoring peace and order and preventing further destructions of Lace frames and machinery the SDM received a route to march for Sheffield and see what kind of metal the Grinders were made of. As the regiment had done so well at Nottingham they were equally successful at Sheffield where much disaffection and disorder had prevailed.

1812

In 1812 to the 13th Dec. the SDM remained at Sheffield and formed many valuable acquaintances. A squadron of the 15th Light Dragoons [was] commanded by Major the Honorable Lord Waldegrove who there and then resigned his commission whilst stationed in the Horse Barracks. There was also a very good Infirmary at Sheffield managed by a clever House Surgeon besides the Physicians and Surgeons also appointed. Whilst there I first operated for cataract on a soldier. The operation turned out well.

About this time Mr Stanniforth Junr was advised to go up to London and attend the Eye Infirmary [later Moorfields] in Charterhouse Square for three months in order to introduce Sanders [Saunders*] new practice on the eye into Sheffield. Dr Davies, a resident physician, urged on this step and said he would himself undertake diseases of the eye unless one of the Hospital Surgeons would do so. Although Dr Davies was one of the hospital physicians he had little or no encouragement given to him to remain in Sheffield. He therefore arranged to leave that town and settle in London as an Accountant. Letters of introduction he obtained from every friend who could favor his views. Dr D appreciated two letters given to him by myself and had them copied into a book previous to presentation. After some time when I visited him at his mansion in George St. Hanover Square I was perfectly surprised at all I saw and heard. I was ushered into a splendid Drawing room handsomely furnished where I saw Mrs Davies seated on one couch and her mother, Mrs Hall [Hale?] on

12   A young turkey.

the opposite side. This was such a contrast to the small house occupied by them in one of the streets of Sheffield.

Whilst at Sheffield I sold my arab pony and bought a famous mare from Capt. T who sold her because he wanted a pair of curricle[13] horses to cut a dash in Sheffield in order to win the affections of Miss Mackenzie, an only child of the Revd M, supposed to have had a good fortune besides Church preferment. The Capt. married this lady who did not live many years. When she died he returned again into Yorkshire to get a second wife, of course with money. Capt. T and I had not been very good friends after the settlement of the bet at Shorncliffe. He had fallen ill on the march and had been attended by the Assistant Surgeon without benefit and had consulted a Physician at Nottingham. Still continuously ill he consulted me at last, who put him to rights and after the purchase of the mare became again friendly. Capt. T having succeeded in paying his addresses advised me to try my luck with Miss Cadman, a niece of Mr Cadman silversmith who had taken out a patent for a toast rack to be folded into a small space, also for other articles. This niece was the only apparent heir to a large fortune. Three or four times a day I had to pass Cadman's dwelling house on my way to and from the Mess Room. Overtures were made and opportunities afforded which I in those days was too shy to accept and so was blamed by my brother officers.

The Regimental Hospital was formed at an old coaching tavern in Sheffield once well conducted by Mr Peach before his death and afterwards superceded by the Tontine Hotel and Hostelry on a much grander scale. Mr Peach, the veterinary surgeon at Sheffield, was the active representative of his family from whom the hospital apartments were rented. A most friendly intercourse was the result of this occupation between the VS and the MRCS. Each party communicated with the other upon any particular operations on man or beast that were going forward. Before this intimacy I used to bleed and physic officers' horses and my own, having studied a little farriery under the able VS James White of Exeter, author of various treatises. Blistering, firing, and nerving lame horses constituted some of these operations.

A private soldier of the SDM having died, his body was inspected and a question put to me by a Surgeon present as to the time it would take to tie the femoral artery.[+] The answer was – not 5 minutes. A bet was offered that I the Dr would not do it in the time but I performed it in two minutes and further said that I could tie all the arteries except the aorta on the dead subject within an hour. I then gave satisfactory proof of my assertion.

Chesterfield Races were approaching which some officers wished to attend. One officer had a well-bred flashy mare that was dancing and fidgeting about and induced the owner to remark what a showy leader she would make for a tandem. Someone present remarked that no-one could drive such a mare tandem with safety. The owner then offered to bet his 10 guineas that he would name an officer present who [could] drive his mare leader of a tandem to Chesterfield and back. This bet was taken by the Col. and the officer chosen for this task was me. As a rehearsal a tandem harness was put on the mare and my new purchase was to be the wheeler in the tandem trap for which the driver of the Manchester Mail was hired to make their first experimental trip. They drove out a short distance over the Chesterfield Turnpike road and returned in dashing style, meeting several officers who had come out to watch

---

[13] A two-wheeled chaise, usually drawn by a matching pair of horses.

the performance. Nothing could exceed the style and steadiness with which the two mares returned, the mare so fidgetty under saddle was quite gentle in harness. This successful rehearsal induced the Col. to cry off the bet to which they all assented.

The Doncaster races took place in September 1812. A party of SDM officers hired a carriage and four horses to drive from Sheffield to Doncaster on the St. Leger day, a distance of [twenty-two] miles, but the wild Captain and I agreed to ride there; we did so and took up the best position in our opinion for witnessing the race near a road crossing the course. Several false starts had been made to no purpose whilst we continued on the inner side of the course. We then thought of going to see the outer side but found before we had got half way over the road that the race horses, 23 in number, were coming swiftly upon [us]. Hastily we returned and saw the troop of racers pass like a charge of cavalry and one of them dropped and fell by jumping over the road. The fallen rider was soon up again but his chance gone. Quickly we returned towards the winning post and saw a fine bay horse win, he proved to be Otterington the property of a Yorkshire farmer called Hobb who won, it was said, ten thousand pounds that day on the race. So little was this horse thought of that his name never entered the listing ring, but the rider on leaving the saddling ground was taunted by another jockey for riding a farmer's horse and was offered two hundred guineas to two guineas that he did not win. 'Well' said the rider 'I can bear the loss of two guineas and so I will take your bet.' Mancealle[?] was the first favourite for this year but she stood eighth at the finish and Callon, another favorite, came in thirteen out of the 23 that started. The Capt. and I, after the race, rode back to the road crossing the course where the horse fell and saw distinctly the spot where the horse sprang from one side to the place where he fell on the other side of the road – the intermediate space being measured again and again at 11 paces or 33 feet. Hunters have been known to jump this distance in crossing canals, brooks etc. We saw another race ran for stakes by three horses and won by Slender Billy, a chestnut all legs and wings apparently but no carcase and very speedy. After the races we rode back to Sheffield from Doncaster.

During the year of [blank] preceeding our visit at Sheffield, a county election had taken place for the West Riding of Yorkshire, and a smart contest ensued between Lord Milton son of Earl FitzWilliam of Wentworth House, and the son of the Earl of Harwood. Not only thousands but tens of thousands, nor did a hundred thousand suffice to pay the Election expences, one voter was brought up from Cornwall in a post chase all the way to Yorkshire and fed librally all the way and promised money to vote for one candidate, and so unprincipled was he as to accept a larger bribe and vote for the other party.

[There follows a selection of 'laughable verses' written by 'a Barrister named Wade', which are less laughable than execrable, and have accordingly been deleted.]

Grouse shooting, as sportsmen well know, is fixed for the 12th August. Some of them went out on the Yorkshire moors and saw scores, perhaps hundreds, of grinders with guns in their hands in pursuit of game. They would take no denial, and when grouse arise volleys are fired at them and should a bird fall a race begins for the prize and first who comes has it.

The SDM remained nearly 10 months at Sheffield, having arrived the 16th May, and left by a War Office order for Pennestone and Huddersfield. During the summer of 1812 in June I obtained one month's leave of absence to visit my friends in

Devonshire and whilst there agreed with a brother officer Lieut. H at Exmouth to return together to Sheffield. Lieut. H therefore came up to Woodbury to dine with me and to meet his sporting friend Tom G at dinner. Also a neighbour's daughter was invited to tea to meet the party of young men, who could do no less than escort her home in the evening. Her agreeable manner so pleased me as to induce me to say she is the prettiest girl in our village and would make an excellent wife. These words left a memorable impression on TG who visited this young lady frequently after the departure of the SDM officers, who learnt by letter soon after their departure for Sheffield that an offer had been made and accepted by the parties who afterwards married and lived near Ottery.

On the 17th day of December 1812 the SDM marched in two divisions for Pennestone and Huddersfield. Snow set in heavily on those two days, and was so deep in the high roads as to render the work laborious for men and horses dragging carriages through it. The SDM left a good character behind them in Sheffield for their orderly and sober conduct at their billets in quarters which the men occupied at many small inns as there were no infantry barracks. At Huddersfield the men were billetted about at inns as at Sheffield. The officers first messed at the George Inn and afterwards at private rooms rented for the purpose. I engaged an empty house for an Hospital and private apartments for my own accommodation.

Riots had run higher at Huddersfield than at Nottingham or Sheffield amongst the mechanics and cloth workers who had broken quantities of machinery, attacked several mills to destroy the looms and had shot one cloth merchant returning from Huddersfield Market in the afternoon to his house about a mile on the Manchester road. He was shot in the groin by some men concealed in the plantation near the turnpike road. Considerable hemorage came from the wound and could not be staunched by the local surgeons so that Mr Hey* from Leeds, one of the most celebrated surgeons at that time, was sent for. As he did not or could not venture to tie the external iliac artery,+ an operation then scarcely attempted or known until Mr Abernethy* first performed it, Mr Horsfall* died from hemorage. Rawfall's Mills for working woollen cloths by new machinery was threatened with a hostile attack from the mob and was prepared accordingly for defence by its spirited owner Mr [blank] who kept an armed force there by night for the protection of his property. One night the rioters came in a great body armed with muskets and other weapons suited for the destruction of the new machinery contained in this mill and regarded by them as the means of depriving themselves and families of their daily bread. The doors and windows were first attacked by the rioters who were warned by the master and defending party within that if they did not desist they would be fired upon and that the first person who entered the mill would be shot. This threat was carried into execution [and] firing then commenced from within and without by the attacking and defending parties. The latter, encouraged by their gallant and high-spirited master, were successful in saving their property and their lives from the destruction of those misguided and ignorant cloth weavers. Much blood was found outside on the mill walls on the following day so that many of the mob must have been wounded but the wounded persons were for a time unknown. The rioters were called Luddites because one Ludd was supposed to have been their leader.

1813

In these troublesome times rebellion was not far off but the militia force was a prophilactic settled at Huddersfield with a good regimental hospital. The usual casualties and sickness among the soldiers billeted about the town occurred. A dragoon was sent into the hospital with a fractured thigh occasioned by his walking in the dark across a hay loft with a hole in the floor through which his leg passed and in falling an oblique fracture of the thigh bone near the neck was produced. The poor fellow became insane and died and the fractured bone was preserved, showing the process of union which had commenced. Scrofula[+] and diseases of the eye prevailed extensively in Huddersfield and the neighbourhood. In visiting a sick soldier one day at his quarters I there saw a child with chronic ophthalmy[+] and disease of the eyelids for which I gave the landlady a prescription for some ointment and collyrium[+] which cured the child. This cure was spread about amongst others so afflicted who came also and received their cures. These results were made known far and wide so favourably as to induce many patients afflicted with complaints in the eye to come to our Regimental Hospital for relief. Amongst others were four children, one almost an infant and the oldest about fourteen years of age, blind with congenital cataracts from birth. Happily I succeeded in removing all these cataracts and restoring them all to sight. The oldest girl afforded a matter for reflection, she had learnt to know common objects of the household solely from touch, such as plates, cups, saucers, knives, forks, spoons all of which she could name. But when these articles were presented to her sight she could not give their names without touching them. These successful cases brought other patients afflicted with divers diseases and so numerous did they become at all times as to induce me to fix on three days a week for giving gratuitous advice to patients in Huddersfield and the neighbouring parishes. I was obliged to do this in order to prevent crowds of people from interrupting me from performing my medical duties at the Regimental Hospital.

There was a walking curiosity, a man apparently with two heads (bicephalic) who sought my advice. He had an immense tumour weighing about seven pounds in the back of his neck where it was still increasing as to prevent him from keeping on his hat comfortably or wearing his coat. As other surgeons had seen and not offered him their advice for its removal he came to me and I fixed a day for the operation, which being fixed and known many persons came to witness it, amongst whom were two County Magistrates; many merchants, several tradespeople and others crowded the room. The first incision was a long one about 14 inches from the back of the head down the space between the shoulder blades, some blood flowed from this wound which appeared so ghastly as to occasion fainting to my particular friend Mr Hugh Lothers. No difficulty presented itself in removing this great mass of fatty matter and no bleeding of any consequence followed the operation. The wound healed in about a week to the great delight of the bicephidal patient and to the astonishment of my acquaintances. The new appearance of this well-known person acted like an advertisement in sending other patients afflicted with tumours, cancers and the like.

A well-known begging woman with cancer in the breast had shown her disease to many surgeons and kind benefactors without relief. I removed her diseased breast and thought that a cure was effected but after two years Dr Walker informed me that it had returned. A man had received a violent blow in the back part of his arm just above the elbow joint. Some time before his application to me the swelling had increased to such a size as to oblige him to wear a large sleeve to his coat and I thought it a tumour and proceeded to remove it, when to my surprise the quantity of pus near a pint flowed out and left a dense sack which I had some trouble in removing.

I was obliged to remain at the head-quarters of the regiment with the commanding officer and staff as the small division was sent to Halifax where disturbances had begun. Assistant Surgeon Tucker was attached to this division. The detachment was also sent to Homefirth [Holmfirth] and smaller detachments to other places where a mischief was suspected or arisen. A small guard with a sergeant and a certain number of men were billetted at Mills Bridge, the residence of Mr Radcliffe* who was the only acting magistrate who had fearlessly done his duty during the Huddersfield riots and sent off many culprits to York Gaol for trial at the ensuing Assizes. Mr Radcliffe was so much hated by the rioters and frame-breakers as to be exposed often to the danger of his life. More than once or twice on going up his staircase to bed where he could be seen through a window from a person outside the house, he was shot at and the ball hit his shoulder but missed the substance. A sergeant's guard was therefore constantly kept at Mills Bridge.

To show the surly and coarse manner of the lower classes at Huddersfield it may be mentioned that soon after the arrival of the SDM there Lt. Col. Lang, commanding, thought it his duty as etiquette to call officially on the chief Magistrate and therefore invited me and other officers to accompany him. This invitation was accepted and attended by all, who had been previously cautioned against the prevailing custom there of drinking wine to excess. All the guests had been put on their guard and the wild officer particularly cautioned, but he asserted that no man should make him drink more wine than he liked or he would call him out. Thus guarded the SDM officers sat down to dinner with the worthy magistrate Mr Radcliffe,* his third wife and a young female friend, in all 22 in number. Dinner over, toasts were proposed according to the usual custom after the retirement of the ladies. These toasts were continued with the word bumper annexed after the circulation of the bottles on the left side of the table and down the right. The president asked his right hand neighbour what was the toast. His reply was negatively that he had forgotten or did not hear, couldn't say, thereupon the president had established certain rules in his house and one of them was to ask his neighbour on the right after the return of the bottles what was the last toast and if he could not name it then he was to fill a bumper and ask his next right hand neighbour to name the last toast, and he then also forgetting was commanded by the rules of the house to fill a bumper, and then ask his neighbour on the right, and as every one present almost had forgotten the toast, the bottles were sent backward until they came again to the president's left, who then repeated it and observed that this had been the custom of his house. Afterwards the wine was circulated two or three times without a toast. Gentlemen in those days did not always return to the ladies' drawing room after dinner. Excess of wine drinking was then the common custom with Englishmen; the gouty Lord Chancellor Elgin it was said drank his two and three bottles of port daily. Mr Pitt Prime Minister at the early age of 27 followed this example and proved himself the greatest statesman of the age; he could not speak well it was attested without drinking previously a bottle of port – the most brilliant orations were delivered under the influence of 2 or 3 bottles of port.

In dining with Lord Rolle* once at Bicton, Lord Elgin's grandson Scott was present. Rolle, about to take his accustomed nap, said 'I leave you two young men to take care of yourselves. I give to you the same advice as King George the Third gave to Lord Elgin and myself when dining with his Majesty, who said to us, "follow my example and stick to port and you will live to four score years of age."' Such was the custom of drinking Port Wine to excess in those days. The motto was: in vino veritas.

During the stay of the SDM at Huddersfield a marching party was told off with some dragoons to escort the bold and intrepid magistrate from Mills Bridge to Assizes, where the Judges paid him the highest compliments that language could convey for his gallant and excellent conduct in times of riot, anarchy and disaffection which had prevailed and so long manifested itself amongst the lower classes at Huddersfield. The Home Secretary of State advised the Sovereign to confer on Mr Radcliffe* the honour of a Baronetcy free of office fees, the highest honour that could then be conferred in the handsomest manner. Of his bold and numerous acts of intrepidity and courage one was particularly mentioned. During the riots at Huddersfield and the meeting of Luddites many magistrates had assembled at the George Inn, Mr Radcliffe among them, in order to devise measures for quelling these disturbances. There were no police in those days and the common constables were fearful and timid. It was proposed to call out the local Militia of which Mr Scott, one of the Magistrates present, was Colonel, to whom Mr Radcliffe appealed for a guard and received for answer that if he obtained one from such a source, Mills Bridge would be pulled down about his ears. To this remark he replied: 'Mr or rather Colonel Scott there the ruin shall remain an eternal disgrace to you and your corps.' On leaving the George Hotel on horseback Mr Radcliffe was hooted and hissed by the mob and one man was seen to throw a brickbat at him, whom Mr Radcliffe saw and dashing forward seized by the collar and held until a constable appeared and then said: 'constable, confine that man and release him at your peril.' The mob at this sight slunk off, they did not attempt to overwhelm this courageous magistrate in the exercise of his duty. His hospitalities and kindness to the officers of the SDM were often repeated during their stay at Huddersfield and left an indelible impression of his manly aristocratic and truly English conduct.

By this time I had become very popular and successful in drawing numbers of sick people from the surrounding parishes for my advice at the Regimental Hospital and some from Wakefield, Leeds, Liverpool, Manchester and Sheffield. One man had a tape worm for which I could find no remedy, and for whom two ounces of the Spirit of Turpentine were prescribed to be taken on an empty stomach, but the druggist refused to give it unless I was present, so I was sent for, the turpentine swallowed and in a day or two the tape worm was voided 12 feet in length, now preserved in a bottle. An interesting little boy had a white swelling on his knee and discharges from the joint. These had wasted him down to a skeleton and induced his Medical Attendant to offer no hope; he was too weak to suffer amputation in the thigh. Being called in I amputated the little boy's thigh who afterwards recovered most rapidly his health and strength and grew fat. Two workmen employed at the Cloth Hall in raising heavy bailes had their legs broken by one of these bailes slipping off the machinery upon them. One was attended by a resident practitioner and the other by myself with a compound fracture of both bones, and strange to say that man recovered sooner than the other. Not many miles from Huddersfield there were men called bone-setters, by name Whitworth Doctors.[14] These quacks were looked upon as more successful than the regular practitioners for setting broken bones and reducing dislocations and it was said of them that when bones were ill set or not set firmly they would break them again and reset, thereby proving that surgery had not been very successful in that part of Yorkshire with the general practitioners.

Patients from all quarters flocked to Huddersfield for advice and took up many hours a day from 10 o'clock am to 2 o'clock pm. The druggists who made up the prescriptions were also unusually busy on public days and one in particular declared that he was obliged to sit up after midnight in preparing decoctions and infusions and other medicines ordered. Quinine was not known in those days and so decoctions of bark of which quinine is the essence was given, they used to say, not by the bottle alone, nor by the gallon but by the hogshead. Often with the addition of oxymuriate of mercury[+] which together worked great cures in scrufolas[+] complaints and proved a most effective though unchemical remedy.

The resident practitioners of Huddersfield petitioned the Colonel and threatened also to petition the War Office against the practice of drawing away their private patients to the military hospital. One surgeon declared he was losing practice at the rate of 200 a year and another of 100 a year, but their petitions were unheeded.

So matters ran on during the stay of the South Devon Militia.

A blind man appeared who had been operated on in the Leeds Infirmary for cataract by the celebrated Mr Hey,* who had invented a round shape needle for punching and depressing the cataract. This operation had so often been repeated as at last to excite inflammation of the iris. With the iris scalpel invented by Adams I made a sufficient aperture to restore sight sufficient for him to walk about, and thus succeeded by one operation in restoring vision after the failure of 13 previous opera-tions – success in such cases fast augmented applications from patients living at a great distance from Huddersfield.

Lieut. Fowler, SDM, had been sent on detachment to Homefirth about 7 miles off to protect a mill there threatened with an attack from the rioters and whilst there tippled a little too freely one day of port wine. The weather very frosty with snow on the ground; on the following morning he was found dead in his bed and the report of his death brought to head-quarters at Huddersfield where the Colonel directed me to go and inspect the dead body. I proceeded accordingly and took with me the assistant surgeon to Homefirth. The head was examined and a large clot of congealed blood found in the ventricals of the brain where it must have been poured from some ruptured blood vessels so suddenly as to occasion almost immediate death. After this inspection the two doctors rode back to Huddersfield cold and hungry enough and arrived soon after the mess dinner was over, and found the officers drinking their wine in the mess room where dinner was provided for the doctors of such viands as could be soonest warmed. Among other things remaining were the fragments of a brace of pheasants which were too high for the pampered appetites of the officers, but which were greedily devoured by the greedy doctors to the great merriment of the mess and declared most excellent.

Sudden deaths were not uncommon in those days amongst aldermen and free drinkers of port wine and were generally found to result from effusion of blood into

---

[14] The Taylor family of Whitworth, near Rochdale, were blacksmiths and farriers who demonstrated an unusual ability for treating animal fractures and later began to treat humans, gaining a widespread reputation as bone-setters.

or upon the brain. Corvisart, an eminent French physician, had written a treatise on diseases of the heart[15] but in our Post Mortem examinations such diseases were rarely met with, excepting the sudden death of a private soldier in the hospital at Chatham, of which I had the sole charge during the absence of the surgeon, my predecessor. That man had been admitted an in-patient of regimental hospital for catarrh; he had a cough, difficulty breathing, swelling legs and other symptoms of pulmonary[+] obstructions but no danger was apprehended. He died suddenly in bed and I inspected his body but found no disease anywhere until I opened the heart in which I discovered a rupture of the three semi-lunar valves of the aorta, so that the function of these valves or floodgates intended for the passage of blood one way and not again to return were rendered useless. I had never seen such a case in any museum nor read of it. I made a preparation of this specimen in spirits of wine and took it with me to London to show to different anatomy professors who had never met with the like. I possess this specimen still in perfect preservation after the lapse of 55 years, having taken it with others that I could collect during all the regimental marches until I settled down at headquarters in Plymouth.

At Huddersfield officers of the SDM received great hospitality from the neighbouring gentry, the wealthy merchants, manufacturers etc. most of whom had acquired great wealth in their several trades and had built good modern mansions; quietness and order prevailed amongst the populace from the time the SDM were stationed at Huddersfield. After the spring assizes held at York, many rioters sent there as prisoners by Mr Radcliffe* were condemned to death and hung and their bodies brought back to Huddersfield and their corpses exhibited in their respective abodes to passers-by.

Of public amusements there were few or none at Huddersfield; it was a new town raised in the midst of the moors, there was no theatre, assembly rooms or place of public amusement excepting the best room at the George Inn, where a private concert was got up and attended by the SDM officers who were shy-faced fellows in general, having seen very little of ladies' society for several years. At this concert one young lady sung the song of 'Fly not yet' and 'Is there a heart that never loved'. Some of the words, such as: 'twas Rosa's lips, twas Rosa's eyes that caused this sigh' excited a good deal of mirth and much conversation and a question arose whether there was a heart present that never loved, for which one young officer present said: 'I have a heart that was never in love'. This remark went the round of the room in a laugh which excited the attention of the young lady who, being so informed, looked more particularly at this officer than at the others, being so marked out he was occasionally met by this young lady in her walks with a pleasing smile.

There was only one married officer whose wife was with him living in lodgings at Huddersfield where she happened to be ill and required medical aid. On her this young lady called and offered such things as she could send to a stranger in a strange place. There she often met me in attendances until her recovery was affected. Then I fell ill with quinsey,[+] a sore throat to which complaint I had been frequently subjected from my youth upwards; this information being communicated by the married lady to her fair visitor who thought she might continue to send some

---

[15] J. N. Corvisart, *An Essay on the Organic Diseases and Lesions of the Heart* (Philadelphia: Anthony Finley, 1812).

raspberry vinegar through this channel as a gargle for me, receiving back the usual compliment of thanks.

About this time General Ackland[16] came on a tour of inspection to Huddersfield, and then examined the books of the SDM and ordered them out for his inspection in the field. The Regiment was accordingly formed into a solid square previously to their being marched off to the training ground. Whilst so assembled in one of the broad streets of Huddersfield a young lady appeared and attempted to cross, but appeared confused and hesitated which way to go. This being noticed I was desired to offer her my services, as all the other officers had fallen into their places in line with their respective companies and there was no one left but the colonel commanding and me to perform this gallant rescue of the lady, who proved to be the fair songstress at the concert. Various comments were made subsequently on this lady's difficulty and my gallantry. Being out on duty I could not then quit my post but my services were fully acknowledged as the sequel will show.

The regiment went through their field-day in admirable style, which could not have been surpassed by any regiment, but received no praise or commendation from the General. On the return of the regiment back to quarters further scrutiny was made by this Tartar General into the various accounts, billets and quarters and finally asked the men if they had any complaints to prefer. Having found all the faults he could do in order to annoy the Commanding Officer the latter said: 'I hope, General, you are satisfied with the Regiment in the field.' The General indignantly answered: 'I was sir, but that good drill was owing to your adjutant and sergeant major and not to yourself.' The acerbity in the General's temper might have been attributed to some unpleasantness between Col. Lord Rolle* and himself pre-existing had he not obtained the character for such harshness with other regiments. When the men were asked if they had any charges to prefer or any complaints to make, all answered in the negative but one man who had been flogged for not going to his duty, which he said he was not able to perform by means of some simulated complaint in his loins which I disbelieved and therefore had a consultation of other surgeons before the flogging of Rippon. This was a literary man and had been a hawker of pamphlets prior to his enlistment in the S Devon and was suspected of communicating secret intelligence to the emissaries of Sir Francis Burdett and Major Cartwright. These emissaries were also suspected of casting the fire branch of tumult and disaffection into manufacturing districts in order to create riots and tumults with the people. To prove the correctness of my disbelief in Rippon's disorder this man, on the homeward march of the regiment back from Huddersfield into Devonshire, was understood to possess some pugilistic science which some officers prevailed on him for a sum of money to try with Molyneux* who was giving lessons in pugilistic art at Uttoxeter, a place in Staffordshire where the regiment halted for the night. Rippon's sparring with Molyneux was admirable and much applauded by the officers who liberally rewarded them and from that time he threw off the hospital garb and became one of the smartest men in the regiment. So much for the diagnosis of a simulated disease.

The S Devon regiment remained at Huddersfield until June 1813 when a route arrived for them to march in two divisions southward back through Penniston and Sheffield. This was a trial time for sweethearts and wives. My medical fame was now

---

[16] Lieutenant-General Wroth Palmer Acland, KCB (1770–1816) was notable for his role in the Peninsular War (ODNB). Several documents relating to his involvement with the Luddites are reproduced verbatim on www.ludditebicentenary.blogspot.com

at the highest, my success had obtained for me an introduction into the wealthiest families around Huddersfield. Sir Joseph Radcliffe* and his lady promised me their interest and support. Mr Haigh, a millionaire cloth merchant, offered me a cheque book to draw on his banker for any amount of money that might be required to establish myself in Huddersfield. Old Mr Holroyd offered me a yearly salary, sick or well. Mr Staple, the Allens, Walkers and other rich residents too numerous to mention promised their support and interest. What was to be done? How were these bright promises to be acknowledged? There were two contingencies: one was this young man of 22 would be obliged to resign the Surgeoncy of his regiment in order to settle at Huddersfield as a surgeon. My appointment had been so far most agreeable in marching from place to place and afforded me an opportunity of knowing men and their manners. By settling at Huddersfield I would give up a certainty for an uncertainty; for all the work I had done in healing the sick, curing their diseases and performing surgical operations gratuitously I had not received £50 in presents or fees, which I was not allowed to accept as fees.

Zeal for professional knowledge and improvement followed by the gratitude of many were the object and aim of all these extra labours in addition to my ordinary military duties. There was again another tempting offer made to me by an old retired physician, formerly a surgeon at Huddersfield, a complete hypocondriac, fearing sudden death from imaginary disease of the heart. He had resolved to leave Huddersfield for a year with his wife and go to the South of England. His furnished house and the use of a servant during his absence was also offered and gratefully declined, but the greatest of all these determinations remain to be told, viz: a wife. I had been engaged for a short time to Miss Louisa H, youngest daughter of Mr & Mrs H living at Spring Grove in much apparent comfort and respectability, keeping a close carriage and servants after his retirement from practising the law. How this engagement with Louisa H was brought about it is not easy now to tell. After the concert she had no doubt set her mind on winning the heart never then in love. [She made] frequent visits to the lodgings of Mrs A the Captain's wife where she often met me, and led me one day to escort her from thence over the path field towards the rear of her father's house, and whilst shaking hands she looked unutterable things! We often took leave and seemed loth to depart, at last drawing nearer our lips came together and a kiss was the result. An engagement was thus made and Papa was spoken to who promised to place her fortune on an equal footing with his other daughters. Time soon arrived for the departure of the SDM from Huddersfield according to the War Office route received. The regiment marched in two divisions, the Band remaining with the Staff and playing the tune of 'The girl I left behind me'. The people of Huddersfield cheered the regiment on their departure from Penniston and Sheffield. Devonshire soldiers had acquired for themselves a good reputation at Huddersfield by restoring peace and order among the rioters by their good conduct in quarters and by their soldier-like appearance in the field.

I remained behind one day after the departure of the regiment and then took a parting leave with Miss LH after the regiment had finished its march. In riding hastily from Huddersfield to Sheffield on a Yorkshire horse which I had purchased there, the horse fell and proved such a bad bargain as to induce me to leave the animal for sale at Sheffield with my veterinary friend Mr Peach who in time disposed of the horse at a loss. On the following morning early the SDM marched from Sheffield to Bakewell in Derbyshire where a halt enabled them to get a little fishing in some beautiful streams and to visit Chatsworth the seat of the Duke of Devonshire. This march was performed on foot as my other horse had been lent to the Paymaster.

Homewards the regiment daily marched until their arrival at Tewkesbury where Mr Dangerfield the surgeon, a fellow-student of mine in London had invited me, the Colonel and Captain Oliver to dinner instead of our messing with other officers at the Inn. After a good dinner the party disposed of about seven bottles of Port, not an excessive quantity in those port-drinking days.

At Newport near Berkeley Castle the regiment halted on a Saturday night and the Colonel and I visited Mrs and the Missess Whitaker who had often admired my charger. A ride was proposed on the Cheltenham Down to see some objects there and horses were got ready for the party, a side saddle procured for the young lady who was to grace the Colonel's charger. It so happened in cantering over these Downs the lady was leading a little in advance and her palfrey, seeing other horses following, playfully kicked up her heels and threw her rider who hung by the saddle. I, being younger and nearer the lady, dashed forward, caught her horse by the reins, sprang off my horse and rescued the young lady from the threatened danger of being dragged some distance. After this rescue the writer's vanity may be excused from thinking that this young lady looked more favourably on me, although knowing my engagement to her friend, than on the gallant Colonel.

Mrs Whitaker was subject to gall stones and disease of the liver for which she had gone to Cheltenham and intended afterwards to winter in Bath.

On Sunday night the Col. and I rejoined the last division at Newport. On the following morning, Monday, the last division marched for Bristol at 5 o'clock and took with them my horse whilst I and the Col. were asleep in bed. At 7 I started on foot having given the regiment two hours grace, overtook them on the road and got into Bristol to order breakfast at the Inn one hour before them. I could then walk 5 miles an hour. Halting at Bristol one night, marching was continued daily to Ottery Barracks which they had previously occupied and after a few days resumed their march westward through Exeter, Moreton and Dartmoor Prison which then contained a number of French prisoners. Arrived at this melancholy place I obtained leave of absence and returned to Huddersfield to see my lady love and some old friends. Living in her father's house was a young Irish Esquire, brother to the doctor who had married her sister. Suspicion of a rival quickly arose and proved to be well founded although devised by the lady herself. Her sister and brother-in-law, Mr & Mrs Haigh were apprized of my return and prepared to receive me into their house instead of living at an Inn. A proposal was made by Mr Haigh to visit Harrogate for a week and accordingly a brace of Hunters were sent forward whilst he and I posted all the way through Leeds to that watering place. Kind as Mr Haigh's proposal was, his object was clear to get me away from his sister-in-law who had no doubt transferred her affections to the Irish squire. On the journey Mr Haigh did everything in his power to make matters agreeable, he found all the money and paid all the expenses at the boarding house and gave me a ride with Lord Darlington's foxhounds, but all this kindness did not assuage the miserable feelings of his companion. Harrowgate and Scarborough would not have been visited but for this trip. The Harrowgate waters smell like rotten eggs and contain quantities of sulphur. These have acquired great repute in curing diseases of the skin, rheumatism and chronic affections.

This trip was made during the month's leave of absence during November. We remained a week at Harrowgate and returned to Huddersfield where I acknowledged the liberality and kindness and took leave of Mr Haigh himself and family and returned towards Devonshire. Whilst travelling on the top of a coach a conversation was overheard about some sick person who had been to Huddersfield for advice without relief and said: 'what a pity it was that she had not gone and seen the soldier doctor, as he had cured so many patients before the regiment left.' I looked at the parties as if they knew me and convinced myself that they did not, neither did I make myself known to them for all their praises.

After my return to Dartmoor Prison and rejoining the regiment some good hunting was afforded by the Harriers of Mr King, then residing at Spitchwick Park some eight miles off. Some of the officers shot a number of Woodcocks and Snipes and one or two Heathpoults.[17]

The French prisoners shewed ingenuity in carving and converting bones and cocoa nut shells into useful and ornamental articles for sale, such as Ladies work-boxes etc. Their conduct was orderly and good.

From August 26th to December 3/4th in 1813 the SDM remained in barracks at Dartmoor Prison where nearly all the sick soldiers recovered their health. On the 3rd and 4th day of December the regiment marched from Dartmoor to Plymouth where they were billetted at Inns for a short time as the Barracks were filled with Regular soldiers, and the Officer's Mess was at the Commercial Inn kept by Congdon who catered bountifully with all the good eatables that the town afforded.

Soon after their arrival I was laid up in bed at the Inn [with] quinsey+ and whilst there a note was brought to me signed by the name of Welsford stating that they had heard from Mr Barnes* at Exeter of the arrival of the SDM at Plymouth and requesting that I might be called in to see Mr Welsford who was suffering greatly from Ophthalmia+ following the operation for cataract performed on him by Mr Barnes at Exeter. On receipt of this note, I got out of bed, dressed, enquired of the officers if they knew of a person called Welsford, to which question the good old Paymaster replied: 'yes, I know Mr Welsford, he is a distant relation of mine and one of the three partners of Arthur and Rosedew at the Abbey Wine Vaults. Why do you ask?' Answer: 'Here is a note to visit him.' Paymaster: 'I will go then and introduce you.' I found Mr Welsford labouring under gouty irises with both pupils closed shutting out the light and producing almost total blindness. His nights were restless and disturbed by intense pains over the eye brows and in the eyeballs. If sleep could be procured by any means before midnight he was sure to awake about two in the morning with intense pain and restlessness afterwards. My judgement was quickly given; I said plainly 'I can be of no service to you, Sir, all the mischief is done that can be done, all your patience will be tried until these nocturnal pains and gouty attacks be removed or transferred to your feet and other parts.' The fee was then presented and hesitatingly received with the observation that I was merely acting for Mr Barnes as his locum tenens, but on being pressed again with its reception I took it with the intention of transferring it to Mr Barnes at the first opportunity.

Captain Hawkins then retired leaving the house without any intention of calling again. On the following day another note was received soliciting his daily attendance during Mr Welsford's severe sufferings which I endeavoured to palliate by all the known remedies then in use, as topical applications or internal anodynes. Days, weeks and months passed before any permanent ease could be obtained. Meanwhile,

---

17 Peregrine falcon.

Mr Barnes* came down from Exeter to see his patient who was advised to return to Exeter in the ensuing summer for further trials by means of operations to recover his sight. Before leaving Plymouth, a fee of 20 guineas was paid by the directions of Mr Barnes himself. Mr Welsford remained some weeks in Exeter but no further operation was advised, his case being deemed hopeless. With great gloom he and Miss Welsford came back to Plymouth and pressed me repeatedly to perform some operation on his eyes, but this experiment I refused and coincided with the judgement expressed by Mr Barnes.

1814

The SDM removed from quarters into the Citadel where they were located happily for the winter which had by this time began most vigorously by sharp frost and heavy falls of snow, such as were never before seen by the oldest inhabitant. So continuous and rapid were the snow-falls to block up all the high roads and streets and cover the fields to a height exceeding that of the hedges, and persons might walk over the snow and the hedges almost without knowing it but for the tops of the bushes. The turnpike roads to Exeter by degrees were choked up but cleared by numerous workmen, or rather made passable so far as Ivybridge where further progress was entirely intercepted for days and weeks so that carriages and carts were there stopped with their contents. Such a large accumulation of materials, eatables, and drinkables, fish and luggage of different kinds was never before seen in Ivybridge. The depth of snow on the high roads was supposed to be in certain places from 6 to 12 feet. Numerous workmen were employed to cut through these snowdrifts and much time and difficulty were required in certain places. Every species of cattle usually grazing on Dartmoor in winter as well as in summer were destroyed by the frost or buried in the snow. The Dartmoor pony was the only animal found alive, other quadrupeds as the Hare, the Sheep and nomad cattle and birds were found dead and discovered by their skeletons. No living person, Octogenarians or Nonogenarians, ever remembered such a winter before and yet longevity on the borders of the Moor especially near Ivybridge was proverbial where two females sisters had lived above 100 years and died at the respective ages of 103 and 101.

Whilst stationed in the Citadel I had a great wish to visit the family of my friend Dr Leach* living at Woodlands about 4 miles off. I had waited some weeks until the Tavistock turnpike road was cleared for travelling. Out of this road I had to turn down a narrow lane where the snow lay still very deep and the mare I rode often sunk in the snow and plunged to get out of it rendering my sword a very inconvenient appendage on this occasion. General Brown, commanding the Western District, had issued an order that all officers were to appear in uniform in the streets of Plymouth, and therefore I was obliged to ride this journey in regimentals which I seldom wore, and returned to the Citadel in safety after a hospitable reception from Mr, Mrs and Miss Leach.

The SDM continued in the Citadel and performed Garrison duty in turn with the Marines, the East Devon and other regiments until they were disbanded. Whilst standing in the street one day with some of the officers a person walking stepped on my foot and occasioned me to look around when I saw a soldier a woman and a child. I asked: 'cannot you see how and where you are going?' and received for answer: 'no, Sir, I am a blind Chelsea pensioner.' Looking at his eyes I saw one was sunk and the other had a cataract which I thought might be removed with advantage: 'would you like to see me?' I asked and was informed there was no chance for him as Staff Surgeons had examined him and considered his sight irrecoverabley gone before his pension was granted. I continued: 'will you be at the Citadel Hospital any forenoon after 10 o'clock and enquire for me. I will tell you what hope remains for recovering your sight.' I operated on his eyes and restored his sight so completely as to enable him to read and write and post bills against the walls of Plymouth and earn half a crown daily besides his pension. His name was Sergeant Jackman who had a wife and family to maintain. The success in this case spread throughout the Garrison and encouraged many veterans in the receipt of pension to apply for similar help in case of blindness or disease. Other blind pensioners were operated upon with success. These results reached the Chelsea Board who ordered an Inspector down who examined and reported on the vision of the pensioners with the view, it was feared by some, of taking away their pensions.

Sergeant Jackman was one day posting a Bill at the corner of a street through which Sir Israel* and Lady Pellew were passing who had heard of his restoration to sight and thus enquired: 'are you the pensioner who was blind?' 'Yes, M'am' was the answer. 'But were you quite blind?' 'I was.' 'And can you now see to read and write?' 'I can.' 'How did you recover your sight?' 'By an operation, M'am, performed by the doctor of the militia regiment in the Citadel.' 'And what did you say for it all?' 'Thanks to Mr Butter and God Almighty.' This quaint answer much amused her Ladyship, at his placing the doctor before the Almighty.

The Welsford family was so well pleased as to introduce me to the widow Mrs Symons who was blind from cataracts and gutta serena+ mixed. She had consulted other oculists and been dissuaded from an operation but her desire to have an operation performed was so great as to submit to a trial. I accordingly operated on both eyes in the presence of Dr Woollcombe,* Mr Tottan her son-in-law and her daughters. Hopes were entertained after these operations for the recovery of her sight and hailed with delight at the prospect. Her gloom and despondency were changed into cheerfulness and she said: 'if I should recover my sight he shall have 100 guineas.' She began to see the archway the opposite side of the street and shadows of passing objects. These had much encouraged her hopes. About this time I left Plymouth for Woodbury and remained many days there when a letter from Miss Welsford apprised me that Mrs Symons was considered in much danger, owing to the formation of a carbuncle which had spread rapidly over the back. In my absence she was obliged to call in her family surgeon, Mr Seccombe, who with Dr Woollcombe continued their joint attendances until her death which speedily ensued.

Mr Tottan was a good man and charitable, he proposed and would have assisted in the formation of an Ophthalmic Institution in Plymouth if I would attend to it, but I could not then promise to do so whilst I remained Surgeon of the SDM, which regiment might be ordered to Ireland at any time. Many curious cases were hunted up by Mr Tottan; one was the first case of hydroopthalmy+ which I had seen and which I tapped several times with a needle having a groove to let out the water. The distended eyeball filled and refilled so that there was no hope of a cure but the extirpation of the eyeball which I did not recommend.

There was a man called Davies blind in both eyes with opaque cornea+ which I thinned off and enabled him to see a little at one point. Miss Dorothea Symons made a beautiful drawing which I still possess of this man's eye. Davies had the wonderful faculty of finding his way about through the streets and roads in the country wherever he was sent, and I believe once went as far as Manchester on foot. His wonderful faculty may be compared to that of Holman[18] the blind traveller who alone had visited the four quarters of the Globe and published an account of his travels.

Knaresborough Jack, alias Metcalfe,[19] was still more remarkable for his faculties as a blind man. At 6 years of age his sight was destroyed by the small-pox; deprived of vision, his other four senses enabled him to achieve wonderful exploits. He became in turn a guide to travellers over the Yorkshire Moors, a carrier, owner of horses which he rode and drove fearlessly, an Engineer, Architect and Contractor for making new roads, bridges, culverts, drains and the like. He is said to have planned hundreds of miles of Turnpike roads uniting Yorkshire and Lancashire, and in one place to have succeeded where others had failed in crossing a deep bog. His plan was to cut deep trenches on either side of the space allotted for a wide road, then to employ a number of hands in cutting heath and furze bushes and other growths across the bog to be trodden down so that horses and carts might be drawn over them and as these sunk or were forced down into the bog others were supplied or were forced down, so that these faggots of heath at last became consolidated and then over them was carted thick layers of stone until the whole became a solid mass in width according to the space required for the road. This scheme was the invention of a blind man and the example probably of inducing George Stephenson to carry a rail road across Chat Moss by purchasing a great number of empty barrels at Manchester and Liverpool and sinking them in the mud in such quantities as to bear weights of heavy stones and other materials for a railway without further sinkage.

I also couched an old man blind with a cataract in each eye, the father of Mr Elliot of Barley House. One eye only was operated upon and in that sight was restored and sufficient for all the purposes of life. Sometime after his sight was restored he remarked that the sight of the other eye was returning likewise and so it turned out in the end for that cataract loose detached and flocculent and spontaneously absorbed leaving good sight on that eye also. Such a spontaneous disappearance of a cataract I had never before seen, but curiously enough it was soon followed by another.

Admiral Bedford consulted me about a cataract in one of his eyes on which I was to have operated when the sight of the other eye then very dim was gone. The Admiral visited me occasionally and one day remarked that his sight in the cataract eye was returning. On looking at it I perceived that the cataract was floating to and fro out of its proper situation and adhering only to one part of the vitreous humour.[+] It ultimately became absorbed, disappeared and the sight of the eye returned. I had read of such cases but had never seen one until these two occurred and therefore I drew up a paper on the 'spontaneous dispersion of cataract with operation' and placed it before the Royal Society of Edinburgh of which an extract appeared in Brewster's* philos[c] journal.[20] Mr Gunning, Deputy Inspector of hospitals had become officially known to me and heard of my success in restoring the sight of blind pensioners. Captain Bray of the army was then sent to me for inspection by the Deputy Inspector. The Captain was so blind as to be led about the streets by a

[18] James Holman, FRS (1786–1857) was born in Exeter and joined the navy, rising to the rank of Lieutenant. He was invalided out in 1810 with a rheumatic illness, which was followed by blindness.

[19] John Metcalf (1717–1810).

[20] *Edinburgh Philosophical Journal* 6 (1821–22), pp. 135–40.

boy. His blindness was produced by an attack of purulent ophthalmy [trachoma[+]] in Egypt where he was regarded as a bold and dashing officer who had done some very extra-ordinary exploits, one of which was climbing Pompey's pillar[21] to a greater height than any other man. The surfaces of his eyeballs were covered with a network of red vessels carrying blood and depositing opaque matter between the lamine[+] and the cornea.[+] He had paid 50 guineas to Sir William Adams* for little or no benefit and therefore wished me to try what I could do for him. He was a resolute determined man full of blood. I therefore bled him to fainting and found that the red vessels over his eyes became pallid like those of a calf blooded in order to make white veal. Low diet and blisters behind the ears enabled me to try such topical applications as promoted absorption. Our famous ointment made with lard, the nitric oxide of mercury, was applied at night to his eyeballs and a solution of nitric of silver by day. Granulations[+] were repressed by the sulphate and acetate of copper, also Gowlardes extract.[+] These applications had the desired effect of promoting absorption and reproducing the natural whiteness of the eye balls. Thus was the supply of red blood suppressed and absorption of the deposits promoted. After much perseverance his sight was sufficiently recovered to enable him to walk about and travel without a guide. He was further enabled to resume the sports of the field and to shoot at a partridge flying. I attended a shooting party with him and saw him shoot a rabbit running although he did not kill a woodcock.

Success in the Captain's case induced the Deputy Inspector to ask me to visit the military hospital at Stoke and give my opinion as to the number of soldiers there admitted for diseases of the eye, especially granulations (corneites[+]), which were said to be the sequel of Egyptian Ophthalmy [trachoma[+]] which had prevailed in our armies ever since Sir Robert Abercrombie's attack in 1801. This purulent or Egyptian Ophthalmy had decimated the ranks of many regiments and rendered more soldiers non-effective than war itself. So great was the number of blind and half-blind soldiers in our army as to induce Sir William Adams* to propose, and Lord Palmerston as Secretary of War to construct an Ophthalmic Military Hospital, to which were ordered such soldiers whose sight was defective or insufficient for military duties. After these patients had been examined and treated with variable success, the hospital was given up by the Government as no longer useful to the country. Diseases of the eye became more generally studied by young surgeons entering the Army and Navy and thereby such morbid changes as granulation, purulent[+] ophthalmy and other defects of vision were frequently prevented.

In the beginning of the present century no hospital or ophthalmic institution existed in Great Britain for the exclusive reception and treatment of diseases of the eye. In 1805 Mr Sanders,* a Devonshire man from Barnstaple became demonstrator of anatomy at the Borough hospitals in London and proposed the formation of a London Eye Infirmary under the auspices and by the advice of his master, Sir Astley Cooper* and Mr Cline.* Great opposition was raised by the faculty in London against Mr Sander's proposal. So great were his exertions and so anxious his studies in getting subscriptions to defray the expenses of an ophthalmic institution that his health broke down and an attack of apoplexy[+] deprived him of life. He died before he had time to publish his new method of restoring sight by the removal of cataracts

---

[21] A Roman triumphal column, just under ninety feet tall, erected in Alexandria between 298 and 302 AD in honour of Emperor Diocletian.

both in adults and infants. The adaptation of his new operations applicable to children and infants in arms was quite new to the surgical world. The ordinary operations for cataract at one metropolitan hospital were few and far between and were twofold, consisting either in depressing the opaque body out of the axis of vision in the vitreous humour[+] or in extracting it at once from the eye ball. Mr Sander's new and third operation consisted in passing a spear-pointed needle through the cornea into the eye, drilling a hole into the centre of the cataract, breaking up the interior of its structure and detaching it from surrounding adhesions so as to leave it a loose body exposed to the solvent power of the aquaeous and vitreous humours. Professor Scarpa* of Pavia whom I visited in 1817 and whose books I purchased, had invented a curved sharp-pointed needle which he passed through the [s]clerotic coat[+] into the eye and depressed the cataract out of the axis of vision and thus restored sight at once in favorable cases, but in others a cataract rose again and again and rendered further operations necessary and sometimes failures.

I found Scarpa* a most intelligent and accomplished surgeon fully deserving the high European reputation awarded to him. His drawings and writings on diseases of the eye, club feet, and hernia[+] were exquisite and unsurpassed by any other European production. Mr Hey* of Leeds was best known to the profession as one of the most experienced and able surgeons out of London, he had also obtained much reputation as an oculist; his round-shaped needle for depressing the cataract was one of the most awkward instruments ever used and so obtuse as not to pierce or cut. Extraction he believed he never attempted. This operation of extracting the cataract was, he believed, confined to London.

Baron Wenzell,[22] however, from Germany came over to London occasionally to extract cataracts from blind people. He used to say that a man must put out a hatful of eyes before he could acquire the greatest expertness in performing this operation. Baron Wenzell's words were translated into English by Mr Ware[23] who practised with much success the operation of extraction in London. Mr Phipps was also an oculist very expert and successful in extracting cataracts, he had the good fortune to operate on the Baroness Howe whose sight was obscured by cataracts. The Baroness was so delighted at the recovery of her vision as to confer on him her hand and her fortune. One proviso however was made that he should relinquish the practice of an oculist and take the name of Waller. The Baroness and oculist were united in the bonds of wedlock and known in the fashionable world as the Baroness Howe and Sir Wathen Waller.* They gave the most sumptuous banquet at their Twickenham Villa.

Mr Adams* with Mr Milford's aid established the Exeter Eye Infirmary for the West of England in 1808 and drew thither a number of ophthalmic patients from Devon and Cornwall. His reputation increased so he extended it towards London where he desired to succeed his fellow apprentice and Tutor, the late Mr Sanders,* whose merits he forestalled by publishing Sander's new practice before Dr Farre, the editor of Sander's post-humous work, could get it through the press. The consequence was that Adams was rejected and Benjamin Travers selected to fill the

[22] For more information see A. L. Wyman, 'Baron de Wenzel, Oculist to King George III: His Impact on British Ophthalmologists', *Medical History* 35 (1991), pp. 78–88.
[23] James Ware (1756–1815) was a prolific writer and philanthropist who founded a charity school for the blind in London. He translated *A Treatise on the Cataract; With Cases to Prove the Necessity of Dividing the Transparent Cornea.... By M. de Wenzel, jun. Baron of the Holy Roman Empire* (London: Dilly, 1791).

office of Surgeon oculist to the London Eye Infirmary with Dr Farre the physician. Adams however made a successful excursion to Dublin and other parts of Ireland from whence he obtained a charming woman for a wife with a good fortune. It was asserted that Adams had realised about £100.0 [£1,000?] which he lost by unsuccessful speculation in the South American Mines worked in the search of the precious metals. Machinery, it was supposed, would supersede the toil of hand labour to which the peasantry was subjected in bringing up bags of ore to the surface, which bags were so heavy as to try an Englishman's strength in lifting. These natives lived chiefly on flesh of Bullocks, Buffaloes etc and were uncommonly muscular and strong. Speculators went out from England with costly steam machinery to work the South American like the Cornish mines but in this scheme they were greatly disappointed. After purchasing the exporting steam engines and conveying them over land to their places of destination, great was their disappointment not to find any water in the land to convert into steam. The whole speculation therefore became a bubble into which Adams and others were ruinously drawn.

Mr Sam Barnes* became sole surgeon to the West of England Eye Infirmary after Adam's resignation and continued the office from 1813 to 1846 when he resigned and two of his pupils, de la Garde* and Edye* succeeded to the office.

1814 by Orders, the SDM was disembodied at Plymouth on the 9th of August 1814. The Staff were retained at Headquarters and the men dismissed to their respective homes. The Staff consisted of one Adjutant, one Quartermaster, Paymaster and Surgeon. The two latter joined in taking lodgings and lived comfortably together during the remainder of the year. Captain and Paymaster John Hawkins was as honorable, kind hearted and friendly a man as ever lived. The want of a good Mess dinner daily, and the loss of our brother officers' society afforded a striking contrast to the melancholy change of living in a dirty lodging almost in solitary confinement, with only a casual friend dropping in now and then, and expecting perhaps a bit of dinner which generally consisted of a chop or a pork griskin[24] instead of a joint which neither could be boiled or roasted at the lodging, where the mistress and her children and two other lodgers were all to be attended to by a hard-working slave of an old widow woman passed 60. Good lodgings at that time were not obtainable in Plymouth.

What was to be done in Plymouth at this dull time? I was a stranger there in a strange land without relations, connexions or friends. I kept my horse at an Inn and my favourite setter bitch Juno occupied the same rooms with myself by night and day. Besides the sick of the Staff I had several private patients who paid one little or nothing. My 2nd assistant surgeon, John Churchill, whom I had enlisted in the preceding year when the regiment was marching through the street at Exeter for Dartmoor, also settled in Plymouth and obtained an appointment as one of the two apothecaries at the Dispensary with a salary of £40 a year, added to his half pay of £45 which with his private income enabled him to save and invest a small sum in the Funds yearly. Whilst he was paying his addresses to Miss Cookworthy, sister to Dr C, he wished one day to show her how well he could ride and borrowed my horse for the purpose. I tried to dissuade him by saying the horse was apt to run away with a stranger and without proper caution might run away with him. Churchill being so eager to shew his lady love his equestrian performance accompanied me

---

[24] The lean part of the loin of a bacon pig.

to the Commercial Stables where the following dialogue occurred after the horse was saddled and led out in the street to be mounted. Churchill asked the hostler if the horse was quiet: 'yes, Sir, he is very quiet in the stable but you must mind he doesn't run away with you sir!' 'Oh I will take care of that with a good double rein bridle. Now for the saddle, John. Girths all right?' 'Yes, sir.' Churchill being portly in person had some difficulty in mounting by the stirrup which he had lengthened or shortened according to his fancy, rising in his stirrups and reseating himself in the saddle according to fancy. All being ready for a start he turned round and said: 'how do I look John on horseback?' John with a hem answered: 'you look well enough for what I see, you won't look so long if you don't mind that horse.' Thereupon he chirped and started whip in hand using it a little and the horse started off wondering, we supposed, what sort of a rider was on his back. To Broad Street he went and paraded up and down before the lady's window, looking at and admiring him as he was vain enough to suppose. Then starting up the street in a canter and whipping the horse round the corner facing the Guildhall they both came down together and Churchill's head received a blow from the kerbstone which stunned him for a time, when he was carried back before his lady's door to his own lodging and there treated for concussion of the brain. The horse made his way back to the stables where the hostler in his quaint way said: 'I thought it would be so.' This horse was a very fine animal once purchased of Rookes the dealer by Sir TT Drake for £20 as a match horse with three others to draw his carriage. Owing to bad management the horse had been made very nervous and when checked from starting would rear and plunge and not stand quietly. Whenever he heard the carriage door open or shut he pranced and jumped and reared until they were all off together, and once all four horses ran away beyond the postillion's power of restraint and smashed a handsome carriage in the wall of a bridge.

Finding this horse so unruly the Baronet and his postboys were one day debating whether they should not shoot the horse, but my father arriving with another horse that would match the Baronet's team, an exchange was thus effected. My father's first trial of the horse was made with Lord Rolle's* hounds, and when the hounds started a hare and other horses followed them this horse jumped and plunged a little and being light in his carcase jumped through his saddle loosely girthed, and so left my father behind him, thus was the horse further condemned. When I arrived at Woodbury from Plymouth I was induced also to ride the horse out with the hounds which started in full cry after a hare. I followed with the other riders, this horse pulling tremendously. After rounding Woodbury Castle the hounds took upwards and Major Hull of Marpool[25] a capital horseman rode up to me and said: 'now let us see what speed your horse has,' accordingly we had a race for a few hundred yards, neck and neck, when suddenly he fell back without my knowing the reason and I followed the hounds down to the road where there was a check. I wanted to pull up my horse there but no he dashed through the pack making some hounds howl, but not killing any. When in the road he ran furiously down towards Woodbury Village I pulling all the time hard at the reins to stop him. I knew there was a sharp turn in the village where we should come up. A thought suddenly struck me to relax the steady pull at the reins to let go to the right and grasp the left suddenly so as to pull the horse into the ditch, where his head came against the hedge and so we were stopped.

[25] Marpool Hall, Exmouth.

My arms were aching pretty much at this time when I was a mile at least from the hounds which I wished again to rejoin, but the horse was disinclined to a retreat and swerved from side to side, but a rap over the ears with my whip let him know that I would be master. When I returned to hounds Lord Rolle joked me about the injury done to several dogs, and others wondered what had become of me and the horse, and on my enquiring for Major Hull I was told that he had gone home with his horse blown up as a butcher blows veal almost to blindness, his horse having ruptured some of the air cells of his lungs. From that time forth this horse never attempted to run away with me again but could be rode anywhere with the lightest snaffle. He would however not do so with other people. My brother afterwards rode the horse which ran away with him down a hill too fast to turn a corner so that he went plump against the hedge where he stopped, and my brother went over his head into a wheat field, thereby occasioning a laugh that the horse knew better than his rider that he was not to trample over new wheat. It was said that I and my horse afterwards used to waltze in the streets of Plymouth with a dashing young lady on horseback who rode beautifully. On another occasion at Dartmoor I rode the horse over the turnpike gate and broke the girths in so doing, without a fall. Blindness however ultimately was the cause of the horse being sold as a poster.

The Paymaster's daily amusement was to read Sir W Scott's novels between breakfast and dinner and throughout the evening lest any friends dropped in. After some weeks reading I found him one morning re-perusing a book which he had returned and again got back. 'Why' I said 'you read those books some weeks ago!' He replied: 'I did so, but I have forgotten the contents and so I read them over again.' In these uncomfortable lodgings we passed our time until the year 1815 when the SDM was re-embodied and sent into George's Square Barracks, Plymouth Dock on the 7th day of July.

1815

The regiment was quartered in George's Square Barracks but the regimental hospital was fixed at Frankfort Barracks, Plymouth so that the sick were sent there and I had to visit them twice daily at 10am and 8pm. Here I performed my first operation for Litholomy+ on a Cooper Angel of Holne sent down by the Leach family, who had changed their residence to Spitchwick Park near Ashburton. This man was above 70 years of age and, the stone extracted by aid of scalpel and finger, some alarming haemorrhage ensued but the old man recovered perfectly cured and enabled to take three voyages to Newfoundland afterwards, and died at the age of nearly 80 at the Frankfort Hospital. I also allowed a number of poor private patients to attend, especially those afflicted with diseases of the eyes. Here also I performed an operation for hernia+ and by this time had successfully performed nearly all the capital operations in surgery. The litholomy patient from Holne put me to £3 expense besides his hospital lodgings as I was anxious to perform this operation. Another instance for litholomy soon occurred, a poor boy sent down from Aveton Gifford on whom the Kingsbridge surgeons had failed after a long trial to extract the stone. That operation was also successfully performed as well as five others in after years making a total of seven litholomy patients who all recovered.

As I had the advantage of a stable in George's Square Barracks for my horse and dogs – a brace of beautiful black setters, Juno and her half brother Otho – as

September arrived I obtained leave to shoot over an estate at Ermington favorable for game. Thither I and Captain Toll went on the 1ˢᵗ and shot many brace of birds having started with sunrise and not returning before 4 in the afternoon. Notwithstanding this day work I walked to and from George's Square to Frankfort hospital after 8 o'clock in the evening. Deputy Inspector Gunning in admiring these black setters and enquiring about their breed staunchness said 'I wish you would come out one day to Hemerdon early at breakfast and accompany me over the moors in search of Heath Fowl.²⁶ I own a kennel of dogs not good but I have one famous dog which shall go with yours and the three together may find a Heath Fowl for which I have tried in vain. Mr Treeby of Goodamoor is accused of shooting a greater number of the pack before the day but some are left.'

At 7 o'clock on the day fixed I arrived on horseback with the dogs at Hemerdon but found scarcely anyone up. After breakfast we started on horseback taking with us 2 men and 3 dogs. After some trial on the moors the Inspector said: 'why do you allow your dogs such a wide range? I keep mine within gunshot.' 'Oh' said I 'let them go where they like and find game if they can.' After a walk of some 2 hours he observed: 'there is one of your dogs standing by the side of the hill. I wonder if he is staunch.' 'The result will prove that,' I said, 'let us hasten to the spot.' As we drew nearer Otho saw the bitch standing and immediately dropped by backing her. When they got within 2 or 3 shots of the bitch, Gunning's dog went up and passed before her head without ever backing or stopping at any game. Thereupon Gunning said: 'I can depend on my dog – there is nothing before yours.' 'So here' I said 'I think either your dog is worth nothing or mine is worth nothing. I must attend to her.' So I went forward and Otho came up backed his sister and lay down. It was a beautiful spectacle to see how staunch the bitch was and how well the dog lay. On going ahead up whirled a heath fowl and flew swiftly away, which I brought down at a long shot. Down was the word as I loaded, then went on and picked up a fine hen heath fowl, which I put into my pocket, and looking around saw the dog standing which I supposed might be another heath fowl, but on going up a cock partridge rose and flew swiftly away. This bird likewise dropped before my gun. Taking a circuit around and finding no more birds I went down the hill to Gunning. 'What do you think of that?' 'Think!' he replied, 'one of the prettiest sights I ever saw, I would have given a guinea or two to have shot that Heath Fowl. Let us look at the bird,' he said, 'it is a beautiful old hen, and the partridge is a fine old cock, how remarkable that these birds should have lain so close together.' 'Well,' I said, 'What think you of the dogs now, and what excuse can you make for the ill behaviour of your own dog, which paid no deference to mine?' 'Ah well,' he said, 'there is nothing more here so I must be getting homewards. There are some snipe down in the bottom, let us try for them and you will see how my dog will behave.' Juno pointed at one and Otho at another but his dog stood not at all. Gunning fired two or three shots and missed. I killed one snipe only. He then said, 'excuse me I must be gone. I promised Mrs Gunning to return soon after noon and drive her to Plympton but you can make out your day here with snipes and perhaps other things. I will not take you away but will order a luncheon to be provided for you by Miss Fuller, my wife's sister on your return to Hemerdon.' Not finding many snipes or any other game I beat backwards and in passing by Treeby's rabbit warren I saw two or three rabbits out, one sitting on

²⁶ Grouse.

his hind legs and wiping his face with the fore paws. I thought it a long shot but let go at the rabbit and to my surprise turned over a couple; with these I beat backwards to Hemerdon House, put my dogs into the stable and went into the house where I found a luncheon laid out and Miss Fuller, a lovely girl, to receive me. She and Mrs Gunning were the daughters of General Fuller. I deposited the rabbits, partridge and two snipe having no use for them at the Mess and took with me the coveted heath fowl which I stuffed and preserved, good to this day, Janu^r 22nd 1866, as a memento of this memorable day.

About the end of September Captain Braddon, SDM, tempted me to accept an invitation from Mr Justice Morgan and son who kept a pack of hounds some miles from Tavistock where they had a fine range of sporting granted by the Duke of Bedford. We were fools enough to start soon after 3 o'clock in the morning from George's Square Barracks for Woodovis, which we reached about 7 or 8 o'clock in time for Breakfast. The old squire and his son who hunted his father's hounds were astonished to find us there so early from Plymouth Dock, and remarked that we could not expect our dogs to hunt after such a journey, but that he had an old pointer and a young setter which might serve our purpose. After an hours rest we started with four dogs and three guns and killed a few brace of birds all of which nearly had been found by my own dogs. After dinner we halted two or three hours, and left soon after 7 for the Barracks. On returning, Braddon's horse, a young animal which he had purchased, knocked up tired at Roborough Down and obliged Braddon to walk back the greater part of the distance. I rode on followed by Juno, but Otho was too tired and so accompanied Braddon and his horse who did not reach George Square Barracks [until] a long time after myself. The distance by road forward and backward must have been nearly 40 miles, and it was computed that the dogs must have gone double that distance by ranging widely over the Downs and hunting 6 or 7 hours afterwards. This was a wild excursion which I am ashamed almost to relate.

A propos of the dogs – sometime afterwards I had shot some pheasants and hung them up in my stable meaning to distribute them to certain friends, but some members of our mess thought they would like to taste them and therefore entered the stable to take away the birds, but Otho stood at bay and forbad their entrance. There was a laugh about the fidelity of the dog afterwards. The condition of these dogs was admirable.

During my morning visits to the Frankfort hospital in George's Square the dogs accompanied me, and remained in the dead house during the performance of my hospital duties. One of my private patients there was a butcher employed in killing beasts for the contractor who supplied the troops with meat. In cleaving a bone one day a splinter flew into his eye and cut the cornea$^+$ almost through. The wound was healing favourably under the application of a lotion and bandage, but one day hoisting a pulley the block fell with violence against his damaged eye and burst it like a gooseberry squashed. He was a poor fellow and unable to pay for my advice and attendance, so I took out my fee in kind by getting offal for my dogs who enjoyed many a repeated meal of nice warm flesh from a recently slaughtered bullock. After this daily repast they returned with me to George's Square in time for our mess dinner, after which bones and scraps were saved for their supper. In this way their condition was excellent.

In those days Plymouth Marsh was a swamp over which the Union Road now passes and on which the houses East and West of the Octagon are now built. Snipes in abundance were found [there] during the winter. It was amusing to see the fondness of these dogs for hunting and pointing at these snipes. There were dikes for the conveyance of water on the sides of which snipes often lay. Otho one day in jumping one of these dikes caught the wind of a snipe just as he had made a spring and fell with his under parts under the water and his fore legs on the opposite bank, his head being turned round to one side, and his tail showing out of the water. In this attitude the dog paused until the snipe arose; it was a beautiful sight to see him.

One frosty day I went with my gun to the marsh, there was snow on the ground, the dog stood, a snipe rose and flew lowly under a bank. I fired, killed the snipe and peppered a horse screened by a thorn bush growing on the bank, and before I had time to load I heard a hue and cry from Stonehouse Lane, and saw two persons running towards me and exclaiming: 'you have shot two children and broke two panes of glass.' I said 'that is impossible,' but on looking again I found that the window was exactly in the line with my shot but at an incredible distance. I said 'come to me at my lodgings, you shall be paid for the glass.' Thus I shot a snipe, a horse, frightened two children and broke two panes of glass. Some sceptics may call this a Baron Mancaesen's[27] story but it is true.

1816

Feb the 8th the SDM was again disbanded at George's Square Barracks. Dock Sergeant Huxham engaged for me Rowe's lodging, 1 Cornwall Street where the mixed business of Druggist and Grocer was carried on. A number of poor patients visited me there and got their prescription made up in the shop below. I made myself as comfortable as I could do in these lodgings and conferred advantages on my landlord by my prescriptions far beyond the amount paid for my lodgings.

The times now in Plymouth grew awfully dull, there was a total stagnation of trade, the merchants were slack in business and the banks would not promote their speculations. Professional men, especially the Medical were badly paid by their patients and obliged to do a great deal of work for nothing. My brother visited me in May and arranged a plan for settling at Limpstone where he afterwards practised for 17 years until broken down by cholera in 1832.

Whilst at dinner one day eating some pork griskins which my landlady Mrs Rowe cooked remarkably well, a man called Dawe, living as a servant with Mr Tingcombe the banker, wished to speak with me. He stated his object and said I had been sent for to see his brother who was dying of a rupture strangulated at a place called Lewe Down, 9 miles north of Tavistock and near Mr Tremaynes at Sydenham. Dawe reasoned thus: 'I can do my brother no good whether he be dead or living but you perhaps may save him as you did Lieut Black at Shorncliffe Barracks, who was otherwise doomed to death by the Military Surgeons.' Dawe continued: 'I cannot pay you for your journey but I will provide a post chaise at my own expense and take you there and bring you back free of cost, further than this I cannot do as I am only a servant.' My brother and I packed up our instruments whilst the post chaise was got ready. We started and reached Tavistock at about 9 or 10 at night and then took fresh

[27] Baron Karl Friedrich Münchausen (1720–97) was a German soldier in the Russian army, addicted to telling stirring tales of his exploits. These were expanded and fictionalised by Rudolf Raspe and others, and Münchausen is now synonymous with the telling of tall stories.

horses for Lew Down where we got lost and wandered about failing to find out the poor man's cottage until two o'clock in the morning. On entering the hovel we found two or three old women and a nurse seated around a wood fire expecting Dawe's death. The brother who had piloted us there told his sick brother who I was and what I had done and begged him to follow my advice. The old women, especially the nurse, were loth for me to meddle with the case. Three doctors they said had given the man over and if Dr Harness of Tavistock, in whose skill they had unbounded confidence, gave the patient over, no other doctor would be likely to succeed. On examining the patient I found a strangulated rupture on the left side somewhat large but not painful; it had been down for 15 days and no passage through the bowels had taken place, he had been constantly sick, and unable to retain anything in his stomach. I said to the patient 'your case is clear and simple an operation can save your life, will you undergo it?' He answered: 'I will Sir.' I replied: 'get ready hot water and sponges.' On cutting down through the hernial sack I discovered a portion of the bowel mortified and the rest adhering so firmly as not to be easily separated from the sack. The stricture I divided and the contents of the upper bowels escaped freely. In this state I left the patient under my brother's care, promising to return again in a day or two if the man was alive. On the following day my brother brought back to Plymouth a favorable report which encouraged me to revisit Dawe twice or thrice a week. My journeys were performed in this way – Symons's 3 horse coach took me to Tavistock rather under three hours, then I had to hire a horse to ride 9 miles to the patient and 9 back, in time to catch the coach returning to Plymouth. Thus were 10 or 12 hours a day spent about this patient. A question soon arose how my expenses were to be paid. The Overseers of Milton Abbott parish, to which the man belonged, met in vestry and decided on guaranteeing my expenses but the Rev Doctor alone objected by stating that it would be a bad precedent to make the sick poor dissatisfied with the parochial doctor. Thus the rector overruled the ratepayers, but only for a time. Mr Justice Morgan at last advocated my cause and said he would report it to the Duke of Bedford unless my expenses were paid. The Duke's brother it seems died of strangulated hernia at Woburn where the Country Surgeon would not operate and before Sir Astley, then Mr Cooper,* could be fetched from London. The Duke's case was hopeless. Dawe recovered and told his tale where ever he went but the wound in his groin from which his stools were discharged [remained] for many months until Dupuytren's* operation was tried for enlarging the passage so that the contents of the bowels might pass through their natural channel. Whatever fame I got by this bold operation I have always thought that it was hardly earned as my expenses were never paid and every journey accompanied by rain which wetted through my clothes. Ultimately on my return from France in 1817 I found a letter from the Rector's son, the Rev J stating that the parish officers had voted twelve guineas to defray my expenses in journeys made for the recovery of their parishioner Dawe, whose wife and family would have become chargeable on the parish. Thus the Rector's son atoned for the obstinacy of his father in some measure, but the money came with such a bad grace through the hands of Captain Morgan and his father, the Justice who had received it from the parochial officers, that I determined not to accept it as money, although I was then poor and in want of ready money. The sum of twelve guineas was therefore laid out in the purchase of a silver salver.

In 1816 Plymouth was one of the dullest towns in the Kingdom. Wars, horrid wars, were ended, pensioners and sailors quitted the port and lived in other places leaving Plymouth in a deserted state and the tradesmen without business which wars had created, and a total stagnation existed with dispondency in every countenance. The merchants were few in number and not prosperous excepting those concerned in the corn and liquor trades. Grass grew in the public streets quite green, and property of all descriptions both house and land fell to a considerable discount. An acre of land which then could be bought for a £100 or less has since been sold at the rate of £4,000 and upwards. No respectable lodgings could then be obtained in Plymouth. The Royal Hotel built by Tontine at a cost of £40,000 could not get a tenant for a long time. Windsor took it and failed, Congdon then tried and paid a £100 to be released. Then the Widdons from the Pope's Head entered the hotel at a nominal rent. Times took a turn in their favour they prospered and in the course of years realised several thousand pounds, which [they] imprudently invested in the Butterford Estate and to complete the purchase were obliged to borrow several thousand pounds. This purchase ruined them in the end and obliged them to lose all the profits of their Hotel.

From 1816 to 1820 Medical Practice was at a very low ebb in Plymouth, scarcely a surgeon apothecary and not above one or two kept a horse, their visits were paid on foot and sometimes by the aid of dock dillies.[28] One Guinea per week was then the ordinary charge and that sum there was often delay and difficulty in getting. Dr Woolcombe* was then the leading physician, he kept one black horse and rode his journeys dressed generally in top-boots and knee-breeches. His death was occasioned by gangrenous erysipelas[+] on the [blank] day of 1822. A marble tablet is placed in St Andrews Church Plymouth recording his many virtues and medical attainments.

I had many patients to visit daily but few that paid me anything. I was heartily sick of Plymouth and of my professional practice, from which I could get only a small remuneration. I kept my horse however and black setters, which I would have sold all but Juno which I determined never to part with.

Much of my professional time was occupied with the Welsford family. Mr Welsford was blind; Mrs Welsford occasionally alarmed about her hernia;[+] their second son George unable to walk without a man's arm; their youngest daughter Louisa scarcely able to speak or stand without help; Miss Jenny Smith the companion and house-keeper troubled with spasms which obliged her to drink laudanum by a wine glass and to have down quart bottles at a time; lastly there was Miss Welsford the oldest daughter who had devoted her time and thoughts by day and by night to her afflicted father and family. For two years she had scarcely gone out of the house except with her blind father for a short walk. There never was a more dutiful daughter or a warmer friend. In the summer of the year 1816 she was induced to walk 3 or 4 miles into the country on a visit to the Leach family. This journey brought on inflammation of her right hip joint for which repeated cupping[+] and leachings were required and constant repose in bed on a mattress; in this posture she was confined about 3 years before she could be considered secure from abscess and ulceration and shortening of the limb. Of these maladies numerous instances could be found in Plymouth. A little girl called Esther Ralph, daughter of Jewish parents, came under my care with

---

[28] Stagecoaches or some other form of wheeled transport presumably, in this case, originating in the docks.

disease in both hip joints, in which abscesses had formed and matter burst into the bladder and worked its way out through fistulas[+] opening in front and back.

Whilst stationed in the Citadel [in] 1814 Mrs Trewman consulted me there on account of her sight; one eye was sunk and lost and the other affected with amoroses[+] almost to blindness. She had paid a Quack Dr called Williams £10 for his advice and a bottle of drops which were of no service. This rapacious Quack was said to have carried away many hundreds of pounds from Plymouth by advertising his drops and advice which he would not give without £10 previously paid. From my advice Mrs Trewman derived so much benefit as to lead her subsequently to send for me at a time when she was pronounced by three medical men to labour under a disease of the heart for which she was strongly advised to go to Bath and drink the waters. I visited her and said: 'Ma'm, there is no disease of your heart and there is no necessity for your going to Bath. I can put you on a plan of treatment which I hope will be successful but you must first speak to your medical advisers.' They retired and I took upon myself the sole treatment which consisted of doing away with all medicine, except a little Bluepil Rhubarb occasionally. Bark and alcoholic drinks were cast aside, a milk diet was enforced, she recovered perfectly and lived for many years afterwards and when she ultimately died of brain disease I opened her body and found her heart as sound and perfect as nature had formed it. She had two daughters and one son. One day in going to visit her I met her son going to school with his satchel and pallid not shining morning face, limping and crawling unwillingly to school. I said: 'little boy, what is the matter with you?' He said: 'Dr S has attended me and said my hip was affected.' I saw at a glance that his hip joints were perfect and that his spine must be affected. I asked the mother her reason for concealing the little boy's complaint from me and received for answer that her son had been attended by a doctor who pronounced the complaint to be the hips. On examining the child I found that abscesses had formed in the loins and burst through many sinuses on the back and groin. I said: 'Ma'm, there is no disease in this boy's hips, he labours under lumbar abscess owing to decay of the back bone and vertebrae. He must lay up at once if you wish to prolong his life, on a mattress and on no occasion to get out of bed.' He was ordered to live well and to take little or no medicine; an issue[+] was put in the back over the suspected caries[+] of the bone. He must have been then 13 or 14 years of age; some property hung on his life and hope was expressed that he might live to become of age and to make a Will, but no judge could suppose that his stamina would ever enable him to reach that period of life. The Almighty however saw fit to preserve him to manhood, but his appearance never assumed a manly aspect. Many of the old sinuses drained off matter but some closed up and many of the lumbar and vertebrae[+] seemed to be compressed from joints into one bony mouth. Having attained the age of 21 years and made his Will, he was removed from Plymouth to Ivybridge where he regained much health and strength which enabled him to walk a little and to drive about in a gig for many hours during the day. Horses and gigs became his hobby and on them he spent his income freely and lavished his resources imprudently. After many years spent in this way he died but I had no opportunity of examining his body.

Whilst in lodgings I employed much of my leisure time in stuffing birds according to the rules of Taxidermy which I first learnt at Sheffield for a guinea paid to a bird stuffer there for that information, which I imparted to Drew at Rock who made a fortune by this employment but died of disease of the heart.

One of my patients informed me that Mr Coram of Compton, a notorious cock-fighter, possessed an old hen which had changed her plumage from a dusky brown for the more beautiful feathers of a cock, that she crowed like the cock, had spurs and wattles, which latter were cut off to make her look like a fighting cock, and had also the arch feathers in her tail. I tried to purchase this bird and therefore induced Mr Coram junr to call upon me at Rowe's lodgings. At first he asked a large price for this curious hen but ultimately came down to my terms after drinking a bottle of gin. I learnt more from this man than I had ever before heard or suspected of the low practises by gamblers in cock fighting, horse racing and card playing. Having secured my wished-for prize, my next object was to get a drawing made of this remarkable bird and I was fortunate in finding a young lady, Miss Mary Gosling of Leigham, where she resided with her mother, brother and sister with Addis Archer Esq who bought them up, educated and maintained the family until his death, leaving his property amongst them. Mary Gosling was a pretty little clever and delicate girl, her accomplishments were many. She could shoot a bird first and afterwards draw it. She could also fish in the river Plym, she rode well on horseback, and she had often led the Plympton Orchestra with a violin. Her drawing of Coram's hen was afterwards engraved and published by me in the Transactions of the Wernerian Natural History of Edinburgh, of which I became a member in 1817.

My time therefore was industriously filled up from morning to night with a number of unprofitable patients from whom my landlord reaped some advantages by dispensing my prescriptions. My regimental pay was 6 [shillings] per diem [which], with such additions as my practice afforded, sufficed to keep myself my horse and black setters. I never was in debt in any part of my life either at school where I generally had a shilling at the end of the term when other boys had nothing although they brought with them a great deal more money than was allowed to me. I often wanted more money than I possessed and curtailed my desires frequently to purchase an article until I could pay for it. On Sundays at home I generally had the same dinner – baked mutton, potatoes and pudding and invited an additional companion to partake of it. Juno was always with me by day and by night on the hearth rug or blanket, but her brother more rude in manner and boisterous in his ways was a companion of the horse in the stable. On Sundays Otho was invited to partake of my Sunday's dinner. When seated after grace, the first word given was 'Down' at which one on either side lay down, the bitch silently and gently but the dog restless and requiring often the word 'Down'. He would sometimes lash the floor with his tail, look up at me with a delighted countenance, lick his lips and drool at the mouth at the savory meat I was eating; the remainder was squeezed with potatoes and pudding and placed before each dog with the word 'Down'. Juno obeyed patiently but Otho was eager and restless, but neither touched their meat until other words were given, such as 'Now then'', at which they would begin their meal, Juno picking out all the flesh and leaving potatoes and pudding for the last and sometimes refusing both, but the dog gobbled up his dinner voraciously, licking his plate and then asked for more but with a fine grateful countenance which marked the indulgence shewn to him.

Applications were made to me to sell the dogs. Juno I determined never to part with, although I was offered a Spanish Horse valued at £25 and £15 to boot by Sir Wm Beattie* Lord Nelson's surgeon on board the Victory. During the winter I was invited to spend four days at Horswill near Kingsbridge by Mr Peter Ilbert, who was well known for his wit, humour and hospitality as the Paymaster of the North Devon Militia. He had fractured his high thigh some years before and had one short leg, as English surgeons in those days wanted the skill of the French in setting straight fractured bones, and therefore many patients were turned out of the London Hospitals after their fractures had been badly set in a way which induced Sir Astley Cooper* to say 'here is another of our ram's horns'. Mr Ilbert's fondness for shooting and inability to walk well induced him to invite me to see what sort of dogs mine were. I spent four days with him, two in shooting two in hunting, frost and snow were on the ground. Whilst walking across a meadow a snipe arose and dropped into a further corner of the field around which my setters were galloping. Mr Ilbert exclaimed: 'oh, I wish these dogs could be stopped, then I might have a chance at the snipe.' 'No' says I and both dogs stopped. 'Now Sir, don't hurry, go up quietly and take your shot.' I standing and the dogs looking at me, a snipe arose and Mr Ilbert fired both barrels missing the snipe; I fired, crippled the bird which flew over the hedge and dropped into an orchard. I said: 'Sir how could you miss that bird which I have wounded?' He replied: 'if your dogs can find that bird I shall pronounce them very good.' Getting over the hedge alone and passing up the orchard the dog stopped suddenly pointing around an apple tree where the dead snipe lay. When he saw the dog with the snipe in his mouth he began to say 'put down, let me have it,' but I remarked: 'don't say so Sir, for neither you or any one here can take that bird from the dog.' 'But he is biting and crushing the bird, do take it away from him.' 'He will not hurt the bird' said I. 'Otho here, down' the bird he delivered up to me. 'What say you to that Mr Ilbert?' I enquired. 'A sportsman all my life' he said 'I have had scores of dogs but never saw anything like this. I must buy this dog.' After a capital dinner and abundance of wine he tried to deal but could not. My price was unalterably fixed at 25 guineas. Mr. Ilbert offered me £15, a pointer which I would not accept in a gift, and several couple of wild ducks which I did not want. After four days pleasantly spent and hospitably treated at Horswill I returned to Plymouth and resumed my various avocations.

Mr Bird a Barrister had settled in Plymouth and heard of my dogs which he wished to see in the field; we accordingly took a walk over the snipe ground about Plymouth. He was much pleased with the dogs and disposed to purchase one of them. He invited me to dinner and said: 'your price for the dog is I believe 25 guineas.' I answered 'yes,' thereupon he placed before me that sum viz: £26.5. He kept the dog so long as he continued a sportsman and then sold him for £15 to Mr Irvin Clarke of Efford Manor.

About this time I gave two lectures on Natural History and one on Comparative Anatomy at the Plymouth Atheneum, and when going through the doorway followed by Juno the Porter tried to exclude her, but I said: 'without the dog you get no lecture.' So she was admitted pro tem an honorary member and much caressed by the members present. Her symetary of form, beautiful condition, gentle manners, docility and gracefulness attracted universal attention. When I was speaking of quadrupeds she looked up occasionally without approaching the desk on which I was speaking.

I could just keep my head above water and pay my way in this doleful dismal deserted town of Plymouth, and therefore I determined to visit the Continent in the following year. I had not learnt French and was therefore obliged to put myself under the tuition of Abbe Grizel to purchase a French Grammar and Dictionary and so to learn the French language, but though I had learnt to read and write a little French I found that I could not speak it, and that further time and practise would be required to make myself intelligible. However, I made what progress I could in reading and writing French. Thus ran on the year 1816.

1817

February. I started on horseback for a tour through Cornwall through Tavistock and by Launceston where I dined with Captain Braddon SDM by appointment and met his friends Par, Hockin, Rowe, Spettigue and another and played a rubber passing the evening very comfortably. On Tuesday the next day I started for Bodmin and encountered some of the fiercest winds that blow over the Moors at this season from WNW. I reached Bodmin in time for an early dinner; whilst that was preparing and the horse feeding, I strolled towards the Gaol and enquired about the prisoners. I had forgotten at the time that my old school fellow and student at Exeter, Donald, was confined there for the supposed poisoning of his mother-in-law Mrs Downing of Falmouth. I desired to see him whom I found cheerful and in good spirits with his nice-looking wife, both as comfortable as could be expected under the grave charge hanging over Donald's head. He begged me to attend his trial at the Assizes and said that his Exeter friends were coming down for the purpose of giving him a good character. I believe I promised also to attend. After dinner I rode on to Truro and slept that night, then next day, Wednesday, I reached Penzance and saw what I could in that place, the museum, Dr Paris,[29] and other things of note. On Thursday I returned from Penzance to Truro, on Friday I passed through Lostwithiel and halted at Liskeard and on Saturday reached Plymouth. At Scorrier I was much gratified with Mr William's collection of minerals, and was sorry that my time would not admit of my descending the shaft of any mines. This hasty and superficial view of Cornwall enabled me to form some general ideas of the immense masses of subterraneous wealth which were brought to the surface annually by the armies of work-people under ground.

In March I attended the Bodmin Assizes according to promise, and slept over-night at Mr Brendon's between Tavistock and Launceston. He lived not far from Dawe, about whom he offered me every assistance. Early on the morning of trial Mr Brendon and I rode to Launceston where the stables were so crammed with horses that we could only find standing room and a little hay for our horses. I quickly joined the Medical Staff from Exeter at the Inn where I found Dr Miller, Mr T Luscombe, Mr J Tucker, Dr Cookworthy of Plymouth and others. I was about to enroll my own name when some parts of the evidence came out and determined me to withdraw. I appeared however in court with Donald's friends.

The trial lasted all day. Dr Edwards, a Physician and Chemist of Falmouth, appeared for the prosecution. He had analysed the contents of the stomach and discovered arsenic therein but he had not reproduced the metal according to some new experiments possibly unknown to him or thought unnecessary. Counter-evidence was set up on the other side by the medical friends of Donald. They attempted to prove that onions of which she had partaken during the day would produce similar

[29] Dr John Ayrton Paris (1785–1856) was one of the founders of The Royal Geological Society of Cornwall in Penzance in 1814. He was the Society's first secretary.

results in appearance to arsenic with the same tests. Counsellor Pell for the prisoner made what use he could of this evidence and dealt forcibly on the impossibility of poison put into a cup of coffee which had been handed round with other cups at a party of whom Mrs Downing was one. Donald had not appeared to meddle with the cup nor to be near his mother-in-law when she drank the contents which soon produced sickness and vomiting followed by death. Counsellor Giffard who afterwards became Lord Chancellor acted for the prosecution and the Judge's name was Abbott. The trial lasted until the evening when the judge summed up the evidence in such strong terms against the prisoner as to leave no doubt in the minds of the court of his guilt. Tucker had stood by the side of Donald during the greater part of the day and after hearing the judge's summing up gave up his post and begged me to take it saying: 'it is all over, I must go and prepare his wife for the worst.' I took up his post and saw the judge place his black cap on the desk and witnessed Donald trembling before the jury pronounced their verdict. On the foreman rising the Clerk of the Assaigns asked: 'Gentlemen of the Jury, what say you. Is the prisoner at the bar guilty or not guilty?' The foreman answered: 'Not guilty.' The question was repeated and the same answer returned. The prisoner was then acquitted. I never saw a greater change from despair to happiness than that exhibited by Donald whom I accompanied back to his cell where his gyves[30] were struck off his legs and then walked with him to his wife's lodgings. The poor woman was lying on a couch almost insensible or inaccessible to the belief that her husband was acquitted. She had been bled and her arm was tied up to prevent evil consequences; there I left the parties with others in the room to attend to them.

I had eaten nothing for the day and was therefore glad of some supper of which Mr Brendon and I were partaking when the foreman of the jury, well known to him, entered the room and we asked him how he could acquit the prisoner against such strong evidence and received for answer that the jury had no doubt Mrs Downing had been poisoned by Donald but as no-one saw him meddle with the coffee cup or put the poison into it they acquitted him. Some time afterwards I heard that Donald had called the following morning upon his counsellor, Sergeant Pell, and thanked him for his able and successful defence. The Counsel received him coldly and said: 'Thank your God, Sir, and not me, to your gracious God and a merciful jury you owe the salvation of your life.' Soon after midnight I left Mr Brendon and rode to Plymouth, a distance of 26 miles, having an appointment at Totnes at 11 o'clock on the same forenoon. I reached Plymouth between 3 and 4 o'clock in the morning, gave my horse some water and corn of which he stood in much need after a day's starvation at Launceston. I lay down two or three hours and then started the same horse for Totnes in time for the meeting held there to pass recruits for the militia. I there dined and gave the horse 3 or 4 hours rest and returned to Plymouth the same day, having ridden the same horse about 75 miles. Thus I had toiled two days for two guineas.

My time in Plymouth was now fully occupied in stuffing birds, putting up anatomical preparations and visiting unprofitable patients. I had now determined to visit the Continent this year, and arranged a plan to accompany Mr & Mrs Proctor, two infirm patients of my fathers. We agreed to start during the first week in May from London to Dover. On the first of May I accordingly left Plymouth on

---

[30] Shackles.

horseback, taking with me a knife given by Miss Welsford then confined to bed with a nose complaint. On my road to Ivybridge where I slept that night my horse fell lame having a stone in his fore foot; in getting it out I broke off a part of the picker of the knife, this circumstance I mention to show a remarkable circumstance that after 30 years I had occasion to use the same picker within a gunshot of the same place and for the same purpose for another horse I was then driving. This said knife I still possess in good condition as one of the most useful articles I ever saved, never having been without it in my pocket for a day during the last 55 years during my travels over France, Italy, Switzerland, Scotland, Ireland and nearly all parts of England and having performed some surgical operations with it. This history of the knife I relate to shew that I have always been a Conservative.

On the 2nd May 1817 I rode to Morley, passed recruits for the Militia there, and then accompanied our Major Seale, afterwards Sir John H Seale* Baronet to Mount Boon, Dartmouth, where I slept that night, started next day for Woodbury through Totnes and reached Woodbury on the same day having obtained leave of absence for four months from Col. Lord Rolle*.

[An inserted piece of paper records the following]:

1817 May 4th. On my way from Woodbury to London through Bath my father desired me to call on his Uncle Barnard[31] and enquire for him & Mrs Butter. I was graciously received by them and informed that some years before they had desired Mr Tucker of Lyme to invite me there from Ottery Barracks but that I had not heeded their invitation. On hearing my intentions to visit Paris and possibly Rome Mrs Butter requested me to write her a letter from one or both of these capitals and to revisit them on my return to England – I promised to do so. On the following Sept I repeated my visit at Bath and found that my letters from both capitals had been received with satisfaction. Enquiries were then made as to my future movements; I replied that I must now return to headquarters at Plymouth having been indulged by Col. Lord Rolle* with 5 months leave of attendance, and that if I could get another month's leave I hoped to visit Edinburgh before I settled down permanently in practice, so we parted and hence a correspondence ensued. On the following Nov on my way through Bath for Edinburgh I repeated my visit by invitation and found another gracious reception, also on my return from Edinburgh about the end of November.

[end of insertion]

I met Mr & Mrs Proctor in London where they had bought a light travelling carriage and fitted it up with every conceivable article for a long journey or for a barren country producing neither food nor raiment for the want of man. They proceeded to Dover with their female servant with this carriage and agreed to await my arrival there in a day or two. I called at the Bank of Herries, Farquhar & Co[32] and deposited with them £100, the amount of my savings at Plymouth and the first £100 I could call my own. I called on Mr Abernethy* and several friends and left my

[31] Butter refers to him throughout the Memoir as Barnard, but most other records, including the signature on his will, clearly indicate Bernard.
[32] Established in 1770 as London Exchange Banking Co. by Robert Herries.

address at the Grecian Coffee House where Dr Johnson was said to have spent much of his time. In the evening I was surprised by a visit from Mr Abernethy who walked into the Coffee Room, looked round, saw me and sat down to the same table where we partook of a lobster salad, some porter and drank two glasses of punch each, which we did not exceed. 'Well,' he said, 'you are going to France, you have written to me for letters of introduction, but I have not brought you any as they are unnecessary. How are you going?' he enquired. I replied: 'with an old invalid gentleman and his wife.' 'What are you going to get from your journey?' I answered: 'nothing beyond the payment of my travelling expenses and diet.' 'Oh' he said 'you ought to have had some fees.' We passed a few hours together most pleasantly. Mr. Lawrence had previously favoured me with some letters of introduction to Blainville etc., and Dr. Leach,* with whom I had previously dined at the British Museum where he was Zoologist, also gave me letters to Cuvier,* Count Lacépède,* Blainville, and others. The bankers letters of credit which I took from Herries & Co sufficed for Paris and other parts of the continent.

Having thus accomplished the object of my visit to London I proceeded by the Dover Mail for that place. On the following morning I found the Proctors at the Ship Inn and agreed for our passage across the Channel from Dover to Calais, where we slept that night. Our passage occupied between two and three hours, the wind being westerly drove our vessel forward with great speed from mid-channel. The next day we ordered post horses at Calais to take the carriage onward to Abbeville on route to Paris. We halted a night there and had some fried eels which are kept in large casks for use. Mrs Proctor was the speaker and banker for our party and well she performed her task. Having paid the inn keeper liberally and spoken pleasantly to them the Maitre de Hotel advanced gracefully and saluted Mrs Proctor with the words 'permettez-moi ma chere Madame' – who was certainly no tempting beauty. Mr Proctor and I standing together witnessed this salutation, upon which he exclaimed 'D… that French fellow his impudence to kiss my wife. I will pay him off for that.' The bar maid, a pretty French girl possessing very pleasing manners stood near and so Mr Ambrose Proctor advanced towards her and repeated the words of the host: 'permettez-moi Madame,' upon which she frisked and lifted and turned about exclaiming 'je ne suis pas Madame, je suis Mademoiselle, a votre service Monsieur' so Ambrose had a smack at her cheek and so retorted 'now we are quits.'

We reached Paris safely and took our abode at the Hotel de Saxe, rue de Colombier, Faubourg St Germaine. We spent three weeks there most pleasantly in company with Mr and Mrs George Eastlake* who had induced me to meet them there. His visit to Paris was professional on behalf of several Plymouth persons who had invested monies in the French Funds, from which they desired to recover the principal if not the dividends. The Eastlakes were of great service to me in speaking French and interpreting on various occasions. Mr E accompanied me to the residence of Baron Larry,* Chief Surgeon of the French Army, to whom I presented a written introduction from Monsieur Blainville, and from whom I received the following laconic order, to visit the Military Hospital over which he was Chirurgeon en Chef at 6 o'clock in the morning. Monsieur Blainville also introduced me as a visitor to the National Institute of France where I saw many of the learned and most distinguished men of Paris.

Whilst at the Jardin des Plantes one day, where I had visited Cuvier* and his brother Frederic, I heard an eloquent lecture delivered on fishes by Count Lecépède* who had resided for a time on the sea-coast to get information on Ichthyology.[33] I was much impressed with the order and arrangements of the Museum on comparative anatomy and natural history. On another morning at 6 o'clock I went to the Hotel Dieu and there saw the celebrated Surgeon Professor Dupuytren* excise an enlarged tonsil from the throat of a young girl. I had never before seen this operation which was performed so adroitly and so neatly as to excite the applause of a large body of students assembled. Dupuytren had also invented an instrument for closing an artificial anus which sometimes occurs in the groin after strangulated hernia[+] and mortification[+] of the portion of the gut. I likewise visited the hospital for cutaneous[+] diseases ably conducted by Monsieur Alibert.

As time drew on and the temperature increased we were warned to leave Paris and move southward to Lyons. I suggested to Mr Proctor the propriety of examining his carriage well and ascertaining if possible the rattling noise we had often heard on the road toward Paris. When he opened his large trunk fastened to the back of the carriage surprised was he to find all things in disorder. Everything had been nicely packed in London, but on the eve of starting a friend thought that a whetstone might be necessary to sharpen his knife should he be induced to go over the Alps. This whetstone he incautiously put in the travelling chest loosely over the other things. The rattling of the carriage occasioned frequent motion of this whetstone which by degrees had broken glass bottles, battered in tin cannisters, and so mixed the contents of papers and parcels that the whole of the contents were mixed up together: Tea, Sugar, Medicines, Cordials, Condiments, Spices and a variety of other articles, enough for a month's use had we been going over Alpine or the deserts of Arabia where these necessary articles could not be procured for days or weeks together. The alternative was this travelling trunk and all its heterogeneous articles were left behind in Paris. I also found it necessary to leave my leather trunk at the Hotel until my return, and to purchase a petit sac for 7 francs into which I put my toilet of two shirts stockings and a surtout[34] coat; with these few articles I contented myself in addition to the clothes on my back. Thus lightened of our burden, we started with post-horses for Lyons. Four persons inside were too many so I took to the dickey and left Mr and Mrs Proctor and servant inside. This servant was not merely useless but actually an incumbrance. She knew nothing, neither could she learn French or repeat such words as Mr P told her. The sun shone most fervently through the greater part of this journey and so scorched the skin of my face as to occasion bladders and pealing of the cuticle.

On arriving at Lyons we were all suffering from the heat of the journey. Mr & Mrs P determined on giving up their proposed excursion into Italy and to retire to Geneva, there to pass some time. Minding my desire to see some parts of Italy they considerately said: 'We will release you as we are in tolerable health and likely to preserve it. We have just heard that a diligence[35] will start in a few days for Turin and pass over Mont Cenis. If you like to go without us, this opportunity is most favourable.' Whilst at Lyons I heard that an execution of 3 criminals or traitors would take place in the large square at such an hour. I saw the guillotine erected on a stage or platform raised 6 or 8 feet above the ground affording sufficient room for a cart to be placed under

---

[33] A branch of zoology: the natural history of fish.
[34] An overcoat.
[35] A public stagecoach.

a trap-door through which the heads of the culprits and their bodies were cast after the execution. The guillotine consists of 2 upright posts fastened by a cross beam on the top and fixed into a stage below and between these poles was a table on which the criminal would be fastened whilst the knife, suspended many feet above with a heavy weight attached to it, would fall on loosening the pulley to have kept it up. The knife in form was something like a hay knife sharp at the point and wide at the base, large enough to run in a groove of the pole. The sharpness of the edge and the weight attached to it caused it to descend quickly and cut off the head as we should slice a turnip. The head fell forward and the headless man bleeding fiercely rolled back over the table with the carotid arteries pumping blood and sprinkling it about like a gardening water-pot. One man thus disposed of, a second and the third prisoner was brought up in succession and decapitated in similar manner, having previously witnessed the first execution. This added to the horror of the previous feeling and quite unnerved the third man who was faint and overwhelmed with horror to such a degree as to appear half dead when forced on the table by the attendant. Each man had been brought to the place of execution in a separate cart attended by a catholic priest whose manner seemed to engage the culprit in earnest prayer.

I visited several hospitals in Lyons and found nothing worthy of record.

Having secured my place in the Dilligence and taken an affectionate leave of Mr & Mrs Proctor, who charged me to write to them post restante Geneva should I want money or wish to communicate with them, I started for Turin, passed over the rapid Rhone and Mont Cenis and reached Turin without accident. Turin is a very fine city built in crosses and squares and the hospitals capacious and cleanly. We arrived at Milan in safety and together inspected the magnificent church and tower there, more worthy than any we had before seen. The hospitals also at Milan are magnificent, spacious, airy, clean and well kept in every way conducive to health. The wards are very large and well arranged with beds placed in double rows through the middle, head to head, as well as singly by the side walls. Milan is a fine city replete with everything fertile and conducive to the health of mankind. Here I took leave of Mr Sams with his Irish party, they were bound for Rome and I for Pavia, 18 miles off, to visit Professor Scarpa* whose writing and drawings had surpassed all others and rendered his name famous not merely as an oculist but as a scientific surgeon throughout all Europe.

After breakfasting on the finest caffee au lait and the best bread I had eaten on the continent I engaged a Vetturino[36] to convey me from Milan to Pavia. I found he wanted a party of four to complete the number for payment of the conveyance. I was going in front with the driver when an elderly gentleman with three smart young ladies offered to give up his seat for mine, which I accepted after a little parley. Whilst seated with these three lovely young girls in the carriage I commenced conversation, first in bad French at which they shook their heads, then in English, but Italian was the only language they could speak of which I knew not one word scarcely. Never had I found myself in such a puzzle before; fortunately I had an English and Italian dictionary in my pocket. This I took out and received my first lesson in the Italian language from these three young ladies who were as eager to teach as I was to learn. They wore neither hats nor bonnets but each had a veil and their hair beautifully cleaned and perfumed was gathered up into a ball at the back

---

[36] A driver of a vettura – a four-wheeled carriage.

through which a large pin was fixed with a knot at either end fastened to a metal resembling gold in colour.

On arriving at Pavia, after dinner I penned a note in French to Professor Scarpa.* Scarpa's name was so celebrated in England that I determined to visit him if possible. I found him a tall elegant rather thin man, with a fine intellectual countenance, residing in a Palace near the hospital; he could speak sufficiently well for me to understand him. I said I had a great wish to see him and buy his books, at which he laughed heartily and replied: 'some of my books are very large, how can you possibly take them?' I said: 'in a packing case.' He continued: 'I do not usually sell my own books, which are disposed of by the booksellers to whom I could refer you,' but I replied I wished to be able to say I bought them of himself. He hesitated and said: 'where are you going from here?' I answered: 'to Florence and possibly to Rome.' 'What will you do with the packing case?' I said: 'take it with me and forward it by water.' Scarpa again paused and properly remarked: 'you will find that plan troublesome and expensive. Let me send them direct for you.' I relied: 'no I will take them. When I left England I determined if possible to see you and purchase your books.' He smiled gracefully but seemingly with a doubt whether or not he ought to assent. He continued: 'I have given up my professorship and declined practice on account of my age', which I supposed to be something under 70, but he continued: 'I will introduce you to my successor who will show you the Museum, Hospital etc.' I paid Scarpa for his works and got them secured and placed into a packing case. Further he said: 'if you are on a Tour I recommend you to see my native place Venice, most worthy of your notice and inspection as differing from all other cities and towns in Italy.'

At Pavia the hospital is small and the museum select. After two or three days detention there I started for Genoa and passed near the plains of Marengo where Bonaparte's great battle was fought. At Genoa I enquired for the Bank of Gibbs & Co at which I presented one of Herries and Farquhar's drafts for 20 gold Napoleons and spoke a few words in French at which the attendant said: 'you may speak English if you please Sir, I am also an Englishman from Topsham in Devonshire, from which county I presume you also come.' This remark startled me as my dialect, I thought, was not provincial. He then asked: 'are you related to Mr Butter of Woodbury, seeing your name.' I said: 'yes he is my father.' 'Gibbs is my name, my Uncle Gibbs is the head of this Bank. I must introduce you to him as he is also a Devonshire man and brother of Sir Verney Gibbs.' We adjourned into a private room where I found a fine well-dressed old gentleman who joined his nephew in offering me advice and assistance during my stay, saying: 'will you dine with me on Sunday at such an hour? We will take a drive in my carriage and visit such places as may be worthy of your notice.' I was too glad to accept such an invitation and surprised at my good fortune in forming such acquaintances. Being asked as to my future movements I said I was bent upon Florence, and that after reading Moore's account of Italy at Plymouth, where I resided, and his florid description of the anatomical cabinets there, I startled a friend present by saying suddenly: 'there I will go and see them.' Messrs. Gibbs advised me to engage a berth on board a polacca[37] bound from Genoa to Leghorn preferring a sea voyage to the rugged and hilly roads over the Carrara Marble Mountains. A polacca was engaged

[37] A three-masted sailing vessel.

for me but I had not previously inspected it before embarkation. I was the only passenger on board. I disliked the appearance both of the vessel and the sailors. It was thought with a fair wind my voyage over the south Mediterranean would not be long. We made short headway at first and were becalmed all night. No sleep however could I obtain, having kept in my clothes from a dislike to the dirty berth allotted to me. The sailors stunk so badly of garlic and onions as to prevent a near approach to them and when I reclined I was beset with a number of unwelcome visitors, hopping and dancing and sucking my blood whenever they had a chance of supplying their wants. I need not describe these animals in entomological terms as they are well-known under the English name of fleas, lice, bugs and mosquitoes. My alternative lay between these troublesome gentry and the strong-flavoured sailors. After two days and one night I was eager to be put on shore at the nearest port and to abandon my plan of reaching Leghorn.

When we got off the port of Lerici within the gulf of Spezzia, a boat fortunately hove in sight and luckily came to our signal. I was too happy to be released from my prison and unwelcome society and so I took to the boat which landed me safely. My first question almost was to enquire for a warm bath, which fortunately I obtained and derived much relief from the itching and heat of my skin. A clean shirt added much to my comfort whilst the other, well specked by my unwelcome companions, was sent to the wash. At the Inn I got comfortable meals and lodgings and agreed with the mail-carrier for a seat in his trap next day for Pisa. The drive was beautiful through woods of olive trees and sweet-smelling flowers.

At Pisa I obtained comfortable lodgings and found time to inspect the inclined Tower, the beautiful marble baths and other objects of interest to the traveller. Florence however was the city which I was most intent on reaching and therefore lost no time in going there from Pisa instead of Leghorn. I took up my residence at the Albergo de York kept by Mr & Mrs Sambolina. Happily for me I soon ascertained that Madame Sambolina was an English woman, a native of Barnstaple where her husband first saw her when on an official visit as Messenger sent down officially by Mr Pitts' Government. He spoke English, Italian and French fluently. My apartments there were splendid and fit for My Lord Anglis, as they call them. My object was now obtained and eagerly followed up by an early and close inspection of the Florentine galleries of pictures and by the 13 cabinets of wax-works exhibiting all the natural structures of the human body modelled in wax. These preparations surpassed anything that I conceived of their beauty, accuracy and usefulness to the anatomist and surgeon. Anatomy is thus made easy to students without the nasty and unhealthy practise of dissecting dead bodies. Zumbo[38] was the first artist who succeeded in modelling the effects of the plague in Italy; his models strikingly illustrate the horrors and destruction of the human body afflicted with this direful scourge. I had once before seen in England specimens of anatomical preparations in wax, and that was at Sir Charles Bell's* Museum in London. If I had never dissected a human body I might have learnt human anatomy here and not destroyed my health and risked my life as I had done in 1810 at the foul dissecting room at St Bartholomew's Hospital. Operations in surgery at Florence are performed by young

[38] Gaetano Giulio Zumbo (1656–1701) was renowned primarily as a creator of scientific wax models.

men and students; I understood from a medical practitioner the hospitals there are well conducted by eminent surgeons.

A splendid edition of S.... on the absorbents I was tempted to purchase and add to Scarpa's* plates and books which I had brought so far with me. John Bell[39] the celebrated Professor of Surgery at Edinburgh I found at Florence with Mrs Bell and Miss Maghee their travelling companion. I was vain enough to ask him to dine with me at the Albergo de Yorke where we had a nice Italian dinner and some delicious Florentine wine which we both enjoyed. He told me that the young King of Rome, Bonaparte's son, had arrived in Florence and lodged on the banks of the Arno for the purpose of having his fangs sharpened with his teeth polished, by which he was thereafter to bite the world! The dentist who performed this work was very celebrated throughout all the continent.

Florence, now the capital of Italy, I found to be a lovely place, comfortable as a city and charming in its locality surrounded by a luxuriant country with vineyards, fruit and olive trees. I could have prolonged my stay there comfortably for months. My desire however to visit Rome was now entertained and a conveyance sought. The owner of a Vettura applied and said he should be ready to start in a few days when his number was made up. A young American physician, also called John Bell, arrived in Florence and enquired his best way to Rome. We agreed to go in the same carriage with others who made the number. For so many dollars, each person was to be conveyed to Rome and dined and lodged by night without extra charges.

Arrived at Rome, Bell and myself visited the public buildings and hospitals of which a repetition here after so many publications may be unnecessary. The weather now was very hot so that the Romans said that none but English-men and dogs ventured out at noon day. In passing through one of the principal streets I observed on the opposite side a gentleman walking whom I quickly recognised by his dress and manner as an Englishman whom I had often seen in Plymouth. He also knew me and although we had never spoken, we hastily crossed to shake hands with each other. After a short parley we were about to separate when I said I was going to Eastlake's studio where he said he was also going and so together we walked and found Eastlake* at his work. Thus did we three Plymouthians meet: Captain Fanshawe* of the Navy, Charles Eastlake and myself. Captain Fanshawe was a great name in Plymouth and the Navy. Admiral Fanshawe, the father, had been Commissioner at Plymouth Dockyard and had great interest in raising my companion to the rank also of Admiral and ultimately to that lucrative and eminent position of Port Admiral of Plymouth with a splendid income of £4,000 a year which he had scarcely time to enjoy before he died.

At Rome we all three aspired to fame and to fortune, two of the three reached the pinnacle of their ambition, the third was left behind. I was doing well in my profession but had nothing great to aspire to, little did I ever think of the privation in store for me. I had saved and restored the sight of hundreds and thousands of my poor afflicted patients but I never dreamt myself of becoming blind. The Almighty however decreed otherwise; in my 64th year I was deprived of sight in both eyes by a translation of rheumatic gout from the extremities to the eyes. I could not but draw a comparison of my humble lot with that of my distinguished travellers. One placed at the head of the Royal Academy and the other of the Royal Naval Port of Plymouth.

---

[39] Brother of Charles Bell (see preceding paragraph).

These eminent and highly favoured individuals are now gone before me and here am I left to tell the tale. How mysterious are the ways of Providence.

Whilst in Rome I was much impressed with an account of the dreadful fever which occasionally broke out there, attributable to the Malaria wafted over the Pontine Marshes into the city. This fever was intermittent and resembled Ague and was curable by the same means, by bark and arsenic, as quinine was not known in 1817. In passing over these Marshes on our route from Rome to Naples with my companions Bell and Baldwin, we were advised to halt on approaching these marshes and take some warm coffee, eau de vie or any other cordial with a view of protecting our health against the malaria. We saw numerous herds of cattle, pigs and horses grazing in our route. The malaria arising from these marshes is supposed to be owing to stagnant water and the rudiments of decayed animal and vegetable substances therein contained and kept back by lands under the level of the seas. Judicious draining however may remove this evil.

All swamps in all countries are calculated to produce in the human race the same sort of intermittent fever. In many parts of England wet lands adjoining rivers, lakes and even the sea, especially shrouded by trees, were formerly notorious for the production of ague and typhoid fever. These places are now known to be healthy and free from epidemic disorders owing to judicious draining and other sanitary improvements. The rot in sheep, whose lungs become ulcerated and whose livers were infested with fluke worms and other diseases produced by their depasturing on such unhealthy soils, can now graze on them without the risk of incurring such destructive maladies. The sirocco wind is the agent which brings the poisonous maleria into the streets of Rome. In Africa and India and America such fevers arise under similar circumstances and produce the most fatal consequences, especially amongst Europeans and travellers in these Countries. Certain names such as the jungle fever, the Bulam fever, the African fever, the bilious, intermittent, remittant, yellow, and typhus are given according to the places and the fatality with which they occur. Fever is fever in every form and place, wheresoever found; some are called contagious, putrid, petecrial [petechial[+]], scarlet, rheumatic, and designated by other names. No fever begins with typhus but all fevers terminating fatally may be called typhus or typhoid. Fever means heat, un-natural excessive heat generally following shivering or a cold stage, after which comes the re-action of heat. Fever in English is called in Latin Febris, in French fievre in Italian febio, in Spanish and in Portugese [blank].

The Walcheren fever[+] took its name from its destruction of one half of the British Army sent out under Lord Chatham to Flanders in 1809 and the banks of the Scheldt river in order to take Antwerp from the French, in which project they were defeated and driven out of the low countries back to England at a loss of one half of the Army and the expenditure of millions of money. Fever & dysentory broke out amongst the defeated troops of Sir John More after his retreat from Corunna where he lost his life. Fevers therefore are often more destructive than the sword. The rinderpest as it is now called, 1866, begins also as fever: there is a shivering fit followed by heat, the secretions dry up and become altered in quality, the natural dew and moisture about the muzzle & nostrils of the Ox are first checked and then changed into a catarrhal efflux of a whitish purulent[+] discharge. The eyes look glassy & watery, the brain no doubt is affected, the mouth and tongue and probably the throat are sprinkled with Aphtha or small ulcerations which probably tend downwards into the stomach and bowels, thus showing that some maleria or poisonous air has entered the body through these passages and thus excited fever with its excessive heat. By some French authors this malady is called contagious typhus; the word contagion cannot be always sustained or well applied, because it implies contact or inoculation through the agency of some poison such as that of small pox, cow pox and the like – whatsoever the poison be, or from whatever source derived, the early symptoms shew that it has entered and passed into the body through the nostrils & mouth; how then can this be contagious? When the disease first breaks out in a locality miles distant from an infected district and attacks the first cow a natural question arises – how came it to attack No 1 and not the rest of the herd? After the attack on No 1 we can easily understand the processes of contagion or infection extended to the rest of the herd, but herein our reasoning may be wrong because we cannot reason or state the objection why the first cause which attacked No 1 should not also affect the others in succession without contagion passed from No 1 to No 2 and to the others in succession. The same maleria which engenders in man fevers of all kinds may also produce this kind of fever called Rinderpest, a term rather objectionable because the Cow pox may be called with equal propriety Rinderpest. Whilst its pathology is uncertain our treatment will be unsuccessful. How it came into England first we scarcely know but conjecture that it was imported from the Steppes of Russia. To this day we are ignorant how the Cholera came into England, or what caused to its first appearance in Plymouth; between the first and second instances of Cholera which occurred here there was a distance of nearly one mile, and the third case had no communication with the former two, although the Cholera was more fatal in Plymouth in 1832, and 1849 more fatal than in any other place in the kingdom according to the population, excepting [blank] in Staffordshire. There was scarcely an instance of a medical man being attacked, and not one who died of Cholera in Plymouth. What are we to say of infection and contagion after this?

Influenza or epidemic catarrh followed the Cholera in the ensuing year and proved more fatal than the latter disease. Can we ascribe to infection or contagion the origin, continuation and disappearance of Influenza? I know not. These two words contagion and infection are so alarming to the public, so accredited by medical men and so countenanced by the government of this country as to lead to heavy restrictions and impositions on the unfortunate possessors of diseased Cattle. The prayers too offered up in our religious ceremonies for our protection and relief against infectious diseases shew the alarm and dread in which it is held by the community. I have heard of only one instance of a medical man supposed to be affected with the rinderpest, from desection of a dead animal, in which he scratched the back of his hand, where a bladder formed, and ran[?] the usual course of vaccination desicating about the eighth day. He presented himself before a medical society who decided that the cattle plague was analigous to small pox and might be prevented from spreading by vaccination. Emenence [immense] demand therefore was created for vaccine limph in a greater degree than could be supplied by the vaccine Institution in London. Lord Claringdon [Clarendon], as foreign secretary, was implored to import vaccine from France, but this application might have been unnecessary if medical practioners had vaccinated certain cows in our different dairies from which they might have obtained vaccine limph enough in ten days to innoculate all the people of Europe. Vaccination therefore was no antidote against the cattle plague. Serious reflection might have prevented this error. If the cow be capable of furnishing an antidote against the poison of small pox in human beings why should not the cow protect himself against the infection of small pox? Could it be supposed that the cow could furnish an antidote to protect human beings from small pox, and yet not be able to protect herself? Of medical practioners we may say as a master of Fox hunting may remark 'We have made a bad cast and we must try back again. What are there to do' and how are we then to treat this disease? The Government have legislated for us and said the pole axe is the remidy. Kill away all diseased animals, & others suspected of disease. Stamp it out of the country wheresoever it appears. This order of councel upsets all further trials of a remidy. This is the only safe or depending plan as a profilactic against the further progress, and this is founded on the credence of the highest veterinary authorities. Our Veternary College therefore ought to have for its motto: Rinderpest opprobrium medicina Veterinar…[40]

Having passed over the Pontine Marshes in safety we halted for the night at Terracine which is the boundary between the pontifical and neapolitan states. Bell and I being pretty fresh ascended through brushwood a hill which over-looks these marshes and the beautiful coasts along the Mediterranean.

Passports procured we started early on our forward journey on the 21st July 1817 and observed numerous specimens of the cacti, myrtles, heath and other ornamental plants seen only in hot and green houses at home, but here in their natural element. We reached Naples on the 23rd July 1817.

As my journal contains particulars of this journey I shall not recapitulate them here. Two or three circumstances however may be mentioned. One was the ascent of Vesuvius then bursting forth in flames and explosions greater than any that had been witnessed since the year 1794. From the summit of Vesuvius after a dark night and driving fog we beheld the sun rising out of the deep waters of the Mediterranean as it were and shining beautifully over Naples Bay where two Ships of War at anchor lay, one the Albion commanded by Admiral Penrose and the other, the Washington, an American man of war. The Shannon and Chesapeake Bay were thought of. I said to my American companion: 'Dr Bell, here you and I are representatives of two nations, and there lay at anchor those two vast engines of war, peaceful and quiet awaiting only some latent opportunity, some call of patriotism or necessity to put forth all their beauty and their bravery and awaken their dormant thunder.' We afterwards visited these two ships and received such attention and hospitality as hearty sailors know so well how to confer.

One thing on board the American ship struck me forcibly at the time. It was a swivel gun with 7 barrels which rotated on their own axis and could be fired separately at 7 distinct times. I little thought then that this curious gun would be piloted some 20 or 30 years afterwards and brought before the public in the name of a revolver.

From the top of Vesuvius we could almost see the Islands of Ischia and Nisida which are no doubt of volcanic origin. The Grotto del Cane is likewise a curious place in which carbonic acid gas is generated in abundance. Amidst all the gases to which man is exposed more or less pernicious to human life the carbonic acid and sulphurous gases are perhaps the most detrimental. Dr Beddoes* of Bristol formerly attempted to cure consumptive cases by confining them to closed rooms in which

[40] The Latin is hard to read and the word endings unclear. Butter might perhaps have intended 'Rinderpest opprobrium medicinae veterinariae', 'Rinderpest, the disgrace of veterinary medicine.'

they could breathe artificial gases and atmospheric air divested [of] some portions of oxygen. Sir Humphrey Davy however succeeded better than any chemist in his day in elucidating the operations and different properties of certain gases inhaled by man and animals. Chloroform is a new gas obtained from ether and alcohol; when inhaled effectively chloroform gas overpowers the brain and nervous system so effectually as to render the body insensible to pain. Previous to operations on living bodies chloroform is administered generally to patients who are the subjects of painful operations which can be performed under its influence without the knowledge of the patient. Fatal effects occasionally occur from the inhalation of chloroform. The patient thus deprived of consciousness swoons and sinks and expires especially when labouring under the disease of heart. The heart's action it was once supposed depended on the stimulus of the blood which it contained and circulated, but later the experiments of Brodie* and Legadol shew that the celiac plexus[+] of nerves have much to do with the heart's actions. Divide the par vagum[+] or the pneumo-gastric[+] nerve and you convulse the expiratory circulating and digestive organs, thus shewing the way in which these functions are performed and death produced by chloroform. Happily these fatal results are few and unavoidable in certain trials made with the greatest caution and circumspection.

My journey homeward from Naples to Rome was commenced on the 3rd day of August 1817 and ended on the 6th August. From Rome I started on the 6th day of August and reached Florence on the 11th August, returning through the same places I had gone forward. At Florence I remained well catered and provided for at the Alberge de York by Mr and Mrs Sambelino. I soon quitted the gaudy apartments assigned to me for the more convenient and comfortable position of being considered one of the family by dining at two o'clock daily with them and taking a seat in their private carriage for the casino on fine evenings. I was here brought to a standstill for lack of money. My £100 had been entirely expended in travelling from Lyon to Rome and Naples and back to Florence, in buying books, wax preparations and other things.

I explained my position frankly to my host and hostess who made no difference in their attentions and hospitality. I told them that I had written a letter for a remitance of money to the Lady and Gentleman with whom I had travelled from England to Lyons, where I left them with a good understanding that they would proceed and halt at Geneva, where a letter would find them directed poste restante. To this address I had dispatched a letter but received no answer, and that I had written a second time and now awaited a remittance of money. They smiled and said they were not afraid to trust me.

My delay at Florence was profitably employed in visiting the hospitals, museums, cabinets and galleries of paintings, palaces, churches and public buildings, but the want of money threw a gloom over all my proceedings. Ample time having been allowed for my getting an answer with the remittance from Geneva, and none arriving, I became very uneasy at the thought of my longer detention of Florence where I must remain or borrow money to return homewards. Great was my relief one morning when the waiter came and said that an English gentleman had just arrived from Malta homewards bound for London and enquired if there was any English gentleman in the Hotel wishing to return to England and having no objection to join him in travelling. The waiter replied yes, there was a gentleman, an English doctor. An introduction thus effected led to mutual statements from each other. He said his name was Richards, travelling for the great Birmingham house of Richards & Co, of world wide fame for all sorts of hardware and iron works manufactured at Birmingham. He said that he was returning from Malta on business, had landed at Leghorn and came up to Florence with the view of passing through Italy and visiting Venice in particular. I replied that scheme would suit my wishes but one great obstacle stood in my way: 'my money' I said 'is all done. I have waited here in vain for remittance.' 'Oh' said he 'that shall be no obstacle. I have plenty of money for us both. I can draw twenty Napolians here, twenty at Geneva and more at Paris if required. You shall be banker and go with me at once to the Bank.' So we went together and drew the money with which I was entrusted with this remark: 'You can speak perhaps French and Italian and know the ways of the country which I do not. I have already travelled into the four quarters of the globe but was never before in Italy or France.' My companion had a dog, Kalych by name: 'a white haired curly kind of poodle dog has been my travelling companion, you will have no objection to the dog I hope.' 'No' said I 'I have been too fond and famous to my own dogs to object to such a good tempered animal as yours.' We agreed on all points, being about the same age, disposition, requirements and desire in the pursuit of knowledge of men, manners and countries. I was now enabled to pay off all my debts at the Alberge de York and to thank Mr and Mrs Sambelino gratefully for all their kindness, hospitality and attention to me, a stranger.

On the 21ˢᵗ day of August 1817 at 3am Richards and I and the dog left Florence for Bologna, which we reached on the 22ⁿᵈ day of August having slept the night at Masculi[?]. Bologna is a very ancient fine old city affording the following places and objects for my consideration. The inclining tower displays the skill of the architect who designed and built it. One of the Abbies [Abbés] here is said to write and speak twenty-seven languages. The market place is good and abundantly supplied, in it I saw a great number of quails for sale in baskets and cages, also quantities of frogs legs beautifully white in clean water. Bologna sausages are famous delicacies prepared for immediate use of an epicure. The hospital is also most worthy of inspection, being exceedingly well conducted, clean and healthful; the resident physician most civil and obliging in explaining the successful practice of Professor Tomas Jinis's new theory of medicine. The Apothecary's shop was most neat.

Sept. 10ᵗʰ Richards and I were joined by Andrews and Rogers in hiring a carriage for seven and half Napolians for eight days, to take us to Paris with post horses hired at different stages, the distance being from Geneva to Paris about [336] miles. Started at 4 o'clock pm and appointed me purse-bearer, and we went two posts and were stopped for passports; as the director of police was gone hunting, waited until eleven o'clock for his signature then went to bed until 2 o'clock am, when we started on the eleventh and ascended a tremendous hill whilst the sun was rising, and bringing into view the most beautiful scenery on both sides of the road. The sun had just begun to appear over the snowy white mountains of the Alps, amongst which Mont Blanc stood pre-eminently high. Our route was continued onwards all night till we reached Dole the following morning at six o'clock.

12ᵗʰ Sept. pursued our course from Dole to Dijon a city celebrated for its champagne, Burgundy and other wines, of which we partook freely at prices fully equal to those in Paris. Dijon is a fine town and very considerable in the time of the vintage. Fine old cathedral, palace, halls on the promenade etc., old church completely stripped by the French Army, a triumphal arch, neat streets and many pretty women in them, the surrounding country bounded with vines trimmed low like hedges.

13th Sept. through Burgundy and Champagne all day but could not get over more than 18 posts in 24 hours. Halted at Sens a little and reached Ville Greniard to supper and good wine, where we also slept. Inn good.

14th Sept. Started at 6 o'clock and posted at a good rate through Gossard to Fontainbleau where we breakfasted near the forest, saw a covey of 5 partridges, longed for a pop at them. Met an English gentleman and a pretty demoiselle. Thence to Paris where we arrived at 5pm, having seen sportsmen in the adjoining fields. Our companions rather aristocratic. Richards and I arrived at the Hotel de Sax and to my great joy found 7 letters long wished for: those from Mr Proctor fully accounted for their not receiving or answering my letters as they travelled from Lyons to Geneva, Berne and other parts of Switzerland. From the 15th to the 19th we remained at the Hotel de Sax as Richards wished to see something of the city and its environs. Our travelling companions called and settled accounts amicably. I wrote sundry letters to Mrs Welsford, Miss Leach, Mrs Butter at Bath and lastly to my father requesting him to transmit £60 to my credit at the London Bank of Herries, Farquar & Co without delay, there to await my early return to London in order to reimburse my excellent friend Richards for his advances of money. Richards and I made good use of our time in Paris being much together but sometimes apart when he wished to visit public institutions often seen by myself, or when I visited hospitals or medical persons not interesting to himself.

With Mons. Brechet I was introduced and I believe elected a member of the Society of Emulation[41] in Paris. Mons. Blainville also introduced me to the Royal Institute of France, where I saw a very full attendance of the literary and scientific men of Paris, to some of whom I had the honor of introduction. I renewed my acquaintance also with Baron Larrie* at the Military Hospital, and whilst there a wounded chasseur[42] was brought in stabbed in the breast by the sword by a comrade with whom he had fought a duel. The poor fellow was paled faint and bloodless; being stripped, the Baron taking a clasp knife out of his pocket and thrusting his forefinger into the wound between the ribs of the right side, several pints of clotted blood were let out and the man's breathing much relieved, but he died from internal haemorrhage. In going through the wards I saw the usual number of Irons heated in the fire, one of which the Baron took to friz and fry a phagedenic+ ulcer of the leg to bring on sloughing+ to new action. Another poor soldier had a lumber abscess to be opened, for this work the Baron took a sharp pointed heated Iron and putting himself in a fencing attitude, with all things ready thrust the heated iron into the abscess and whilst the matter was escaping he continued a circular motion of the iron until the aperture was enlarged from the size of a sixpence to that of a crown piece, and so this poor fellow was left with dry cloths put over the wound to absorb the remaining quantities of matter. How different I thought was this practice to that of Mr Abernethy* whose plan is to open the lumber abscess, discharge a certain quantity and carefully close the wound to prevent the ingress of air which is supposed to lead to hectic fever of a most fatal kind.

41 Société Médicale d'Émulation de Paris.
42 A light cavalryman.

From 6 o'clock in the morning until midnight during these five days my time was fully occupied with study or pleasure. We dined at the Palais Royale, where I met Dr Bossi Granville* for the last time, visited the Cafe Desmille Colonne, the theatre and opera, which seemed inferior to La Scala at Milan and to the gaudy appearance of the Opera at Naples. Having secured our passports from the French and English Ministers and booked ourselves on the coach for Dieppe we spent our last night in Paris.

19th Sept. By the diligence we left Paris at six o'clock booked for Dieppe at 25 francs each paid. On arriving at Rouen the next morning with a full coach of passengers, we found others booked also from Rouen to Dieppe, and the proprietors wished to unseat us and place others on the coach. 'No' said I 'that won't do, possession is nine points of the law, we will not give up our places.' 'But' said the proprietor 'two English gentlemen are booked to go from hence and here is one of them.' We were both mutually bent on contesting the seats, our argument was that we were booked all the way from Paris to Dieppe and their argument that they were booked at Rouen. Both parties were waxing warm and inclined for a contest when I looked on my opponents's face and said: 'surely Hemdleby you know me.' Surprised he looked in my face and said: 'no I do not recollect you.' 'Have you forgotten our boyish days at Exeter School?' I enquired. Startled again he replied: 'I do not recollect your person or name.' 'Do you not remember John Butter?' Now suddenly the tone and temper of our meeting altered, instead of a fight we were ready to embrace each other. Room was made on the coach for all the English and so we journeyed safely into Dieppe, where we arrived at 3pm and after 2 hours preparation embarked in the packet, Lord Wellington, Captain Cole, bound to start for Brighton, which place we hoped to reach on the following morning. I had just time enough to put on my legs 8 pairs of silk stockings and round my waist some silks and satins which might have been deemed contraband goods. On board the packet were Sir Charles* and Lady Burrell and her two sisters, the Miss Wyndhams, daughters of Lord Egremont, a Scottish family and many others.

Becalmed all night, heavy shower about 10 o'clock, afterwards a fresh breeze sprung up followed by another calm on the next day, so that we did not reach Brighton till 10 o'clock the next night, having been on board 30 hours. My legs ached very much with the number of stockings on them and my body was very uncomfortable. In my hurry to get out of the boat I accidentally knocked down a man in the way. We took up our quarters at the Ship Inn where I was heartily glad to undress and relieve myself of so many supernumerary articles. We enjoyed an excellent supper consisting of true English fare, roast beef, porter and punch; Miss Robinson, her father, Hemdleby, Richards, Leith and a French colonel who was at the battle of Waterloo; many school stories related by Hemdleby and myself. A very pleasant evening, the only cause of regret that I felt was that it would be the last I should spend with my good friend Richards.

22nd Sept. Brighton. Rose at six, had a good bathing in the open sea, fine beach and water but no quays or harbours so that large vessels dare not approach near the shore and boats are required to take passengers to and from the ships. Got my things from the Custom House for 4s 6d; a small print of 2 quails was seized but afterwards given up. We had time to look over Brighton and the Pavilion which the Prince Regent and his companions occasionally visited.

18 coaches were said to leave London daily for Brighton and 18 return from Brighton. We booked ourselves by one of them and started at 3pm o'clock for London which we reached about 9 o'clock having dined at Reigate. Left Richards at the Elephant & Castle and promised to dine with his father the following day, whilst I went on to the Golden Cross, Charing Cross where the coach stopped and not far from the Cannon Coffee House where I intended to sleep that night. My luggage consisting of a leather trunk, petit sac and some minor articles were conveyed hither from the coach office. On entering the Cannon Coffee House I ascertained the loss of my surtout coat left on the seat of the coach. I desired the landlady at the bar to take care of a bottle of Marascino which I had brought all the way from Milan, and the porter to remove my luggage to a bedroom whilst I made all haste back to the coach office in search of my coat, but lo and behold how great my surprise to find the coach gone, the coach office locked and no official at hand from whom I could get any tidings. This was the only article I had lost or missed in my Continental tour.

Bad luck and good luck they say come together. On my return to the bar of the Coffee House I asked if my luggage had been taken to a bedroom and then enquired for my bottle of marascino, but the lady at the bar with whom I had entrusted the bottle was no longer to be seen and the other female attendant seemed to know nothing about it, or rather to hesitate in her answer. I became imperative and demanded the return of my bottle or to see the female to whom I had entrusted it. Hesitation and confusion arose, and after a little delay my bottle was produced with the cork drawn and half the contents drank. Angrily I enquired 'where is the lady who had charge of it?' Apologies and excuses were made with regret and sorrow that she drank enough to intoxicate herself and had gone to bed drunk. I threatened to bring her up and expose the transaction on the following day, but being desirous of a good night's sleep I did not leave the house as I ought to have done that night.

23rd Sept. went to the Bank of Farqhuar Herries and Co [to enquire] if any remittance had arrived for John Butter. The answer was 'yes, what sum do you expect?' '£60' answer. 'Be pleased to sign your name for that amount.' I signed my name in full, John Butter, this excited suspicious looks counselling amongst the clerks. I was then asked if I was the same John Butter who had signed his name in May last for their Bills of Credit. Answer: 'yes.' A clerk then said: 'your two signatures do not correspond, but we perceive they are the same handwriting and therefore beg to suggest that your future signatures be made in the same way.' I thanked them and took the money which made me very happy to find myself in a position to repay with thanks the obligations I was under to my honourable friend Richards, with whom I afterwards dined at his father's residence, settled accounts and took leave with the best feelings of gratitude and friendship for my travelling companion who had really proved himself to me a friend indeed.

From London I went to Bath the next day and, according to promise, called on my father's uncle Barnard Butter and his wife living on St James' Parade. I was expected and graciously received and with them stayed a day or two, after which I left for Woodbury to spend the remaining days of the month with my parents before reporting at Plymouth on the first day of October.

After a day's coaching from Bath to Exeter where a saddled horse awaited my arrival, I rode to Woodbury where I found that Lord Rolle* had made anxious enquiries as to my return. I had exceeded my leave of absence and, as there was a favourite Sergeant of his staff lying seriously ill at Plymouth, his Lordship wished me to attend him as soon as possible on my return. Having refreshed myself and horse, I started for Bicton, about 4 miles off, the same evening and found his Lordship with a friend or two drinking their wine after dinner. His Lordship graciously received me, and remarked that I had rather exceeded my extension of leave but hoped, indeed urged, that I would return to Plymouth without further delay and report upon the condition of the Master of the SDM Band.

Thinking over this request, or rather command, from my indulgent Colonel, I proposed to my father and mother to start at once, it being 10 o'clock at night, on horseback for Plymouth. 'Of course' they said and did everything that fond parents could do to dissuade me from riding over 50 miles of ground at midnight after the journey from Bath and 8 miles ride over Woodbury Common to visit Lord Rolle.* I knew the time the Down Mail would stop at Ashburton and therefore contrived to reach that town about that hour in order to get a feed of corn for my horse. This object accomplished I was enabled to reach Plymouth at 6 o'clock in the morning, being myself more tired than the horse, but I had taken more out of myself in my journey from Bath to Bicton. I thought I should have fainted whilst this famous horse seemed fresh enough for more work. This was the same horse which I rode from Launceston after the assizes to Totnes and back to Plymouth nearly 80 miles in about 20 hours. I visited the sick Sergeant attended by a Physician and Surgeon in Plymouth and reported favourably on his condition by the post of that day to Col. Lord Rolle who graciously acknowledged my letter, commended my exertions and attributed the man's recovery afterwards to my presence and attention.

Thus ended my Continental Tour from the 1st of May to the 1st of October 1817. I had taken pretty much out of myself from first to last as the reader may guess and therefore required a month's rest to recruit my strength and decide on further plans.

Previous to my departure I left behind me many patients variously afflicted who again returned for my advice and excused my runaway propensities. One lady was confined to her bed with a hip complaint for 3 years under my care and ultimately recovered the perfect use of the joint. A little boy with Lumber abscesses and caries+ of the spine lay a bed 7 years under my care and ultimately recovered and reached manhood.

During my travels on the Continent I had frequently derived much comfort and advantage from warm baths in which I was occasionally indulged with a cup of coffee floated on a board and drank whilst in the bath. When much fatigued by exercise and incapable of further exertion for a time a warm bath has recruited and refreshed my muscular powers in such a way to enable me to endure further exercise for hours. Bonaparte it was said never would have reached Paris after his defeat from Moscow in such a rapid manner of travelling night and day without the aid of baths and coffee. Impressed with this experience I wrote a letter published in the Plymouth Newspaper and signed 'a semi resident' urging the establishment of baths under the Hoe.[43] This letter excited a good deal of table-talk at the time and at last received the attention of the Earl of Morley,* who presided at a meeting assembled for the purpose of forming a Committee and fixing on a site under the Hoe for Baths there to be constructed according to the plans and specifications of Mr John Foulston, the celebrated architect of Plymouth. Soon after the Committee meeting held at the Guildhall and the approval of Foulston's plans by the Earl of Morley as Chairman,

43 *Plymouth and Plymouth Dock Weekly Journal*, 1.7.1824.

and before operations were actually commenced, the awful gale of the 23rd of Nov. 1824 had set in and committed such fearful havoc and destruction on the Breakwater and ships in the Sound, of whom 26 were said to be wrecked on the line of our coast, and the sea could be seen dashing its waters not only over the selected site for Baths but even to the top of the Citadel walls so that the members of the Bath Committee were dispersed and the plan dissolved and hopelessly abandoned. A subscription however was made to remunerate the architect for his trouble and expenses. Thus a period of seven years from Oct. 1817–1824 were occupied in the projected scheme of baths abolished by this frightful storm. Good baths however are now in existence in another part of the coast under Westward Hoe, less exposed than the former site.

Arrears of pay and the receipt of professional fees enabled me to take a journey to Edinburgh for which purpose I obtained another month's leave from Col. Lord Rolle.* On the 1st Nov. I started for Bath and slept one night at the house of my great-uncle and aunt from whence I started the next day for Oxford, visited Stratford-on-Avon, Warwick, York where I visited the Minster, the Asylums, Hospitals and public buildings, and again travelled by night to Newcastle-on-Tyne, Berwick-on-Tweed, Darlington, Durham and so on to Edinburgh, which city I reached on the morning of the 8th by mail.

This long journey I had performed on the outside of coaches and mails, chiefly by night with only one night's rest in bed, and passed the days in viewing the cities and towns through which I had travelled. At daybreak on a cold and frosty morning, whilst on the outside of the mail travelling between Darlington and Durham, I beheld a novel and curious sight of several carriages laden with coals and linked together ascending an incline up a hill with no living body or animal power apparently near them. In this district first began the idea of rail roads by George Stephenson.

At Edinburgh I took up my abode at Berkley's Hotel, near the University. Intending to remain a short time in Edinburgh, I entered my name in the Album of the College and according to rules took two tickets of admission, one for Professor Monroe,* lecturer on anatomy, and the other for Dr Holmes* on Materia Medica. I attended however several other lectures for a short time viz: Professor Playfair* then at the height of his fame on Natural Philosophy, also Dr Browne successor to Dugald Stewart* on Moral Philosophy, Dr Gregory the oldest Professor in Europe on the practices of Medicine, and Dr Duncan.* I delivered letters of introduction from Dr Leach* to Professor Jamieson* on Natural History, to Dr Barclay* a private lecturer unattached to the College, also to Wilson the celebrated bird stuffer. To Mrs Grant of Laggan, an authoress of poems and letters from the mountains, I was likewise introduced by Mary Grant her oldest daughter, whom I had known in Devonshire whilst she was on a visit to Miss Leach. Mrs Grant conferred on me a great compliment by personally going to Constable's the great booksellers and there introducing me to several savants discussing the subject of Capital Punishment, whether hanging ought ever to be resorted to or not for the expiation of crime. I was bold enough to join a little in this discussion to the amusement of Mrs Grant before such men as Jeffery, Sidney Smith, Browne and others. I did not see Walter Scott there but at the Session House afterwards. On our return to Prince's Street Mrs Grant wished me to prescribe for her daughter Moore[?] Grant, who had been given over by her medical attendant. She was well pleased enough with my advice and prescriptions.

My stay in Edinburgh was limited to a fortnights time, enough to keep my first out of three terms required for graduation by paying the fee of registration and taking two Professor's tickets.

Dr Duncan* Junr. also conducted the Edinburgh medical and surgical journal; on him I called with a specimen of the stethoscope which I had brought from Paris and being the first in Edinburgh which served as a model for others. Auscultation had sprung up as a new science in Paris for detecting diseases of the heart and lungs, to which Professor Laennec* was the first to draw particular attention. I also delivered to Dr Duncan a drawing with a description of a heart which had been penetrated by a ball at the Siege of Corunna, in one of our soldiers who afterwards came to Plymouth and died under the care of Mr John Fuge, who with other supernumerary surgeons humanely attended to the sick soldiers of this defeated army whose numerous sick filled the hospitals and barracks to over-flowing, so that numbers were forwarded by waggons to the barracks at Exeter. This extraordinary case was published in Dr Duncan's journal for 1817, No. 53.[44] I also left for publication in No. 53[45] an account of a lady who had swallowed 2 ozs of nitre, saltpetre and had recovered from the effects of the same although pregnant. No miscarriage took place from the excess of vomiting of blood and liquids for nearly 30 hours. St Vitus Dance+ however ensued during her convalescence and became most formidable for a considerable time. Ultimately she recovered her health and produced a fine healthy son in the following October. She lived many years after this accident although I have read and heard of many other persons who had died from smaller doses of nitre taken by mistake for Epsom Salts.

My short term of residence in Edinburgh having nearly expired, I started for Glasgow which city, as well as the Hunterian Museum there, I had a great wish to visit. Mrs Grant had favored me with some letters to her friends at Jordan Hill whom I had not time to visit as I wished to inspect Harley's celebrated Cow-houses capable of containing it was said of 1000 cows which number could not easily be kept up, as two or three cows frequently died when that number was obtained. The city of Glasgow was however abundantly supplied with good milk and fine herds of cows. Time now shortened and I hastened my retreat homewards on or before the 1st of Dec. From Glasgow I coached over the Caledonian road to Carlisle, Liverpool, Manchester, Birmingham and Bath where I halted for the night at St. James Parade with Uncle Barnard and Mrs Butter.

Plymouth I reached in time for the monthly return on the 1st of Dec. having travelled over that long distance by slow coaches and inspected the two great capitals of Scotland and heard distinguished Professors in the short space of 30 days. Now for a long rest at headquarters until the following Nov.

1818

Many of my old patients returned to me and new ones came to hand so easily as to induce a Lady to say I could whistle back my patients after my return.

Uncle Barnard and Mrs Butter generally passed the summer at Lyme Regis in Dorsetshire where she gave an Annual Ball to the visitors. I was summoned to attend

---

[44] *Edinburgh Medical and Surgical Journal* (April 1818), p. 131.
[45] *Edinburgh Medical and Surgical Journal* (January 1818), p. 34.

one of these assemblies in 1818 as Master of Ceremonies, but I was so ignorant and awkward in discharging the duties of my new office as to induce me to wish myself at any place but there – 7 years before I had seen little of ladies society. I rode the distance on horseback from Plymouth to Lyme Regis and back and sent on my traps by coach.

Mary Anning, a poor girl but comely, contrived to maintain herself and mother by exploring the rocks and coasts in which were embedded casts and models of extinct mammals and antediluvian remains. She got up carefully many specimens of Ichthyosaure (half fish and lizards) and plesiosaure. Her celebrety extended far and wide into the universities through the patronage of professor Delabeach in London and Dr Buckland at Oxford, two eminent lecturers on Geology and the sister sciences. Sir William Delabeach[46] was arrested in his scientific career by an attack of pleurisy or affection of the lumber and sacral nerves. Dr Buckland became Dean of Westminster, but enjoyed that high dignity for a short time owing to one attack of insanity or mental imbecility. This illness caused a great loss to science which his son however has since pursued with ardour and success. Frank Buckland, so well known in scientific circles by his numerous contributions on Ichthiology, especially on the hatching of salmon from collected ova and on other subjects in natural history, is likely to render great service to science.

After my return to Plymouth I was consulted by many new patients chiefly about diseases of the eyes and joints. I had patients enough to give me a better income than I received, as Plymouth had been much deserted by wealthy people and the residents generally expected their bills which I was not in the habit of making out. I got money enough however to pay the expenses of my second visit to Edinburgh, which University I reached in Decr 1818 and attended studiously until Feb. 1819 when I again returned to Plymouth. During this second session I was proposed by Professor Jamieson* and admitted a member of the Wernerian Society which was then considered the Natural History Society of Scotland. I read before the Society a paper on the change of plumage of old hen birds with a drawing made by a young lady of Plymouth and afterwards published in the Transactions.[47] This paper was so well received at the time and reported on by Mr Divett, our late member for Exeter, as to be very gratifying to my father and friends.

In No 54 in Dr Duncan's* medical journal[48] I also published a memoir on the compression of cancerous breasts, which paper was favorably received by medical men and serviceable to me in my future practice.

1819

After my return to Plymouth I amputated the thigh of a wealthy Brewer of white ale[49] who had waited for my return some months on account of a white swelling of his knee joint which he was unwilling for any other surgeon to remove. The operation

---

[46] Not William but Henry de la Beche.

[47] Butter seems a little confused. He actually read the paper in two parts, the first on 10 January 1818 and the second on 15 January 1820. *Memoirs of the Wernerian Natural History Society Vol. 3, 1817–1820* (Edinburgh: Archibald Constable & Co., 1821), pp. 183–206.

[48] *Edinburgh Medical and Surgical Journal* (1818), p. 498.

[49] Traditionally flavoured with orange peel and coriander, also possibly with peppercorn and ginger.

went off well but secondary haemorrhage ensued and obliged me to reopen the stump and tie in all 13 arteries. The wound healed beautifully and the result was most favourable.

During the year 1819 from Feb. to Dec. my receipts from practice had increased and enabled me to invest a little in the Funds, from which I afterwards transferred to the purchase of land. I wrote a 3rd paper for Dr Duncan's* journal on the use and abuse of mercury in the treatment of specific diseases,[50] and there described the remedy as worse than the disease itself having seen sailors who had been salivated times over and left with loss of teeth, rotten bones and ruined constitution.

Fever and ague in the autumn assailed and laid me up for weeks owing to my getting especially wet at a shooting party and not changing my clothes and not taking proper stimuli to prevent a collapse. I had suffered severely two or three attacks of paroxysm[+] on alternative days without understanding my case and had called in Dr M and Mr H who blooded me twice with disadvantage and then I understood my condition and took bark and Port wine every hour beginning 6 hours before an expected return. This succeeded well and carried me safely over the time of an expected paroxysm and securely I felt myself for 48 hours. By omitting the bark another paroxysm ensued and obliged me to forestall the next by 6 hours in the way I had previously done. Nauseated by the bark owing to the swelling of my legs, I substituted doses of 4 drops of Fowlers solution[51] of arsenic in mutton broth previously to my next expected attack. This remedy succeeded as well as the former but nauseated me; whenever I left it off another attack of tertian ague[+] returned. I have already published these particulars in 1825 in my book *On irritative fever or Dock-yard disease*, and therefore need not recapitulate my malady here.

Determined to carry out the work I had begun in two preceding sessions, I started on my second journey to Edinburgh by coach in which I thought I should have died under a smart attack of ague whilst passing over Haldon where my back ached, shivering was more severe than on any former occasion. I halted for a night at Bath and proceeded northward by shorter journies sleeping in bed during the night and travelling during the days. The further northwards I got the better I felt myself and experienced no further attack until I reached Edinburgh where I found most comfortable lodgings kept by the widow Gillies at No 2 Nicholson Square. Her son was a physician out of practice who resided occasionally at his mother's, where also were lodged and boarded the following persons viz: Stanford, surgeon of the 29th Regiment stationed at Armagh in Ireland, Joshua Harvey of Dublin, Thos Fisher of Limerick and Ogilvie from the Orkney Islands and myself. We were truly the happy family; Mrs Gillies with the aid of one Scotch lassie managed the whole house and provided a good Scotch dinner daily, consisting of soup or haddie,[52] haggis, some animal food and occasionally game, which is cheap in Edinburgh. We dined together daily at 4 but breakfasted apart on all days, Sundays excepted. I breakfasted by candlelight alone in my private apartment where I also kept a little wine and spirit as we only drank at our dinner water or weak Table Beer at a penny a bottle. I had taken all the requisite tickets from the college Professors and attended only a few lecturers as I thought myself equal to give as good a lecture on anatomy as my friend

---

[50] *Edinburgh Medical and Surgical Journal* (1819), p. 195.
[51] One per cent potassium arsenate used as a tonic.
[52] Haddock.

Professor Sandy Monroe.* My first sally forth daily was to hear a lecture delivered by candlelight at 8 o'clock on Moral Philosophy from Professor Browne;[53] at 9 o'clock Dr Gregory* gave his lecture on the practice of medicine which contained a multitude of facts worthy of remembrance. I had previously consulted him about my own health when I took out my ticket for his lecture, and then offered him an additional fee which he refused saying he never took a fee from a pupil. In his discourse on ague and intermitting fever subsequently he mentioned my case of which he had taken notes very properly.

I attended Professor Hope's* lecture on chemistry, this was the most fashionable and crowded of all the classes. Hope was the best lecturer I had ever heard and I had never heard a bad one in London or in Paris. He was so accurate and precise in all his experiments and descriptions as to convey the most distinct and clear notions in everything he handled or said. He had never failed in making an experiment until the frost set in severely when his assistant had omitted to warm or heat sufficiently the glass vessel under which the Professor performed the experiment of burning iron wire in oxygen gas. So vivid was the flame and so intense the heat as to occasion the bursting of the glass, on which Hope's countenance changed and turning round with a look of censure to his assistant the whole class burst out with one universal applause, to the great consternation of the Professor who was reported in the next Blackwoods Magazine[54] as having at least failed in one experiment.

1820

After a weeks holiday at Xmas, it is usual for the classes to applaud the several lecturers on their return to duty. At 8 o'clock am Professor Home was greeted with this salutation. At 9 o'clock Dr Gregory* entered his class room and whilst stumping the steps to his desk, holding his [a]esculapean staff[+] in one hand, 2 books in the other, received the most hearty applause and responded in the following manner: 'well Gentleman I presume this is your way of wishing me a happy new Year. Wish you the same, with all my heart.' Hearty applause was echoed for this laconic speech. The Professor then, with spectacles on nose and pouch on side, full of wise saws and modern instances, thus began his daily oration. At a former meeting we were considering the subject of fever and of allowing patients such remedies as they expressed a particular wish for, and when these requests were allowed the word Halient[+] was entered in the prescription. In the Edinburgh Infirmary there had been a patient suffering from fever running a long course and making the patient dissatisfied with the ordinary nurses. The clinical physician was informed that the patient was frequently craving for his wife, who had been kept away, but on this occasion the word Halient was written, the attendance of the wife allowed and the patient soon recovered.

At 10 o'clock Professor Hope* entered his class-room and received a perfect ovation from a theatre crammed to excess with students and visitors. Silence being momentarily procured the professor, in an attitude corresponding to the word, thus began: 'Gentlemen, Can I believe myself in a theatre devoted to sciences' (applause). 'Dramatic representations ought not to be exhibited here' (great applause). 'I thank

---

[53] Thomas Brown (1778–1820) was joint Professor of Moral Philosophy with Monroe.
[54] A wide-ranging magazine produced monthly in Edinburgh by William Blackwood.

you for this earnest proof of your good wishes (cheering). Do let us proceed with our scientific work in hand' (renewed cheering).

Soon after my attendance at these three lectures I returned to my lodgings and remained there employed in writing or reading until one o'clock, when I returned and attended Professor Jameson's* lecture on Natural History. Afterwards I attended Dr James Hamilton's* lecture on Midwifery and the diseases of women and children. His lectures were practical and good, and his fame as an Accoucheur⁺ known throughout Scotland and extended even to London, but it never rose to that height which has since been obtained by Professor Simpson* as the discoverer of chloroform which then was unknown as an anaesthetic. There were two Physicians named Hamilton, one known for his book on purgative medicine and the cure of diseases by attention to the digestive organs, and the other an obstectric physician. Liston* and Lizzard, two rival surgeons had also commenced private lectures on anatomy unconnected with those of the College. Liston soon became known for his bold operations in surgery and subsequently removed to London where he became one of the surgeons at the University Hospital. He wrote a paper for the Medical Society of Edinburgh where it was freely discussed by several members, some for and some against it. I took part in defending Liston's practice. Many years afterwards whilst on a visit in London I renewed his acquaintance which he remembered and I attended the University Hospital on one of his operating days at the request of a student. I met him on one of the wards where he took me by the arm and ushered me into his operating theatre, filled to excess with young men, and placed me on a seat behind his chair, by the side of one of the surgeons of St George's Hospital. I never felt myself more unexpectedly honoured. There were only two operations, for dropsy⁺ and lithotomy⁺ on a man and a boy, both of whom were narcotized by Dr Snow* who was considered the most safe and skilful person in administering chloroform. Liston had mistaken the man's disease which he considered a cancerous tumour and proceeded to remove it with a knife which plunged unexpectedly into a bag of water and placed him under considerable difficulty in removing the sack. Liston however preserved his equanimity and presence of mind although the looks and shrugs and buzz which ran through the assembly might have upset many operators. My neighbour whispered to me he could have done as well as that at St George's. Next came the little boy for lithotomy placed under the chloroform. An incision was made into the groove of the staff into which the fore finger of the left hand, not the smallest in the room, was forced into the bladder, tearing and not cutting the parts for a sufficient aperture to extract the stones which came out with a flush of water on the floor and picked up. This work being over, my neighbour whispered a remark whether Liston would say anything to his class, which he soon addressed thus: 'Gentlemen, you see how easy it is for the most experienced to be sometimes deceived. I had taken the usual precautions to discover this disease whether it was hydrocele⁺ or sarcocele,⁺ solid or fluid. I was deceived and put to a little more trouble than I expected.' This candour and manly explanation was received with great applause. Many of us left the hospital with a satisfactory feeling that we could have done as well at Plymouth as the first operator in London. Liston soon afterwards died from the bursting of an aneurysm into his windpipe, soon after an operation on a patient for a similar disease. He had been a bold rider to foxhounds and injured himself about the clavical and neck by a heavy fall from his horse and never felt right afterwards.

Mrs Gillies dinner hour daily was at 4 o'clock when we all met but had not seen each other perhaps before that time. On Sundays we breakfasted and dined together between church hours, we were all Protestants or Presbyterians following places of worship accordingly. I generally attended services and was accompanied on one Sunday by Mrs Grant of Laggan to whom I had applied for a motto in Scotch or Gallic for a snuff box composed of moss agate and ribbon stone set in gold as a present to my very kind aunt Mrs Butter of Bath.

George Bidder* the Devonshire calculator breakfasted with me on another Sunday. The University of Edinburgh to their honor be it spoken, maintained Bidder and gave him a gratuitous education. They had sent a sum of money twice to induce his father at Moreton to bring or send him thither. I told him that I had been present in the Plymouth Guildhall when his father brought him there and submitted him to the test of many calculating persons who were surprised at his facility of doing sums and figures by his head more rapidly than they could do on paper. Bidder at this time is perhaps the most eminent Engineer in England having been a pupil of Robert Stephenson.

Dr Gillies, the only living child of our Landlady had taken out his diploma but had not fixed on any place of settlement. He had been to London lately and studied opthalmy[+] at the London Eye Infirmary with advantage. On his return to Edinburgh he wrote a paper *On Irises* for the medical society of which he was a member and to which he introduced me. In this well-written paper he had expressed doubt whether or not Gout and Rheumatism ever assailed the eye. I happened to be the only person present who appeared to have seen or known an instance, as in Mr Welsford, of gouty irises. My commentary on his paper was favourably received although I delicately pointed out this omission. Thereupon I was proposed and subsequently elected a Member of the Society. About this time I was introduced by Mr Patrick Neale to a meeting at the Royal Society of Edinburgh and left with the Secretary a Memoir on the spontaneous dispersion of Cataract in two patients whom I had attended at Plymouth. This paper received some notice in Dr Brewster's* philosophical journal[55] afterwards, but was not published I believe in the Transactions of the Royal Society. My next duty was to write a Thesis de Opthalmia[56] in Latin and send in to the Dean of the Faculty in order to get an early examination. In this thesis I had suggested the formation of an Eye Infirmary in Edinburgh.

Agreeably to my wishes I attained an early examination at the house of Professor Monroe,* one of my examiners, with Professor Hope,* Home and Duncan* in the midst of whom before I was seated. The questions and answers were all conducted in Latin for the space of one hour, beginning with circulation of the blood in the adult and infant, the composition of the blood, the secretions of the body, their chemical composition in health and disease and the remedies appropriate to their cure. Nitre or nitrate of potash I happened to mention as a febrifuge[+] without guessing the length of questions likely to arise. Professor Hope then took up the examination by asking [in] how many different forms were Oxygen and Nitrogen united? I answered, atmospheric air, nitric and nitrus oxides, nitrates of potash, and soda also of metals

[55] *Edinburgh Philosophical Journal.* The article mentioned has not been found, although the *Journal* did print 'Remarks on the Insensibility of the Eye to Certain Colours' (vol. 6 (1821–2), pp. 135–40).
[56] John Butter, *Disputatio Medica inauguralis, quaedam de ophthalmia complectens* (Edinburgh, P. Neill, 1820).

etc. Professor Hope then took me up in this department of Materia Medica and asked the class and order of Ipecacuanha,[+] which I had mentioned, its common dose and of other powers, whether the dry or moist should be given in the larger dose.

From this period in the month of May to the 1st of August when all successful candidates must be present to take up their diplomas I thought it hardly worth while to run down to Devonshire and back for the space of a couple of months. My indulgent Colonel, Lord Rolle,* granted me a further extension of leave for that period. The winter courses of lectures had now ended and the summer began. Professor Leslie,* successor to Playfair, gave a course of lectures on Natural Philosophy which I attended.

One of my domestic companions at Mrs Gillie's was Mr Stanford, surgeon of the 29th Regiment stationed at Armagh in Ireland to which place he had returned and had given me a hearty invitation to visit him there should I decide upon going to Ireland. At this period I hesitated how to dispose of myself for the months of June and July. My friend William Speke of Jordans in Somersetshire had been a resident at Bishop Sanford's with Montague Baker Bere of Tiverton and some other young men studying general literature or science. Speke had been introduced to me by his brother-in-law Mr T Barnes of Exeter. His plan was to remain in Edinburgh until August and then make a tour of the Highlands on a sporting excursion in which he wished me to join as a companion. I agreed and so instead of going to Staffa, Iona, and the Highlands I decided on taking a trip to Ireland. To Glasgow I went and there got a berth on board the Rob Roy steam vessel, then a novelty. At 8 in the morning, Saturday, we weighed anchor and left Glasgow and whilst steaming down the Clyde I asked the Captain at what time he thought we should reach Belfast. He replied, the weather being fine and the tide running down so many knots an hour, he thought that provided no unexpected obstacle arose in crossing the Irish Channel we might reach Belfast at about 5 o'clock on the following morning, Sunday. I remained on deck until dark and then went below.

At daybreak in the morning I saw a fleet of little sailing vessels cruising off Belfast Loch endeavouring to make that harbour by frequent tacking, but failing owing to the wind and tide being both against them. It was delightful to see how easily the Rob Roy steamed through the little fleet against all opposing obstacles and landed us at the Pier exactly as the Exchange clock struck 5. I complimented the Captain and called [him] the best calculator I had ever met with on sea or land. Comfortable quarters I found at an hotel frequented by numerous travellers who found out each others pursuits and passed away the Sabbath Day pleasantly.

Next day I proceeded through County Antrim by mail to Carrack Fergus and there took a jaunting car for the Giant's Causeway of which I had seen drawings and specimens in England and Italy without deriving the pleasure and astonishment of beholding such wonderful formations of nature. Having satisfied myself with this personal inspection, alone I returned by way of Loch Foyle to Londonderry where the sight of the long bridge reminded me of Bideford, and from thence I came back to Belfast where I remained for that night. By mail next day I passed through Castle Stuart to Armagh where I found my hearty friend Stanford ready to welcome me with every hospitality. Horses were provided and servants too, and the Officer's most gentlemanly set of men. We visited the Lord Primate's Palace and other beautiful places in the neighbourhood, dined daily at the Mess and passed our evenings in agreeable conversation.

After those pleasant days spent at Armagh I took the mail again to Dublin. In Dublin I took up my abode at Gresham's Hotel in Sackville Street and there found every comfort. I visited the different hospitals, the lying-in charity, the asylum and public institutions including the Post Office which was one of the most capacious I had ever seen, as the mail coaches could be driven through one doorway into a large area or court where the letter bags could be taken up and piled away and at the appointed hours leave through the opposite gate-way to all parts of Ireland. I visited the Wicklow Mountains but brought away no gold, which can be dug up there according to tradition. Joshua Harvey had furnished me with a letter of intro-duction to Mr Todhunter, a merchant who had married his sister whom I found to be an amiable pleasing woman. I dined with them and heard a good deal about the Citizens and Institutions in Dublin.

When satisfied with my hasty trip to Dublin and after viewing Phoenix Park and O'Connel's residence in Marion Square I hastened back by mail on the same route as I had come to Belfast, where I halted for another Sunday expecting the arrival of the good ship Rob Roy, but was disappointed with many other people who could not account for her absence and feared that some accident had befallen her. In the afternoon when the mail started from Belfast for Donaghadee I was persuaded to become a passenger as the distance across the channel from Donaghadee to Port Patrick was the shortest known route. After a most pleasant drive I enjoyed a roasted fowl and cheek of pork at Donaghadee and engaged a place in the mail packet, on board of which I found myself a solitary passenger.

In the 1st mile or two the sailing was delightful before the wind and as we got further into the Channel the packet began to lean off on one side, and the sailors put on their north-westers in which attire two of them came to me without speaking so that I asked if they were going to heave me overboard. They replied no but were going to conduct me below into their cabin. I objected at first to go and said I was very comfortable, but they asserted that I should not long be so or even safe in my then position. I did not know my state until I trod the deck over which I might have fallen in my rambling without their assistance. I had not long been in the cabin without parting with my comfortable dinner and without the power of standing. The craft lay more and more on one side, the whizzing and bouncing of the waters became more audible, the plunging, rising and dipping of the vessel caused a whirlwind in my head and the sails such a rattling in my ears as to occasion a privation almost of my other senses. The ship's motion became at last altered into a rocking motion, the sailors began to talk and other voices were heard in the distance, so I was encouraged to look up and contemplate a sight fearful to my view. On either side and before were fearful rocks against which the foam of the sea was dashing and the people on shore seemed eager to moor the vessel. 'Thanks be to God' I said 'I am once more on terra firma,' but I rambled and reeled like a drunken man and the sailors looked like mermaids washed all over with sea-water. I got up to the Inn with my baggage but could not stay in the house or sit down until I had walked about in the open air and got rid of my nausea and giddiness. We had crossed the Channel in about 2 or 3 hours. Having got a little steadier in my gait I retired to the Inn for the night, took tea to comfort my disappointed and distressed stomach, and retired to rest, but none could I get for a more restless night I scarcely remember. At early dawn I got up and took a place on the coach for Dumfries, where there is a monument erected to Robby Burns the poet. From there I coached back to Glasgow and Edinburgh where I passed the months of June & July.

Some years after, I was dining with the Earl and Countess of M when a conversation was brought by a facetious Lady about names long and short. It was suggested that Lady Londonderry should be called London in England and Derry in Ireland, and as it was known that this Lady indulged sometimes too freely with the bottle the witted Countess immediately asked what you would call her half seas over!

The printing of my Thesis de Ophthalmia in Latin was beautifully executed at the printing office of my friend Patrick Neale. It contained a suggestion about the establishment of an Eye Infirmary in Edinburgh[57] on the model of the London Eye Infirmary. Mr Wishart,[58] Surgeon, had translated Scarpa's* treatise on diseases of the eye and had therefore proved himself the best person to bring before the public such an institution, which he was disinclined to attempt. Dedications were customary in these Theses by the authors to such benefactors and friends as had assisted them in obtaining the diploma of MD Edinburgh. I therefore made 5 dedications: 1st to my great aunt Mrs Butter of Bath; 2nd to my patron and friend, Col. Lord Rolle;* 3rd to my esteemed friend Lieut. Col. of the SD Militia, Sir JH Seale,* Bart; 4th to my respected friend John Abernethy* Esq.; 5th to my valued and kind friend Dr Wm Elford Leach,* zoologist to the British Museum.

Without my colonel's leave of absence I could not have absented myself from headquarters for a month without losing my pay of 6/- per diem less 10 per cent income tax. Lieut. Col. Seale* lost no opportunity of befriending me and therefore merited my acknowledgements. Mr Abernethy* cheered me at starting for my diploma from the College of Surgeons in London, without which I could not have obtained the surgeoncy of the SD Militia. My friend Dr Leach* introduced me to his influential family and relations at Plymouth where I was doomed to live half a century and upwards, he also introduced me personally to Sir Joseph Banks* and to the scientific visitors to his house; he also furnished me with letters in introduction to several naturalists and scientific men in Paris and established a lasting friendship between his parents and family with myself to the end of their days. Of that excellent and good lady Mrs Butter of Bath, my great uncle's wife and therefore no blood relation to myself, I could not speak too highly. When she married my great uncle she possessed no fortune of her own but after the lapse of years inherited her brother's fortune above £40,000 made in the iron trade. The unexpected possession of such a large sum bequeathed to her so late in life led her to think how she could dispose of it by her will. On going to bed one night at their house I saw on the dressing table a beautiful gold watch, chain and seals containing a fine specimen of Cairngorm stone she said that that is my present to you. In the preceding December too I slept at their house in St James' Parade and received a sum of money carefully wrapped up with her good wishes and hopes that it might prove sufficient for my last trip to Edinburgh. The dedication to her of my Thesis was well deserved and not overcharged for such generous bounty from a kind hearted lady.

After the 1st August 1820 Mr Wm Speke and I commenced our Tour into the Highlands. He had provided things necessary for us both, a horse and gig, pointer and setter, double guns and ammunition. From Edinburgh we drove to Glasgow and

---

57 Established in 1834.
58 John Henry Wishart (1781–1834).

there fell in with Col. Leach and his eldest brother George, with whom we dined at the Mess of the 95th Regiment of Rifles. The Col. and his brother were also entering on a similar excursion, to Fort William by water. From Glasgow we travelled so far as we could go before the 12th of August, via Dumbarton, Loch Lomond etc. and slept overnight at the King's road house where we got ready for the field and engaged a guide for the opening day. We walked some 4 miles over bog and heather and had moderate sport until we approached a glen from which a column of smoke was issuing as from a chimney. Then we saw a man hastening towards us, as we thought a game-keeper to warn us off that district and prepared ourselves accordingly but our guide assured us there was no such intention. He held something in his hand, afterwards found to be whisky in a raw state from the still contained in a bladder. This was the illicit still and the distiller fearing exposure and conviction he came to pacify us with a bribe of his liquor. He talked gallic which our guide understood and interpreted to us in broad Scotch which we could barely understand. We all of us sipped a little of this raw and ardent spirit which increased our desire to drink according to the quantity taken. I cautioned Speke again and again against its potent effects, but he was so cheered by it as to form some plan by which he could transport a quantity to his family seat in Somersetshire. We all drank too much but the guide and I were able to walk homewards. Speke was overwhelmed with stupor, so I sent the guide back 4 miles for one horse and remained with Speke whom I could not rouse; thus broke down our first day's sport, just as we had got onto the thickest of the grouse. I tried unsuccessfully to make him sick or to swallow water but he seemed quite insensible and deaf to my applications. I never saw a man so overpowered by alcohol before. Impatiently I waited for the return of our guide with the horse and when we placed Speke on the saddle he could not sit there without my holding him. We had to cross a mountain stream, and whilst succouring him I fell into a deep pool of water which wetted my gun and powder and dress, so that now an additional trouble met us. We reached the Inn, undressed and put Speke into a warm bed in his insensible state. I became very uneasy about him, fearing apoplexy,[+] so I went into another bed in the same room that night and never heard him speak until 5 o'clock on Sunday morning, when he cried out 'Water, water oh my head'. For dinner we had nice Highland mutton and grouse, of which I ate heartily, but poor Speke was entirely off his food. Thus disappointed in our trip and shortened for time we thought it prudent to beat backwards, especially as there had been an annual fair held there on the following day during which people were coming from all quarters and disturbing our rest at night by forcing open our bedroom door.

We returned to Calendar and halted there at the Inn with the intention of visiting the Trossachs, Loch Katrine and Benlomen. A terrific toothache seized Speke at Calendar and obliged him to keep his bed. We sent to the Parish Doctor to extract the tooth but found that he had not been in the habit of performing that operation, and moreover that he possessed no instruments for the purpose except a rusty old and imperfect German key which he would not use. Neither could I make sure of extracting a tooth with it but I succeeded and left Speke in bed whilst I drove with the dogs and guns to the Trossachs, where host Stuart was most attentive and obliging. I was bent on going on the lake alone, but learning from our Host that there was a fine pack of Heath Fowl on the road to Aberfoyle about a mile or two off I repaired thither and bagged some of these fine birds when a brawny old Highlander came up to me and said: 'this is Lord Breadalbane's property.' 'Oh yes', I said: 'alright you have done your duty so here is a half-crown for you', and so the gamekeeper walked off leaving me to my sport. When I returned to Calendar with some fine birds Speke was so elated as to forget his toothache and former ailments and to wish for a repetition of the journey on the following day, when I went a second time to the Trossachs and saw Benvenne and Benledi with Speke more bent on Heath Fowl than on scenery or lakes.

We returned to Edinburgh via Sterling where we inspected the castle with its romantic scenery. Having adjusted our money matters at Edinburgh I was eager to travel southwards whilst Speke remained behind at Bishop Sandford's. I thought myself a good walker equal to any man, but having been shut up in the University for so many months at my studies and having undergone no training I found myself totally unable to compete in pace with Speke or the brawny Highlander. I settled all my affairs with Mrs Gillies comfortably and got ready my baggage including two surgical apparatuses which I had procured. The first was Nasdom's[+] long splint, extending from the hip to the heel, with a foot-board to be placed on the sound or opposite extremity in case of fracture of the thigh. I presented one of his splints to the Devon and Exeter Hospital and the other I took with me to Plymouth where I found it of great value in my future practice.

Whilst walking the London Hospitals formerly, I observed the bad success of hospital surgeons in treating fractures of the thigh which were generally placed on their side without fixed extension, and so the muscles contracted, the fractured ends over-lapped and the limb shortened 2 or 3 inches with a feeble union liable to a re-fracture at any time. Whilst in Paris in 1817 I had observed the practice at the Hotel Dieu and other hospitals of managing fractured thighs more successfully than in London. The patients were laid on their backs and the fractured thigh permanently extended and kept steady from spasms by means of a long splint extending from the pelvis to some inches beyond the foot with a screw at the end to slacken or tighten the bandage attached to the ankle and foot. Nasdom's splint however seemed to me preferable to Boyer's because in cases of compound fractures attended with discharges, the injured limb was more easily dressed and bandaged whilst the splint remained fixed on the opposite or sound limb. This splint was well spoken of by the Surgeons at Exeter and Plymouth. Baldy, the Surgeon of the Plymouth Workhouse, turned out several fractured thighs straight. Sir Hayton Drake's Coachman had his thigh broken by the kick from a coach horse and suffered severely from spasms which obliged a nurse to sit by his bedside and hold the limb by night and by day. The application of this splint procured immediate ease and comfort and so nicely steadied the fractured bones in juxta position as to secure a speedy and firm union without shortening of the limb, so that after his recovery he was enabled to ride as postillion. The coachman of Colonel Morshead of Widey Court was riding a run-away horse back from Plymouth when his knee came in contact with the post of the Turn pike gate and his thigh-bone was fractured in more places than one. He suffered greatly afterwards from muscular spasms and shortening of the limb although placed under the care of a very skilful surgeon who at last desired me to see him and helped to apply Nasdom's splint which kept the fractured limb steady and comfortable whilst the reunion went on and a useful limb restored.

I brought back also from Edinburgh an ingenious instrument for extracting a barbed fish-hook out of a boy's throat. A shepherd's boy was watching his master's flocks grazing on the mountain side by the side of a river in which the boy amused himself with fishing. He had a rod and line and rather a large barbed hook united by twisted wire to the end of his line, and whilst attempting to do something to the line he put the fish-hook momentarily into his mouth from which it accidentally slipt over the tongue into the Aesophagus, from whence the boy tried to drag it back and so fixed it into the flesh that it could not be drawn out by any known means. The boy was sent up to the Edinburgh Infirmary where his case puzzled all the surgeons and obliged them to consult an ingenious instrument maker who got a facsimile of the hook and then procured a round ivory ball with a hole made large enough for the fishing line to pass through. A long piece of whale-bone was fastened into the ivory ball. The successful operation was thus effected: the fishing line hanging out of the boy's mouth and attached to the hook in his throat was then passed through the hole in the ivory ball and on this line the ball was forced down the throat by the whale-bone until it reached the hook. Force was then applied to detach the hook and the barbs from their hold fast, and when so detached the string was tightened and the points of the hook brought against the ivory ball and so the hole, the ball and hook were thus brought up together. Ingenious and successful as this instrument was I have never had occasion to use it but this notice may be useful to others.

At Bath I was well received in my backward journey and pleased to find that my Latin dedication to my aunt had been faithfully translated by a classical young surgeon of her acquaintance.

To Plymouth as Headquarters I returned for the winter of 1820, thinking and preparing for my new career as a Physician as well as a Surgeon. Many of my old patients now wished to know in what light they were to regard me, as a Physician or as a Surgeon. My reply was that I should make no difference to my old patients but continue my professional attendance on former terms, but that with new patients I should expect a Physician's fee. This answer was pleasing and acceptable and then it was said I had whistled back most of my old patients. The time had apparently arrived when I ought to come forth more publicly than I had done during the preceding 10 years when I had lived either in barracks or obscure lodgings without the fixture of my name over the door. The only two lodging I had occupied were Rowe's the Druggist's and Mrs Hallett's the poulterer.

1821

I moved into Rosie's lodgings in George Street in July and had my name printed over the door which afforded some public comment although done after the example of Mr Abernethy* in London. Two sittings and the bed-room with a stable comprised these lodgings. Furnished for £60 a year, they had been previously occupied by an itinerant Oculist who was said to carry away with him more money than I ever received in one year at Plymouth. Old Mr and Mrs Rosie were peculiar people; he had been a purser in the Navy and was now a money-lender to Butchers and other tradesmen requiring small loans of money for a short time at high interest. Old Mrs Rosie led a singular life; she generally sat up by night by the kitchen fire and went to bed by day, still kept her house in decent order with one servant. I moved into these lodgings from Mrs Hallett's, foreseeing that George Street would become a great thoroughfare on the completion of the Union Road to Stonehouse Dock.

I was very successful there in my practice and increase of fees. I had many patients at Teignmouth and Ashburton, to which places I generally rode on horseback from

40 to 50 miles a day. My famous horse had gone blind and been sold for a poster during my absence from Plymouth and my setter Juno remained with my mother until my return, when she related the following circumstances. During the wheat harvest at Woodbury she and a female servant walked out taking with her Juno and a spaniel dog which was recovering from the distemper which had dreadfully shaken the dog's nervous system and produced subsultus tendisuum or a sort of St Vitus' dance.[+] This spaniel had been much petted and brought to fetch and carry things as a retriever. On returning from the cornfield my mother and servant observed that the dogs were missing. Whilst returning homewards the spaniel overtook them with a partridge in his mouth which they took from the dog and expressed their surprise as to how the dog could have caught the bird. During their deliberations the dog escaped from their notice and disposed them to call the dog which they soon saw coming with another partridge. The 2nd bird being also secured, the dog again left them with all speed and they followed him but not fast enough before the dog had secured a 3rd partridge, making three in all. They then went backwards where Juno had lain all this time before the covey, of which the dog might have brought other birds had he been allowed to do so.

Whilst occupying my new lodgings I had Juno and a fresh horse which I sold for 50 guineas.

One morning I was requested to visit a clergyman's wife who had come from the country to consult me at her friend's house. She had a cancer of her left breast which I said ought to be removed without delay. She asked: 'will you do it sir?' 'Why do you ask Mam?' She replied: 'because you are a physician a doubt arises about your operating. If you will perform the operation yourself I will appoint a day for the purpose, otherwise I will go to London and have it done.' 'Agreed, to whom am I indebted for this introduction.' A: 'To Dr Marshall of Totnes who has read and approved of your paper on this disease.'[59] 'Then, Mam' I said 'Dr Marshall ought to be invited to attend the operation; and who is your country surgeon?' A. 'Mr Gest of Woodbury.' 'He ought also to be present, being nearer than myself to your residence, in case of anything untoward.' We all three attended and I removed the breast to the satisfaction of all present, the wound healed beautifully as one seam. She was a grateful and warm-hearted friend and subsequently rendered me good service in my Profession. She attended concerts and balls and parties and dressed so well as to defy an anatomist to discover the loss of her breast; after a certain period, however, a furious haemorrhage from the uterus occurred from time to time and completely exhausted her powers until death ended her sufferings.

The year 1821 proved more than usually prosperous in my profession but I could not do without surgery which enabled me to get many large fees which I should have otherwise lost by acting as the mere physician.

I had long meditated in Edinburgh and in Plymouth if I settled there to attempt the establishment of an Asylum for Lunatics of whom there were many, or an Eye Infirmary. The former establishment I could not get up without a large sum of money whilst the other was more suited to my means and reputation. I therefore resolved on the latter and drew up the following letter[60] dated 4th of November, and published my address, read before His Worship the Mayor, Edmund Lockyer* Esquire, a bench of

---

[59] *Edinburgh Medical and Surgical Journal* 14 (October 1818), pp. 498–507.
[60] This has not been found.

Aldermen and Magistrates, a large meeting of country gentlemen and Townspeople in the Plymouth Guildhall on the 6th of Dec. 1821.[61] All the rules and regulations framed by myself were read and passed at this meeting. The Mayor then proposed that Dr Butter be elected the Physician and Mr Edward Moore as Surgeon to the Plymouth Eye Dispensary. Then came the election for a second Surgeon for which office three candidates started. Mr John Luscombe, John Hele,[62] and Mr Tracey. The latter soon resigned and after a smart contest Mr Luscombe was elected by a majority of 20 votes. For the 7 preceding years from 1814 to 1821 I had monopolized the treatment of Ophthalmic patients as no resident Surgeon or Apothecary had paid particular attention to these diseases or had ever operated or seen an operation performed with success for the cure of cataract or restoration to sight, but I was not disposed to continue in this course single-handed without establishing a distinct Institution for the treatment of Ophthalmic diseases. I therefore selected Mr Edward Moore, a young surgeon who had previously applied for the appointment of Assistant Surgeon in the South Devon Militia at Barnstaple, he therefore became my assistant or colleague in raising subscriptions for the new Institution. When my letter was published much commotion was excited amongst the Medical men at Plymouth and especially those at the Public Dispensary who offered all the opposition in their power to my plans, and after their unsuccessful opposition one of the Surgeons offered himself as a candidate for the office of 2nd Surgeon to the Eye Dispensary. This appointment of two surgeons I opposed for a time but my colleague prevailed on me at last to open the door for a 2nd Surgeon which brought forth many candidates and gave me an infinity of trouble and abuse which might have been avoided.

Predictions soon got afloat that the new Institution would not stand above a year or two and one of the wealthiest subscribers withdrew his name from the list. Some years afterwards the Mother and Sister asked me if the report was true that their relation had withdrawn his name as a subscriber. I said 'yes.' They replied: 'then double our subscriptions' and before these good ladies died a legacy of £100 was given to the Institution and £25 to myself, thus showing that my public conduct which had given offence to one member of the family had gained the support and generosity of others.

One of my foolish acts committed in this year I ought to mention for the guidance of others. As no practising Surgeon could obtain a fellowship from the Royal College of Physicians in London without resigning his Surgeon's diploma which I had no wish to do, and as I had to run a race with another honorable competitor for public favour who had obtained a fellowship from the Royal College of Physicians in Edinburgh, I must now do the same at the cost of £95, which was money entirely thrown away, especially as I had already obtained my medical degree from the University of Edinburgh at a cost of several £100, of three long journies in the winter season, and three years loss of surgical practise at a time when I was beginning to rise in the ladder of reputation. But I had two games to play; one was to obtain a livelihood from my professional practice in Plymouth and the other was to keep up the favour and good opinion of my relations in Bath. These two objects clashed

---

[61] John Butter, *An Address Delivered in the Guildhall, at Plymouth, on the 6th Day of December, 1821: At the First General Meeting of the Subscribers to the Plymouth Eye Infirmary* (Plymouth: Rowes, 1821).

[62] He was John Hele Fuge – see Introduction.

at times and prevented me from gaining that large share of surgical practise which might have otherwise fallen into my hands.

Another bit of good luck had fallen to my lot. One morning a letter of introduction was brought to me by Mr Stokes, a naturalist and friend who had arrived at the Royal Hotel in company with Mr and Mrs Hatchett* and Mr and Mrs Chantrey.* They were proceeding on a Tour through Cornwall. Mrs Hatchett was an invalid for whom I prescribed. Mr and Mrs Chantrey, Stokes and myself visited the marble[63] quarries at Oreston in order to see the trucks on which large blocks of lime stone were transferred from the quarries to the Breakwater barges. This conveyance was more interesting to the eminent Sculptor and receiver of large Carrara marble than to ourselves, however we passed a pleasant day in going to the Breakwater and other places without seeing Mr Wilby FRS, who was the chief director of works, and who had travelled round the world with Cooke and Vancouver. Something more suitable than rocks to our distinguished chemist was fished up out of the Sound; it was a cannon ball of iron, converted by sea-water into plumbago,[64] of which our scientific friend afterwards published an account. We all dined together at the Hotel on a dinner served up in Mrs Whiddon's best style. Mr Hatchett was acknowledged to be one of the best chemists of the age. He had published numerous works and memoirs in the Transactions of the Royal Society, especially on the anatomy of bones, shells etc. He was a most cheerful and delightful companion full of jokes, wit and repartee, as well as a scientific enquirer whose labours had been checked by the acquisition of a large fortune which he dispensed with a liberal hand. Finding me in a lodging where he called daily although I could show him no hospitality, Mr Hatchett evinced much good will towards me and a desire to promote my prospects.

One day he said: 'I think we must have you in the Royal Society, would you have any objection to be proposed as a candidate?' 'No Sir' I said 'but I have not sufficient pretensions yet for attaining such a huge honour.' 'Oh' said he 'I think we may manage it for you. When I go back to Town we will put up your name as a candidate in a list which should be signed by as many medical men as you can get.' At my request I believe the following names were subscribed after Mr Hatchett:* John Abernethy,* Astley Cooper,* Wm Lawrence,* WE Leach,* M Brand, Mr Hatchett's son-in-law, Francis Chantrey* and other friends of Mr Hatchett.[65]

During the month of May of this year the SDM were assembled for 21 days training at the Longroom Barracks, Stonehouse. Lord Rolle* and several officers were quartered at the Royal Hotel where we messed. The weather got very warm and the duties oppressive for young officers who had to walk there for an early morning drill and return to Breakfast and repeat the journey once or twice during the remainder of the day. One of our recruits, Capt. Jno Yarde Buller,* brought on an attack of fever, which appeared to be simple continued fever for a week and then typhoid symptoms appeared. He grew worse and worse and by night delirium came on so that he got out of bed and wandered about the passages alarming the servants of the Inn who got him into bed and sent for me. His glassy eyes, dry and dark-coloured tongue, parched skin, low and frequent pulse forewarned me of his danger which I reported

---

[63] Not marble, but limestone.

[64] Black lead or graphite.

[65] Butter became a Fellow on 21 March 1822. *List of Fellows of the Royal Society, 1660–2019* (London: The Royal Society, 2020).

to Col. Lord Rolle in Command, who replied 'you must then call in some other Physician in consultation.' His Lordship kindly observed that 'were it my own case I should be perfectly satisfied with you, but this young man's life is of great object to the country as well as to his family. His mother resides in Staffordshire where we must send for her and I must act as his father.' Dr Woolcombe* was therefore called in and agreed with me perfectly in the treatment of the case. Many persons urged me to bleed him but I refused to do so, observing that his strength was fast failing him and that the loss of blood would only expedite his death. Dr Woolcombe fully agreed with me in that opinion and confirmed my treatment. His powers of strength were reduced so fast as to oblige him to have two beds, one for the night and one for the day, and as his weakness was too great for him to walk I was obliged to carry him like a child in my arms from one bed to the other. We sent over the country in search of grapes, to the different hothouses, without procuring any, and therefore trusted to such lemons and oranges as could be procured. His mother arrived and proved herself to be such a charming woman as we had heard of her. The greater part of my time by day and by night was spent in Capt. Buller's bedroom, where every wish and want was attended to, but still I found time to visit the sick soldiers. After the lapse of five or six weeks the fever ebbed and the tide of recovery began to flow and enabled him to recover by slow degrees his appetite and strength, which enabled him to recover or rather to cripple[?] out of this fever.

The period of training being over, officers and men returned to their respective homes and left Capt. Buller* sick at the Hotel; after 6 weeks he was sufficiently convalescent to return to Lupton near Brixham. I escorted him as far as Ivybridge on his way and returned again having received a handsome fee of 20 guineas from his good mother. I could not then foresee my future advantages in saving the life of such a promising young man who has never forgotten my services to the present day. He has lived to represent Lord Rolle* in the Colonelcy in the SDM and to place his son the Honorable John Buller in that high office. He married a sister of Mr Wilson Patten MP for [Lancashire], became a Baronet at the death of his father, and subsequently a peer of the realm during Lord Derby's administration.

1822

Dr Woolcombe* died on the [blank] day this year and the tablet is deservedly erected in St Andrew's Church to his memory. His loss was felt by the Town and his situation as Senior Physician at the Dispensary was subsequently supplied by the election of Dr James Yonge* who was brought down from London by the family to supply his place, deservedly it may be said as the descendant of the late Chas Yonge, the founder and largest contributor to the Plymouth Dispensary. No other Physician in Plymouth was encouraged to offer himself as a candidate except Dr Bellamy, an old Naval Surgeon whose excuse was to show the public that he had not retired from practice.

I was summoned to Bath professionally to visit my great-uncle Barnard Butter, said to be dangerously ill with water in the chest following an attack of pleurisy which seized him at Lyme late in the preceding year and increased after his return to Bath. My predecessor, Mr Tucker, who had married and settled at Lyme as a surgeon advised him to be blooded, but he refused as Tucker unfortunately squinted and let him fear that he might not open the vein properly. Finding his difficulty of respiration and cough getting worse he hastened back to Bath and the journey accelerated those symptoms which timely bleeding might have relieved. Mr White, a Bath surgeon in whom he had confidence, considered that the time had gone by for bleeding and therefore followed suit with the Bath fashion of that day in filling and not emptying overcharged blood vessels, producing dropsical effusions: my uncle, finding his breath more and more embarrassed, wished me to be sent for. I found him in bed unable to lie back, coughing and breathing heavily with an anxious countenance portraying danger.

On the [blank] day of [blank] 1822 my uncle breathed his last at the age of 84 and his remains were interred in Alverton Church, which is opposite Warlegh Mansion where he resided for a number of years. I attended the funeral and found that my brother, sister and I were each left an annuity of £20 after the death of Barnard Webber, to whom an annuity of £60 a year was left. My good aunt under this will received an annuity of £300 a year which sum she did not want and therefore assisted me annually with a portion of it.

In March my good friend Mr Hatchett* invited me to come up to London to be present at the Royal Society's rooms during the ballot for my name. I was agreeably surprised to find that good arrangements had been made on this occasion. Mr Hatchett's residence at Belle Vue, Chelsea was my headquarters. Various dinners I was invited to attend, and I was present in an adjoining room when Mr Hatchett came from the ballot in great glee and said: 'I congratulate you as FRS, elected without one single black ball, but Rennie had several and others were entirely excluded.' I was then asked whether I would pay down £32 at once or 2 guineas a year. I was glad to have it in my power to pay down the full amount at once in lieu of annual instalments.

My good aunt had supplied me with a little more money than I wanted about which I consulted Mr Hatchett,* who said 'I should stick to the funds. Although they pay less interest than other stocks, still I would feel secure there and prefer a smaller income with security to a larger one attended with risk. I will give you a letter of introduction to my Banker, Fauntleroy, one of the firm of Marsh, Tracey and Fauntleroy, who will advise you better in money matters than I can.' I took Fauntleroy's advice and invested a few hundreds I possessed in Danish and Spanish Bonds, both of which turned out badly, especially the latter which I kept for years with little or no interest then grew tired and sold them at a discount, from which they rose in a week or two and nearly doubled the price. I have never had any faith in Spanish Stock or Spanish credit from that time. Apropos of these investments, whilst dining at a friend's house soon after the settlement of the Spanish question, a discussion arose at table about the better condition of Spain. One gentleman present distrusted the Spanish Government as well as myself and thought that as they had once broken faith with nations they would do so again and render their Government imbecile and their national credit bad. A more eloquent gentleman present, who often read up subjects likely to be discussed at dinner parties, took the opposite side and argued that the Spanish nation was now settled on a firm basis by the Cortes[66] and that their national faith would be respected and trusted by other Governments. He had no doubt the balance of argument in his favour and of silencing the former speaker by making the worse appear the better. Still so completely was this argument

[66] The Spanish Parliament.

ex absurdo conducted as to induce one of the company lately possessed of a few hundreds to embark his all in Spanish Stock where it came to nothing. Henry Fauntleroy was afterwards hanged at the Old Bailey for forgery on the 30th day of Nov. 1824.[67]

Two leasehold houses were advertised for sale, one on the north and the other on the south side of George Street Plymouth. I was strongly persuaded to buy the larger house and premises on the South side, but my own inclination led me to prefer the smaller on the north as being pleasanter to the view and more suitable to my means and wishes. I bought it for £610 besides fees for the attorney of £24.4s and paid down £50 on Nov. 15th as a deposit and the remainder of the purchase on the 23rd Dec. I had been beating about the world for Eleven or twelve years in Barracks or in Lodgings and therefore felt the necessity now of settling myself in a House of my own. No. 28, now 55, in George Street was a very pretty little house pleasantly and conveniently situated, well fitted-up with mahogany doors and cupboards and a small garden plot extending backwards into George Lane. My first object was to build a bath-room, water closet and Museum in the rear, and subsequently a stable for three horses with a loft over. I had collected many specimens of natural curiosities and stuffed birds, some of my own shooting, and had put up many morbid preparations, some of great interest in glass bottles containing spirits of wine. My idle time and spare money had been spent in getting up these preparations so that I soon exhibited a tidy little Museum. I had two human skelitons of the male and the female; the skeliton of the little pony which beat the mail coach in travelling from London to Exeter in 1805, 172 miles in 22 hours; the skeliton of a domestic hen which in old age had assumed the cock's plumage and which came into my possession too late for presentation like the other, or Corham's hen. I had several infected preparations and wax models of the brain, eye, ear, and foetus brought from Florence, also calculi,[+] seven in number taken from patients between the ages of six and seventy years without losing one by death. These alterations and extensions afforded me great pleasure for a time until they were completed and then I thought it desirable to purchase the fee simple, then offered at the price of £100, for the conveyance of which the attorney had the conscience to charge £30 in addition. Property in George Street is however so much increased in value that a house then let for £40 a year now fetches from £100 to £120. I could only furnish my house by degrees but all my furniture was chosen of the newest and best manufacture and paid for at once for a discount. I had borrowed of my brother at five per cent interest £100 which was transmitted through an Exeter Bank to that of Shields and Johns at Dock, now Devonport, and before I could draw out any part of it to pay for my furniture, the Bank failed and I lost both principle and interest, viz £105 repaid at the end of the year without the least advantage. When Lord Rolle* heard of this circumstance he told my father that he was surprised at my trusting another Bank when there was such a safe and respected one as that of Sir W Elford & Co. at Plymouth, which I afterwards trusted for £50 and lost that sum also on the failure of that Bank in 1825.

During the summer of 1822 I had three commissions from Bath to obtain furnished houses or lodgings for three families who bound me to only one circumstance, viz: that the windows might overlook the sea. Without a trial I should have had no idea

---

[67] He was one of the last people to be executed for forgery before it ceased to be a capital crime in 1836.

of the difficulty of fulfilling such a condition unless I had gone up to Stoke or to the Baths under Mount Wise. I secured one furnished however in Durnford Street over-looking Stonehouse Pool. This I engaged for my Aunt, but could not obtain two others for the families of Mrs Horsfall and Mr & Mrs Bill, the latter keeping a yacht with which they left for Southampton and the Misses Horsfall for Weymouth, so that my Aunt remained at Stonehouse without her party from Bath. She had brought introductions to General Vinnicombe, then Commandant of Marines, and made friends enough for a quiet rubber of whist at night. There being no Dentist in Plymouth at that time she made a party with Miss Allen and myself to drive up to Exeter and consult Groves about her teeth. We had a pleasant journey there and back, she also gave a dinner excursion at the Inn near Mount Edgecumbe and invited a number of my valued friends on this occasion. We made likewise an excursion to the Tavistock Races so that she contrived here to pass through her widowhood very agreeably until the fall of the year, when she returned to Bath for the winter.

On the 19th Nov. I was consulted by Sir Alexander Cochrane,* then Port Admiral in command at Government House, Mount Wise. On a preceding evening he was playing at Whist with Lady Cochrane and a party and induced by some circumstance to close his right eye, when to his surprise he found himself in total darkness. He repeated this trial several times with the same result. Astonished thereat he exclaimed: 'Lady Cochrane, do you know that I am blind in one eye?' 'Oh no' she said 'you deceive yourself.' This announcement astonished all persons present who severally looked at the blind eye without discovering inflammation, alteration or any defect whatsoever. The Surgeon of the Ordinary was sent for but saw nothing. Mr Hammick of the Naval Hospital was consulted but he saw nothing and conjectured that a cataract was forming, but this did not account for blindness and therefore Admiral Wise advised my attendance. I pronounced Sir Alexander to be in some danger of his life, to the astonishment of all present, and said: 'this blindness is the token of a forthcoming storm; cataract has nothing to do with the case, there is none. The vessels within the eyeball are congested and so are those of the head and brain, forewarning us with apoplexy.+ The disease is Amaurosis,+ commonly called Gutta Serena, the treatment must be active to prevent further mischief. Cupping+ or Bleeding or Leeches must be resorted to and blisters to the neck or behind the ears, a moderate diet must be enjoined with small quantities of wine, and the feet kept very warm to entice a fit of gout if any be floating in the system, and the head kept cool and the mind free from all speculations or excitement. These are my views and treatment proposed', to which Mr Hammick dissented and objected. 'Then' said Sir Alexander 'will you draw up my case with your views and plan of treatment?' 'Certainly' I said. That having been done, three copies were ordered to be made by the clerks in office and sent to three eminent Professors in London, viz: Wardrop, Guthrie and Travers, who all three returned prompt answers confirming my views and treatment but thought I might carry it further than was proposed. 'What say you to this Mr Hammick?' asked Sir Alexander: 'Oh,' he replied, 'all this is against me but my opinion remains unaltered.' 'Well then I must try and do something. Cupping cannot much hurt me and may relieve my head, [which is] often confused,' and so cupping was performed by Mr Bailey, Surgeon of the Flag Ship. He performed the operation well and willingly obeyed all other injunctions, but impartially declined to offer any opinion.

At 8 o'clock every morning Sir Alexander's carriage took me up at my new habitation in George St then drove to the Royal Naval Hospital for Mr Hammick and conveyed us together to the Admiralty House, where we breakfasted, consulted and remained for an hour, when we were driven back again. One morning Lady Cochrane took me aside alone and said: 'if you and Mr Hammick do not agree and go on pleasantly together I will desire him to cease his attendance and leave Sir Alexander's treatment entirely in your hands.' 'Oh, Lady Cochrane' I replied 'don't do so. Although Mr Hammick's opinion is at variance with my own, his experience and skill as a hospital surgeon may yet be of use to me in treating such an important case as Sir Alexander's. I wish him to continue his visits with my own until Sir Alexander's condition is improved.' Then she enquired: 'you wish Mr Hammick to continue his visits with yourself?' 'Most certainly My Lady.' There was much snow on the ground during the winter of 1822 and the mornings were cold for my early visits. The sight of the blind eye could not be regained, but the warning symptoms in the other with those of the head had been so far removed as to render the sight of the sound eye safe and his life secure from apoplexy.[+] In the following year he repaired to France and lived for many years, having presented me with £50 previous to his departure. Sir Alexander Cochrane* was one of the most delightful persons I had ever met with, gentle and kind and hospitable to all persons about or under him. His word was a law and his command of fleets and stations both temperate and judicious; every sailor loved and feared him and all persons respected his authority.

The 1st Annual Report of the Plymouth Eye Dispensary was made up at Xmas 1822 and the number under treatment was 707. This result was a pretty decisive answer to its opponents and staff at the Dispensary, who had opposed its formation by their statistical report for the 7 preceding years during which only 114 patients had applied there with ophthalmic diseases, or about 17 in a year, whereas 224 patients had been registered within 2 months at the Eye Dispensary. Our corner house in Cornwall St did not suit well our purposes on account of the noises during market days and times of the fairs. We thence removed our Institution into Westwell St where the business was carried on for many years and where we might have longer remained had not the Committee been blind or perverse in allowing the premises to be bought over our heads.

[There follows a description of the attempted purchase of a property in Princess Street which is repeated and expanded in the entry for 1844.]

1823

The affairs of the Eye Infirmary, the furnishing of my new house, the Militia meetings and my private patients at home and at a distance fully occupied my thoughts and time. Some patients at Kingsbridge induced me to attend a Ball there and to stay up all night for want of a bed. Next day I visited some patients and left to ride to Plymouth in a dark and dirty November day. My horse and I were pretty well covered with mud. I dressed for dinner, dined with one friend at his party, danced at another party, visited the Admiral at Devonport and another Admiral at Stonehouse and then returned home into bed about 10 o'clock.

Some remarkable instances occurred during this year. So fast as I could get money from my profession or otherwise I expended it in furnishing, repairing and adding to my house. Being a raw student at this work I was soon taught some practical lessons. The 1st was to get a table and some chairs and a carpet for one room. I bought a mahogany table large enough for four persons to dine on for which the upholsterer asked 5 guineas, but by paying down £5 I had it as a favour. In visiting the various Upholsterer's shops I ascertained that I could get a mahogany table of the same size and form and nearly as good as the other for £2, at which I purchased it; this was one of my first lessons. The next was to provide fire irons and fenders for my two rooms with folding doors. I saw a very pretty brass fender in a shop and asked the price, which was fixed at £2 10s Being no judge of its value I inquired if that was the lowest ready money price and received for answer: 'yes.' I then enquired if he could get another of the same pattern for my two rooms opening with folding doors. His answer was he did not think another such fender would be found in the Town, so I paid for it. Some days afterwards in passing Pomeroy's shop at Stonehouse I saw a fender of exactly the same pattern but 3 inches longer, which difference exactly suited the other fireplace. 'What is the price?' '30/-.' 'Any discount for ready money?' 'No Sir, we make but one price and that is what we ask.' Money paid and fender delivered. I then sent for the other Ironmonger and asked his opinion as to the difference between the two fenders. Suspecting my reason he quickly turned up the second fender and saw the shop mark not erased and exclaimed: 'surely Sir you did not get this for 30/-?' 'I sent for you to ask and not to answer the question, tell me what difference there is between these two fenders.' 'None Sir' he replied 'they are the same pattern and quality.' 'Look again' I said 'and tell me if their length be the same.' 'Why Sir, this is 3 inches longer than mine.' 'Does the additional length add to or take from its value?' 'Sir I am quite willing to refund this over-plus which you paid to me, as I was deceived in thinking the pattern could not be matched in the Town.' 'I will not ask you to refund your overcharge, which is a downright imposition and a warning to me never more to deal with you, or any tradesman whom I suspect of trickery and dishonesty.' These two examples made me more cautious in future how I paid ready money.

I was much indebted to one of our SDM Officers, Lt John Carne, for purchasing a good dinner service still in use, also plated and silver articles which I had no time to buy for myself. He frequently dined with me and pointed out such articles as I required. When we had salt cellars we found we wanted salt spoons; a mustard pot, no spoon; gravy in our dish, no gravy spoon; fish, no slice; soup, no ladle; bread, no basket; butter, no dish etc. so that at the end of the year I still found something wanting. Mardon had furnished my kitchen utensils at a cost of £34.

In the course of this summer 1823 my good aunt was pleased to have a new carriage and horses etc in Bath, to provide herself with some splendid dresses and ornaments consisting of diamonds, pearls and jewelry etc and to attend the Gloucester Musical Festival in September and to invite me and Lt Benjamin Sadler, then the only representative living of his family, to be her pages or guards of honour. She had set her mind laudably enough on shewing the Gloucester people, who might have remembered her in her native town or at Thornbury where she conducted a country school, how fortune had at last smiled upon her and blessed her with happiness in the evening of her days.

Just before the appointed time of my leaving Plymouth for Gloucester a violent tooth seized me. A wise Tooth had sprung up and jammed itself between the angle of the lower jaw and the last molar tooth. My tooth ache obliged me to apply to a young dentist who tried to extract it but the claw of the instrument slipped and nearly pulled out the sound double tooth. In another trial he broke the wise tooth into 3 parts one of which only could be extracted. Violent inflammation set in but did not prevent me from going on to Exeter that night, where the pain increased more and more and obliged me to get out of bed at 5 o'clock a.m. and traverse Northernhay until St Peter's clock struck 6, when I rang the bell and called up Groves the dentist, who after many trials got out from the swollen gums another piece of the tooth and said: 'I hope you will never again ask me to draw one of your teeth as they are so firmly fixed.' This additional operation increased the inflammation and pain so much that at Bath I must give up the journey altogether, but being expected I made another effort to reach Gloucester where I expected nothing less than a locked jaw. A dozen leeches, fomentations, medicines, and soft gruel administered by my very attentive and kind rival as he was called, warded off fatal consequences and confined me to bed during the whole of the musical festival. My aunt was also kind to visit me often in bed and shew her beautiful dresses and ornaments which she so well graced. When I was convalescent I returned with her to Bath on a Saturday and walked to the Bath Market to get a Dory for Sunday's dinner, and there I saw laid out 40 or 50 salmon which I supposed had been caught in the River Severn until the owner informed me that they were all Devonshire salmon caught in the River Dart, and sent up by his agent Mr Cumming of Totnes. The price varied from 9d to 1/3 which I thought very cheap, especially after hearing that no salmon had been sold at Plymouth for less than 1/6 as it had been very scarce in the market.

Having spent a few days in Bath on our return from the Gloucester festival my aunt, Ben Sadler and myself left Bath for Fonthill Abbey where the sale was going on, and where we arrived on the 22nd day of September and attended the sale the next day, when we bought many articles through a broker who introduced himself to me and presented his card with his London address. He politely offered to purchase for us any article we required at 5 per cent brokerage, and said there were many of his profession at the sale who had agreed amongst themselves not to bid against each other, but to run against bidders for articles going under their value and then asking a profit from 5 to 20 percent. I had no hesitation in trusting this man with my commissions. I fancied an Ormolu clock, a repeater which he valued at £25, a sum too large for my pocket, but I should not mind £5 or £6 for it. He bought the clock for £5 and 5/- was his fee; a set of chessmen of oriental ivory, valued at 30 guineas, he bought for £9, a beautiful painted coffer box lined with satin for 5/-; these articles I still possess. There were many other things, china etc. bought for my aunt and sent to Bath, also a Chinese compass and another article for Miss Bewes of Plymouth to my care.

We paid extravagantly for our board and lodging, being thickly crowded with strangers. Having surveyed such parts of the Abbey and the Tower as were visible to the public, my aunt departed next day for Wardour Castle, Wilton and Salisbury. Sadler returned to Plymouth to go on board his ship the Harlequin. At Wardour there was not much to be seen but what was old and out of fashion, it was the property of Lord Arundel. Having arrived at Wilton we put up at a small Inn there, ordered our dinner and fed the horses. While these preparations were going forward we strolled out as far as the Lodge Gate of Wilton House and enquired of the porter if we might be permitted to inspect the House and Grounds. He answered that the family were there with many Visitors and that Strangers could not then be admitted unless personally known to the noble owner, the Earl of Pembroke. My aunt was rather disappointed on her way back to the Inn as she harboured some pleasing reminiscences of Wilton House, the Statuary and Paintings seen by her in her youthful days. We repaired to the Inn, where I wrote the following letter addressed to the Right Honourable Earl Pembroke, Wilton House: 'Dr Butter presents his respectful compliments to the Earl of Pembroke and begs his Lordship's permission for himself and friend to visit Wilton House as they have come from Fonthill and Wardour Castle with the hope of being permitted also to see Wilton House', dated from the Inn and sent to the Porter at the Lodge, requesting its immediate deliverance. The Porter soon returned and enquired for Dr Butler and being shewn to me said: 'My Lord has sent me to say he was going out for a ride with a party staying in the house and cannot conveniently stop to answer your letter, but if you are related to his particular friend Dr Butler of Harrow, he hoped you will partake of any refreshment at the House.' The Porter, looking at me, enquired if I was Dr Butler or related to his Lordship's friend. 'All right,' I said, and so we returned, gave the Porter his fee and then proceeded over Wilton House in which there is much to admire. My aunt seemed to have a good recollection of the quadrangle and walk under cover, the Statuary, the Van Dykes and other paintings, and the beautiful views of the Park from the different windows. The family being out we were admitted to see almost all the sitting rooms until we came to the Banqueting apartment, where the cloth was laid for dinner and on the sideboard there were many bottles of wine of which the butler dressed in his silk stockings etc., required us to partake by the desire of his Lordship, to whom we returned our thanks and presented a half crown to the gentleman in Silk, and so we returned to our dinner at the Inn and afterwards repaired to the Antelope at Salisbury for the night.

On the 25th we slept at Devizes and on the 26th returned to Bath from whence I hastened back to Plymouth to be present at the return day on the 1st of October. About the middle of Dec. I returned again to Queen Square, Bath by special invitation from my aunt to play an active part on one of her gay soirees composed chiefly of Whist-players, Quadrilles, Bagamon[68] and Chess, with some music and a supper but no dancing.

I returned once more to Plymouth in time for Xmas.

1824

In the year 1824 my professional income increased both at home and abroad. I had many patients at Teignmouth and intermediate places which I visited on horseback. One evening I was called upon to visit Sir Edward Buller of Trenant House just in time to cross the Tamar on the floating bridge with Mr Cole the Steward then living in Durnford St., Stonehouse. On arriving at Torpoint a question arose how we were to get forward to Looe as there was no carriage to be had. A servant had rode up a favourite Lady's horse, Miss Buller's palfrey before she became Mrs Elphinstone. Mr Cole hired a hack and gave up the servant's horse to me. From Torpoint to Looe there are two roads, one for carriages and a shorter one, a bridle path over the cliffs. I had only to follow my guide but I often found myself unpleasantly near the edge

[68] Backgammon.

of the cliffs as I guessed from the roaring of the sea. Moreover my famous animal as I supposed continually tripped and inclined to stumble especially when we came down across the Looe River in the darkness of night. We arrived at Trenant House about midnight, and on alighting the groom asked me how the mare had carried me: 'Why' I said 'she kept tripping and stumbling in a way which I should not have suspected from so fine an animal.' 'Oh!' he replied 'she has always done so since her blindness.' 'Blindness' said I 'have I rode a blind horse from Torpoint to this place?' 'Yes sir.' 'Then I thank God she did not go over the cliffs with me, or tumble down as she was several times inclined to do.' I remained at Trenant during the night, left Sir Edward in a dangerous state on the following morning under the care of Mr Rogers, Surgeon at Looe, and returned to Plymouth in safety.

So fast as I could get money I laid it out in articles of furniture, household expenses and the keep of the horses. I ordered a slab to be made of Devonshire marbles and other stones arranged in the form of a chess and backgammon table; the squares of course were made of Italian white marble for chess and long triangular pieces of Sienna marble interspersed with dark marble for backgammon. I also inserted a square of verdantique[69] picked up in the streets of Rome, polished panale[?] and specimens of calculi[+] which I had extracted from the bladder of my patients; all the other specimens were Devonshire marbles forming a table mounted on castors with 2 drawers, cost me £21. The following motto was ingrained on stone: 'Turpe est in patria vivere et patrionum ignorare' which being translated means 'it is shameful to live in a country and to be ignorant of the products of that country.'

Some of my chimneys smoked which the mason advised me to raise 3 feet, which being done my neighbour, Mrs Gasking, widow of the late Dr then complained that I had caused her chimneys to smoke, and so she had her chimneys raised above mine and thus we ran a race. These chimneys had attained a formidable height and apparent danger to the public during the violent storm which raged on the 23rd and 24th of November when twenty-six vessels were wrecked along our coast, and when I feared both the windows of my house would be blown in as well as my chimneys down. Neither of these fears however were realized of this unprecedented storm so often described and represented in drawings. Never supposing that I should live forty-one years longer to witness a second edition of a similar storm on the 24th November 1865.

Another table I had made of a variety of woods, of which 40 or 50 different specimens were given to me by Mr Couch, timber master in the Dockyard. The design formed was to represent the four feet of a zebra, carrying on his back a pedestal of oak supporting a circular table 3ft in diameter, the chess board of wood, alternately of white and black, and drawers for cards, curiosities, objects of vertue etc.

1825

During this year I had many long and fatiguing rides in Devon and Cornwall in keeping up my increasing practice. Two colts bred by my father and sent down to me on the preceding year I had now got to good saleable condition and sold one for 70 guineas and the other for 100 sovereigns. The latter a black mare was much admired

---

[69] A decorative facing stone.

for her strength, good temper and docility, in proof of which at a Plymouth regatta I rode her by the side of one carriage and conveyed a glass full of wine across the course from one Lady to another without spilling any.

My servants consisted only of two persons, a man and his wife at a salary of £20 a year besides board and lodging, gratuities, etc. Sergeant Jones SDM was one of the most upright and conscientious men I had ever met with, and I believe as honest as the Sun. He had never been accustomed much to horses before he came into my service but since his time I have never succeeded in getting my horses into equal condition. All my furniture was new and the mahogany chairs and tables made of the best Spanish wood which was saturated with cold drawn linseed oil over night and rubbed off early in the morning. Sometimes as early as 4 o'clock he would rise and polish the furniture and then take out the horses for an airing till 6. His wife was not so highly principled but quick and active and particularly clever at giving answers and messages at the door. She could roast a leg of mutton or a fowl but was not a professed cook. My bachelor's dinners I obtained from the Hotel from whence Mrs Whiddon sent them in good style. Ladies used to ask me sometimes, whose husband had dined with me, to give receipts for puddings, entremets[70] and made dishes with a remark that I must have an excellent cook.

During this year a number of provincial banks failed, by two of which I lost money. Soon after the hurricane I dined at Saltram with Lord Saumerez* and Captn Pipon* his Flag Captain, where a discussion rose by damages done not only to the shipping and to houses, but to the breakwater and to the embankment at Laira constructed by the Earl of Morley* and enclosing 70 acres of marsh land, for which his Lordship obtained a gold medal.

During this year I published an octavo volume on Irritative fever, or Dockyard disease, printed at Devonport and sent to Messrs Underwood in London for sale.[71] The journals and reviews favourably noticed my book but the subsequent failure of the booksellers entailed me a loss of 200 copies, exceeding £60, so I gained no profit and very little fame by my book which had taken so much time and money to get sufficient evidence for publication.

On August the 3rd I returned from a tour in Wales where I had gone with my aunt so far as Tenbeigh and Pembroke Dockyard, from which we saw the launch of a ship and then visited Lord Cawder's beautiful domain of Stackpole Court which is worth a journey into Wales to see. We went from Bath to Gloucester, Ross, Monmouth, Abergavenny, Brecon, and returned by way of Newport, Swansea and Neath, and visited Tintern Abbey, and Wyncliffe, descending 365 steps backwards, zig-zag course, holding my aunt's hand, into the beautiful prairie below on the banks of the Wye. Here I saw for the 1st time a grass turner, a sort of roller with spikes in it drawn by one horse and shafts adapted for scattering abroad swathes of grass for turning hay. 30 years had elapsed from this time before another such implement was seen by me in Devonshire, so slow is the adoption of machinery.

---

[70] A sweet offering traditionally served up at banquets as a treat between savoury courses.
[71] *Remarks on Irritative Fever, Commonly Called the Plymouth Dock-Yard Disease; With Mr. Dryden's Detailed Account of the Fatal Cases, Including that of the Lamented Surgeon, Dr. Bell* (London: Underwoods; Edinburgh: Black; Dublin: MacArthur, 1825). There is a very long review of Butter's book in *The Lancet* (1825), pp. 283–94, which reproduces much of his material and praises it as likely to become the standard work on irritative fever.

1826

This year was the most important and successful of my life. I had now laboured for nearly 16 years in the practice of my profession and had not settled myself in life with a partner. The lady whose breast I removed in 1821 had befriended me from that time to the present and had interceded in bringing about an engagement between Miss Veale and myself and effectually promoting our marriage. My good and excellent aunt had died on the 31st day of Jan. of this year and buried on the 8th Feb. at Bath where I remained a week.

She bequeathed to me a sum of money and on Lady's Day I went to London, called and dined with Sir Francis Ommanney who accompanied me to Sherwood's[72] office in the borough and saw me receive £8,900 after the payment of £1,000 legacy duty, which sum I brought away in my pocket through the streets of London and opened an account at Child's Bank,[73] accompanied by Francis Ommanney to whom I felt much obliged. I have now therefore banked with Child's for 40 years without a mistake.

On the 30th of May 1826 I married Elizabeth White Veale at the parish church of Ugborough Devon, and left on a tour for London, having posted to Torquay for the first night, thence to Exeter for another night and on the succeeding day so far as Bridport, where we took the Mail for Salisbury and there remained 2 or 3 days with Doctors and attorneys, feeling heartily glad to get rid of Post Chaises, Post Boys, Taverns and Turnpikes which kept my hands constantly in my pocket. In London we occupied Mrs Leuchard's lodgings in Piccadilly and remained so long as time and circumstances permitted, with a view of seeing the sights of London until we were tired and glad to retreat into the country as the temperature of London became very hot.

We saw Oxford on our way to Cheltenham where we arrived on the 26th of June. The Plough Hotel was so full as to prevent us getting apartments therein, we therefore got accommodation the opposite side of the street. The weather at this time was sultry and hot and the nights very oppressive. Soon after midnight in the silent stillness of early morning of the 27th we suddenly heard a door open opposite our own and a person with a quick step going along the passage, opening another door and throwing up a window suddenly, then exclaiming 'Police, Police, a Surgeon send for a Surgeon.' I jumped out of bed quickly and putting on a dressing gown went into the passage and then into a room where I saw two ladies standing up by the bedside of an old gentleman lying down and snoring heavily. I said: 'what is the matter, Ladies?' They replied: 'we want a doctor or a surgeon, Sir, would you have the kindness to go for one, do Sir go.' I answered: 'I am one.' 'Are you Sir?' 'Yes.' 'What shall we do for our father, we cannot rouse him, he snores and sleeps so heavily.' Feeling his pulse strong, full, bounding: 'your father has a fit of apoplexy.[+] I must bleed him, give me something to tie up his arm, a piece of tape, ribbon or a garter.' 'Sir, we cannot consent to that, he must not be blooded. All his physicians have opposed bleeding.' 'I tell you again he must be blooded or he will soon be a dead man.' 'Oh, Sir, we cannot consent unless a doctor be called in.' 'I tell you again, I am one.' 'But we don't know you Sir.' 'I dare say not, but you may see that I am not trifling but serious, and

---

[72] His aunt's solicitor.
[73] A private bank, the oldest in the United Kingdom and third oldest in the world. It was founded in 1665 and is now part of the Royal Bank of Scotland.

if you wish to save your father give me a bandage to tie up his arm.' Murmuring and hesitating, they reluctantly consenting, I drew off about a quart of dark blood from his arm into a wash hand basin and caught a little in a glass to see whether it was inflamed, buffed and cupped. When this was done, he opened his eyes, looked around and enquired what was the matter to the great joy of his affrighted daughters: 'There now' I said 'I told you so, and you see that I was right.' By this time the hue and cry had been sent abroad and a surgeon procured by the name of Averile. On hearing particulars he said to the ladies: 'this gentleman has saved your father's life.' Mr Runell was the patient's name, a rich merchant of Bristol, big and burly and full of blood, his veins ventricles of the heart. The sinus of the brain seemed to have been all gorged with blood and distended so much as to cause heavy pressure on the brain and produce temporary insensibility. His recollection and speech having returned, and the ladies recovered their composure from their alarm, I retired by saying that they would find me if I was required on the opposite side of the passage. Nothing further occurred until breakfast time when we all became acquainted with each other's history. Mr Runell had been pampered and fed and nourished with good things by desire of his doctors in Bristol, Bath and Cheltenham, who sent him about to drink the waters and cautioned him never to be blooded. The manifest benefit derived from blood-letting gained the confidence of the whole party, and both the patient and his daughters would have rewarded me with a handsome fee which I declined to accept, and therefore presents were made to my bride, whose position by this time had been revealed. For some time after our return to Plymouth a correspondence was kept up expressive of the great confidence they had acquired in my advice in so promptly relieving their father from impending danger.

From Gloucester we went to Berkley Castle and saw the room in which Edward the 2nd was murdered, and whilst strolling about the grounds met Mr Henry Woollcombe, one of our Plymouth Aldermen, a most excellent man who, being out of health, was returning from Cheltenham. Berkley was the birthplace and residence of the celebrated Dr Jenner, whose practice lay amongst the dairy farmers of that agricultural district from whom of their dairy-maids he had learnt that such persons who suffered from the cow-pox were never attacked with small-pox. Jenner has been rewarded as he deserved by the British and Continental Nations for his discovery. In going to Thornbury afterwards, where my aunt had conducted the school before her removal to Bath, we dined and slept at the house of Mr Newster the Surgeon, son of Mr Newster who had been my aunt's principal adviser and friend and who was, as she believed, and as Mr Newster asserted, the first person medical who discovered and reported to Dr Jenner the fact that such persons as had taken the cow-pox were never known to have small-pox afterwards.[74]

On the 28th of July my wife and I took leave of Mr Runell and his daughters and left Cheltenham for Gloucester where we inspected the cathedral and public buildings. At the Guildhall I was reminded of a former visit there with my aunt to inspect some beautiful paintings which she had remembered in her youth and desired again to see. At the Guildhall door we saw an elderly man standing like

---

[74] John Fewster (not Newster) did discover vaccination before Jenner (who quite possibly heard about it from him), but he did not realise its true significance: L. Thurston and G. Williams, 'An Examination of John Fewster's Role in the Discovery of Smallpox Vaccination', *Journal of the Royal College of Physicians of Edinburgh* 45, no. 2 (2015), pp. 173–9.

a Mace bearer; we asked him if we could see the Guildhall. 'Certainly' he said 'I shall be glad to show it to you.' We followed him up the stairs through the different rooms, listened to his descriptions and thanked him for his civility and attention, and when about to take our leave and present him with a half-crown I observed people passing and touching their hats respectfully to our guide, whom I thought could not be a Common Officer of the Corporation. Stepping aside to speak to a person who seemed to know our Guide I asked who he was and to my surprise found that he was no less a person than James Wood* the Banker, the richest man in Gloucester, and perhaps the humblest, for he would often stand behind his own counter and receive pence from his customers with an expression of thanks and a humble bow. We left the Guildhall and the Half-crown I returned to my pocket. I mentioned this circumstance afterwards to a person who knew Mr Wood well and who said: 'I wish you had offered the half-crown for he would certainly have taken it and I would have teased him for his penury as I have often done.'

Leaving Gloucester on the 30th of June we returned to Exeter. On the 1st of July we visited my parents and family at Woodbury where the bells rang merry peals for us, as the Parish bells of Ugborough and Brent had done on the day of our marriage, and as the bells of St Andrews and Charles were rung on the 11th of July when we returned to Plymouth, thus making in all 5 sets of parish bells at a cost of 10 guineas to celebrate our marriage. After a cordial reception at Woodbury we left for Ugborough and remained there for a short time to visit our friends preparatory to our final return home, which we reached on the 11th of July.

My house and furniture and wedding had taken away all my loose cash and left a feeling of satisfaction that I had accomplished these three great objects of life and remained free of debt. Great was the gratification at welcoming the numerous friends who called on us and made parties for us. The Bridesmaid Miss Laura Bartlett rendered Mrs Butter great service on this occasion. Previously to my marriage I had purchased two very fine young mares, 6 and 7 years old, and had them well broken during my absence so that we were enabled to return the visits of our country friends on horseback, sometimes riding 20 miles a day.

On the 28th of August our good friend Mrs Bartlett died.

On the 13th of September I was sent for by Mr Bayntun to visit a dumb man, a great wrestler labouring under strangulated hernia+ requiring an operation in which I assisted. Whilst riding on the road rather fast I was hailed by a gentleman and lady in a post-chaise whom I found to my very great surprise to be Mr and Mrs Abernethy* of London, posting to Plymouth in order to visit his brother, living about 5 miles off, on the following day. I was surprised at seeing Mr Abernethy and said 'I should as soon of thought of seeing the King of England as the King of Surgery.' 'Why' he said 'I wanted to see my brother who is much better, I understand, for your advice and treatment. I will call and see you tomorrow.' I returned late from the operation. On the following morning before I was up, whilst the servant was cleaning the front door, Mr Abernethy came, asked if I was up and received for answer that I might be gone out to visit a patient. 'Now' he said 'don't tell me a lie, you know your master is not out of bed. Take up this card to him and say that I will call again tomorrow.' The card being brought up to me with a message the servant said: 'there has been such an odd man Sir, enquiring for you, he called himself John Abernethy, here is his card. Did ever you hear of such a man Sir? He said that I told him a lie and looked so odd at me, I have never seen his like before. Must I admit him if he calls again?' 'Most certainly' I said. On the following morning about breakfast time Mr Abernethy called and left Mrs A at the hotel. Whilst walking about the room with a serious look he thus began: 'I visited my brother yesterday at Doctor Ware's and met him walking in the garden and before I was near enough to speak to him he stopped, paused and looked steadfastly at me but before we were near enough to exchange words he staggered and fell to the ground with muscular agitations and twitching of the face and eyes. "Apoplexy[+]" I said. Ware replied: "bleed him. Sir, bleed him, let us take off his coat and bleed him." I answered "it will be of no use." Ware said: "if you will not bleed him I will bleed him myself, Sir." I then blooded him from the arm so long as blood would flow and then we carried him a corpse into the house. The shock was almost too great for me to bear, I myself became violently sick, unnerved and weak enough to weep over my deceased brother. I have not yet recovered the shock which was so awful and unexpected and disappointing of the object and pleasure of my journey.'

Mrs Butter was charmed with Mrs Abernethy, she was one of the most delightful women I ever saw and a most devoted wife to her exemplary husband. Mr Abernethy's brother had suffered for years from chronic ophthalmy[+] and Ectropion[+] which I had almost cured by operation etc. Sudden death I had known to occur previously in two men afflicted with chronic inflammation in their eyes which I had learnt to regard as ominous and indicative of fullness in the vessels of the brain.

On the 28th of Sept I attended the annual meeting of the Exeter Grammar School conducted by the Rev. Dr Collins, who had appointed me, Thos Snow and two others Stewards for the year. To my surprise I was elected Chairman at the dinner at which I endeavoured to make the best speech I could do impromptu without study, and received congratulations from the Headmaster and company.

On the 13th of April I had again gone to Bath for the purpose of escorting down a young female friend who had gone thither from Devonshire to try the waters and Physicians for the recovery of her health and the use of lower extremities which had been semi-paralyzed owing to the affection of the lumber and spinal nerves. As she gained no benefit at Bath, her friends desired to get her home safely and therefore requested my services, which were required for putting her into and taking her out of the carriage. We posted with four horses from Bath to Exeter where we halted for one night and reached Plymouth on the 16th of April. Suffice it to say that this lady has perfectly regained the use of her limbs and lives to the present day, the only survivor of a numerous family of whom she was thought 40 years ago to be the most delicate member.

1827[75]

After the failure of the Banks in 1825[76] many sales took place of Bankrupts' effects in 1826 and 1827 and gave me an opportunity of purchasing such articles of plate, pictures, wine etc. required for my household establishment. At a sale of Shield's and John's lands at Mutley in the preceding Aug. I was induced to bid for a

[75] This was the year in which Butter had a lengthy letter on the subject of erysipelas, a skin disease, published in *The Lancet* 9, no. 224, pp. 444–6.

[76] A fraud involving stock market investments in a fictitious South American country called Poyias led to the collapse of a large number of English banks.

field called Ford Park and unexpectedly bought it at a price of £1,180 besides the conveyance of £40, which made the sum of £1,220 paid for at Michaelmas 1827. This payment obliged me to disturb my investment in the Funds which now began to rise in value. The purchase was thought rather dear at the time, but I speculated in order to recover the £100 lost by the failure of the Bank and as I have since sold the land for building purposes I have no cause to repent this purchase. My professional income had increased during this year. I planted above 20,000 larch and fir trees in the preceding Nov. and paid for this work in the preceding year. Agricultural operations now came in for a portion of my time and attention and afforded me health as well as occupation.

1828

Little mare died of locked jaw.

1829

24th June Militia Staff disbanded, pay reduced 1s per diem.

1830

Bought Hosking's Broom Parks & Map & Lawyers	£450
Bought 500 Consols at 92 3/8th	£462 10s
Purchased Corringdon for	£5,000
Lawyers Tozer & Tucker	£98
Houlston Builders	£248 3s 0d
Juno died at 17 years.	

Piles operations Moore & Roberts £21 – Suffered much from abscesses etc.

1831

Received of Norrington for House at Mutley	£200
Sir R Lopes	£22 10s
Rendle 22,000 Trees	£17 6s
Lucian Bonaparte's Sevres china[77], 440 pieces J.L.B.	£25 1s 3d
Consols 3 pr cent 600 @ 82	£498 6s 6d

1832

Powley for Owley cottages	£25 7s
Carriage to Bulston Aug.	£29 1s 1d
Reduced boys hips 14th Nov.	

[77] Lucien Bonaparte was Napoleon's brother, and in 1800, during a short period as Minister of the Interior, he appointed Alexandre Brogniart to save the Sèvres Porcelain Manufactory, which was then failing. Brogniart succeeded admirably, but exactly what pieces of Sèvres china belonged to Lucien, and how they came to be sold to Butter, is not known.

As the year 1826 had been the happiest and most prosperous of my life, so the present 1832 proved to be the most disastrous and nearly fatal of my life. I had not quite recovered the warnings of 1830 when my complaints brought on by riding long journies and much sitting troubled me much and rendered rest in a horizontal position necessary by day, sometimes as well as by night. Sore throats or cynanche tonsillaris had frequently attacked my throat from boyhood and led the way to feverish attacks and rheumatic pains in the limbs. On the 21st of June the first instance of cholera was reported to me by Mr Baldy, Surgeon of Plymouth, who generally conferred about any rare or extraordinary case under his treatment. This case was observed at Coxside on the eastern part of Plymouth near the water's edge and being compared with the description given and the figure drawn in the Lancet confirmed my belief that it was a case of Cholera such as neither of us had before seen. The 2nd case occurred at Millbay on the western side of Plymouth, also near the water's edge, in a Marine and his wife who both died. The 3rd case heard of was on the northern bank of the Plymouth Leat at the foot of New Town. On this bank I saw 9 patients dead or dying one morning before breakfast, after which my health broke down. My disease began with soreness of the throat, fever, and rheumatic pains in my back and limbs with swelling of the joints so that I could scarcely turn in bed or help myself in any way. The symptoms for two or three days were exhibited in the heels and carves of the legs in a manner to prevent my walking or standing on first getting up. My neighbour Dr Cookworthy kindly visited me and advised a mixture composed of colchicum,$^{+}$ magnesia and hartshorn in camphor julep. 5 doses brought on nausea, vomiting and purging so that from that time I loathed all food and relished nothing which I swallowed. So weak and ill had I become and so loathsome was the contaminated air of Plymouth as to convince me that I should not long live here, and therefore hired a carriage on the 29th of August and drove to a farm-house near the Moor at South Brent. I had not eaten flesh for some time but on the 2nd day after my arrival there I was enabled to partake moderately of a roasted leg of mutton and from that time my health began to return, so that with moderate exercise on horseback and a little shooting I got better and better until the 12th of October when I again returned to Plymouth, but there I found myself unequal to the laborious task of a medical man and so I returned from time to time to the farm-house according to my feelings, and from that time to the present I have made annual excursions to and from Plymouth and Brent, with the feeling that health was always preferable to wealth.

On the 14th of November 1832 Mr Phillips the district surgeon of Brent called on me at the farm-house and said that as he knew I had had much experience of hip diseases he very much wished me to see a farmer's apprentice with a dislocated hip about 2 miles off, which he and Dr [blank] of Totnes had twice endeavoured to reduce ineffectually with the aid of pulleys. I was weak and frail at the time and disinclined to encounter the dreary weather, but on reaching the house I was ushered into the boy's bedroom where he set up such a yelling and crying and abuse as quite startled me. Looking at his distorted position in the hollow of a bed sacking I saw in a moment the dislocation of the boy's right hip with limb inverted, shortened and the head of the femur on the dorsum of the ilium.$^{+}$ I said to Phillips: 'I see that limb is dislocated.' 'Do you think so?' he enquired. 'We have not tried anything for that. The dislocation on the left side we have directed our efforts to reduce ineffectually.' 'We must have the boy out of this pit and put him on a mattress' which, being procured and the boy placed on it swearing and crying all the time, it was then quite apparent that both hips were dislocated, the left downwards and inwards and the right upwards and outwards. 'Now,' I said, 'we must have a couple of running towels such are seen behind kitchen doors often on a roller.' These being procured one was fixed on the pelvis and held by two men behind the boy's head, the other I fixed on the right ankle and gave to the surgeon and the farmer so that the four pulled against each other and when the head of the bone was judged near the edge of the socket I took hold of the ankle and turned the foot outwards and instantly the head of the bone was heard to slam in the socket. Great joy beamed on all countenances and the poor little sufferer exclaimed 'Oh God bless Dr Butter, he shall do anything to me that he asks, there was no pain.' The towel being shifted from the right to the left leg, extension was made in a similar manner and the head of that bone drawn to the edge of the socket where the surgeon said it had been frequently drawn before, but they could not get it into its place. 'Now get it in' I said, and then took hold of the boy's ankle, inverted the foot and returned the bone into its socket with an audible sound, both hips reduced within the hour. I never saw greater joy depicted on the countenance of the attendants nor more speedy relief afforded to the little patient whose cries and yells had been converted into ease and comfort. 30 years after this event this patient was working on the rail road near my farm and came to show me how perfect his limbs were and how glad he would be to assist in the operation of haymaking or any work in which his services could be useful. He never would or perhaps could say how the accident occurred, he had been sent somewhere with a cart and two horses which returned home without the boy, who was found afterwards lying in the road helpless and unable to stand; a probability was that he had been riding on the shaft of the cart and dragged in some way so as to occasion this double dislocation. His name was [blank] Rowlands.

The Plymouth Eye Infirmary, established on the 6th of Dec. 1821, had now began after 11 years existence to decline in the number of patients from 715 in the 1st year to 30 in the present[78] owing to the illness and absence of myself, to the death of Mr J Luscombe the 2nd surgeon, and to the busy occupation on cholera patients of Dr E Moore, so that the attention and treatment of the patients generally fell on the Dispenser, John Elliott, Sergeant-Major of the South Devon Militia, who shewed much tact and good management in the absence of the Medical Officers.

On the 16th of Nov. we returned to Plymouth and on the 21st I experienced a smart attack of fever preceded by shiverings, sore throat and pains in the limbs, which induced me to be blooded from the arm and to apply 16 leeches to the throat. Rheumatic Gout then developed itself forcibly with pain and swellings of the hands, heels, knees, back etc. Whilst thus laid up in bed the funeral of my colleague took place at Yealmpton on the 22nd day of November, and left a gloomy impression in my mind that I should soon follow his fate. I was confined to bed more or less the remainder of this year but was much consoled by the visits and good wishes and presents of numerous friends. Until then I had never tasted pheasant soup, which I thought excellent and relished beyond anything else.

The Reform bill was carried in this year by Lords Grey and Russell and proved means of returning three of my friends for Cornwall, and some for Devon. My friend

---

[78] The annual report for 1832 is missing, but the total number of cases reported in the first three quarters amounts to exactly 750. Perhaps the fourth quarter was particularly bad and clouded Butter's memory.

Leach contested Devonport unsuccessfully against Admiral Sir Edward Codrington who had fought the battle of Navarino in 1827 aided by the Russian fleet and destroyed the Turkish ships of War.

[There follows a rambling and not entirely comprehensible discourse on the events leading to the Crimean War, which has been omitted].

Three remarkable cases of recovery from pulmonary[+] disease occurred during this year. One was that of my own brother, who was a medical practitioner at Limpstone where the cholera had broken out and obliged his patients to call him up for 16 successive nights and thus to bring on an attack on his lungs, probably of a gouty kind, as an abscess had formed and occasioned a terrific cough with night sweats and hectic fever so that his life was despaired of. His father had seen a great number of consumptive patients in his practice and said: 'I consider Jacobus labouring under an incurable consumption.' 'Then' I replied 'I will take him to Plymouth and shut him up in two rooms for the winter.' I ordered a closed carriage from the New London Inn, Exeter and posted with it all the way to Plymouth having relays of horses at Chudleigh, Ashburton and Ivybridge. The motto on the carriage was remarkable 'Dum Spiro Spero'.[79] After two months confinement from breathing cold air all his symptoms abated favourably and he became convalescent, but being tired of confinement he broke loose one fine day and without permission went into the stable and saw my two horses in fine condition and ordered a saddle and bridle to be put on Mazeppa and rode off without my knowledge. On his return I was surprised to learn that as the day was fine and the horse pleasant to ride he had actually gone to Tavistock and back, a total distance of 20 miles. I was perfectly surprised at this outbreak and wonderful performance and was inclined to censure him for rashness and disobedience of orders, but he joyously laughed off my censure and said that the ride had quite renovated him. From this time forth he lived to May 1846 when he died of diseased liver and dropsy[+] for which he had been tapped 3 or 4 times. His body was inspected by Dr Price, who succeeded to his practice at Limpstone, and by Dr Brent of Woodbury. Thus his life had been preserved for 13 years after the time when his death was considered inevitable.

The 2nd case was of a similar kind, occurred in the late Mr T King Esq. of the Manor House, North Huish. When I was first consulted about him Mr Gest the Surgeon had pronounced his disease to be in the heart, called angina pectoris,[+] but I said: 'this is gout floating about the system and disturbing the action and pulsations of the heart.' Some time after his convalescence Mr King exposed himself at a Cattle Sale to severe cold which brought on shivering, fever and cough for which he was treated in the usual way, but at last symptoms of great alarm arose, and whilst in a fit of coughing something burst in his lungs and a quantity of purulent[+] matter was expectorated over the bed and clothes so suddenly that it could not be caught, and was so offensive that no person but Mrs King could possibly bear it. I was sent for in haste and told by Mr Gest and the ladies that I should not be able to bear the smell of his expectoration, but of course I distrusted such an idea supposing that nothing of the kind could be too bad for a medical man to bear. Whilst feeling his pulse however such an effluxion arose from his breath and expectoration as almost

[79] 'While I breathe I hope.'

to stagger me and to make me sick if I had not quickly gone into the open air. I was never too much upset before by anything of the kind. At first death seemed inevitable but as his stamina appeared to be good his removal from the country to Plymouth was decided on and whilst changing horses at Ivybridge the landlady condemned the doctor for getting down his patient to Plymouth to die. Mr King however made favourable progress at Plymouth and after some weeks residence returned convalescent to Huish where he lived till 1843, when he died from that form of typhoid which frequently attacks gouty patients advanced in years.

Mrs Abernethie, wife of the Col. Commandant of the Marines, had been a patient of mine for entropium or inversion of the eye-lashes of which complaint I cured her by an excision of a large portion of loose skin under each eye lid. The Col. also had been a patient of mine for an accident to his leg by his charger slipping up with him during his command of the regiment on a field day. The tibia was not fractured but considerably injured so that many inches of the surface exfoliated. During this process my opinion was solicited in addition to that of Dr Kein the venerable and respected surgeon of that Corps. During the year [blank] Mrs Abernethie had an attack in her lungs followed by cough and much expectoration for which she was sent into the country, but as she grew worse and worse there I was hastily desired to go out in her carriage and bring her back to the Barracks as death seemed inevitable. On our way back we halted occasionally to administer some wine to prevent her sinking and when in her house I reasoned thus, here is a thin little woman with a rapid circulation of blood which meets with obstruction in its circulation through the lungs, her pulse is strong, quick and bounding and the superficial veins distended with blood. I conferred with the Assistant Surgeon of the Corps in the absence of the Doctor and suggested the propriety of taking away 4 or 5 ounces of blood from the arm, this was found to be highly inflamed both cupped and buffed. It afforded much relief to our patient so on the second day blood-letting was repeated with further relief and after a few days a third bleeding was still more efficacious in abating the cough and expectoration and rendering the respiration more freely. Suffice it to say that this charming lady survived this formidable attack and afterwards removed to Exeter with the Colonel on his retiring from the Service. I have used the word charming for my good old lady patient because she had survived her three husbands, an English, Irish and Scotch and died at last a widow in the 74th year of her age.

After these three recoveries I have entertained hopes of other patients supposed to be dying of incurable maladies.

Thus ended one of the most trying and nearly fatal years of my life.

1833

During this year I was presented with a silver snuff box with the other medical men by the Mayor of Plymouth G Coryndon Esq. for our services during the cholera which raged here with greater violence than elsewhere according to the bills of mortality except for Bilston in Staffordshire, where the fatality exceeded that of Plymouth.

Mr Kerswile Jun., son of a much respected surgeon at Devonport, came to me with his father to have a piece of copper cap removed from the cornea[+] of his eye where it had been lodged by the snapping of a cap previously to going out shooting. Before I could get ready an instrument to remove it, it had worked its way into the antechamber of the eye, which had been rendered flaccid by the escape of the aqueous humour and had rendered the extraction through a section of the cornea tedious and difficult. The sight of his eye however is still preserved after 33 years lapse of time. I published his case in the Edinburgh Medical and Surgical Journal no. [blank][80] from which it has been copied by Dr Mackenzie of Glasgow in his excellent work on diseases of the eye.[81] I also removed the eye-ball of Mr Hutchinson, steward to Mr Pendarves, MP for Cornwall and purser of a mine. A shot had lodged in the optic nerve of his left eye for 6 ½ years, deprived him of vision in the left eye and produced incipient Amaurosis[+] in his right confusing his vision and depriving him almost of his occupation; this case was likewise published in the same journal.[82] This patient was also recovered and retained his sight in his right eye.

Let the Covingdon Estate to Thos Smerdon for £100 a year retaining possession of the plantations, woods, etc.

My father and Jas Ashford visited me in June and returned much pleased with their journey. The Duchess of Kent and Queen Victoria at Plymouth presented Colours to the 89th Regiment. Sir George Magrath* fractured his leg on the 1st of Nov. in walking through Union St hastily and slipping his foot on a kerb stone rendered greasy as stones often are.

Slept at Owley 1st time.

1834

Mr Bacot, Secretary to the Apothecary's Company in London, had prosecuted a Mr Sargent, a medical practitioner at Callington for attending patients without a licence from the Apothecary's Hall in London and obtained a verdict against him at the Cornish Assizes in March 1834. On his return homewards through Plymouth to Ivybridge he there hired a Post Chaise and pair of horses which were rather flighty, and on passing through the populous town of Buckfastleigh to a hill where horses generally walked, the driver descended to whip off some boys behind the carriage. The horses, hearing the whip, dashed off with a furious pace so that the driver could not regain the reins to stop them. Finding themselves unrestrained at the top of the hill they galloped down the descent, passed over Dart Bridge, through the Turnpike gateway and on the turnpike road for two miles until they came within one mile of Ashburton, where it was supposed that the horses were winded so that the carriage went in a zigzag manner which led Mr Bacot and the little boy with him to look out of the windows to see if the expected driver was following near them. Whilst in this attitude the horses swerved the carriage from the middle of the road towards the hedge-ditch where a solitary oak tree pollard inclined outwards, and this not being perceived Mr Bacot's head was caught between the edge of the carriage window and projecting tree, and thus was the skull smashed like an egg, the right parietal[+] bone was carried up and the brain ousing out. He fell back senseless into the corner of the carriage but the little boy could get no answer from him. The horses on arriving at

---

[80] If he did, it is not indexed anywhere, and a subject search has produced no trace of it. It is possible that it was published as a snippet and that the accreditation has not been recorded, or that Butter's memory misled him and it was published in a different journal.

[81] William Mackenzie, *A Practical Treatise on the Diseases of the Eye* (London: Longmans, 1833).

[82] As for footnote 79 above.

the Golden Lion Inn, Ashburton, stopped of their own accord according to custom, and when the people of the Inn came out they were surprised to find no driver but a little boy crying within the carriage and a Gentleman seated in the corner bleeding from the head with his hat off. Startled at this circumstance the Gentleman was removed in an insensible state, placed on a bed and a surgeon sent for, who prudently called in other Surgeons, viz. Messrs Mogridge, Gervis, Hele and Soper, Surgeons of the town, and in their deliberations sent for me at midnight. The poor man seemed to be conscious, kept his eyes open, looked at the people in the room but spoke not, neither could he answer any questions put to him, although he apparently noticed us. The right parietal bone was ripped off its sutures and the dura mater[+] left bare with a rip in it through which some brain protruded. No pressure seemed to exist on the brain as in cases of compression. Violent concussion had no doubt stunned the sense of hearing and power of speech, but the eyes seemed to be free and his breathing was not laborious. He died after 30 hours, on the 3rd of April, from the accident.

Mrs Bray, the Authoress of various publications, Warlegh or the fatal Oak, Trelawn[83] and others, consulted me about her eyes which had been seriously overworked in reading, writing and mental exertions which had much disturbed the functions of the retina and laid the foundation for future Amaourosis.[+] Rest, however, and cessation from literary labours alleviated these foreboding symptoms.

In March I removed the breast of Mrs B at Torpoint and succeeded very satisfactorily in the presence of her son and of other medical men. She was much relieved for a time both mentally and bodily but ultimately died of that peculiar form of dyspnoea or difficult respiration which frequently occurs sooner or later after such an operation, and therefore Celsus wrote that these tumours should be left to themselves. Her son Mr B was himself a very clever surgeon but breathed only by his right lung; he was himself sure of this fact and desired me to be sure of opening his body after death. One day he was sent for in much haste to visit a neighbouring patient and after walking up a hill quickly and reaching the stile of a footpath a sudden gush of blood took place from his mouth and he died on the spot. On opening his body we found his prognosis perfectly correct, his left lung was consolidated into a solid mass resembling liver or boiled lights, the air cells were destroyed and the venica[?] had burst into the wind pipe.

Mr Lanyon's letter from Camborne led me to visit my patient Mr Hutchinson, whose left eye I had extirpated and whose sight in the right eye had not been regained sufficiently without creating some uneasiness. I therefore visited him at his residence near Camborne, Cornwall. During my absence on the 8th of May my wife had stepped on a chair to open a window and entangled her foot in her dress, pitched on her right leg and broke both bones, tibia and fibula, about 6 inches above the ankle. On my return from Cornwall to Torpoint and New Passage I met my man with horses and learnt from him this sad accident. After the usual inflammation had subsided and the fractured bones adjusted by bandages, union was speedily effected and her recovery in the use of her limbs unusually quick, so that she was able to walk nearly as soon as Sir George Magrath* could do after confinement to his bed from the preceding November without his bones uniting. In his case reunion of the fractured bone was retarded by his very abstemious habits and low diet which

[83] Anna Eliza Bray (1790–1883), the wife of the Vicar of Tavistock, was a prolific author. The full title of *Trelawn* is *Trelawny of Trelawne*.

prevented a sufficient quantity of bony matter being deposited at the seat of fracture, whereas Mrs Butter was allowed full diet after the first week. My brother officers Mr J H Fuge and Dr E Moore, whom I found in attendance after my return, deserve our gratitude and thanks for their skill and kind attentions.

1835

Jan. Mrs Luscombe of Coombe Royal near Kingsbridge I visited on the 2nd of Jan. in consultation with the late Mr Elliot, surgeon there for many years. She had an encisted tumour at the back of her neck into which a puncture had been made and some fluid discharged, followed by Exsipelaus+ which overran the head and face and produced fever with delirium. I split the tumour into two halves to remove tension and wished to have removed both but Mr Elliot objected and therefore Mr Barnes* of Exeter was brought down and confirmed the treatment. Our patient recovered and lived many years afterwards. The value of incisions had been sent forth 10 years before in my book published in 1825 on the Dock Yard Disease, and had been the means of saving many patients from death by removing tension and facilitating the escape of dead cellular substances underneath the skin.

In April Scarlatina maligna appeared in detached places and proved very fatal. At Bulston in Brent three out of four children were attacked. The 1st Mary B, a grown-up girl, a farmer's daughter was attacked with a sore throat and rash in her skin accompanied by fever for which a country surgeon was consulted who saw no danger and promised to revisit her on the following day. Fatal symptoms soon set in with delirium, sinking of pulse and purplish hue of the skin; she died on that night. The distress of her parents was great and excusable for blaming the doctor on account of his want of foresight in not pronouncing danger. The younger brother then sickened from the same complaint and disposed the parents to send for me but before my arrival he also was dead. The elder brother then was attacked with sore throat and redness of skin and fever. I was immediately sent for and in riding hastily over the stones of Plymouth was near a serious accident by my horse slipping up all fours and nearly catching my leg under him. I remounted without injury and reached Bulston, 16 miles off, in time to behold the third patient in a dangerous condition surrounded by his parents and friends expecting also his death. His eyes were glassy and wandering, his skin covered with an effervescence inclining to a purple, his pulse extremely weak and frequent, his tongue dry cracked yellow, his lips jaws and throat covered with a slimy and thready secretion, his tonsils and uvula a darkish red inclining to slough,+ his thoughts wandering and anxious, and his wishes to be allowed a glass of cider which was immediately granted. One tumbler full of half cider and water was given which he took with tremendous hands and eagerly swallowed expressing a most anxious desire for another tumbler, which after some minutes was allowed him and more he would have drunk had I not paused to witness the result. He soon became quieter and inclined to doze so that the parents thought him dying and questioned the propriety of granting him so much cold liquid. His face and arms were sponged over with cold vinegar and water and by degrees he got into a sound sleep mistaken for approaching death and asked for more cider, which was again granted with benefit as it carried down the solids from his tongue and throat and left those parts comparatively clean and moist. From this abuse of danger he gradually recovered his health and strength and now lives after 31 years in the active pursuit of cultivating a farm near Exeter.

A very respectable farmer living about 10 miles from Plymouth about this time had 3 out of 4 daughters attacked successively in a similar way with a malignant Scarlatina and died. I was sent for but not being at hand another Physician was called in for the first girl, but seeing no danger, promised to revisit her on the following day. But before that day had closed the girl was dead and a message sent to the Doctor to that effect. When the 2nd daughter was attacked I was again sent for and again was out of the way. She also died and her sister, being afterwards attacked also died. Thus the parents lost 3 out of their 4 daughters from Scarlatina. So much for the epidemic in the year 1835.

I saw an instance of a united fracture within the capsular ligament$^+$ of the hip at Paris preserved in the École de Médecine. The French surgeons had long proved themselves more successful than the English in the treatment of fractures of the lower extremities. The former kept their patients on their backs with a long splint extended from the hip beyond the toes, whilst the English placed patients on their sides with fractures of the femur, and hence arose an over lapping of the fractured bones and a shortening of the limb.

On the 15th of October Mrs Bewes died aged 83, one of my most respected and valued patients. She had always [my fee] ready made up in paper for my visit and on the day preceding her death she presented one to me with her own hand in a pathetic manner which let me infer it would be the last fee I should ever receive from her hand and so it proved. On the 29th I lost another valuable patient, Mrs T King of North Huish, whose family have continued on the most friendly terms with us to the present time. A valuable mourning ring was presented to me by Miss Bewes.

[An inserted piece of paper records the following]:

One of my patients Mrs Iredale a Widow Lady and a stranger died in Plymouth in the year 1835. She had lived here in a forlorn and unhappy condition which no medical art could relieve for years having been a castaway so far as her family were concerned. She was a Baronet's daughter and was sent out to ride on horseback attended by a groom whom she married to the great annoyance of her family who henceforth cast her off and refused ever more to take the least notice of her. Her husband's elevation drove him to drink and drink to madness, for which he was confined in the Retreat at York, where he died leaving his widow a disconsolate, miserable being. She had no disease but a malade imaginaire, arising from the want of good society. Such is one of the dangers of temptation to which young ladies sent out with young grooms are exposed. Another such example has occurred lately in Surrey where a clergyman's daughter, 18 years old, was sent out on horseback attended by a young groom, two years younger than herself, with whom she fell in love and married. I cannot but condemn this dangerous practice of sending young girls out on horseback from Boarding Schools attended only by a smart young groom.

[end of insertion]

1836

Bought Merrifield Estate £1375 less Mr Woodley £108 12s 7d

Mr Edmund Lockyer*, Mayor of Plymouth, died aged 87.

Feb. the 3rd Mr Gest sent for me to attend Miss Mary Luscombe, labouring under strangulated inguinal$^+$ hernia$^+$ on the left side. As there was no reducing it by ordinary means I operated on her, divided the stricture and returned the bowel with perfect success. This Lady had previously, in a former year, fallen down over some steps and fractured the neck of the thigh bone which happily united without shortening of the limb, the fractured ends having been kept in juxta position by Hagsdoris[?][84] splint so that she was able to walk well for years afterwards. In the year [blank] she had removed to Plymouth with her nieces where she became the subject of strangulated hernia[+] on the right side for which she was again operated on by Mr Square and myself. A large piece of omentum[+] was excised during this 2nd operation which she again survived and lived until the year [blank] when she died of a pulmonary[+] attack.

A fire took place in the Plymouth Citadel within the Barrack rooms of my old patient Major Watson and burnt the building with the Major and his two daughters before the fire was discovered by the sentinels on guard. These buildings are very low and small so that the wonder was that the Major and his family had not escaped from the windows. His surviving son became a patient of mine on account of his eyes, the sight of which was almost obscured by disease of the cornea[+] and lens. Adjutant Chapple of the SD Militia I found on my return from the country in a state of apoplexy[+] and unconsciousness. I opened both of his temple arteries and let them bleed considerably until his consciousness returned. He recovered this attack and died some weeks later aged 62, and although one of the best Sergeant Majors in the Militia Service, yet as Adjutant he was unfit to manage the accounts and correspondence attached to that office.

Lost two patients in consumption both being under 21 years of age in this month of March.

May the 19th Horticultural Meeting: as President I delivered the Annual Address. Visited Wm Langmead, the Ward of Mr France, late.

Sir R. Lopes* and myself at Ottery School and returned by way of Woodbury.

10th of July, Mr George Hunt of Burleigh became very ill and having slept there two nights and found that I could not relieve his complaints – attacks of colic – as heretofore, I thought it right to apprise him of his danger and to desire that some other medical man should see him with me. He positively refused this proposal and said 'I must, then make a new Will, but don't give me up, you have never done so before and you may still succeed.' I replied: 'there is some opposing obstacle which I have never before met with.' 'Then' he said 'I must alter my Will.'

[The following section has been contracted to eliminate tedious detail.]

… I was present in the room … when the Testator dictated his Will. He asked my permission to insert my name as a Trustee and Executor; … I assented, not dreaming of consequences or such evil events as thereafter ensued … Mr G Hunt, aged 69, died on the 11th July and was buried at Pennycross Chapel on the 19th … After death I inspected his body and found so far as the bowels were concerned the obstructions had all been removed, and only some sandy deposits in the head of the large bowel. His aorta I found dilated and its coats ossified[+] also the coronary arteries of his heart, constituting the disease called angina pectoris,[+] of which disease the usual premonitory symptoms had been deficient. His fainting and sickness had been accounted for by undigested food in his stomach, from which the contents were vomited seven

[84] As with Nasdom, there is no apparent record of either Hagsdoris or his splint.

hours after breakfast ... As I had no legacy nor beneficial interest in the Will I did not trouble myself much about it, especially as I had received a handsome present of a hackney saddle, which was about the 6th part of fees due to me for extra journeys, attendance, operations and sleeping in the house to the neglect of other patients.

[George Hunt's nephew] WA Hunt's profligacy soon got rid of the ready money ... An alarm was then given to me that the Trustees, Oxenham & myself, should be brought to some loss, but in what way I could not imagine until served with a notice of a Chancery suit to show cause why the Annuities had not been paid to the three servants ...

So this case passed through the Court and left us to pay the cost of the suit, Counsel's fees and two years' arrears due to the annuitants, besides the bills of our attorney and his London agent. These bills altogether amount to the sum of £[blank] one half of which I paid, and on every quarter day since the [blank] day of [blank] on the eleventh day of the month at eleven o'clock in the forenoon, I have been called upon for the payment of £11 5s od being the quarter part of £45 a year demanded by these two servants, not in the humility of their former capacities with thanks, but with the air of a legal demand on me, as their due. The example thus set of myself I hope will operate as a beacon or warning to other Medical Men, and prevent their falling into a lawyer's trap which inflicts greater pain or penalties than an Hornet's sting.

[This ends the edited section.]

My friend Dr Leach* died at Piedmont of cholera on the 24th of August 1836.

Oct. the 5th Tommy Horse, a very handsome animal suited to saddle or harness took a large spike nail into his hind foot in the Turnpike Road near the 14 mile-stone from Plymouth. I got out the nail, which had passed through the frog and skin above the hoof, with some difficulty and drove on the horse without much lameness in a carriage. I foretold dangerous consequences; as the horse was in fine condition and the weather sultry, every precaution was taken at home by the removal of the shoe, opening the wound and poulticing the foot and giving the horse a dose of purging physic. I ought perhaps to have added blood-letting, and when the leg began to swell to an enormous size I ought further to have fired the leg for removing the tension and discharging sloughs underneath the skin, but being obliged to go to Exeter I placed the horse entirely under the management of my kind friend Gabriel, a veterinary surgeon of much skill in whom I trusted, with a remark that the horse would die and baffle all his efforts. He did not think so but paid the greatest attention to the suffering animal which he thought better late in the night of the 4th day and found dead in his stall on the morning of the 5th, five days after the accident.

Nov. the 18th I went by coach to Lostwithiel and thence in Mrs Wyond's carriage to Bodmin, where I visited Miss Kempthorne, an elegant and accomplished young lady dying of consumption, and on my way back visited Mr Nex's family at Restormel Castle.

1837

Influenza was epidemic in the early part of this year, heads of families and servants and horses were attacked. All our household suffered in turn. My valuable horse Mazoppa was prostrated with the malady and so great were his sufferings as to dispose me to despair of his recovery, but the skill and perseverance of Mr Raddell VS, added to the care and nursing of us all, succeeded in warding off death but the poor animal never was himself entirely after this severe attack. He was a fine specimen of his Mother, by Gainsborough, and his Sire Grey Comus.

After Adjutant Chapple's death, Capt. Fisk* was appointed Adjutant of the South Devon Militia in April 1837 and continued to discharge the multi-form duties of that appointment with consummate ability until he took brevet[85] rank as Lieut. Col. in the army, retiring from the Militia with a splendid testimonial presented to him by Col. Lord Churston and the Officers of the SD Militia.

On the 15th My good and excellent mother broke the neck of her thigh-bone by slipping over a paved court and falling heavily on her right side. My Brother's letter on the 16th hastened my visit to Woodbury by mail on that day. I found the dear good creature laying on a feather bed and suffering much pain with shortening of the leg. I had her placed upon a mattress until I could return to Plymouth on the following day and send up a water bed[86] and Nasdom's+ long splint. These were all the suggestions I could offer for her comfort in addition to the services of my Father and Brother. On the 28th of May I revisited my Mother at Woodbury by coach, remained over the 29th administering every comfort and benefit I could think of and returned to Plymouth on the 30th, which was the 11th anniversary of my wedding and the 43rd of my sister's birthday.

The 2nd of June my brother's letter apprised me that the splint had galled the leg a little. The 5th another letter from my brother on the same subject and again on the 9th. On the 11th by Quick Silver Mail from Plymouth to Exeter and Woodbury, adjusted the splints and left her more comfortable and easy on the 13th when I returned again to Plymouth by the night mail. On the 18th, Waterloo Day, my brother's bulletin gave a bad account of my dear mother and induced me to revisit her on the 19th and found her dangerously ill with a flushed and feverish aspect owing principally to a sloughing+ which had began about the nates,+ owing to some difficulty in relieving her bowels etc. The fractured limb had kept in a proper position by means of a splint and had been disturbed only when relief of any kind was necessary. Her pulse had become much harried and her countenance so anxious as to forebode the fatal result. My feelings were much overpowered by her anxious manner of clinging to me as her last hope of comfort in this world, and reluctantly assented to my leaving her again for Plymouth although I assured her that I could do no more than my father or brother were doing for her relief. I remained at Woodbury on the 20th and returned to Plymouth on the 21st, the longest day, by the evening mail and bringing the intelligence of the death of King William the 4th.

My brother's letters on the 23rd and 24th did not lead me to believe that my presence was again required at Woodbury and as I had many patients and engagements at Plymouth I could not conveniently absent myself from home. On the 27th accounts better, the 28th accounts reversed. On the 29th I drove up a gig to Ashburton and reached Woodbury on the 29th when I found my suffering mother almost insensible. On the 1st of July she died at 4 o'clock in her 77th year; thus departed the life of a virtuous religious woman, of as faithful a wife and as good a mother as ever

[85] A military commission conferred especially for outstanding service, by which an officer is promoted to a higher rank without the corresponding pay.
[86] In 1833, Dr Neil Arnott invented his Hydrostatic Bed, designed to prevent bedsores. It was essentially a bath of water with a covering of rubber-impregnated canvas sealed with varnish.

lived. I remained at Woodbury until the next day, Sunday, and started after dinner to Countess Wear bridge where I took up Mr Counter and drove to his residence, Waye near Ashburton, on Sunday night and on the following day reaching Plymouth 9 at night. On the 6th I returned to Exeter by mail and hence to Woodbury for my mother's funeral on the 7th, when her body was interred in a vault within Woodbury Church where I erected a tablet to her memory. On Sunday the 9th I attended with the other branches of our family except my father who was too much overpowered to trust himself so far. On the 10th I returned by coach to Newhouse where my gig awaited my arrival and took me to some places in Brent and to Ugborough from whence Mrs Butter and myself after tea returned to Plymouth that evening.

My Father's grief was excessive and inconsolable, his appetite failed and his habit of smoking tobacco almost given up. For want of appetite his bodily strength was much wasted. He however went to Church once and received the Sacrament kneeling, but could not again raise himself without the aid of Admiral and Captain Woodbridge. Frequently he would say that he should not live a year after his wife's death and true was the prophecy, for he died on the 8th of June in the following year 1838.

Early in October I attended James Cornish Esq. of Black Hall near Brent, a stout and burly man and a hearty feeder but drinking nothing but water. His pulse was so forcible as to induce me to recommend blood-letting to which he objected by saying: 'if you take away a man's blood how is it to be replenished?' I said: 'sir your system is overloaded with blood, your blood vessels are too full, and your labouring heart circulates the blood with difficulty.' My reasoning being useless I left him and went below stairs where I was asked by his family what I thought of their father and replied: 'he is in great danger, living on the brink of a precipice. He will not be blooded from the arm and therefore something serious must happen.' Whilst this dialogue was going on the bedroom door was suddenly opened and a person was heard running rapidly over the stairs in the dining room and asking if Dr Butter was gone. Seeing me he said: 'please to come up Sir, Master is dying.' On entering his bedroom I beheld him in an arm chair supported by his coachman holding a wash-hand basin half-filled with dark grainy blood before his mouth, from which was still spouting more blood which reminded me of water spouting from the mouth of a Lion statue often seen on the Continent near water fountains. His pallid countenance and long fainting led me to think he was dead and to remove him quickly from the chair to the horizontal position in bed, where we sprinkled water over his face, mingled with vinegar and stimulants, for nearly an hour when he shewed signs of returning to life. He lived however over a day and a night and died on the 5th of October. Thus was my prognosis verified.

On the 16th of October I had the honour of dining at Bicton with my noble Patron Lord Rolle* who attained his 86th year on that day, and of meeting Lady Rolle, Miss Chichester and the Honorable Mr Repton grandson of the late Lord Eldon. After the ladies had retired his Lordship said to us: 'you young men must take care of yourselves and drink such wines as you like. I repeat to you the same advice as King George the 3rd gave on his Birthday to the late Lord Eldon,[87] Mr Repton's grandfather and myself, viz. I advise you young men to stick to port as I have done, and

---

[87] Butter has previously used this quote, in 1813, when the Lord concerned was Elgin.

you may live to a good old age like myself.' Thereupon Lord Rolle took his usual siesta of half an hour before we rejoined the Ladies.

On every subsequent year one of my greatest pleasures was to supply Lord Rolle* on the 16th of Oct. with two sorts of Woodcock, the Land and Sea Woodcock.[88] It was so early for the Land Woodcock as to call forth his Lordship's surprise that he could not get one from all his manors in the North and South of Devon and so uncertain was the supply of Sur Mullet in Plymouth Market as to oblige me to obtain them from Cornwall or Torcross. However, I was fortunate enough to keep up the custom until his Lordship's death. The Sur Mullet was a fish so highly prized by gourmands as to fetch high prices.

Nov. the 11th Miss Rashleigh, sister to Mrs Rodd and Mrs Gervis Grills of Luxulyan, had been a patient of mine for some weeks on account of her ophthalmic complaints for which she had consulted eminent Occulists in London, Exeter etc. One eye was gone and the other threatened with amaurosis[+] and blindness. She was a thin little lady with a great deal of blood in her system, a strong pulse and visible beatings in the temple arteries, one of which I opened as a forlorn hope in the presence of her friend Miss Welsford and never before that time had I ever witnessed such a furious hem[orrhage]. I divided the artery more than once but it would not contract and the bleeding would not cease until I desired her to sit up and then fainting ensued. I never before took such a great quantity of blood from the temple artery of any patient as from this little lady. After many hours of quietude she recovered and expressed herself greatly relieved from all formidable symptoms about her head and eye. She lived for years afterwards and expressed herself with gratitude and admiration of the operation which she designated a masterpiece of surgery.

On the 20th of Nov. Mr Charles Tanner my old friend and patient, requiring more attendance than I could conveniently give him owing to my frequent visits in the country, led me to place him under the care of Mr Square with a promise to see him occasionally. He had been out of health and, returning from Devonport one day in an omnibus, fell on his back against a kerb stone and received such a severe concussion as ultimately produced paralysis of the lower extremities for which cupping,[+] blisters, Setons[+] and Issues[+] were in turn resorted to during his confinement to bed. The result was a partial recovery of sensation and motion but insufficient to enable him to walk any distances. Thus ended the eventful year of 1837.

1838

Jan. the 3rd. The Rev Mr Edsall, curate of Woodbury, Mr Wells and his daughter-in-law dined with us. He [Edsall] was the most remarkable specimen of wasting of flesh I had ever seen or read of. His weight at one time reached nearly 300 lbs. After losing about 140 lbs weight, he was dining in company with Gen. Lee and two other gentlemen to whom he mentioned this remarkable circumstance, rendered still more remarkable by an expression from the party that neither one of them had ever weighed 100 lbs! This wasting was not attributable to disease or any obvious circumstance as he always retained an enormous appetite for food.

---

[88] Surmullet or red mullet, 'sometimes called the Sea Woodcock' – Mary Eaton, *The Cook and Housekeeper's Universal Dictionary* (Bungay: I & R Chubb, 1822), p. 302.

In Jan. death deprived me of two patients, Arthur Jun. and W P Baldy, Surgeon to the Workhouse, both of pulmonary[+] disease. On March the 11th my old and much respected friend Geo. Furlong Wise of Woolston near Kingsbridge died at 84 suddenly in his bed at night. I revere his memory.

20th March. I visited my former patient and friend Colonel Abernethie RM retired from the service and residing at Dix's Field Exeter with his excellent wife, my former patient who survived his death which was caused by his taking by mistake of the servant a bottle of Goulard[+] Liniment instead of a black draught. This poison brought on sickness, great prostration of strength and mortification[+] of the great toe[?].

On the 27th of March I dined at Brent Vicarage and learnt that Mr James Goodman, a most respectable farmer, wished to consult me about the bite of his hand by a mad dog. His countenance denoted extreme anxiety and fright lest he should become a subject of Hydrophobia.[+] Mr Cornish, the parish Surgeon, lived near the Vicarage and induced me to go there with Goodman for a scalpel with which I excised freely all the wounded or suspected skin and cauterized it with lunar caustic.[+] Afterwards I asked him if he was certain the dog was mad and he said yes, always a docile animal until the day he flew at his master and bit him as well as other animals in his way. The dog was then confined until he died raving mad. Mr Goodman is living at the present time to tell the tale, but so great was his alarm at the time that death might probably have ensued from apprehension had not the operation been performed.

My Father's health had been gradually declining and his appetite failing but my brother's reports did not lead me to revisit him so often as I might otherwise have done on account of my numerous engagements at Plymouth. Some years before he met with a serious accident in alighting from a horse on whose back he had been seated for many hours, and his own knees became stiffened so that he got off to walk down a hill and fell forward nearly under his horse's legs and, pitching on his right arm, broke both bones of the radius alna, which cut the radial artery and produced such haemorrhage as he was unable to staunch the blood. Recovering his legs he walked on the road, anxiously as night was approaching, to the nearest cottage and, seeing a light, called loudly for assistance and there fell faint on the road. The inmates hearing a loud call went out and found him on the ground. They assisted him into their cottage and a man went for a carriage to his own house not a mile off. This accident he recovered from and both bones reunited but he often repeated his belief that the accident had knocked off seven years from his existence. His subsequent grief for my mother's accident and death, added to his former belief, tended no doubt to shorten the period of his life. Both of my parents seemed to have been doomed to accidents and broken bones from horses and carriages. Soon after I had got into my teens as a schoolboy I rode to Woodbury Camp before my mother, who was seated on a pillion, and on our road a shower appeared against which she expanded her umbrella, which frightened the horse but, as we were going uphill I had strength enough to pull him up. She then said: 'how shall I manage to get this umbrella down without frightening the horse?' Arriving on the Camp ground the drums and fifes beat off for Church service which my religious mother was most anxious to attend as there was none at Woodbury Church during this Sunday. Whether or not the drums or the umbrella which my mother closed up frightened the horse I never learnt, but the animal galloped off plunging and kicking until my mother was unseated and thrown violently to the ground with her arm round my waist, sending me over a sumersalt on my head and shoulders to the ground, from which I quickly arose without knowing at first where I was, and seeing all things dancing around me, tents and soldiers all seemingly in motion flitting before my eyes. Then, looking round, I beheld a party carrying my mother into a tent where the Regimental Doctor was sent for who dispatched a messenger to my father for a carriage to convey her home. Poor woman, she was also stunned by this accident and spoke incoherently on the road. Her left leg was broken and her right arm dislocated and she was suckling an infant about this time. The shoulder was easily reduced but the leg appeared so frightful for a time as to create fear of mortification[+] and therefore the advice of other surgeons was thought necessary. Her good constitution enabled her to survive all these trials but many accidents happened to her afterwards with horses in gigs unworthy of repetition until the fatal fracture of the neck of thigh-bone occurred.

June the 6th. I visited my Father and found him in a sinking state, his natural powers had lost their elasticity, his stomach refused food and his life was fast approaching to an end, which terminated on ½ past 12 o'clock at midnight on the morning of the 8th of June, his age 77. I started in my gig at Woodbury for Plymouth which I reached the same night at 11 o'clock.

On the 14th the funeral took place which I attended at Woodbury Church with the other branches of his family. I remained over Sunday the 17th and returned to Plymouth on the 19th. We left for Glazbrook House Brent where we remained until Nov. 12th.

Sept. 29th I received a fee of £100 from my grateful patient Miss Rashleigh with her warmest acknowledgements. Sold Musbury Field to Henley for £900.

Nov. the 15th being at Woodbury I couched Mrs Wheaton.

Miss Leah from Penzance came to Plymouth to consult me about a very large tumour of the Lachrymal sac,[+] the left side of the nose. I opened the tumour from which a large quantity of pus was let out with tears. I overcame the obstruction by a probe passed through the nasal duct to the floor of the nostril, syringed out the tube with warm water and passed a silver pin with its head fastened by silk to the forehead. Fomentations and poultices with solutions of alum soon reduced parts to their normal state. She soon returned to Penzance wired with a pin in the lachrymal duct from which it accidentally fell out and her family surgeon could not or cared not to replace it. So she had to return from Penzance to Plymouth and back again for this simple restoration of the style, done in half a minute.

Lieut. Col. Cambell came under my care at Stonehouse for a most violent attack of rheumatic ophthalmia[+] which threatened total extinction of vision, but by active depletion followed by colchicum[+] I restored him to convalescence in which state he went to London and consulted the late Mr Guthrie, who was pleased to say that I had treated him with consummate skill.

Mrs Henry Counter of Ashburton was attacked with Typhus Fever and attended by Mr Mogridge, Surgeon who advised consultation with myself on the approach of danger, and her friends brought down Dr J Budd from Exeter. During our visit she had occasion to get out of bed and fainted so deadly as to alarm all present, and I think she would have died if I had not caught her up in my arms and quickly laid in a horizontal position on her bed. As I had to remain during this night Dr Budd returned to Exeter with a request to have a letter on the following day stating the time of her death. A plentiful supply of yeast and a liquor called Ashburton pop,[89] which she particularly desired, got her well through the night and improved her condition on the following day so that she ultimately recovered and came to Plymouth for change of air. The mail coach was the fastest in those days and by it I returned to Plymouth from Ashburton a distance of 23 miles in two hours and twenty minutes.

1839

Miss Ann King, a very fine girl about twenty years of age, dined at our house and stepped into a pool of water in passing from her carriage to our house so that she sat with her feet wet and cold uncomfortably during the evening and complained at night of an attack in her bowels with pain in the left groin which seldom left her for many weeks until an abscess formed and burst. Her bowels were regular and appetite good so that no suspicion existed for a time of any communication between the bowel and the abscess, but after some time a currant, a seed and the pip of an apple came that way and convinced us of an opening existing in the bowel which I supposed to be the sicmoid flexure.[+] There was also a sinous which I opened without discovering any foreign body so matters continued rather worse than better for a time, after which I drew up her case and submitted it to Sir Benjamin Brodie,* also to Mr Liston* both of whom considered that I had done everything surgically which the case admitted of. Long confinement to bed weakened her health for which she went to Ivybridge with her sisters and there died. By the wish of all parties a post-mortem examination was made by Mr Gest, late Surgeon of Modbury and myself and proved the existence of an aperture in the small bowel or illyum,[+] and not in the sicmoid flexure[+] of the large bowel as suspected. An internal adhesion of the diseased portion adhered to the integument[+] and prevented the escape of the contents into the peritoneum[+] where more active inflammation would have been set up and death ensured. In talking over the case with Sir B Brodie afterwards in London, and mutually agreeing that medical opinions were often set right by these desirable inspections after death, we spoke of one or two young ladies whose bodies he had been requested to examine after death, one a case of suspected poison, where the causes of death arose from internal ulcerations of the bowels. In my own practice however I could only remember one similar case. During this year I saw Mr Square's patient affected with hydrophobia,[+] of which the poor man died in the usual agonies. I had not seen such a case for 20 years and I never saw but four, of which two were children in St Bartholomew's Hospital in London where I was a dresser.

Besides my medical practice many other subjects relating to agriculture and monetary investments occupied a portion of my time. The parish of South Brent, in which my wife inherited some lands, to which I added other lands by purchase, was submitted to the Tithe Commutation Act. Like all other bargains the Incumbent wished to get as much and the parishioners to pay as little rent charge as possible. I was Chairman of one meeting which agreed to offer the Parson £1,000 a year which he refused, the subject being further argued by the Vicar in possession, and the Vicar in expectation by purchase, and the Parish whose interests were argued by Attornies. An Agreement was ultimately effected under the Tithe Commutation Act for the

[89] A highly carbonated beer.

annual sum of £965 subject to averages variable by the price of grain. Some distant
lands at Musbury, Colyford and Seaton I sold off to purchase other lands in Brent.

Bought Consols £2,100 @ 92 5/8ths

1840

Alice Hosking, a blind school mistress from Falmouth applied at the Plymouth
Royal Eye Infirmary where her case was deemed so hopeless for trial her right eye
being sunk and the left having a cataract complicated with Amaurosis[+] and adherent
to the inner margin of the iris. At her particular request I performed several operations on her eye and succeeded only at the 6th time by detaching the adhesions and
depressing the remaining cataract out of the axis of vision by Scarpa's[*] curved
needle. Her sight was then recovered sufficiently well to enable her to return thanks
in Church and to read and write for years afterwards. Her letters from Falmouth were
full of gratitude, where she resumed her duties as a Schoolmistress.

The Right Honourable Earl of Morley[*] died on the 14th of March at Saltram. His
Lordship's death occasioned such a vacuum as never has been replaced in Plymouth.
On Good Friday the 17th of April I visited the Revd Mr Savage, the Vicar of Harford
near Ivybridge, dying of a complicated disease, thence over the Moor to Brent Dean
and returned to Plymouth on the same horse carrying 17 stone.

May the 17th I lost an estimable friend and an attached patient, Miss Cordelia
Bewes, who gave me a legacy of £25 in addition to ordinary fees and a Benefaction
of £100 to the Plymouth Royal Eye Infirmary – 'Requiescat In Pace'.

29th May I drove to Owley where I had appointed Tommy French from
Widdecombe to aid my men in destroying some foxes. On my arrival I was surprised
at meeting the party, 4 in number, returning from the Chase, Tommy with a great
lusty dog fox under his arm with a dog chain and collar round his neck and his mouth
coped with a strong cord fastening the jaws tightly together. Some of Tommy's dogs
had been severely punished by the fox, especially a game little terrier bitten blind.
There were 3 hounds and 4 terriers, all excellent of their kind. Having shut up the
dogs, Tommy released the fox's mouth and chained him up in a dog's house. My
little dog, half Spaniel and Terrier would not attack the fox when the animal opened
his mouth wide and showed his teeth in full force. The fox was a very noble animal
of its species but died afterwards from the wounds received from the dogs.

The plan of hunting was the following. Early in a May morning when Chanticleer
proclaims the dawn, foxes are on the alert and on the way to the nearest poultry
and they pick up a fowl or a duck and carry to their Lady's love, who are by this
time near their accouchement and unable to fly before their enemies, so they take
shelter in the nearest hole and leave their mates to decoy away their pursuer. The
party therefore had started soon after 3 o'clock with their three hounds and terriers
until they took upon the dray of a fox which generally ran to some hole, where they
followed him and put in the terriers who to battle went and dragged out the fox dead
or, if alive, Tommy quickly caught him by the neck whilst an attendant fastened the
cord round the under jaw and fastened it to the top so that Reynard could not open
his mouth to bite. The cleverness of Tommy French at this work and at all other
kinds of sporting, hunting, shooting, fishing was perhaps never surpassed by any
Dartmoor hero. One of his quaint expressions was against my men not following
his dogs fast enough when they were running a fox, that they were heavy footed

fellows only fit to tread clay. During this week they killed I think 16 or 17 foxes old and young.

My neighbour [blank] Williams, Surgeon, was capsized out of his gig and received concussion of the brain for which Mr Auge and I attended him till death, after which his head was examined and over his brain considerable effusion of water had taken place and some blood in the ventricles.

During this summer a party of us visited the landslip at Axmouth, between Lyme and Sidmouth and there saw an immense mass of the cliff which had slipped down on the sea-shore carrying in its fall a cottage not much damaged. Connibeare's plates and description give a full account of this singular phenomenon.[90]

13th of June the Queen was shot at by Oxford but happily for England not injured.

Wm Templar, groom to my friend Mr Leach, died of rheumatic fever, one of the worst cases I ever saw. Major Kinsman, Paymaster of the Royal Marines also died, of a diseased liver, on the 19th of August.

Oct. the 16th Lord Rolle* attained the venerable age of 89 on which occasion I was glad of the opportunity in keeping up my custom of sending two sorts of woodcock to his Lordship, viz. 2 woodcocks and 6 Sur Mullet.

Jane Smith, companion in the Welsford family died. She was what may be called an opium drinker if not an eater and used to get down Laudanum by the quart from London and pour out ½, sometimes near a wineglass full, of laudanum. I knew another Lady, Mrs W a great botanist and authoress who wrote on the adaptation of particular plants to particular soils who was also a drinker of laudanum, from 1 to 2 oz at a draught. One day whilst I was writing a prescription in a druggist's shop at Stonehouse a poor, miserable, pallid looking woman, thin and ill-fed with ragged clothes entered the shop, put down a small coin on the counter and received in return something taken from a drawer wrapped in a bit of paper and with it she left the shop without speaking a word. I said to the druggist: 'how could you possibly guess the meaning of that woman as to her wants?' 'Oh' he said 'she is a constant customer here whenever she has a penny or two to lay out. She is an opium eater, and the wife of a marine whose clothes she sometimes pawns and gets her husband into difficulties, and with the money she buys opium.' He said: 'I give her the crude and not the purified opium for I might have killed her long since if I had given her the best extract. There are many such cases in our town.' How little do doctors know the private habits of patients when called upon to cure diseases.

The British Association[91] visited Plymouth and tested the hospitality of their Plymouth brethren. Our townsman W Snow Harris and myself entertained many of the members at dinner and gave up spare beds. Brockeden* the artist, whose views of the Alps are well-known and appreciated, said to me: 'can't you give us a paper on some subject; Medical Doctors are generally behind others in providing papers for discussion.' 'Why' I said 'we expect you literary men to entertain us, for we humble men cannot presume to entertain you.' 'Well' he said 'I wish you would provide your section with a paper.' I replied 'I have none ready, but I could offer some remarks on Squinting, for the cure of which a new operation has been introduced into England from Stromere of Hanover and Dieffenbach of Berlin by Bennett Lucas, an English surgeon whose success does him much credit.' After the reading of my paper, which

90 See footnote 93 below.
91 Founded in 1831 as the British Association for the Advancement of Science.

was subsequently published in their transactions[92] a gentleman, a stranger present, came forward and thanked me for my notice of him, saying: 'I am Bennett Lucas of whom you have spoken so favourably as to receive my thanks.'

Queen Victoria was married to Prince Albert on the 24th day of May of this year, and the usual rejoicings by ringing of bells and firing of guns from forts of garrisons and ships in harbour.

Slept at Owley for the first time [in] 1840.

1841

Jan. the 3rd One of my first and oldest patients, Mrs Welsford, died at the age of 86 years. On the 12th the Rev. T Royce sent a boy aged 15 to the Plymouth Eye Infirmary on account of blindness of both eyes, which appeared clear and transparent with pupils much dilated but without opacity. The boy soon died, being the first and almost the only patient who ever died in the Institution. His eyes and brain were examined at a post-mortem and the following morbid changes discovered: there was no lens in either eye, only water of the aqueous and vitreous humours;[+] on the right ventricle of the brain a tumour was found in consistence like blubber or jelly, and in weight about 4 oz; the left ventricle was greatly distended with water. The tumour emanated from the right Thalamus[+] and filled the ventricle to the Pons Varolii[+] and Medulla.[+] It was contained in a cyst not vascular.[+] Such a case I had never since met with.

16th Mrs Hennah, wife of our respected Chaplain of the Garrison died. On the 21st of Feb I was sent for by a Surgeon at Ivybridge to see the driver of the Mail Coach who had been thrown off the driving box some days before and broken his right leg. Both bones were splintered and haemorrhage had continued at intervals. I found him in bed in an upper chamber seldom inhabited at the Inn and thought him in a dying state as he appeared pallid and bloodless, with the pupils of his eyes widely dilated. He appeared almost asph[yx]iated owing to a fire being kept up with Charcoal in the room with closed doors and windows, where he would have died as many others have done from the burning of Charcoal in closed rooms and in limestone kilns. A turnicoat was applied around his thigh to be tightened in case of further haemor-rhage, and in that case I advised amputation of the leg. For this purpose I set out my amputating case after my return to Plymouth and awaited a further summons in the event of haemorrhage, which occurred within a few days, when an Express arrived for me and when I arrived within a mile of Ivybridge, which is 11 miles off, a gentleman informed me that the Coachman had just died. I proceeded however and amputated the fractured leg which I brought back and dissected. The tibia was smashed into many pieces some with sharp points, one of which had punctured the posterior tibial artery from which haemorrhage had ensued. The fibula also was fractured in 2 or 3 places. I boiled and dried the bones and glued all the fragments together and preserved the specimen, now in my collection.

March the 23rd my friend Thomas Gosling died. He was the brother of an accom-plished young lady who drew for me the domestic hen with male plumage recorded

---

[92] It was not the paper itself but a report on it that was published in the 'Notices and Abstracts of Communications', pp. 79–80 of the *Report of the Eleventh Meeting of the British Association for the Advancement of Science; Held at Plymouth in July 1841* (London: John Murray, 1842).

in another place. The Gosling family had been left a very fine Estate near Plymouth by the late Addis Archer Esq. of Leigham, who had adopted them instead of his relatives.

Mr Fulford's Autopsy, April 17. Dr Cookworthy and myself attended the autopsy performed by Mr Whipple of our joint patient Mr Fulford, a successful manufacturer who had died at Plymouth. For many years he had been the subject of a liver and stomach disease with jaundice, for which he consulted many eminent medical men with[out] deriving any permanent benefit. He was at last salavated[93] and thereby relieved of a number of gall stones, from 30 to 40 I think, and therefore [we] looked particularly at his gall bladder, in which one solitary calculus[+] still remained. He was the father of a very fine family, [including] Mrs Henry Caunter of Ashburton, whose remarkable recovery from Typhus Fever has been already narrated. She ultimately died at Plymouth of a peculiar disease of her lungs accompanied with a speccled appearance.

A very pretty little Cornish girl named Asher was brought to me by her relations on account of a peculiar appearance in her left eye which was blind, although in its external appearance sound. When the pupil was dilated a peculiar metallic appearance was seen at the fundus[+] of her eye-ball, near the expansion of the optic nerve and retina. Had I not been previously prepared by reading of such a rare case, which I had never before seen, I should not have been able to forewarn her friends of the danger which might occur by producing fits and death, of which there seemed to be then little probability. My prophecy induced me to pay much attention to this peculiar disease of the interesting little patient, whose poor relations raised a subscription to present me with a silver snuff-box.

Sunday May 9th Miss Rashleigh, whose case has been already described, was partaking of our family dinner when it occurred to me that I had some glass eyes left of those brought from Paris, and looking at them after dinner I saw one exactly resembling Miss R's other eye and accordingly fitted it between the lids of the lost eye, and so nicely did it suit as to please myself and gratify Miss R so excessively as scarcely to believe her own face when reflected in a mirror, before which she looked and gazed and looked again with surprise and delight so intently as to return again and again to behold her dear face in the glass. No child with a toy could have been more delighted. On the following Sunday she sat in our pew at Church and after service a Lady accosted me with this question: 'what have you done to Miss R's eyes? The last time I saw her she had but one eye and today she appears with two, what a wonderful alteration.' 'Ask me no questions' I replied.

May 13th Thos King Jun., only son of Thos King Esquire of North Huish Manor, came of age on which occasion there were great rejoicings. His father's remarkable recovery from abscess of the lungs has been here recorded.

29th the Rev. Mr Savage of Lewksland and Vicar of Harford died, being afflicted with an internal tumour which required many surgical operations.

July 1st Jno Ashford with £500 to Mr Andrews, Solicitor, Modbury for the payment of Glasscombe, an Estate in the parish of Ugborough.

---

[93] Salivation is the production of an unusual amount of saliva, generally by the use of mercury, although this seems somewhat at variance with Butter's aversion to mercury in the treatment of syphilis. Homeopaths recommend a plant called Chionanthus for the same purpose – perhaps Butter used that or something similar.

1st August the British Association held their meeting, the Rev. Dr Whewell President. The Rev. Dr Buckland, afterwards Dean of Westminster, and Conybeare, author of a work on the landslip at Axmouth[94] preached a Sermon at St Andrew's Church, Plymouth.

10th August Eliz. slept at Owley Cottage for the first time and thither we resorted whensoever a change from Plymouth was required for the benefit of our health. The Moor air at Owley was proverbially healthy and invigorating as an antidote against the moist and relaxing air of Plymouth. The change from one place to the other was always perceptible, both air and water at Owley are the purest that can be found. The cottage is situated on a rock facing a valley leading to the South, at the foot of a mountain called the Eastern Beacon, which shelters it from the western gales so that trees grow all around it and afford both shade and shelter. It is located in the centre of a sporting district which would abound with much game but for innumerable foxes. A wide range of moorlands rise to the North and East and afford good shooting of Snipes, Plovers, Ducks, Heath-fowl, and 5 rivers for fishing lay within a mornings walk, viz: The Yealm, the Erme, the Dart, the Avon and the Glaze stream, a tributary of the Avon in front of the Cottage. 3 Railway stations exist from 1½ to 3 miles from the house. The salubrity of this spot has been acknowledged by every Invalid who has ever tried it. Its name arises probably from the number of Owls frequently in the neighbourhood and therefore it has been proposed to call it Minerva Cottage.[95]

On the 24th we made a tour to London and proceeded from Plymouth by the ordinary conveyances to Bath, where we entered a railway carriage of an Express Train for the 1st time. The darkness of the long Box Tunnel gave us gloomy impressions for a time but the speed of travelling afterwards exhilarated us. The distance from Didcot to London is set down at 53 miles which were accomplished under the hour without a halt. It was amusing to hold a watch in our hands and as the minutes passed away so were the mile stones observed; many a mile was passed over within a minute. We were all delighted with our safe arrival in London and surprised on finding for the 1st time the wonderful power of steam produced from boiling water. When Watt first observed this phenomenon by the steam of boiling water elevating the cover of a Tea pot and considered the application of such a force, neither he nor any subsequent philosopher could possibly have contemplated the future application of such an unknown and undiscovered force in propelling vehicles swiftly through the air and ships over the sea against winds and tides, storms and tempests, but we have lived to see such mighty changes which our ancestors would have considered as fabulous and insane to contemplate.

---

[94] William Buckland (1784–1856), born in Axmouth, and William Daniel Conybeare (1787–1857), vicar of Axmouth, were both eminent amateur geologists. Buckland, who was staying with Conybeare at the time of the landslip, had earlier discovered the so-called 'Red Lady of Paviland', an archaeological sensation at the time. They published a book with the catchy title: *Ten Plates Comprising a Plan, Sections and Views, Representing the Changes Produced on the Coast of East Devon, between Axmouth and Lyme Regis, by the Subsidence of the Land and Elevation of the Bottom of the Sea on 26 December 1838 and 3 February 1840* (London: John Murray, 1840). Another of Buckland's works is discussed by Margaret Green in 'William Buckland's Model of Plymouth Breakwater', *Archives of Natural History* 23 (1996), pp. 219–43.

[95] The goddess Minerva is frequently depicted with her sacred owl, which symbolised her association with wisdom and knowledge.

25th I visited my old school of St Bartholomew's Hospital by appointment with my friends Stanley and Lawrence, and there saw a patient, a poor Italian, Genochio, whom I had sent up from Plymouth to undergo the operation of Lithotomy$^+$ for the 2nd time. He recovered the operations and returned to Plymouth where a fresh formation of calculus$^+$ obliged him to undergo a 3rd operation, successfully performed by Mr Fuge and myself. He lived for some years afterwards.

26th Brockedon* and myself attended the sale of the Sharpham Estate at the Royal Exchange by George Robins, whom we had a wish to hear as well as to learn the name of the purchaser of this fine property on the banks of the river Dart near Totnes where my friend was born. The two Estates were knocked down at the price of £70,400 to Mr Durant, a wealthy silk merchant in London and a native of North Devon.

27th our night's rest was much disturbed at the Trafalgar Hotel, Spring Gardens by the incessant noise of carriages and vehicles travelling unceasingly until 3 o'clock in the morning, when an hour's pause occurred, and then began the Carts and Waggons laden with the Earth's produce of food for man and beast, rolling and rumbling over the stones from 4 to 6 o'clock, and afterwards the customary din of people walking and driving about their morning's occupations.

On the 29th we went down to Southampton and visited Mrs Mangles and her daughter Mrs Jerningham. There on Sunday we engaged ourselves to dine with them, but desired to see Cowes as the weather was favourable for crossing the water, and on arriving at West Cowes I was quickly recognized by Captain Baulkly and other members of the Yacht Club known to me at Plymouth. As the Church bells were going for service we hastened to East Cowes Church and there saw our young friend the Rev. K Hannah reading the prayers. He was the son of our respected Chaplain and my long esteemed friend at Plymouth Garrison. We remained throughout the morning service and heard an excellent sermon, after which, and hearing his surprise at our visit, we accompanied him to his house and received all that hospitality for which his father and mother had been always noted at Plymouth, especially to ourselves. We returned across the water from Cowes to Southampton in a dense fog, so that we could just say that we had seen Cowes and no more! We were in time for Mrs Mangold's excellent dinner of which we partook heartily and spent a very pleasant evening. By coach we returned from Southampton through Hampshire visiting Christchurch, the New Forest and Dorsetshire, visiting Weymouth and its harbour with the island of Portland. We there met our Recorder of Plymouth, Carpenter Rowe, who was recovering from Rheumatic Fever and advised to resort to the seaside at Weymouth which was the favourite watering place of King George the 3rd and his family.

19th Oct. General Vinicombe died aged 67, having suffered of late years from a cutaceous$^+$ disease for the cure of which he resorted to Harrowgate in Yorkshire, where the sulphurous waters palliated but never entirely cured his complaints. The General left me one of his Trustees and Executors under his will with Captain Mallack and Mr L G Hunt, solicitor.

Lord Rolle* aged 90; sent the usual present of woodcocks and sur mullet to His Lordship. Mrs Elliott matron of the Eye Infirmary, died aged 71.

29th went up to Exeter with Sir Walter Carew on the coach and attended the centenary of the Devon and Exeter Hospital to which I presented £25, also the dinner at which I made a speech in acknowledging the toast of Lord Rolle's* health, drank in his absence. I slept at Woodbury on that night and dined at Bicton next day with

Lord & Lady Rolle, Sir John & Lady Yarde Buller* and Mr Buck of Daddon near Bideford, member for North Devon. We played several rubbers of whist which the noble Lord enjoyed. I returned to Woodbury having spent a very pleasant evening. I received his Lordship's thanks for my speech on the preceding day.

2nd Nov. Sir Francis Chantrey* died at 60, also the Earl of Harewood 74. The former had been one of my most zealous friends with Mr Hatchett* in obtaining my admission by ballot as a fellow of the Royal Society and for nearly 20 years had shewn me much hospitality and friendship, while the latter Nobleman had been a patient of mine for a complaint on his skin during his visit at Mount Edgecombe. Dr, now Sir Charles, Locock,* with whom I had been in correspondence about a wet nurse for the Prince of Wales, born on the 9th Nov., called on me at Plymouth on his way to Penzance hoping that the journey from London to the Land's End would relieve him for a time from the heavy duties of his profession, and assist in restoring him to health after a convalescence following an attack of rheumatic fever which had much disabled the use of his limbs.

After sleeping one night at our country cottage I drove home to our house at Plymouth at 11 o'clock and then learnt that several patients had called and that Mr Hunt, my opposite neighbour, had sent three times for me to see Mrs Hunt, whom I found in a state of pending apoplexy+ for which I opened a temporal artery on one side. Not getting sufficient blood therefrom I punctured the temporal artery on the opposite side, nearer the ear, and let off some blood which flowed freely, sometimes in jets for a foot or so, and then in a sprinkled form until I had obtained above a pint, which I thought would do but the bleeding would not stop. Then I divided the artery and as the bleeding did not then stop I called in Mr Little the Dentist to assist me in tieing the bleeding vessel, but my patient's fainting prevented further heomerage and so I left her.

On reaching my own house I observed a carriage slowly approaching, and by it walking was Dr, afterwards Sir George, Magrath,* who accosted me in the following manner viz: 'your old neighbour Mr Sims, whilst walking in Old Town St., Plymouth fell down insensible in a fit of apoplexy.+ Here he is in the carriage which I thought fit to accompany to his home.' Assistance being procured he was removed from the carriage and placed on a sofa. My brother Doctor then said: 'we must get him blooded, how shall we get his coat off?' 'Who is his surgeon?' I replied. 'Never mind those things, let me open his temporal artery' which was done on one side immediately, but the blood not flowing freely I opened the temporal artery on the other side where we took off about a pint of blood, after which his conscien- ceness seemed to return, and as there was no paralysis on either side we advised him to remain on the sofa for an hour or two with his head covered with cloths dipped in vinegar and water. Some cold brandy and water was given to him to drink. I lived in the adjoining house where patients were waiting my arrival, and to them I went having opened four temporal arteries in an hour or thereabouts after my return from the country. Both of these patients recovered and lived for years afterwards without palsy, insensibility or further return of that Apoplectic condition of the brain.

Mr Sims was an old man, past 60 and very shaky in his hands and tremulous in his speech, not like delirium tremens but resembling that tremulous manner of a nervous person. His son qualified as a physician and settled at Bridport and his two daughters were married, one to a Plymouth solicitor and the other to a celebrated chemist in London. He was a most gentlemanly and friendly neighbour. I revisited

Mrs Hunt and found her quite relieved, more comfortable in her head than she had been for months. She lived for some years afterwards. Mrs Hunt's complaints had long denoted the tendency to apoplexy[+] which had been warded off or kept in abeyance by regimen and prophylic remedies, advised and directed by myself. Her sister too, Mrs Admiral Lindsay [had] lived in the adjoining house, a total wreck from a former attack of apoplexy. She was unable to walk, stand or feed herself, her sight, hearing, smell and taste were normal, but the free use of her tongue was so far paralysed as to prevent speech entirely, her taste and power of swallowing were still preserved. In her eating and drinking if she wanted anything additional as sugar, salt or savory articles, she would make signs with her eyes or other ways for them. Physiologists and pathologists must consider this a most interesting case. This lady died in my arms [in] 1825.

It may further be remarked that her late gallant husband, Admiral Lindsay, lived in George Street with the present widow and being fond of horse exercise rode one day with the intention of going to Saltram on the Chain Bridge which plied across the river Plym before the erection of the magnificent stone and iron bridge now erected there by the former Earl of Morley* at his sole expense, and designed by the celebrated Engineer Rendle, on which bridge there is an inscription composed or revised by the late Mr Canning during his visit at Saltram in the year 1825. Admiral Lindsay, on arriving at this spot from which the bridge had just been shoved off, hailed the boatmen to stop and put back for him in an imperious manner, fancying himself possibly in command of a ship on the quarter deck and not on horseback. The disobedience of the boatmen brought forth angry expressions from the Admiral, who was noticed to vociferate loudly and swear against the disobedient boatmen and whilst raising himself in his stirrups with his arm upraised in a threatening manner was seen to droop, loosen the bridle reins and swing from side to side until he fell off his horse on the road, from which he was taken up by the bystanders in an insensible state and carried back to Plymouth and placed in his house, where he died speechless. Here was an awful visitation of providence in shewing the uncertainty of human life.

During one of my early visits at Bath, the instance of my great-uncle, Barnard Butter was told me. He had dined out at some public meeting and drank more port wine than did him good. Early on the following morning he was discovered by his good wife to be insensible and snoring heavily in his sleep from which he could not be awoke. His family surgeon was sent for but he, being ill, was unable to attend, luckily perhaps as he, like the other Bath doctors at that time, were advocates generally for feeding and not depleting their patients. The House Surgeon of the Bath Hospital came as his deputy and opened the temperal artery from which blood flowed freely and relieved the compressed brain without the usual concomitant of palsy or loss of sensation or motion. He lived for many years after this attack and died in the 84th year of his age of Hydrothorax[+] from neglected pneumonia, no relief from bleeding.

1842

March 25 Jno Arthur died of consumption aged 43, one of my earliest friends and patients. April 3rd Lord Rolle* died aged 90. I drove up from Plymouth [on] the same horse that day to Woodbury and there took a fresh one for Bicton where I arrived about 4 hours after his Lordship's death.

July 27th Jno Hole died aged 87 at Owley, in one of my cottages there. The weather being fine we made an excursion on the Moor with 3 saddle horses, 2 donkeys, Joe Edmonds as a guide and others. Our route lay up Glasscombe bottom to three barroughs, Ermepound, Huntingdon Warren, Peter's Cross and on the western banks of the Avon River, which we followed back to Shipley Bridge, to Aish Village, home to Owley, after spending a most pleasant day safely and pleasantly.

August 3rd I attended a meeting of the Exeter Province Medical and Surgical Association and dined with Dr Shapter[96] at whose hospitable table I met many of my profession, all brethren, and spent a most pleasant day.

August 10th began the sinking of a well at Owley and after blowing away the rock reached a beautiful spring of water about 10 feet deep beneath the surface.

August 11th having attended the Plymouth Races on Chelson Meadow my attention was directed to a Tradesman who had been thrown from a horse in attempting to ride over a rope. He was much stunned by the fall, and not coming quickly to his senses I blooded and sent him home, where he recovered and called some days afterwards to thank me for the great benefit he had derived from my bleeding him promptly on the spot.

Sunday 25th Sept. attended Brent Church.

September 29th Sheppard's Windsor Villa No. 7 paid for this house

paid for this house	£1,906
conveyance	33 18s 0d
alterations	73 9s 3d
	£2,013 7s 3d
new stable	200 0s 0d
	£2,213 7s 3d

October 2nd dined at Owley, Brent Church pm, Mr Lowe tooth ache, extracted two teeth with a gimlet for him, having no better instrument.

Dec 5th off at 6 o'clock by mail for Lostwithill to see Mr Golding Inn-keeper with Epistaxis.$^{+}$ His nose had continued to bleed in spite of all efforts to stop it. A piece of lint rolled in flour and alum passed through the floor of his nostril nearly into the throat, where it remained for two or three days and effectually stopped the haemorrhage. In a hired gig back to Liskeard and afterwards by coach I reached Plymouth about 9 at night.

December 14th dined, and on the 15th slept at Windsor Villas for the first time.

Dec. 18th I was attacked with Rheumatic Fever and laid up more or less to the end of the year in bed. This was my 2nd attack in 10 years, the 1st having occurred in 1832 during the raging cholera, of which an account has already been given. Of medical men it is remarkable that Dr Cookworthy, Sir G Magrath* and myself should each have had two attacks of rheumatic fever, besides other medical men of whom I have heard.

---

[96] Dr Thomas Shapter, a physician at the Devon and Exeter Hospital, who published a pioneering work entitled *The History of the Cholera in Exeter in 1832* (London/Exeter: John Churchill/Adam Holden, 1849).

1843

Much honour prevailed in those days between the medical men of Plymouth. I lived for 19 years and 9 months in George Street, which I reluctantly quitted for No. 7 Windsor Villas, within one door of my professional brother and school fellow Dr Cookworthy, without the slightest altercation or jealousy. Necessity obliged me to leave this comfortable house as shops were opened in all directions and society so much improved as to induce me to obtain a larger house or give up society altogether. Dr Cookworthy and I lived for many years in houses divided only by one other, always on the best of terms and in readiness to serve each other.

Sir G Magrath* and I were friendly rivals for the same favours and professional patronage. He had the start of me in years and experience. Our acquaintance began on the Turnpike road between Plymouth and the Dartmoor Prisons where he was going on promotion from Millbay Prison, of which he had been Surgeon. He used sometimes to remind me of this meeting and of the outrageous green feather which I wore in my cocked hat. Whilst Surgeon at the Dartmoor Prisons in care of the sick of American prisoners who had replaced the French in 1814 a row or riot occurred. Governor Shortland ordered the troops to fire on the rebellious Americans, of whom many were wounded and comforted by the skill and attention of Surgeon Magrath, to whom was presented a memorial of thanks signed by numerous prisoners after the cessation of hostilities between England and America. Magrath then settled in Plymouth, not as a Surgeon but as a Physician, and obtained many friends and patients through the interest and recommendations of Naval Officers. One recommendation was that he had been Lord Nelson's Surgeon on board the Victory, which ship he quitted for a better appointment on shore as Surgeon of a Naval Hospital. He had been surgeon to a line of battle ships at the early age of 21, and always suffered from sea sickness which induced him to relinquish sea service and appoint his friend Beattie, afterwards Sir Wm Beattie,* to the vacant Surgeoncy of the Victory, Nelson's flag ship, on board of which he was shot at Trafalgar and the ball was preserved by Beattie, who generally took it with him and shewed to the company wherever he dined. Magrath was a smart, well-grown man 20 years my senior, very active in his habits and calculated to make friends. His language however was stiff, overstudied and precise. This kind of language, being unusual, took with many patients who had consulted other doctors. Sick people are generally given to change doctors unless they get well speedily. One doctor may be deserted for being too stern and uncourteous, another for his reticence and caution, but Magrath's courtesy and frankness soon made him popular. He always pronounced on a disease at once and considered almost every complaint as hepatic or seated in the liver. Being asked by the sister what was the disease of a sick girl, what was her complaint, he answered that there was a good deal of hepatic congestion, which terms, not being found in the lady's vocabulary, she again enquired and received for answer that there was also derangement of the chydo-pro-ietic [sic] viscera. Derangement being the only word understood by the anxious and enquiring sister she replied thus: 'derangement, Sir? I assure you, sir, my sister was never deranged.' 'No Miss, by that word I did not mean mental hallucination.' Again puzzled observed: 'I assure you her mental faculties are right. What diet should we observe?' 'Farrinaceous Ham.' 'Do you mean Milk diet?' 'Yes, coagulated milk again.' 'What kind of milk is that?' 'I believe you have some Devonshire term for it.' 'Do you mean junket, Sir?' 'Just so.' This kind of proceeding from a handsome and exceedingly well dressed Physician took very much with the public. He also became a member of the Freemasons and rose to a high rank among that body, having a number of initials annexed to his medical titles. He was a bon ami, spoke out loudly, and laughed heartily as though he was on a stage speaking words and sentences to be afterwards repeated.

One night at the Plymouth Theatre I dropped into a very thin house where I saw two Freemasons, Sir G M and Mr Councellor Parham seated in a box by themselves, which I entered and got into conversation with them. Between the acts they drew my attention to a lady and gentleman seated alone in a box on the opposite side. Parham said: 'that is a lady and gentleman living in lodgings and spending their honeymoon in Plymouth. We have watched their proceedings and considered that they have had a quarrel as the gentleman repeatedly accosts the lady who turns her head aside and back towards him refusing to answer his remarks.' 'That is an odd way' said I 'of spending the honeymoon.' Upon which remark Sir GM sighed and said 'oh dear me! Connubalism has its acerbities' upon which Parham roared and laughed so vociferously as to be heard across the theatre during the absence of music and to rouse the attention of the quarrelling Bride and Bridegroom, who thereupon seem to speak to each other as much as we could guess and say 'we are observed' whereupon the lady smiled and looked towards us. 'Oh' said I 'quarrel if any is mended as the lady uses her fan and smiles around.' 'Yes' said Parham 'she certainly does smile at last!' Sir GM then pulled out his glass and looking towards them replied thus: 'I perceive the smile of pacification.'

After my 3 years absence more or less from Plymouth from 1817 to 1820 I returned to Plymouth in my new character as Physician and learnt that Magrath* had made considerable headway amongst his Naval brethren and had been often consulted by the patients of Dr Woollcombe* who then enjoyed the best practice in Plymouth. I had therefore to take my stand with these formidable opponents as Physicians of such renown before me. I soon found that I should not get bread and cheese if I relinquished operations, some of which, especially those on the eye, have been performed successfully by myself alone for many years. Having taken up my new abode at Windsor Villas, never before occupied or indeed properly finished,[97] I had much to do to put this house in order suitable to my wants and wishes.

Whilst confined to bed with rheumatic fever a summons arrived after midnight for me to visit Mr Charles Wheeler's son at Stonehouse, but as I knew no such person there and was too ill to walk I declined of course to go or send a deputy. Some time afterwards Mr Wheeler called and informed me that when our acquaintance was first formed in 1810 at St Bartholomew's Hospital his father and himself were the Apothecaries at that Institution and both friends to me. Being a member of the Yacht Club and now a man of fortune he had taken up his residence at Stonehouse. I dined at Stonehouse with my old friend Wheeler, and there met the Secretary of the Yacht Club and many members who had all suffered extremely from their perilous voyage from Cowes to Plymouth and were unfitted to enter for any of the prizes given by the Plymouth Club. Wheeler's son was a poor decrepid paralytic boy from his youth upwards owing to teething which produced fits and palsy of the limbs. The poor little fellow died at Stonehouse on 18th day of August in 1843 in fits. Many instances

---

[97] This seems a little strange. Foulston, who designed the villas, died in 1841, and English Heritage dates them to the 1820s or 1830s.

I have known of a partial or similar kind in children from teething but I never saw an instance of greater aggravation.

May 1st Sold out some Trust money with advantage and advanced £3,700 on the Whifferton Estate to Mr Henry Simmons who was a Land Surveyor and a man of sufficient education to give lectures on Agriculture, but who soon ruined himself by his improvements in draining, levelling and irrigating lands, his model farm and building a good farm house being done with borrowed capital. He was unable to keep up the interest, which being added to the borrowed capital soon reached the value of the estate and left the other creditors in arrears and his own family, including himself and wife, with the loss of their private property. Disappointment and death then destroyed a good scientific farmer.

During my illness in bed I was sent for by my friend John Allen at Coldridge near Kingsbridge to visit his wife and family who were laid up dangerously ill from Scarlet Fever, which proved fatal.

Scarlet Fever is a very deceptive and dangerous disease, my prognosis was always gloomy whenever I saw a patient with Scarlatina Maligna. Lately we have heard of a melancholy instance where a London Barrister who had married one of our friends and became the father of four children thought it prudent [to] take them from London to Super Mare for a change and whilst there all his four children died from Scarlatina which was not attributable to the place or the sea air but to the dormant poison laid in their systems before leaving London.

After my convalescence Parham and I went to Owley Cottage and whilst there inspected the Monksmoor Estate offered for sale. I was inclined to purchase it foreseeing the SD rail must pass through it, but as my ready money was gone on Mortgages I consulted my brother with the desire of purchasing this estate for £3,000, one half of this sum to be provided by myself the other half by himself and for the survivor to possess it. His disinclination was strengthened by the advice of a neighbour and so he refused my offer. Immediately after my answer a farmer bought the estate chiefly with borrowed capital and cleared a £1,000 by a resale partly to the Company and partly to another person.

March the 7th Uncle Barnard died at Ottery at 81 and was buried in Ottery Church Yard, leaving his property to my brother.

April 11th Thos King Esq. my good friend and patient died at the North Huish Manor House at 54.

May 16th began the stable and coach house at Windsor Villas.

Sir David Dickson's* daughter became my Patient on account of amaurosis[+] which was nearly cured. She married and became a Widow, retaining her sight almost to perfection.

Sept. 20th died my patient J Tillie Coryton Esq. at Pentillie Castle and in London Jno Buttell Esq. of Glebe House from effusions of water into the pericardium[+] and the pleura.[+]

Seeing a gentleman in the street lately become a resident in Plymouth with very red eyes and everted lids constituting ectropium[+] I said to his friend: 'I wonder that gentleman does not get his eyes cured.' 'Oh' he replied 'can that be done.' 'Yes' I said 'by an operation which I will perform on any morning when he shall call upon me.' This result was accomplished but excitement and a [?] diet would produce occasional attacks of chronic ophthalmy.[+] This gentleman after the age of 80 years broke his thigh at Cheltenham in crossing a street and by a good appliance recovered the use of his limb and lived for many years after the accident, thereby proving the soundness of his Constitution which had been much tried in the West Indies.

Mr Lowe, my old friend, died at Glaze Brook House, South Brent of ossification[+] of the arteries about the heart.

1844

Mrs Genl Vinnicombe aged 83, died Jan 27th, leaving Captn Mallack RM, Warwick A Hunt and myself joint Trustees under her will and protectors of her orphan grand-daughter Mary Ann Vinnicombe, living with her widow aunt Mrs Thorpe. The Revd Mr Oxenham, Vicar of Cornwood, Prebendary of the Exeter Cathedral fell ill and required my professional services until his death, which took place on the 23rd day of February at 73. He was an educated man.

March 12th I was sent for to visit Mr Solomon Tozer of Ashburton who had fractured the neck of his thigh bone by being blown down in attempting to close some window shutters during a violent gust of wind. In returning from this visit in my gig and passing through the upper part of Ivybridge towards Harford and Cornwood I met in the road a person who desired me to look at Betty Hamlyn, living in Mr River's cottage by the roadside. I had never before seen a cottage with so bad a floor, full of pits and holes without any flags or wood as a flooring. In one of these pits the old woman fell and hurt herself some weeks before this time and had never been able to stand afterwards. I saw her in bed upstairs doubled quite up in a hollow of the sacking with the right leg much shorter than the other, and the thigh bone evidently fractured near its neck. The accident had not been discovered and consequently no surgical appliances had been made. She was then above 102 years of age, lived many years after the accident and died at 105. She was a thin spare looking little woman with a shrivelled skin like a lemon in colour, but her intellects were all clear. I asked her how she had lived to attain such an age, and her answer was, like other people in low circumstances she never refused anything good in eating or drinking offered to her. Her sister Mary Burley also died at 94. Besides these two instances old Mrs Rivers, their nearest neighbour, lived over 90 years and Mr and Mrs Pearse of Broomhill each nearly attained their 90th year. In the small parish of Harford with a limited population there could then be found such an extraordinary number of old persons. I may here observe that of all the parishes in which I have had patients within 30 miles of Plymouth I have never met with so many instances of longevity as in this little parish of Harford, with 188 persons, which I believe to be one of the healthiest in Devonshire.

Betty Hamlyn's case is here recorded as a contrast against Mr Tozer's and my own Mother's. Nothing whatever had been done for her undiscovered fractures, but nature was left to herself whilst in the two other cases everything was done which skill and humanity could suggest and both patients died from sloughing[+] of the hinder parts. Two other parallel cases are recorded in my memory. A Workman standing on a cart in pulling away some faggots desired another man not to move the horse without first speaking to him, but the animal moved of his own accord and pitched the loader off the cart on his head and shoulders. He was taken up helpless and carried to his cottage in a sort of paralysis of the lower limbs, leading the parish doctor and other surgeons to believe that the fracture of the cervical or dorsal vertebra had taken place. After a long confinement to bed, above a year, sensation and motion began to return, contrary to all expectation and the prognosis of medical men who considered his case hopeless. He so far recovered as to be able in time to walk about and do light work in his garden and he lived some years after the accident. I have heard of another case of a man who was loading hay on a waggon during hay-making season and when the load was nearly finished the horse moved off with the loaded waggon without notice so that he fell off head foremost, broke his neck and died on the spot in the presence of his master and the hay-makers, to their great sorrow and surprise.

Two daughters of a wealthy Baronet returned from India, and being fond of horse exercise rode out over a Down to a cottage near where one young lady stopped for a short time whilst the other rode forward. She then set off at a canter to overtake her sister, and the horse being fresh in condition sprang and jumped in a way as horses will do to overtake each other, and threw her off on her head and shoulders, producing concussion if not a fracture of some part of the vertebral column, so that she was taken up from the ground helpless and paralytic in her lower extremities. Sloughing[+] of the hinder parts ensued and carried her off at the end of many weeks from the date of her accident. What shall we say of this contrast of cases? The poor survive but the rich die! Let us not however disparage or cast a doubt on surgical skill brought to such a high pitch of eminence in England, but rather let us suppose that poor persons who feed themselves with food convenient for their bodies and breathe pure air, not contaminated with the taint of towns or mid-night revels, take their rest of night and enjoy sweet 'sleep the lot of the labouring man', and thus does their blood keep more healthful and fit to repair damages done to different parts of the body.

March 20th the Plymouth Eye Infirmary had now been worked most successfully with increasing results above 23 years, and had for a long time created a desire with its founders and committee to build or buy an edifice more suited to its wants and purposes than the tired old dilapidated house in Westwell Street. Annual, biennial and quarterly discussions arose about the purchase of another house or building on the present site a new Infirmary. A plan brought forward at one meeting and approved of was generally upset at the next meeting of committee. Tired of these wearisome disappointments for many years, at last I fixed on a house in Princess Square lately inhabited by a famous dentist and agreed to purchase it for the price of £1,200. I assembled the Committee, 13 in number, at my own house where we all unanimously agreed to buy this house. Circulars were accordingly printed and sent to the different subscribers, signed by the secretary appointing a day for a general Meeting to approve and confirm this decision. The circulars were scarcely issued before a storm commenced amongst the inhabitants and residents in Princess Square of whom some persons raised curious objections. One attorney descanted on the loss and great disadvantages such a public Institution as an Eye Infirmary would do to his freehold property, which in course of time turned out to be mortgaged some hundred pounds above its value. Another attorney said how unpleasant it would be, the sight of an Eye Infirmary opposite his dwelling house. I could not but smile in replying that if he looked at home he would see 'Fire and Life Assurance Office' lettered over his own door. A venerable and prosy old gentleman and part-founder of a hospital busied himself most diligently in obtaining proxies against this scheme. He went so far as to call an Eye Infirmary a nuisance on account of the number of blind and afflicted persons brought near his dwelling house, stating what a bustle and noise there would be, forgetting for a moment the Mechanic's Institute at the corner to which hundreds and thousands flock in times of Elections and public meetings, singing, hurraing, cheering, and making all sorts of noises, all of which would be nothing with the site of an Ophthalmic Institution. Then again there was a celebrated veterinarian, with his hospital for diseased horses and his shoeing forge with hammering all parts of the day, thought that his establishment was tolerable compared to the sight of an Eye Infirmary. Then there was the dear good old deaf lady aged 89 roused partly by her own disinclination but chiefly by the clamours of the Square to oppose an Ophthalmic Institution, observing that she would withdraw her opposition if I would establish another for diseases of the Ear, but as I could not make this promise she carried on her opposition in the most energetic manner for such a venerable and benevolent lady. But the most curious of all the circumstances was that the secretary who was present at the committee meeting and agreed to the printing of the circulars with his name subscribed, should say that he never agreed to the plan and thought there were many objections against it. As the day of battle approached the sub-committee consisting of the Vicar, Admiral Wise and other friends waited on me and said that if I persisted in the purchase of the house I should make many enemies and injure the charity. I listened to their advice and agreed that we should ostensibly carry on the war to the hour of meeting when the Vicar as Chairman would rise, comment on the opposition, laud the Charity and praise the indefatigable Founders and then concluding, throw down the olive branch and for the sake of peace give up the much desired purchase. What an unexpected result! What a waste of all those bundles of papers before them with promises and proxies and premeditated speeches, nothing was to be done. I asked the Admiral if I ought to say anything and received his emphatic answer: 'not a word Doctor' so we struck our sails and made peace with each other all in good fellowship. What was to be done now but to revert to the old regime until something else offered.

Oct. the 31st oft defeated but never subdued I inspected another house suggested to me by Captn Fisk.* It was isolated and rather distant from the market and centre of Plymouth but airey and suited to the purposes of an Eye Infirmary. The former tenant gave £60 a year for this house, which I bought of Phillips the builder for £1,275. I then called the Committee together and said: 'Gentlemen, I have been defeated on many years in obtaining a freehold house with a local habitation and a name for our Charity, and I have now succeeded to my own satisfaction. I have purchased Millbay House, which I will transfer to Trustees for the uses and benefit of the Plymouth Eye Infirmary or I will keep it as private property for myself. What say you? Shall it be taken for the Institution or not?' The Committee then agreed to accept my offer and to appoint three Trustees, Sir Ralph Lopes,* Mr John Williams and myself. No one dreamt at that time of its prospective or increasing value from the erection of the Plymouth Railway Station near to it. When first it was suggested that the SD Railway would purchase the adjoining ground for a station, the Engineer was reported in Parliamentary deeds to have said that none but a mad man would think of crossing the Union Road and forming a station on its present site. However, this was done and afterwards two applications were made to me to re-sell the Eye Infirmary. An attorney offered me £500 more than it cost, and another person hinted that he would give £2,000 for the house and premises. These offers were of course rejected for this most suitable house which turns out to be the best that could have been selected in the most desirable part of Plymouth.

1845

Jan. 3rd Mrs Gest died at Modbury at 53 leaving her husband and two daughters. She had laboured under mental hallucinations owing to obstruction in the bowels which Enemas alone could relieve.

14th Jan. met Dymond at Brent on behalf of the SD Railway and agreed with him for land through which the line was intended to run, being about 4a 1r 12p for £700, average about £162 per acre.

Feb. 11th Col. Symons of Chaddlewood died at 68 and bequeathed his property to the son of his nephew, Salton Symons Esq., the present occupier of this beautiful mansion and estate. The Col. entered the SD Militia at an early period of life and, being stationed at Bristol won the affections of Miss Miles whose fortune was very large and whose residence was continued at Chaddlewood after the Colonel's death. She was an amiable and charitable lady, much respected by the inhabitants of Plympton. The Colonel owed this good wife to the SD Militia.

April 5th I visited London and attended the Marquis of Northampton's Soiree as FRS and there met a number of my scientific friends.

The 17th a patient came to me from Cornwall with Staphyloma+ of her left eye which protruded far beyond the lids and much disfigured a comely face. I sliced off a large portion of the protruding ball and closed the lid over the remainder left within the orbit. Violent inflammation ensued and led me to say that I would never risk such an operation again, but would extirpate the whole eye-ball. She however recovered and expressed herself as much relieved and grateful for all I had done for her. My friend Robert Tucker, an eminent solicitor at Ashburton, became so ill as to require my professional visits often repeated. His peculiar vision on the faculty of perceiving colours I have already related in the Phrenological Transactions of Edinburgh,[98] and compared his case with that of Mr Dalton of Manchester and other persons incapable of distinguishing one colour from another.

June 9th the Rev. Mr Edsall of Woodbury dined with us, made a good dinner and repeated his unaccountable loss of flesh without any obvious disease from 279 lbs to 140 lbs, the loss being 139 lbs.

June 12th having slept this night at Owley, we were roused at 2 o'clock in the morning by a messenger from Plymouth sent up by Miss Welsford to desire that I would proceed without delay to visit her brother at Bowden, near Totnes, where he lay dangerously ill attended by Mr Kellock, Surgeon of Totnes. I found him labouring under a severe attack of pneumonia brought on by a rapid walk into Totnes with some post letters and by a hasty return up a long hill of a mile in length to his family dinner. This rapid walk in hot weather produced much perspiration and heat and induced him to sit for a time in a cold hall floored with stone, where he chilled himself and thence began the pulmonary+ disease which so embarrassed his breathing as to lead me to doubt whether or not anything could be done to save him. He had not been blooded and therefore some blood was taken which proved to be highly buffed and cupped and as it afforded much relief, venesection+ was repeated in the course of some hours, again with relief. Effusion however had taken place within the plura+ and pericardium,+ therefore this treatment had come too late

---

[98] 'Remarks on the Faculty of Perceiving Colours', *Transactions of the Phrenological Society* 1 (1824), pp. 209–34 and 'Remarks on the Insensibility of the Eye to Certain Colours', *Edinburgh Philosophical Journal* 6 (1821–2), pp. 135–40.

and so he died on the 15th at 58, much regretted by all who had the pleasure of his acquaintance and deplored by his devoted wife and dutiful children.

July 17th Captain Mallack, RM died of diseased heart and dropsy⁺ produced no doubt by the excitement he endured on finding that his ward may have been tampered with by his Co-Trustee WAE, who had decoyed this girl into his office at noon, when the clerks were absent at their dinners, then locked the doors, took a pistol out of a drawer and threatened to shoot her and himself unless she surrendered all discretion to his wishes, which were accomplished in the form of a rape. Hurried and flushed with dishevelled hair and despoiled dress she returned to her aunt and told all that had happened. The aunt called upon me and related the story which disposed me quickly to summon Capt. M and Major Balchild, a friend of the family. We then sent to WAE and requested his attendance; he admitted the truth of this charge which we determined at first to make known to his wife, but violent words ensued and he threatened if we so resolved to return home, let loose his savage dogs and shoot the first man who attempted to enter his house. These words uttered in anger by such a consummate villain very much agitated poor Captain Mallack in bad health and dismayed Major Balchild, who could not act officially with us. Mallack returned to his home, offered £100 to be superseded and left me to decide for myself. Not long afterwards [WAE] confessed to his wife all he had done and received her forgiveness. His plan apparently was as attorney and extrustee to elope with the girl, secure her fortune above £20,000 and probably get a divorce from his wife.

August 2nd Attorney B died who had kicked up such a shindy against the Eye Infirmary; failed and defrauded his clients for a large sum exceeding one thousand pounds, which was a serious loss to a family of orphan girls.

Oct 1st shooting at Aller near Newton over property of the late Rev. G Baker with good sport.

Nov. 3rd my brother finding himself getting worse at his own home had come down to Plymouth for a change and on the 3rd of Nov. accompanied me in a drive to Owley, thinking he might be able to shoot a woodcock. I halted near Ivybridge to visit my patient Major Templer, late of the SD Militia, and remained a short time, but too long for my poor brother who got tired and cold by sitting in the gig during my absence. At Owley he became comfortable, rode out the next day on horseback and shot a woodcock which delighted him much. He returned after a week to Woodbury where he became gradually worse. He came back on the 22nd, made his will on the 25th, and was tapped on the 26th by Messrs Fuge and Square who drew off 14 pints of water which relieved him much. He remained with me at Plymouth until the 12th of Dec. and again returned to Woodbury where he was tapped for the 2nd time by Mr Price, his successor at Limpstone, who drew off 16 pints of water.

21st of Dec. soon after my dinner the Boots from the Globe Inn called and desired me to visit a lady without delay who had just arrived in a stage coach. My surprise was great on finding the lady in bed with a newly-born infant by her side. She was relieved and smiling enough to tell me that she had been delivered of a child in the stage coach. Such an event I had never before met with and therefore now mention it. She was the wife of a Surgeon stationed at Chatham from whence she had travelled to Plymouth to be near her friends.

23rd Dec. Mr Fox Parham and myself were shooting woodcocks at Corringdon where I left them at noon and said I wished to attend the sale of the late Rev. Mr Baker's lands at 2 o'clock on that day at Brent. Accordingly I changed my shooting dress and presented myself at the sale which was numerously attended. Mr Tucker, the attorney at Ashburton, wished to have bought some fields to be exchanged for a field in Ashburton belonging to the feoffees of Brent, but the prices at which they were knocked down exceeded his valuation. Then turning to me he said: 'I wish you would buy Summers Wood Estate and let me have a field or two to be exchanged for the fields at Ashburton.' My reply was that I had never inspected or passed over Summers Wood Estate, and that I was ignorant of its value or acreage. 'Oh' he said 'Trant, the Surveyor was there he can tell you all about it as he drained and laid out the land for Mr Baker.' 'Well' said I 'Mr Trant, what do you know about this Summers Wood Estate?' His answer was he knew or ought to know more than other men its value. 'It lets for £75 a year. I will engage to get a tenant to give £100 a year.' 'How can you be so sure of that?' I enquired. 'I will warrant that rental' said he. When the Estate was put up at auction I did not bid at first, but when there came a halt at £1,800 I bid £50 which rather astonished the company. After a pause the Parson and his lawyer bid £5 more and I quickly said £1,900. Another pause ensued and another £5 bid, which I quickly followed by £50. Again there was a repetition and my bid was £2,000. The run between us then went on to £2,200, when the vendors adjourned and returned with an answer that the Estate would now go to the country. As the best bidder I remained silent until the Parson's adviser advanced £5 to which I said, 'ditto' and then to me the Estate was knocked down at £2,210 upon which sum I paid a deposit of £231. Immediately after the sale the parson's attorney asked me if I would resell the plantation fronting the Vicarage House on the opposite side of the Avon River. I replied: 'Yes.' 'Will you also sell the field adjoining.' I again said: 'Yes. I have bought this Estate without ever seeing it or knowing its value and therefore I am free to accommodate you and Mr Tucker with the resale or exchange at a fair valuation.' I then returned to Owley and told my companions that I had bought an Estate, much to their astonishment as I had never seen it. Instead of a further application from the parson I received intelligence that he had gone over the river and taken possession of the Plantation which he had previously offered to buy. On this subject we had a subsequent meeting and gathered together such old persons as could give evidence, or remember anything about the planting of the trees there by the former Vicar, who was owner of the Summers Wood Estate and the advowson. The question was whether he had planted these trees as Vicar on the Vicarage land or as owner of the Summers Wood Estate. The quantity of land so disputed was about a ¼ of an acre and with the trees thereon might be worth £40 or £50. As the evidence was conflicting my attorney said: 'What will you do, Doctor? To try this question will cost £2 or £300. You may win or you may lose, and the Vicar and you will henceforth be bad neighbours.' Prudence therefore disposed me to give it up, but this concession did not satisfy the Vicar who then claimed the whole of the river instead of one half for himself allowing me the other half. I had taken many stones out of the bed of the river and had built a boundary wall against my garden without any dispute. I had also cut down a large ash tree on my side of the river and sold it for a guinea. When my boundary wall was finished and the last corner stone fixed I was seated under my veranda after 8 o'clock one evening by moonlight and talking to my man in the garden when we heard splash, splash in the water. I said to him to go down and see what that is, thinking that someone had fallen into the river whilst crossing the stepping stones leading across from the Vicarage to my side. I sat still and then heard the following dialogue: My man Loquiter[?]: 'Is that you Mr

Cole? I did not think you would have done such a thing as to throw down a part of the wall which had been last put up.' As the parson and his man had recrossed the stepping stones and gone back to his own door, the loud voice of my man induced me to go down and enquire what it was all about. I then was shewn the piece of wall with the stones thrown down into the river. The Vicar and his man then returned and met me and my man on the stepping stones of the river. I asked if he had pulled down the corner stone of my wall? Yes, he had ordered his man to do so. 'For what reason' I asked? 'Because' he said, some of the stones taken out of the river belonged to him. I asked his reason why he deferred his claim so late until I built a great number of yards of wall with stones taken from the river, and these were almost the last put up. He said he did not then know his rights to claim the whole river, nor could he define the line of the bank dividing our properties. Angry words then ensued at his threatening to remove the crossing stones and to prevent me or my people from crossing over the river. I confess I was almost inclined to forget myself and give him a ducking but I refrained.

On Xmas Day I revisited my poor brother at Woodbury and partook of the last Xmas Dinner he was ever likely to see with my sister's family. Next day I returned to Plymouth. Thus ended the eventful year of 1845.

1846

May 13th South Devon Railway opened at Teignmouth, quantities of mackerel carted there from Plymouth.

May 19th off by Tally Ho coach to Exeter and Woodbury. Brother very ill, worse since the 3rd tapping.

20th brother died ¼ to 12 noon in presence of myself and niece Julia Ashford, his end was peace at 53. It is remarkable that I, living at Plymouth, the distance of 50 miles from Woodbury, should have been present at these three deaths of my two parents and beloved brother.

21st Post Mortem by Messrs Price and Brent. The whole body was pallid and bloodless, especially the peritoneum+ which had contained the water. I was anxious particularly to see the state of his left lung in which there must have been an Abscess of many years before to account for the quantities of purulent+ matter which he spit up at that time when he had a tremendous cough. There was an indentation in the lung healed over evidently showing the former seat of an abscess, his liver was much diseased and altered from its natural colour by various little tumours studded in and about its structure. The spleen was enlarged, of the two kidneys only one remained and in lieu of the other a mass of fatty matter leaving a doubt whether or not more than one ever existed.

22nd up at 6 sorting papers, started at 10 and dined in Exeter with James and Louisa Ashford, then Plymouth by coach in the evening.

23rd Plymouth all day seeing patients.

25th at Owley.

26th Newton at 12, Dr Avery and Beeching's office to settle the purchase of Summers Wood. Cheque to Bickford £1,829 19s 0d Mr Nicholas and Mary Baker

£254 19s 0d former deposit. Total £2,320 12s 6d.[99] Dined there and drove on to Woodbury.

27th Brother's funeral in Woodbury Church.

28th Woodbury all day. Crudge Surveyor about sale.

29th Left Woodbury at 2, Ashburton tea at 6, Owley 10. Slept there.

30th slept again at Owley.

31st At Plymouth Miss Boyse and Lieut Williams dined at Windsor Villas.

June 1st Plymouth all day.

4th thermometer 84, hottest day.

22nd from Waye to Newton and Teignmouth, thence to Exmouth Baths, Bastin's Fly, Woodbury at tea.

23rd slept at Exmouth, dined at Woodbury with the Ashfords.

24th Exeter, Birds, Abernethie, Waye at dinner. Lost Rover at Haldon.

25th Plymouth.

28th Coronation Day.

July 1st Uncle Ben died at 76. Sheep shearing at Covingdon, gave prizes £35. Sold 1 house Mutley for £700.

15th Mr Seccombe, Surgeon of Plymouth, died at 81. Visited Miss Rashleigh, Cuddra Cottage, St Austell and returned by coach the following day.

20th Proving brother's will. Hatchard and Pridham £100.

16th August Rev. Mr Edsall died at 66.

23rd Cathedral a.m., Teignmouth by rail and back to Exeter. Visit to Mr & Mrs Bird.

24th left Exeter at 10, Owley at 7.

Sept. 1st shooting partridges at Brent with Camiter and Parham.

2nd Mr Thos Baker married Louisa Ashford.

6th called out of Church to visit Rob. Tucker's child at Octagon.

12th Foundation-stone laying, Keyham Docks, laid by Baker contractor, Lord Buckland's speech, handsome dejeuner.

8th deposit at Cemetery £96.

Nov. 9th ditto £96.

Dec. 4th Jacob Butter died at 59, my father's cousin in Plymouth, leaving a widow now [1866] aged 80 years, also a daughter by the widow's sister.[100]

1847

Jan. 12th Edmund Lockyer* Esq. died of apoplexy.[+] Thrice Mayor of Plymouth and founder of new streets and buildings, his residence was in George Street where many other aged persons had died of apoplexy.

14th Henry Woollcombe Esq. Solicitor also died of apoplexy.[+] He practised as a solicitor with much credit and filled numerous offices in Plymouth besides that of Chief Magistrate, which office he filled with public satisfaction during the year 1814. He was also the founder and the principal mover in the establishment of the

[99] The figures, including the deposit of £231, actually add up to £2,315 18s 0d, i.e. £105 18s 0d more than the purchase price recorded previously.

[100] There is no record of Jacob's marriages, but presumably, after his first wife's death, he married her sister.

Plymouth Athenaeum, where he in turn with many others gave lectures on the Arts, Sciences and Literature.

14th Charles Hatchett* Esq. VPRS, my highly esteemed and valuable friend died at Belle Vue House, Chelsea where he had resided for many years. His valuable contributions to science and his chemical researches into the analysis of bones, shells and other articles acquired for him a world-wide fame and a place in every scientific work connected with chemistry. Mr Hatchett's private friendship was most sincere and his hospitality great. I owe much to him for my introduction into the Royal Society at so early a period of my life and for the acquaintances I was able to make through his kind introductions with the President, Sir Humphry Davy, Bart, Sir Francis Chantrey* the Sculptor, the Bishop of Norwich, Sir Everard Home, Bart., and many others.

28th The Rev. Arscott Howard, the respected Minister at St Andrew's Chapel, had laboured for some days under low typhoid fever for which Mr Page had attended him until this morning, when symptoms of delirium appeared and I was called up at 4 in the morning to consult with Mr Page on his condition, which I soon saw would terminate fatally as his vital powers were ebbing slow. During my 6th visit of this day on March the 1st he died and left no doubt in my mind that the air of the Chapelry as well as the water percolating through the burying ground into the well had produced deleterious effects on his health and, added to his close application to study, produced his death. It was remarked that neither his predecessor or followers had ever enjoyed good health at St Andrew's Chapelry, but since the cessation of burial in that ground and the establishment of the Plymouth Cemetery one mile out of Plymouth that low tone of health usually complained of by residents in this neigh-bourhood is now wholly removed.

[The following is a newspaper cutting that has been attached to the Memoir with a pin.]

Death of the Rev. Arscott Howard.
It is our painful duty this week to record the death of this most pious, amiable, and deserving young clergyman, aged 29, who has been the curate of St Andrew's chapel nearly four years. His death took place at the chapelry on the 1st inst. about midnight.

On Sunday the 21st ult. he preached a sermon, his last, we believe, to a crowded congregation, on behalf of the starving Irish and Scotch peasantry, taking his text from St Mark ch VIII. v. 3 and making a most eloquent and effective appeal to the sympathies and aid of his flock. Little did his delighted audience think that this would be his farewell discourse on earth. This sermon was followed by the largest subscription, viz. £61.5.0. obtained at any church in the neighbourhood. In his discourse, he feelingly alluded to the demise of our late townsman Hen. Woollcombe Esq and expatiated on his example and charitable disposition. His sermon struck his hearers as one of the most appropriate and convincing that had been delivered there for some time. The condensed arrangements, the argument, and force of the compo-sition, had evidently cost him great pains and study, and its effect was commensurate with its merit.

Mr Howard was the only child of a disconsolate mother, and she a widow. His father was a native of Plymouth and a successful teacher of Oriental languages, acquired through a self-taught education by an extraordinary capacity for Belles Lettres and classical literature.

The death of so devout and excellent a pastor will be generally mourned by his flock, and especially by that respectable family with whose accomplished daughter he was engaged speedily to be united in wedlock. His constant zeal, devotion and attention to his Christian duties rendered him a great favourite with his hearers and left an awful but impressive lesson to the living of the uncertain tenure of human life, and of that divine truth which says "in the midst of life we are in death."

[end of cutting.]

March 11th B Parham Esq., late Mayor of Plymouth, was appointed Judge of the County Court of the Worcester district at a salary of £1,200. By his removal I was deprived of a good neighbour and a sporting companion, but was glad to congratulate him on so fine an appointment. News of Captn Nicholas Lockyer's death from bronchitis arrived from Malta on the 28th on board his ship the Albion, which ship it was said rolled so excessively as to injure the health of the Captain and his crew.

Our kind old neighbour and friend Mrs Newton died of apoplexy[+] in George Street where we have recorded many other deaths from a similar malady.

26th Mrs Baker, widow of the late Rev. G Baker died at Torcross in her marine villa there of a low Typhoid fever and was buried at South Brent. She was an exceedingly kind hospitable woman.

April 10th Col. Fulford of Great Fulford died of bronchitis leaving a widow and large family to lament this loss. He was Col. of the East Devon Militia and greatly respected not only by the officers and soldiers of his own regiment but all the Militia and Yeomanry in the county of Devon. Great Fulford Park had been in his family since the days of the Conqueror and now it is a wreck, the mansion crumbling down to ruin, all the noble trees of centuries growth hewn down, and a Park of Deer once furnishing the best flavoured venison in Devon all swept off from the face of the earth.

April 26th old Mrs Prideaux the Quakeress and mother of John Prideaux, Chemist, died at 81. She has been a patient of mine during her middle life on account of conical cornea[+] which became flatter in old age with the corresponding improvement of vision.

28th Mr Johns from the Scilly Islands where he resided with his sister as premier in the absence of Mr Smith, the owner of these islands, had been a patient of mine at Plymouth suffering excruciating pain at times in his right eye owing to Staphylona[+] and irregular protrusions of the Chelotric [Sclerotic[+]] Coat. He had consulted many oculists in England and on the Continent and received from them a corroboration of my opinion that nothing but extirpation of the globe of the eyeball could afford him permanent relief. During his last trip to London I said to him: 'you are going there to have the eyeball removed?' And he replied: 'No. No one but yourself shall do that.' Some weeks before he wished to try the effects of chloroform which he attempted to inhale, but it produced such frightful effects on his nervous system as to oblige us to desist from a further trial. On this day however he had summoned his resolution to have the eyeball removed by myself, aided by my colleagues Messrs Moore and Square in the presence of the Rev. Mr Lane, his personal friend. With the scissors and forceps I quickly removed the whole of his right eye from its socket and found the chelotic coat so attenuated and thinned off as to shew that extirpation was the only remedy. He quickly got over the operation, made me a present of 50 guineas and returned to the Scilly Islands healthy, happy and free from pain. This relief from long suffering of many years was not his lot much longer to enjoy. Not many months afterwards I was sent for to visit him at Scilly on account of an accident which had happened by his being thrown off a colt, and produced some injury of his body likely to prove fatal and therefore my attendance was solicited, but as the distance from Plymouth to Scilly was great and the time occupied in the journey uncertain from Penzance across the water to Scilly and back dependant on tide, and as I had much other business in hand I refused to go, and recommended Mr Lanyon who went over from Camborne to Scilly and saw Mr Johns a short time before his death.

June 22nd Miss Clarissa Squire of Teignmouth died at 44, having been a patient of mine for 25 years on account of a hip disease which had not been detected for many months after its commencement in the right hip joint. When I first visited her at Teignmouth I suspected the commencement of suppuration and ulceration within the joint, but as no remedial measures had been attempted I cupped and leeched the most painful parts, from time to time formented the parts, and fixed an issue behind the trocanter$^+$ major; this treatment moderated her sufferings, aided by confinement on a mattress on a bed so as to take all pressure and motion off the inflamed joint. Time soon shewed, after a year, that suppuration had gone far ahead of my treatment and that therefore I must prepare for the bursting of an abscess somewhere in due course, and endeavour to strengthen the powers of her constitution preparatory to such a result. Abcesses did burst in course of time in the groin and back and discharged copiously. As these discharges continued so we supported her strength and prepared for a shortening of the limb, owing to absorption of the head of the bone in its ulcerated socket. After 3 or 4 years various sinusses continued to discharge and the limb became shortened 2 or 3 inches. She ultimately recovered and came to me at Plymouth, having a high heel shoe to meet the shortness of the limb and enable her to walk with tolerable ease. She lived many years afterwards, the comfort and idol of her mother and an assistant in the excellent school for young Ladies conducted by Mrs Squire as Principal and Mrs Fisher as Assistant.

A contemporary and companion of Miss Squire was also attacked with inflammation in her hip joint. Two other incipient cases appeared in this healthy school on the Den but the inflammation was got out of the joint by rest, leeches, issues$^+$ etc. It was remarkable that 4 such cases should occur in the same establishment. The real cause was owing to the young ladies being seated many hours of the day without going out of the house and then on certain fine days they were encouraged to take long walks to which their young joints were not regularly accustomed, and consequently the inflammation, once begun, was promoted to further increase by the friction of the head of the bone in its inflamed socket. Added to this circumstance was a stumous or scrofulous$^+$ habit always favourable for eruptive and cutaneous$^+$ diseases, enlarged glands and other idiosyncrasies peculiar to the female constitution.

July 5th a trip to London, Trafalgar Hotel, Charing Cross.

6th John Ashford accompanied us to Cambridge to witness the Installation of Prince Albert as Lord High Rector of that University. On arriving at the gates of Trinity College I was asked by the Porter at the Lodge for our tickets, but as I had none he seemed to hesitate about our admission. At this moment the Earl of Hardwick, Lord Lieutenant of the County rode through the entrance gate. I happened to say: 'Oh there goes Lord Hardwick,' so the porter, hearing this remark and seeing Jno Ashford behind us whom he might have taken for our servant, passed us immediately through the barrier into Trinity Square where we strolled about and through the buildings, banqueting hall and different apartments and took up our station at the door through which the Queen, Prince Albert and the Duchess of Sutherland made their exit and crossed just before us into the Queen's carriage in the presence of some half dozen people besides ourselves. Col. Macdougall of the Royal Horse Guards was seated on a magnificent black charger close by the rear of the Queen's carriage and seemed to be on good terms with himself. After patrolling the garden walks and observing the magnificent elm trees, crossing and recrossing the bridges over the Cam River, inspecting St John's College and others, our time drew short for return by train to London after partaking of a luncheon at Cambridge, so we performed this journey to and from Cambridge between breakfast and dinner.

On the 8th I attended an auction at the Royal Exchange for the sale of the Butterford Estate in North Huish, Devon. There were three Mortgages on this property and the mortgagees by their officers meddling at the sale made themselves legally responsible for the purchase of the same at a price above its value. This act led to litigation and much money was subsequently spent about it. The history of this estate suffices for hundreds encumbered by mortgage debts. Mr and Mrs Whiddon, who conducted the Royal Hotel at Plymouth, had realised several thousand pounds besides their stock in trade and business by which they were making money fast. On this estate of Butterford Mr Whiddon had worked often in his youth as a plough-boy and when he had risen himself by honest industry, a feeling of pride came over him and created a desire to purchase this Butterford Estate for £11,000. He had half of the money by him and borrowed the other half at 4 or 5 per cent thinking that he should soon pay that off with his prosperous business. He was not the first man disappointed by speculation in land. The immense house at Butterford required much repair, the beautiful gardens required much outlay, the farming stock of cattle, horses, implements, manures and other outgoings made no return sufficient for years to keep up the interest on the borrowed capital. The times went against him, so by this continued drain and expense of farming took away the surplus income from the Hotel and obliged him to mortgage again and again to other parties until the full value of the estate was under mortgage. Then came in the lawyers and the surveyors, crushed the property and broke down the health of the Mortgagor – added to this bad speculation the Whiddons had two sons, the one an attorney at law and the other a clergyman, both of whom were expensive in their way and needy enough to require parental aid.

A remarkable death has lately [1866] befallen the clergyman who was curate of Maker under the Rev. Mr Trelawny, the vicar invalided by disease from performing his parochial duties. On Sunday the 27th day of May, the Rev. Whiddon was preaching his morning discourse in Maker Church at Mount Edgecumbe with more than his usual animation and when nearly arrived at the end of his discourse and whilst uttering the word 'overthrown' he was seen to fall backwards in the pulpit, burst open the door and fall down over the steps on the floor from whence he was taken up quite dead and afterwards pronounced to have died from the bursting of an anuerisum^{+} near the heart.

July 14th Mr Tompson a respectable Surgeon of Totnes resided at my house some days in this month in order to wait in close attendance on a patient, a Solicitor who had come to Plymouth for the benefit of a consultation. His disease was obscure but evidently seated in the abdominal viscera,$^{+}$ suspected to be the Liver or Spleen: at a post mortem examination however the seat of this cancerous malady was found to exist in the pancreas or sweetbread.

The 29th the Plymouth elections took place when two lawyers were elected who have since become Solicitor and Attorney General, and the country Squire Calmady stood no more chance against them than a fox before Mr Trelawny's hounds.

Sept 1st having occasion to visit some patients at Ivybridge, Parham and I started early in the morning in my carriage with dogs, guns, ammunition and halted at the 9 mile stone. I desired Parham to try all the fields over my little Manor there, excepting a large field of small clover between the old and new turnpike roads. I then drove on the remaining two miles and promised to meet them at 11 o'clock. One of my patients with a fistulous[+] opening into the bowel from the groin had gone to Ivybridge for change of air with her sisters, one of whom was laid up in gastric fever. I was then in my professional attire, but young ladies' eyes are very quick and suspicious and therefore they soon guessed that the object of my journey was not limited entirely to the healing art, but that my manner savoured of war and destruction amongst the feathered tribe. I kept my appointment at 11, [and] changed my dress in the carriage, which was sent to the farm house whilst Parham and I with our two dogs, a Pointer and Spaniel, both retrievers, got over the corner of the hedge into the clover field and tried on steadily till the Pointer brought up a fine covey of Partridges of which I shot a brace and my companion one. We scarcely went out of this clover field for the day or seldom beyond 2 or 3 fields from it and back again, and left off shooting with 4 couple of Landrails[101] and six brace and half of Partridges, 21 head in all of which 13 fell to my gun. When we were beating homewards within a gunshot of a gate by the Turnpike road, the Pointer stood again and a small bird arose like a lark or Jack Snipe, twitted a little and flew over the hedge without our firing at it. One person called it a lark or a snipe, but whilst we were debating a second bird of a similar kind arose and flew away and, when too late, I discovered that they were Quails which I had never before seen in England, although in France and Italy, especially at Bologna, I noticed a great number of living quails for sale in the market place. The farmer said: 'I know where to find them Sir, they are not far beyond the adjoining field.' We tried however in vain for a long time without finding these birds which I would have given a guinea almost to have killed and added to the pleasantest and best day's sport I ever enjoyed in this neighbourhood.

On the 5th my old school fellow and friend Jno Newton Esq. died at Bridestow at 55.

20th Sergeant Major Elliot very ill at the Eye Infirmary.

Rode from South Brent to Holne Chase with Farmer Mead to visit his sister, laying dangerously ill of typhus fever in one of Mrs Bastard's cottages close to a stagnant stream and overhanging trees where many others had suffered and died from this fever.

21st Mr Johns died at Scilly.

Dec 9th Liston* the celebrated Surgeon died of anuerism[+] near the arch of the aorta produced by a fall many years before in hunting, of which sport he was very fond as a young man. He had occasionally spit blood which had come through a sinus from the anuerism into the windpipe. Almost the last operation performed by this celebrated Surgeon was on a patient with anuerism.

---

[101] Corncrakes.

Dec 11th Sir Jno Rogers, Bart of Blatchford¹⁰² died. He had been formerly one of the 4 in hand club, with Sir Charles Bamfylde, the Honorable Newton Pellowes and other sporting men in Devonshire.

29th Thos Cole Esquire died in George St.

During this year, 1847, many investments in Railways, and meetings attended relating to cemetery affairs.

1848

Jan 14th Mrs Henry Little, wife of the dentist died of anaemia and her body was inspected by myself and others. Every organ in the body was healthy but pale and blanched bloodless; the powers of the system for making blood seemed to have deserted them and therefore her complaint may be fairly styled anaemia or want of blood.

16th Sergeant Major Elliot of the SDM died aged 67 at the Plymouth Royal Eye Infirmary of which Charity he and his wife had filled the offices of Dispenser and Matron for 26 years to the satisfaction of the subscribers and patients. His disease was purpura haemorrhagia,¹⁰³ his gums were like a person in scurvy and his skin exhibited purple spots and patches and his bowels discharged black grumous⁺ blood. Acids and bark and wine made no impression on his constitutional disease. His lungs were emphysematous⁺ purplish and adherent to the ribs, accounting for his chronic cough. Heart was sound, liver purple, large bowels dark coloured

Feb 1st Mr & Mrs Bayntun were elected at a salary of £33 a year with £7 a year for a Nurse.

April 14th in returning from my professional rounds from Brent in my gig the Stage Coach heavily laden had passed over the road before me. Near the 13 mile stone a number of navvies were at work on the Bittaford Viaduct. As I turned the corner of the road I saw these men rapidly descending and the stage coach which had just changed horses halted in the middle of the bridge and the passengers descending with all speed and crying out for help from a doctor. When recognised I jumped out of my gig and followed the party into the meadow after forcing the lock of the gate. There I found a tall Gentleman dressed in black with his face embedded in the soft mud of a wet meadow. 'What shall be done?' was the cry 'Get him up' said I 'and seat him by the sunny wall of the bridge.' He was asphyxiated – his nostrils, mouth, and eyes covered with mud which I quickly cleared off and called for some water which [was] speedily brought and enabled me to wash out his nose and mouth and to sprinkle some water over his face. As his breathing did not return 'what shall be done next?' was the question. To which I answered: 'get some brandy' which I poured into his mouth on my finger previously introduced. 'What shall be done?' was the cry. 'Loosen his neckcloth and press his stomach whilst I introduce more brandy.' By this time he began to sniff a little and draw in air until respiration was fully restored. 40 or 50 navvies were standing close around me; I said: 'clear away, stand back and give the man breathing room.' When his respiration was restored he

---

¹⁰² High Sheriff of Devon in 1838.

¹⁰³ Purpura haemorrhagia is a rare version of equine strangles, and unlikely to have been suffered by Mr. Elliott. He probably suffered from plain 'purpura', which is a discolouration of the skin caused by haemorrhage from small blood vessels.

complained acutely of violent pain in his back which led me at first to fear that some of the vertebral bones had been broken. 'What shall be done next?' was the question. 'Order a bed to be warmed immediately for his reception.' This done, he was carried to it by some stalwart navvies, stripped and examined carefully by myself, but not a bone of his body was broken. His history was the following – he was a clergyman going down to Devonport to serve one of the new churches built there and to assist the Rev. Mr Kilpack in his duties. £20 of his money was entrusted to my custody with a request that I would immediately communicate with the Rev. Mr Kilpack on my return to Plymouth, and with his mother, residing in Norfolk. I left him in the occupation of the only bedstead in the room, but there were many beds on the floor occupied by the navvies at night at this public house by the road side. The height from which he had fallen off the top of the coach into the meadow below the bridge measured 33 feet. Mr Huchinson completely recovered his health and strength and proved himself a diligent and excellent Pastor. [He] laid the foundation of a new church of St James, Newpassage, with large schoolrooms annexed, enough to contain nearly 700 children; he trained a number of them to music and got up a small band of drums and pipes. After all the good works which he had accomplished he was much annoyed at the taxing master who was come to rate his building and to demand payment thereon. He refused payment and allowed a silver teapot to be taken and sold for the payment of taxes. Mr Hutchison frequently called on me and told me one day that he had certain warnings about his hands and speech, and I told [him] firmly that he ought to be blooded and go away for a time from the place on which he had bestowed such increasing thought and anxiety for the last 17 or 18 years. My advice was unheeded but my prognostic was right for he was knocked down soon afterwards with a fit of apoplexy[+] and speechless for a time with a paralysed state of his right arm and leg. His brother and cousin called upon me and learnt my real opinion of his situation, that a clot of blood had evidently been poured into the ventrical of his brain from which it could not be removed by ordinary means.

17th one of my patients, a promising and handsome young man named John Elliot, only son of John Elliot his father and Lord of the Manor of South Brent, died on this day of hydrophorax[+] and effusion over his heart. Some weeks previously he had exerted himself excessively on Brent Moor in order to kill a fox with his dogs. He sheared 105 sheep in one day, walked 4 miles, 2 gates, 5 bars. Like many other strong fine young men he over-exerted himself which affected his breathing and brought on pleurisy which had not been subdued by bleeding or blistering and was therefore allowed to spread itself over the bags of the pleura[+] and to fill them with water, which in due course accumulated and pressed heavily on the heart and lungs thereby impeding both respiration and circulation. I had a great fancy at one time to tap his chest and let off the water but another Physician in consultation deemed the operation too hazardous and so it was not done. I have ever since felt that it would have given him the only remaining chance for his life.

May 5th the SD Rail opened to Laira from Plymouth.

June 8th after 10 o'clock at night Mr Kellock, now Solicitor of Totnes, came and desired me to hasten to the Inn at Ermebridge, about 11 miles off, to visit Mr Gest, Surgeon of Modbury who was driving a gig with his wife about 4 o'clock in the afternoon and in turning a corner upset the vehicle from which his wife and himself were thrown into the Turnpike Road, where lay a large stone against which his head came in contact. He was taken up senseless and put to bed at the Inn where he had remained for 6 hours without speaking or recognising any person. Of course I guessed a compression on the brain was made by a fracture of the skull and guessed what instruments to take with me for trepanning[+] him, thinking of course that country surgeons did not normally keep these instruments in proper repair. His partner and son-in-law Mr Lionel Roberts was present, also Messrs Langworthy, surgeons of Woodbury. Having made a long incision of the scalp over the depressed bone, I trepanned and took out a circular piece of bone so as to enable me to raise the depressed portion from the dura mater,[+] and so give an outlet to a quantity of clotted blood and fluid laying between the skull and brain. On the removal of pressure he sighed for a moment and awoke like a person out of a heavy sleep, looked about, gazed on all present, recognized everyone and wondered what had happened. I have seen many such cases but not one more remarkable or decided than this; the insensibility, snoring and heavy breathing all transformed quickly into perception and rational conversation. After breakfast I left him rational and comfortable desiring that the aperture might not be obstructed in preventing the escape of further effusions and pressure on the brain. This order was not properly obeyed so that further accumulations took place with similar effects of pressure on the brain. I was rather vexed on being sent for again in the evening when he had again fallen into a slumber which might have been obviated by opening the trepanned bone. He soon recovered his reason and sensibility and after the wound had healed found all his faculties clear and his ability returned to visit his patients on horseback, and he presented me with a salver and testimonial as I could not take fees of a professional brother. He lived for many years afterwards, working like a slave by night and by day in the active pursuit of a country practice, than which nothing can be more trying to mind and body. He subsequently died, like his father, of disease of the heart attended by dropsy[+] of the chest and swelling of the legs.

August 23rd bought Shillingham Barton one of the finest Estates in Cornwall by desire of my friend Mrs Cole for the sum of £14,500.

Sep. the 1st James Norris came from Lady Honeywood's at Torquay as my indoor servant and has continued such to the present time.

22nd Sept whilst dining with my friend the late Admiral Arthur I received a message to start with all speed and cross Torpoint Passage before 9 o'clock, when the passage boat shuts up for the night, in order to visit a gamekeeper of Lord German's who had been shot in the eye, blinded in the following manner. He was out with some young gentlemen shooting rabbits near the cliffs and one of them fired and wounded the keeper, neither of them seeing the other at the time and therefore a shot must have rebounded from the rock, glanced over the hills towards the keeper. I was graciously received and escorted to my bedroom by the Noble Earl, who presented the customary fee for which I could return very little hope of saving the man's sight.

Oct. the 12th my services were required at Fowellscombe, occupied by Mr Servington Savery, about 16 miles from Plymouth, in order to see his nephew Stuart Hawkins, only son of my worthy friend Admiral Mills Hawkins who had inherited the principal fortune of his Uncle Captain John Hawkins, Paymaster of the SDM for [blank] years. He was considered the Father of the SD Militia and by myself a Patron and friend to whose sterling worth I was much attached. Mr Stuart Hawkins, the grand-nephew had been some time labouring under low fever with congestion of the brain, for which I advised some leeches to the head and sinyp[?] to the feet. He soon became convalescent sufficiently well to enable me to allow him some roasted Woodcock at my next visit. I was desired to carve a bird and cut out such parts as I thought to be suited for my convalescent patient. Mr Pendarves, MP for Cornwall and Mrs Pendarves were present at this dinner from which I was requested to send some woodcock to Mr Pendarves. Having cut a leg and a wing with a portion of the back with some tail and toast, I was accosted by Mr P thus: 'you don't know how to carve a Woodcock, I will shew you' and suiting the action to the word rose from the opposite side of the table, took the carving from me, cut off the head of another woodcock and placed the remainder of the body on a plate by a servant who had orders to take that to Mrs Pendarves. 'That's the way to carve a Woodcock' said she. 'I thank you Mam for your instruction, I am always open to conviction and ready to learn' but my carving was never before so censured!

19th December Mr Hele, surgeon at Ashburton wished me to visit Miss Mary Grace Caunter, a lovely girl who had been his patient with low fever for some time. I found her in a very close bedroom with curtains drawn and the respirable air limited to a small extent. I therefore desired she might be moved into a larger room, more airy and, as typhoid symptoms were setting in, I recommended a more generous diet and antiseptic applications scattered about the room. She lived about a week and died at the age of 18, when she promised to be an ornament to her family and a valuable assistant to her mother.

During this year I bought Binnamoor Estate for £600, and the Chief Rents of Broadamoor and Aishridge with the Lord's Rights thereon for the sum of £133: the lawyer's bill £29 6s, total £63 6s.[104] Summers Wood buildings £123 8s 9d.

1849

Jan 6th Mr Parry and his family came to reside in Lockyer Street near us from South America, where he had lived above 30 years as a Merchant, chiefly at Buenos Ayres. Some of his details and histories were interesting. He possessed large prairies and enormous herds of cattle and horses in a wild state along the course of the Plata River and the Pampas, the most fertile of unknown lands perhaps. These animals are killed chiefly for their hides, and horns, of which large quantities are shipped off to England after being well salted, cured and tied up in packages. On one occasion he wanted to freight a vessel back to England with 300 hides which he did not possess and therefore offered a neighbouring merchant 300 head of wild cattle fat for 300 cured hides but his neighbour did not consider that the value of living cattle was equal to the value of 300 hides, so a difference had to be paid. The flesh, fat, and bones of these slaughtered animals are almost valueless as the flesh cannot be all eaten or preserved for human food. The fat cannot be made available and the bones are burnt chiefly to make charcoal and bone ash for chemical and agricultural purposes. Fuel in this beautiful country is so very scarce the inhabitants are obliged to resort to bones, dried dung or any other inflammable substance to supply the want of coal or wood.

Feb 7th Mr Jas Moore died of apoplexy[+] aged 62. His father and mother died at an advanced age, also of apoplexy.

---

[104] Presumably the £29 6s relates to the chief rents, and there was a lawyer's bill of £34 for the Binnamore purchase.

March 29th Andrew Adams, a retired mercer of Plymouth who had, with others, bought Mr Hine's farm of 36 acres at Mutley and sold a moiety thereof to the Plymouth Cemetery Company of £7,000, wished also to purchase my block of building land thereto adjoining and frequently offered me £4,000 for it. We agreed for £4,200 and signed an open contract in an attorney's office for that sum for all my land comprised within a mason's wall, and the purchase to be settled. I took no money as a deposit, days and weeks passed away without any communication and when the day of settlement arrived no preparation seemed to be made beyond a slight examination of my Title Deeds. Surprised at this delay I was one morning visited by the solicitor, who made frivolous excuses for non-payment and said they wanted some other pieces of land external as well as all internal, and that he was prepared to offer me £50 in addition to the sum already agreed upon. I said 'no, take it at the same price as the other land and at 4d a foot these extra pieces will be worth nearly £200.' After a little parley the attorney, on leaving my house with a flushed face, said if I did not take his offer of £50 he would put me to £50 legal expenses. I was rather indignant at such a remark from such a sensible man, but he put his threat into execution by some process of law or filing a bill, and when the expenses were pretty nearly incurred he then agreed to leave it to a reference or decision according to Law and not to equity, and the lawyer was the Umpire. So was my case disposed of according to Law, and not equity and of course against me, and thus was my land stolen from me. My error had been made in signing an open contract as Lawyers call this humbug, which may compel the vendor to prove his title for centuries back instead of 20, 40, or 60 years to which it may be limited. The real fact was that Adams had bought my land with money which he was obliged to borrow, and therefore resorted to stratagem, which obliged him in the end to borrow money at high rate of interest to build costly houses not remunerative and thereby to ruin himself.

April the 2nd the South Devon Railway opened at Plymouth.

June 5th the Bishop of Exeter Phillpotts consecrated the Plymouth, Stonehouse and Devonport cemetery. I had the honor of presenting the petition and escorting his Lordship up the middle of the Chapel, and thought from his pallid look, his semi-bent body, and his general lassitude that he could not be long for this world without occupying a space in some other cemetery, but I have been completely deceived for his Lordship is still living after the lapse of 17 years.

The first corpse buried at the cemetery was Sergeant Prynn of the SD Militia.[105]

The 25th of June, settled with Boger and Bowes for the purchase of Lipson Farm, [?] acres at the price of £2,750.

July 10th Cholera was reported in Stonehouse Lane and other places about Plymouth, also many at Brent and other places where there was filth and food enough for this loathsome disease to feed on.[106] The mortality in Plymouth from cholera during this year proved to be greater than it was in 1832, and sanitary talk and sanitary work had done little or nothing in 17 years to improve the health of these towns. I predicted that the cemetery, by removing dead bodies from the living, would do more

---

[105] The cemetery was opened in 1848.

[106] Mark Brayshay and Vivien Pointon discuss the 1849 outbreak in detail in 'Local Politics and Public Health in mid-Nineteenth-Century Plymouth', *Medical History* 27 (1983), pp. 162–78.

for the future health and benefit of Plymouth than any other scheme yet devised. Already [1866] there have been interred at the cemetery above 16,000 bodies.

17th July we became the guests of Dr Pennell of Exeter, whom I had succeeded as President to the West of England Provincial Medical and Surgical Association.[107] A grand dinner was given on this occasion to the eminent medical men of Exeter, joined by Mr Fuge and myself from Plymouth. The following day, the 18th, certain preliminaries, rules and regulations were made at a public dinner attended at Pratt's New London Inn by a large number of the faculty in the city – Dr Pennell presided. All the proceedings were conducted in the most satisfactory manner. One circumstance arose out of this visitation worthy of note; whilst in Dr Pennell's drawing room, one of his amiable daughters was listening with much attention to the different methods for recovering drowned persons, and some remark made much impression on her and proved in after years the means of saving her life. On returning from India the vessel was wrecked off the coast of [blank] and the passengers capsized into the water. This Miss Pennell prevented herself from sinking like the others by keeping her hands under water and her fingers close together so as to make paddles which prevented her body from sinking, and this plan immediately was brought to her recollection by the discussion of the medical men at her father's house some years before. All the other ladies who lifted up their arms and screamed for help sunk under water and as a matter of course were drowned.

1850

Jan 2nd Sir David Dickson,* Knight, died, formerly Physician at the Royal Naval Hospital at Plymouth, a zealous and ardent cultivator of the medical profession and a particular friend of mine; he was on the retired list.

July 29th I paid my long promised visit to Judge Parham at Hawford Lodge near Worcester. The Bristol station put us to considerable inconvenience in crossing and recrossing lines, descending and ascending stairs and procuring proper tickets for Spetchely, Worcester. We there found our friend the Judge with his carriage and pair of horses proud enough to shew them and prouder still to drive the horses with the Coachman by his side, luckily for us otherwise we might have had a capsize for though BB [presumably Judge Parham's initials] was a good Judge he was a bad horseman and a worse Whip. We had to drive through Worcester that beautiful City before we reached his residence, 3 miles off.

30th we drove to Malvern Wells, but drank little or no water there, but left it for others. People who have no bridle on their appetites and live luxuriously every day flock to Malvern; beyond the priorities of air and water and the regular habit of diet and exercise enjoined, there is nothing further recommendable for invalids and if the old adage was observed 'that he who wants the advice of a Physician after the age of 40 wants common sense which no Physician can supply', they would then not go there or elsewhere but find health at home.

July 31st drove through the beautiful village of Imberley to Westwood Park the seat of Sir John Packington[108] Bart., First Lord of the Admiralty. Our first notice

---

[107] For the meeting of this Association at Plymouth in July 1848 at which Butter presided, and for his lengthy speech reviewing the medical history of Plymouth, see 'Proceedings of Societies', *British Medical Journal (Clinical Research Edition)*, s1–12.18 (1848), pp. 496–9.
[108] Sir John Pakington (1799–1880).

was attracted to a fine herd of deer and some labourers or park-keepers scattered around at certain distances. We observed also some lines of small cord or twine with solitary feathers tied at certain distances and blown to and fro by the air. This novel sight induced us to halt and approach the keepers to learn what it all meant. We were answered that they were about to shoot a fine old stag, and that for that purpose a man with a rifle loaded with ball was sent up to stand on the branches of a large oak tree, around which the deer were to be driven and his orders were not to fire until he could make sure of shooting the selected deer in the neck, behind the head and horns. Whilst the man was so concealed in the tree the other men encircled the herd with this line of floating feathers brought nearer and nearer to stakes. The old deer were thus by degrees got into a narrow circle as they refused to jump over the line of feathers, but the fawns and younger deer escaped by jumping over the line. The deer at last encircled this fatal oak, around which at a distance they were kept by the park-keepers. After an anxious pause the report of the rifle was heard and all the deer galloped off except the selected one, which fell to the ground and had his throat cut as soon as the men could reach him, and blacker blood I never saw from ox or sheep than flowed from this slaughtered deer. It was a noble and fat animal, a haunch of which the head-keeper thought we might obtain from Sir John if we had any personal acquaintance with him, but as the Judge had no such honour politically or officially we had only to move off, much pleased with the novel sight we had witnessed.

In driving to Droitwich we saw five horses attached to one plough, and hard work it seemed to be for these fine animals to perform their labour. At Droitwich there are a number of salt springs from which the solution is taken, the water evaporated by heat over furnaces, and the salt dried for use and sent to all parts of the world at £12 per ton. We returned to the beautiful village of Claines and passed the Churchyard in which the Judge's late wife was interred. We also inspected the large dairy of Mr Webb, who kept cows. On our return to dinner we found the Rev. Mr Aldham and his wife and my nephew Dr Ashford from London. We had an excellent dinner, soon after which the Judge retired to smoke his pipe, preceded by the ladies. The wine had scarcely gone round twice before Miss P re-entered the dining-room and gave us notice that we had taken wine enough, and that therefore she had come to put it away. My reply was that she was too premature and that we had scarcely begun yet to drink any wine, and that we should probably empty the bottles. Before we had done so she retired and her brother returned to take his guests a walk about his fruitful gardens.

August the 1st left Howford for Droitwich, Birmingham, that confused station, from whence we digressed through Stafford to Shrewsbury, where we inspected the monument to Lord Hill and other public places, and afterwards by train to Chester that ancient and quaint old city where we took up our abode for the night at Royal Hotel, which in olden times carried on an immense business as a tavern and hostelry but now showed marks of decay and want of modern improvements.

We then took the L & NW train for Bangor, passing through Rhyl, Broughton, Conway and other places. After passing through the Tubular bridge we got out at the next station, Llanfair, Anglesea and walked back, but the authorities refused to let us pass along the line of rails, and therefore we were obliged to ascend some high steps and walk, or rather crawl, over the roof of the Tube. Our party there were Mr Mrs & Miss Fignes from Plymouth and a young Gentleman. The first sight from the roof of the bridge was most appalling, the height down to the water being quite frightful, with a stiff breeze rendering the step unsteady. The Ladies had the best of it and, being more courageous than the Gentlemen, walked steadily on from one end to the other with their dresses flickering in the air without disturbing their self-possession and onward course, but the Gentlemen were all cowards except two, the young gentleman who was our beau and Mr Vigur, who was somewhat giddy now and then. The Judge was a perfect coward, sometimes walking or crawling with his eyes open or shut, and tremblingly alive to the dangers of falling overboard. I cannot boast of my own courage, for I never could look over a precipice or the gallery of St Paul's Cathedral without giddiness or an instinctive dread to retreat or, blindfolded, to jump overboard. The greatest coward of our party was my nephew who, on first ascending the steps and looking over the prodigeous height cried, 'oh!' and retreated backwards and found his way down to the water's edge where he gave a boatman a shilling to put him across the Menai Straits.

We returned to Bangor, got a good Welsh dinner, surveyed and discussed these gigantic works of Art viz: the Tubular Bridge, designed and built by George Stephenson and the chain suspension bridge by Telford, both embracing one and the same object viz: that of connecting Wales with the Isle of Anglesea. By a return train from Holyhead we reached our quarters at Chester rather late on the same day, regretting we could not visit the Slate Quarries.

3rd John Ashford left us for Town for a reason we afterwards found to sell his little capital out of a Candle Manufacturing which paid him 10 per cent and to purchase Railway Shares which paid him nothing, this was a bad smite[?]. The Judge and ourselves proceeded from Chester to Birkenhead by train whcre we halted and surveyed the skeliton of the embryo town recently laid out by roads and divided lands into building grounds. Sir Joseph Paxton it was said had furnished the necessary plans for increasing the buildings in the rising town of Birkenhead. For a penny each person we crossed the River Mersey in a steamer to Liverpool, where we took up our abode at the Queen's Hotel and made the best use of our time in looking over the docks and shipping, the Albert Vaults, Squares and Public Buildings. We had salmon and salad for dinner of which I partook heartily and got an attack of colic in the night as the salmon was not sufficiently dressed.

On the 4th, Sunday, we left Liverpool by an early train, passed over Chat Moss and thought of the simple and wonderful scheme of George Stephenson in devising a cheap and unknown plan for carrying a railway over a mass of mud and water.

At Manchester we arrived in time to attend the Cathedral and hear an excellent sermon from the Bishop. We then visited Peel's Park and after dinner proceeded to Huddersfield where we quartered for the night at the George Hotel. Huddersfield in 1850 was very different to the place I left in 1819, but the old George Inn, the Cloth Hall and some of the streets were dingy and doleful as ever. The railroad from Manchester to Huddersfield differed widely from the old coach road, designed and executed by that wonderful blind man,[109] the one being level and the other weaving over hill and dale. At the Huddersfield Station I was at a loss to find the Geography until I espied some of my old haunts and houses in which I had received much hospitality with other officers of the South Devon Militia. Spring Wood, Spring Grove and other mansions formerly occupied by friends well known to me were now possessed

[109] John Metcalf.

by persons of whom I had never heard. A doleful feeling came over me on contemplating the extreme changes which mortality had cast over this once disturbed but hospitable neighbourhood. I then knew everybody almost, rich and poor, sick and well, but now alas after 30 years I could scarcely find a person known to me. I was glad to get out of Huddersfield by rail on the 5th Aug. for Pennistone and Sheffield and Matlock to sleep.

6th Haddon Hall, the Duke of Rutland, and Chatsworth, the Duke of Devonshire, where we met a vast number of persons by excursion trains, and had some difficulty in gaining admission without a ticket. However we succeeded and passed in review of the Duke and Mr Paxton, before whom I took off my hat, to which compliment they graciously responded. There was a large concourse of people parading the grounds which were kept in the neatest possible order, and not a labourer or implement to be seen scarcely except a scythe behind the scenes which I espied and learnt from the man that it was fortunate for him that Mr Paxton did not see it. The water works were in full play and very grand they were. The gardens also with Mr Paxton's dwelling house and carriage were all models of their kind. We there saw the Victoria Regia, a magnificent plant in full bloom from the coast of Guinea, also second crops of strawberries and peas and magnificent peaches in their greatest bloom protected by nets from injuries in falling. Everything seemed in place, cultivated to the highest perfection, and there was no bustle or hurry or apparent waste of time.

As Matlock was so full we were obliged to be contented with a garret and clean beds for one night and then moved onwards by train to Derby where a great competition seemed to be passing between the advocates of the Railway Hotel and the Royal Hotel in which we quartered for that night. Of all the hotels that we had met with, none exceeded the Royal at Derby for neatness, comfort, cleanliness, good fare and every other comfort. Being a shareholder in the Midland Railway, whose books I was permitted to examine and also in the Railway Hotel, I ought perhaps to have gone there but taunt[?] led me to the other. The following day we spent partly at Derby in perambulating the Arboretum and pleasure grounds presented to the Town of Derby by the late Mr Strutt of Belper, a wealthy Cotton Manufacturer whose descendant now takes the name of Lord Belper in the British peerage, which Sir Robert Peel, whose wealth had also derived from cotton-spinning, is said to have declined on behalf of himself and his sons. So much for his humility and good sense. The Judge here left us for his own home at Hawford and we journeyed southward from Birmingham to Gloucester where no Tavern accommodation could be obtained on account of the Races and we were necessitated to occupy a lodging for the night in which we were visited by a number of nameless gentry, which afforded Mrs B good sport.

Left Gloucester at 10, Bristol at 12, Plymouth at 5 by Express train. After our return, nothing but a common routine of patients and business occurred.

On the 19th some very curious inhabitants of the Earth called Bosgesmen[110] were exhibited at Plymouth, having been brought from some part of Africa. Their stature was very small and their bodies covered more or less with hair. The little man with his long beard had a very fierce aspect and showed with his club how he attacked

---

[110] African bushmen and women who were exhibited in Britain between 1846 and 1850, essentially as an exotic freak show.

and killed a lion, whilst the female was a meretricious little lady with a very pleasing smile and desire to kiss anyone so inclined.

Oct 12th bought Whifferton for £4,650. Nov 4th sold it to Captain Pent for £4,900.

Dec 13th I attended the Exeter Assizes and took the 3 oaths of allegiance, supremacy and [affirmation] with Archdeacon Downsell who was with myself then elected JP for the County of Devon, for which honor we had each to pay 8 guineas to Mr T Deake, Attorney at Law and Clerk of the Peace.

1851

My old and esteemed friend Richard Dunning Esq.[111] whose medical history at Devonport was characterized by his zeal and publications in promoting vaccination and his correspondence with the late Dr Jenner, was the father of my old school fellow George Dunning and my medical adviser when I was sick on being first quartered in the Barracks at Plymouth Dock, now Devonport, in 1814. He lived to the good old age of 90, blind from cataracts, for the removal of which his gouty symptoms forbade any attempt; much respected by numerous friends.

March the 19th I attended the Lent Assizes at Exeter and had the honor of dining by invitation from the Judges, Lord Chief Baron Pollock and Baron Martin in company with the Sheriff, the late James Cornish Esq. of Black Hall, and my brother magistrates of the county. Mr Praede, our County Court Judge at Plymouth and I generally met in the train and went together to the Assize Court. On one of these occasions he was returning from Exeter to Teignmouth where the Judge owned considerable property, and when about to leave the railway carriage called the Guard and said: 'I report this gentleman for smoking in a railway carriage contrary to orders, which will subject him to a conviction and fine before a magistrate.' The gentleman replied: 'I hope you will not do so as I asked you and the other passengers if there was any objection to my smoking a cigar, and as no one answered or objected I construed your and their silence into permission and therefore did so.' The Judge replied: 'you have broken the law, Sir, and must be detained for the offence.' The stranger said he hoped not as he was going to Plymouth on business to meet a party awaiting his arrival and that his absence would occasion much inconvenience to others as well as annoyance to himself. The Judge again replied: 'we cannot help such a disappointment as Rules and Orders must be obeyed.' The stranger then pleading forgiveness put his card into the Judge's hand on which appeared the Duke of Cambridge and said: 'I assure you my presence at Plymouth will be much looked for.' Upon this the Judge mitigated his sentence and obsequiously remarked that he did not know before whom he was speaking, and with a sort of apology to the Duke told the railway guard that he need not wait as the charge was not further pressed, and so the Judge, on leaving the carriage, wished the Duke a good journey.

April 8th Mr Rose, the present Governor to the Gaol, was elected almost unanimously by a large bench of magistrates, of whom I went up from Plymouth as one to support the son-in-law of Capt. Cole,[112] the former Adjutant of the SD Militia and late Governor of the Gaol, as he had rendered me many a good turn during my early services as Militia Surgeon.

---

[111] Dunning (1761–1851) is believed to have coined the term 'vaccination'.
[112] Edward Hubbard Rose had married Mary Emery Cole in Exeter in 1842.

May 1st the Crystal Palace opened in London.

On the 4th of June John Ashford, my nephew, sold his interest as a general practitioner in London.

July the 14th Mrs B and my niece Mrs Baker and myself visited London and made the Trafalgar Hotel our headquarters for the time being. The Exhibition[113] received many visits from us and excited our admiration that anything so gigantic and grand could have been planned by a gardener and perfected in so short a time. At the Symposium conducted by Monsieur Soyer we dined one day and saw a number of joints roasting not before coal fires but by Gas, which completely cooked the joints but left an unpleasant smack on the meat. On the 16th Mrs Baker and myself went down to Windsor and back by train in order to inspect the Agricultural Show there, in which we understood the Prince Albert had taken a lively interest.

The 20th by the South Eastern train we visited by appointment our good old friend and Trustee Dr Marshall, formerly a Physician at Totnes but then Barrack Master at Maidstone. We found him suffering from certain complaints for which we discussed many remedies, of which one was at last selected to effect a cure of which he had despaired. Mrs Marshall and her sister, Miss P Ford my wife's relation, provided for us an excellent dinner, after which we returned by train to the Trafalgar.

After 8 days thus spent in London seeing everything and visiting all places within our reach, we returned to Plymouth of course much delighted, instructed and improved.

Nothing particularly occurred after our return to Plymouth beyond the usual routine of a professional life until the 8th of October when I was attacked with smart pleuratic[+] pain on the left side of my chest to which 42 leeches were applied and followed by one fomentation and a cataplasm[+] which removed all pain and morbid sensation and put me to sleep, after which I recovered free from morbid sensation with all the feelings of health restored.

On the 11th, during my convalescence, I was consulted by the Rev. G Langdon who had married a daughter of Sir John Ommanney, the Naval Commander-in-Chief at Government House, Mount Wise, where he was then staying. I prescribed for him Lime Water and tincture of Birch. This mixture he was pleased to observe did him more good and inspired him with greater hopes of recovery from his nephrotic[+] complaints than he had before experienced. On comparing notes we considered ourselves related to each other; his uncle was the Rev. Dr. Gilbert Langdon of Dorsetshire, his brother was a clergyman and school master at Brighton and himself was a minister of some Town in Sussex. My paternal grandmother was also a Langdon and daughter of the Great Grandmother who rode 2 miles to my christening after she had spent 90 years of her life. Our mutual relations were not very close although a daughter of the Rev. Dr Langdon had married my Uncle James Butter. I therefore treated him as a sort of relation as well as patient although his malady was too organic to admit of cure. My visits at the Admiralty House were proportioned to the variations of my Patient's complaints, but the gallant and hospitable Admiral Sir John Ommanney extended every kindness in his power towards me and as I had prescribed Ice for his son-in-law he sent to London for a refrigerator[114] for the use

---

[113] The Great Exhibition at the Crystal Palace, designed by Joseph Paxton, head gardener at Chatsworth.

[114] The first practical refrigeration system relied on vapour compression and was invented in 1834. It was not a commercial success, and refrigerators for normal domestic use were not

of his household and another for myself, which I also found useful in making ice during the hot days of summer at my country seat in the following year. Finding my patient's complaints increasing Dr Rae* of the Naval Hospital, now Sir Wm Rae at Newton, a Country Magistrate, united his valuable skill to my own and provided such medicines as were required from the Naval Hospital. On the 11th of Dec. our patient died and was opened by Mr Swaine in our presence, but his organic disease of the kidneys did not sufficiently explain his malady. His corpse was taken to the Dockyard and shipped off for Portsmouth from whence it could be transferred to his parish for interment. The Admiral and I followed the corpse to the Dockyard.

19th Dec. an anonymous letter appeared in the Herald newspaper suggesting a testimonial for my gratuitous services in founding and conducting the Plymouth Royal Eye Infirmary above 30 years. For some time I was ignorant of my friend who was the author of this letter and one day I said before some ladies: 'I cannot think of any gentleman who wrote that letter.' One of the ladies replied: 'why do you suppose it was written by a gentleman? Could not a lady write such a letter?' I remarked: 'I don't think that a likely circumstance.' The lady continued: 'why, I saw that letter in manuscript before it was printed and know that it was written by a lady.' I asked: 'are you the author of it?' She smiled and assented: 'Yes!,' 'My dear Miss Radcliffe, I owe you many thanks for your good wishes.' She continued: 'we have begun a subscription and want a Treasurer, can you name anyone?' 'Yes' I said 'there is a gentleman distinguished for his philanthropy and patronage towards the Eye Infirmary and friendship towards myself.' When the lady asked him the question he peremtorily refused, and then she was obliged to go out of the Town for a Treasurer and invoke the aid of the Rev. Dr Williams, Vicar of Plympton Maurice. He cheerfully undertook the office of Treasurer and gratified Miss Radcliffe whilst he obliged me by getting a number of subscriptions limited to one guinea each, but some of my zealous friends were inclined to subscribe 5 guineas and upwards. Names were valued more than money.

1852

Jan 1st my first New Year's present was a silver tea caddy, massive and handsome, from my good friend Sir John Ommanney, Port Admiral at Mount Wise, Devonport.

Jan 3rd news arrived of the 'Amazon' steam ship having been burnt at sea in the Bay of Biscay and nearly all hands perished, excepting the chaplain Mr Blood and 13 sailors. His relation, the author[115] of 'The Crescent and the Cross' came down here in great dudgeon and censured the naval authorities for their want of promptitude in not sending out fast steam vessels to the relief of such men as took to the boats and might be alive floating on the waters. The Rev. Mr Blood arrived in Plymouth almost without clothes, obtained a good black suit from Mr Derry the Surgeon and preached a most powerful and thrilling sermon at St Andrew's Church in behalf of himself and the cast-away sailors saved with him.

---

produced until 1913.

[115] Butter's memory has let him down. The *Amazon* caught fire and eventually sank on 4 January, and among those lost was Eliot Warburton, the author of *The Crescent and the Cross*. Who 'his relation' really was is not known.

March 8th my good friend Mr Sterling, above 60 years of age, was unexpectedly attacked with small pox, from the effects of which he never entirely recovered. Miss Ougier also died, aged 44, of consumption. She and her two sisters died at different times of the same disease produced by one and the same cause, which was tight lacing. Be it known unto all young ladies that no practice can be more distorting to the female form than corsets too tightly laced, or shoes like the Chinese, too small for the foot. What a dereliction it is in the human mind, especially of females, to attempt the improvement of their natural form by straightened dresses forceably screwed and laced around the waist so as to resemble wasps. One of the sisters who died afforded to me an opportunity of examining her body after death, in which I found the various organs squeezed together, the liver, stomach and bowels compressed into one mass divided by the diaphragm from the contents of the chest, where the lungs were found adherent to the ribs and the heart compressed and ulcerated so that both circulation and respiration were impeded, and their functions carried on by such relief as a troublesome cough and purulent[+] expectoration afforded. This painful description I hope will deter young females now living from resorting to these pernicious practices introduced into England from France and China. These three sisters were daughters of the Quartermaster of the South Devon Militia whom I had safely escorted to the Exeter Asylum, and of their mother whom I had professionally attended for many years until her death from apoplexy.[+] Their aunt also had been occasionally entered on my sick list.

My professional attendance on this family had been gratuitous of course above 30 years. I never received a fee from one of them but considered that as the survivor had been a Governess in different families their circumstances must be low. She had made a will and appointed Sir H S and myself Executors and residuary legatees and given to me a legacy of £300. During her last illness she was in a Lodging House where her cough, especially by night, disturbed her fellow lodgers and disposed the landlady painfully and properly to tell her that she would feel obliged to her to suit herself elsewhere. Not many doors off was found another lodging in which the mistress of the house paid great attention to Miss Ougier seeing that she was dieing fast of consumption, and got out of her more knowledge than I had obtained about her property in the Funds, greater than I had expected. At one of my morning visits I found her in bed coughing much after a restless night, and appearing low and dejected. I inquired if anything had happened to disturb her feelings in any way. She hesitated and said that as she had felt herself getting weaker she had been advised to send for an Attorney to alter her will of some standing and appoint Trustees for some funded property in order to provide an Annuity for her aunt above 80 years of age. I asked her what had brought about this change, and who had advised an alteration of her former will, and soon discovered that the landlady was mixed up in this plot with a banker's clerk and a crafty attorney who had agreed to give her 8 per cent for £400 to be immediately paid over to him. I remonstrated with her for so doing and candidly said: 'you will never live to receive two dividends.' She then asked if I would take the £400 and give her 8 per cent for her life. I said: 'No Miss Ougier, I can't do this dishonest act. If I do I must discontinue my professional attendance and you must send for another doctor. Why have they altered your will without my knowledge?' She replied that she thought I would not like the trouble of acting as a Trustee, and had therefore sent for a lawyer to appoint the banker's clerk, a perfect stranger to her and only known to her for a short time as the husband of her landlady, who together had sifted out the amount of her funded property and sent for another lawyer to make a new will in which my former legacy of £300 was reduced to £100, less legacy duty of 10 per cent to £90, which was all the money I ever got for 30 years attendance and ultimately received after the aunt's death, the residuary amount approaching nearer £2,000 than £1,000. Let young practitioners profit by this painful history and remember the motto which was early instilled into my mind but which I had too often forgotten during my professional life; it was this: 'Accipe dum dolet' – Take a fee when people are sick, or when offered.

April 5ᵗʰ the election of members for Plymouth having been proposed, 5 candidates offered themselves for representation, viz: Roundell Palmer, Robert Porrett Collier, Lawyers [blank] Braine Dick Estcott and lastly Charles John Mare* who appeared with his father-in-law Peter Rolt,[116] MP for Greenwich, and Churchward, Agent from the London Herald Office. The latter party had been unsuccessful in getting a Chairman and rudely expelled from some houses. I had repeatedly refused to identify myself as chairman of any party. Being however solicited by the Vicar of St Andrew's and many influential Conservatives, I consented at last to sit as Chairman at the Mechanics' Institute and to hear what Mr Mare had to say for himself, without pledging myself to support him or any other candidate unless his principles political accorded with my own. A large influential meeting approved of Mr Mare's sentiments and many came forward to his support. An active canvas henceforward took place and many private meetings were held at which I was requested to take the chair. My sentiments being known against the return of so many lawyers in the House of Commons, I objected to the two legal candidates for Plymouth, comparing the voters to so many bars of a ladder for lifting lawyers into profitable positions from which they might bow with thanks to the multitude and enjoy the lucrative profit of office.

Of the two other candidates I said nothing. Mr Mare's* cause and return I advocated with all my energy and influence and soon succeeded in placing him at the head of the poll. During his canvass and the various meetings of his party I contrived generally to be present, but as I had a great deal of private business on my hands at this time, I found it hard work sometimes to attend these meetings. On one occasion the 21ˢᵗ of May I was requested to visit a patient a very old friend, very dangerously ill of gout at Ashburton. My visit there was performed in the following way. By an early train I started for South Brent, there I had some orders to give on agricultural matters, and from whence I took a saddle horse to ride to and from Ashburton in order to return in time for the down express train, which luckily I just caught at the Kingsbridge Road Station, and arrived by it safely to the Laira Station, where owing to some breakage the train came to a stand still and obliged me to walk along the line over the remaining distance to the Plymouth Station, where a large assemblage of persons were waiting anxiously to learn the cause of delay of the Express Train, and were glad to hear from me that the accident was not serious. I was in a profuse perspiration hurried home by several of Mr Mare's partisans who feared lest I should be absent or unable to preside over a large meeting of his supporters. I was of course obliged to change my dress and dine before I could attend the meeting, which was very full and favourable to Mr Mare with slight exceptions.

---

[116] Rolt (1798–1882) was elected MP for Greenwich in 1852. He took over his son-in-law's insolvent business (C. J. Mare & Co) in 1857 and renamed it Thames Ironworks & Shipbuilding Co.

May the 6th my dear good friend the Admiral invited me to dine at Government House and to meet Sir Wm Burnett,* inventor of the disinfecting fluid, who had officially come to Plymouth on nautical affairs. I found him a most intelligent and agreeable man, ready to impart the fullest information on all subjects.

On the 10th political procession of the different candidates took place with the Mayors of Plymouth and Devonport in order to lay the foundation stone of the new pier at Millbay.

On the 22nd of May gave a large dinner party at home.

June 12th a beautiful vessel, the Queen of the South, arrived in Plymouth Sound and received much admiration from nautical men. She was the 1st of 8 vessels intended to be built by Mr Mare* for the Peninsular & Oriental Steam Company of 1,800 tons each for the conveyance of passengers and goods to and from India.

On the 23rd Mr Stafford, one of the Officials at the Admiralty, visited the Dock Yard at Devonport and gave a public dinner which I attended by invitation at Morsehead's Hotel.

On the 8th a nomination of the Plymouth candidates took place viz: Mare,* Collier, Bickham, Estcott, Braine and Roundell Palmer. On the following day the numbers were Mare 1036, Collier 1004 elected, the rest nowhere. The speeches delivered on that occasion were reported in the newspapers. The Conservative candidates returned for the two boroughs had a public procession in carriages through the different streets in a manner which I very much disliked.

12th Sir John Ommanney, of whose hospitality I have so often spoken, invited me to dine at Government House in company with Lord Palmerston and Admiral Bowles who had come down to inspect the Steam and Dock Yards, also other distinguished persons. On entering the Drawing Room and bowing to Lady Ommanney who was my patient and an invalid unable to join the dinner party, I noticed an elderly Gentleman with a hat under his arm who had been speaking to her Ladyship, and when the party had all nearly quitted the room I stepped up and asked Lady O. the name of the gentleman who had been conversing with her and received for answer this question: 'why, don't you know you were invited to meet Lord Palmerston? That was he.' At the dinner table I had the honor of sitting opposite his Lordship. I particularly observed the movements of the Noble Lord; he cut his food quickly and stored on his plate several potatoes at one time, and occasionally looked under his chair to look at his hat which seemed to be with his Lordship an object of especial solicitude. On rising from dinner the hat was replaced under his arm and there kept during the evening. Whilst in the Drawing Room the kind-hearted Admiral and his Flag Captain, Sir James Dunbar, asked me if there was anything I could wish for in Lord Palmerston's powers to grant. I replied: 'nothing.' Sir John then said: 'what think you of a Title? I can get it for you if you wish and the fees of office will be about £200, what say you?' 'I thank you, Sir John I have no wish of the kind.' 'Well,' said he 'at all events I will introduce you to Lord Palmerston.' Thus: 'allow me my Lord to introduce to you my kind friend Dr Butter who is not one of us Reformers but an out and out Conservative.' 'Ah' said his Lordship, taking me by the hand and looking towards the Admiral, 'he is not the worse for that.' I felt then at a loss what to say to so distinguished a Statesman, and for want of some better remark commented on the valuable service his Lordship had rendered as Secretary of War to the service of his country by establishing the Military Ophthalmic Hospital in 1816, under the direction of Sir Wm Adams,* for the treatment of a small army of invalids, blind or injured in their sight since their service in Egypt and India, and then Pensioners of Chelsea and Kilmannac in Ireland. 'Ah!' his Lordship said 'the Army Surgeons were very jealous of this Institution, but it rendered great service to the Army.'

July 16th a country election took place at Exeter for MPs which I attended in compliment to my long tried friend Sir J B Buller* and Sir R Lopes* Bart, who were returned without opposition MPs for the Southern division for the County of Devon.

My neighbour and patient Mrs Mengles, from age and infirmities constantly required my professional assistance. One day she tripped on the carpet and fell on her side from which she experienced considerable pain at the time and long afterwards so that she was obliged to keep to her bed. My first impression was that she might have fractured or injured the neck of her thigh bone but as no crepitus+ could be felt and as there was no shortening of the limb and no eversion,+ I could not detect a fracture. Daily pains around the hip led to a consultation with Messrs Whipple and Rendell who also suspected a fracture but could not prove it by the usual signs. She continued however to suffer much during the remainder of her life.

August 4th Mrs Butter and I started by train for Totnes where Sir Yarde-Buller* kindly sent his omnibus to convey us the 9 miles to Lupton House, where we spent many pleasant days with some County people and from whence we returned by way of Torquay where I called at the Vomero[117] to visit that kind and excellent lady, Mrs Charles English, who had contributed so largely towards the support of the Plymouth Royal Eye Infirmary.

A remarkable circumstance occurred to my tenant's mare, which was always in first rate condition and able to perform heavy work but was suddenly seized with violent illness of which she died in great suffering. Information as they call it and not inflammation was the supposed cause, but when the dead mare was embowelled and sent to a neighbouring kennel something was heard to rattle and several stones taken out of the large bowel which had been completely obstructed by them. The stones were very smooth from triluration[118] with each other but well fitted so as to form one whole stone 7lbs in weight.

18th and 23rd I was appointed local President of the two Agricultural Meetings held on the above days.

21st I passed 17 recruits for the Militia, on the 25th 12 more recruits, and at Morley on the 27th I examined 74 and passed 69.

28th Brent Fair. I passed 4 additional recruits. Plymouth Store room on the 30th, 37 more.

Oct 2nd examined 17 and passed 16. On the 25th 25 and passed 21.

10th Store room, passed 6 men.

18th October Militia embodied for 21 days to Nov the 7th.

25th Dined at SD Mess.

As parties had petitioned against returning Mr Mare* so Mr Mare's party petitioned against Collier for his want of qualification. There is no doubt of the property for which he qualified was not his own but his mother's, who paid rates and taxes on the Grimstead Estate on which he qualified.

---

[117] Named as such by Joseph Marchetti, this was built in 1838 in the Italian style as a gentleman's residence and was subsequently turned into a hotel.

[118] 'Being ground together' (OED).

30th Nov. Speaker's warrant arrived for the appearance of Mr Mare's* friends at the House of Commons for examination, but it was curious enough for the petitioners to let me off as the Chairman whilst they summoned the Deputy Chairman and others acting in concert with him.

On the 17th of Dec. Lord Derby's Budget was defeated by 19 and the Conservative party thrown on their beam ends.

1853

Jan. 16th Lady Forrest, widow of the late Sir Digery Forrest, Knight, died at Exmouth at 100 years. Her ladyship had been a patient of my father for an eruptive disease of the skin, eczema, which had troubled her for years and no doubt preserved her life by casting on the surface of the body an irritant disease to the relief of vital organs.

During this year enlisting for the SD Militia was carried on briskly at different places, at headquarters in Plymouth, at Tavistock, Totnes, Morely, South Brent and Newton and a large number were passed by myself and assistants.

On the 31st of January I met in consultation a Plymouth Surgeon about a hip disease in a little boy under 10 years of age who had brought on inflammation by over-exertion in accompanying a shooting party during frost and snow. I feared that the disease had passed over its first or inflammatory stage into the suppurative,[+] and nothing but rest in bed and counter-irritation could prevent the formation of an abscess. Although I had strictly enjoined the necessity of absolute confinement to bed the parents were injudicious enough to follow others advice and to convey their son in a carriage over the streets of Plymouth to the Baths at Devonport where the disease increased rapidly, and induced me to urge his return home by water. By this time the abscess had increased to a large size and required an immediate opening through which a quantity of pus escaped. The little boy recovered with a shortened limb but ultimately died of another disease.

February the 7th a Committee of five gentleman, subscribers to the Plymouth Royal Eye Infirmary as well as to a testimonial to myself as the Founder and principal Manager of this Charity for 34 years, met and decided on a Portrait to be painted by John Lucas,* an artist of London, at a cost of 100 guineas which was to be hung at the Infirmary.

April the 4th my old school-fellow and patient the Rev. N. Royse died at Dunterton Rectory. He was in common parlance a sporting parson who took a good deal out of his constitution at times by long fasting, tiresome journeys and severe exercise in fox hunting. He had an eruption on his skin which relieved him at times from cough and internal complaints. Inflammation of the lungs or pleura[+] at last attacked him as it had done many other fox hunters. He was not blooded or subjected to any active treatment for the stoppage of the inflammation which had settled in the membranes of his heart and lungs. Dropsy[+] of the chest, hydrothorax[+] and percarditas[+] increased and embarrassed his breathing to such a degree as to prevent his lying back in bed or to converse without coughing. Adema[+] of his legs also required bandages to reduce the swelling. Such a break-up of human health in a strong man may be prevented by copious bleeding and blistering during the early stages, and tapping the chest between the ribs in paracentasis[+] may let off a load of water compressing the lungs and obstructing the circulation of the blood in the great blood vessels of the heart and liver.

On the 5th of April I lost another old and valuable patient in Mrs Mangles whose death was accelerated by a fall on the floor and the probable fracture of the neck of her thigh bone.

May the 23rd a petition was presented against Charles John Mare* for bribery at the Election when he was returned MP for Plymouth at the head of the poll, beating 4 others. As I had been his Chairman I naturally expected a subpoena with which I had been threatened to appear before a committee of the House of Commons, but the lawyers for once let me off easily and summoned the Deputy Chairman George Meunie[?]. Edwin James, however, the leading barrister complimented me on my speech at the meetings and said he had no complaint to make against me but my vituperation of lawyers. During this enquiry at the House of Commons I was a guest of Sir John Yarde Buller,* now Lord Churston, and late Colonel of the SD Militia at his elegant mansion in Belgrave Square. Whilst there I was cautioned not to go near the House of Commons lest I might be summoned upon this enquiry. Sir Jno Buller had most handsomely offered me the run of his house during the time I might be detained in London in sitting for my portrait to Lucas.* On the day of my arrival dinner was served at 7 for the family party consisting of Sir John and Lady Yarde and Miss Buller with myself. About 10 o'clock I was surprised by a question, 'what I meant to do with myself for the evening.' My simple reply was: 'go to bed.' Lady B said: 'we are only going to two parties tonight and shall probably return early.' I then asked what the word early implied and was answered: 'our carriage will be ordered a ¼ to 3.' Sir John said: 'I am going to the House of Commons where I may be detained until 2 or 3 o'clock in the morning. Lately after a tedious debate I did not return before 5 o'clock when my porter was gone and gas put out, so that I was obliged to ring the bell again and again and to walk to and fro the pavé for some time before I could ring up any of my servants.' 'Well, what am I to do?' A sudden thought struck me that I would pay morning [sic] visits, so I hired a cab, drove off to Mr Mare's* house where I found him and his father-in-law, Mr Peter Rolt drinking their wine after dinner, and Mrs Mare and Miss Rolt in the drawing-room. Soon after midnight I returned to Belgrave Square and there found a comfortable bed. The breakfast hour was 9½ o'clock punctually no matter what the bed time was. One o'clock for luncheon and seven was the dinner hour at home. I received here the greatest cordiality and hospitality from Sir John, Lady and Miss Buller, now Lady Lopes.

On the 9th of May Mr Acland, son of that good and excellent Baronet Sir T Dyke Acland,* waited on me with Mr Kidner, an excellent judge of cattle and farming, about the proposed Agricultural Meeting of the Bath and West of England Society of which his father was Patron and one of the local Presidents, to be held at Plymouth.

On the 23rd my wife and I started for Bath where she remained with a friend whilst I returned to London.

24th Mr Mare's* splendid turn out of a carriage and magnificent horses called at Belgrave Square to take me and Miss Rolt to the building yard at Blackwall to witness the launch of the most magnificent ship in the world at that time, to be christened the 'Himalaya' by Lady Matheson whose assistant I became in breaking the bottle of wine. After the launch, which was a most beautiful thing of the kind, Mr Mare escorted me over the East and West India Docks, from there to his lodgings at Cornhill where he and Mr Rolt dressed for dinner given by Mr Mare at the London Tavern, where I was escorted by them and introduced to a number of leading merchants in the City, including Sir James Matheson, Duncan Dunbar and others. Mr Mare presided at the dinner which was one of the most splendid and costly I had ever seen. Quantities of gold plate were exhibited, thirteen different sorts of fishes put on the table, and the best wine of every country in profusion. I could not prevent the waiters from constantly presenting me with different sorts of wines. Thanks to Signor Zorah, the Turkish consule, who seemed to take me under his especial patronage and protection, I was instructed in the true art of dining. After Turtle Soup I was asked by a gentleman opposite to take a glass of wine and induced to select sherry, which my Turkish instructor told me was not right, and said after Turtle punch a la Romain was orthodox. After Ben Loman Trout I was advised to take Madeira, after Whitebait sherry, and after water susdhee[?] hock. After which my gastronomist, whose stomach must have been pretty well warmed with cayenne etc. exclaimed, 'Ah, that was so cooling.' After venison came claret and then champagne, burgundy and other liquors too numerous to mention. 72 persons dined there.

Appendix 1: List of Names

Note: biographical information is taken from the relevant entry of the ODNB unless otherwise stated.

Abercromby, Sir (Robert) Ralph (1734–1801) initially studied law but turned to a military career and became commander of the British army in the Mediterranean. He was sent to Egypt in 1801 to destroy the army left there by Bonaparte, which he achieved at the Battle of Alexandria, but he was struck in the thigh by a musket ball and died from septicaemia.

Abernethy, John (1764–1831) was educated at Wolverhampton Grammar School and in 1779 was apprenticed to Charles Blicke (q.v.), a surgeon at St Bartholomew's, where he remained for the rest of his career. He was hugely admired by John Butter and considered to be the best lecturer in London on anatomy, surgery and pathology. His lectures became so popular that in 1791 a lecture theatre was built within the hospital, thus founding the School of St Bartholomew's. He married Anne Threlfall in 1800, but nothing was allowed to overcome his sense of duty to his profession: 'Egad, I came down to lecture the day I was married'.[1] Although he was more renowned as a teacher than for his surgical skill, he was a man of considerable influence in all aspects of medical practice. He retired from the position of surgeon in 1827 but continued lecturing until 1829.

Acland, Sir Thomas Dyke (1787–1871) of Killerton, was High Sheriff of Devon in 1809–10 and a Tory MP: 'the head of the religious party in the House of Commons'. His statue in Northernhay Gardens, Exeter, was erected 'as a tribute of affectionate respect for private worth and public integrity'.

Adams, Sir William (1783–1827) was born in Morwenstow, Cornwall. He began his medical training as an assistant to John Hill (q.v.) and went to London in 1805 to complete his education at St Thomas's and Guy's hospitals. He attended demonstrations in anatomy by John Saunders (q.v.) at the newly opened London Ophthalmic Infirmary (now Moorfields) and assisted in surgical operations there. In 1807 he was elected MRCS and shortly afterwards moved to Exeter, where he helped to establish the West of England Eye Infirmary. He lived and worked mostly in Exeter and Bath until 1810 when he returned to London to set up a practice there. At times a contentious figure, he made a number of enemies, particularly in 1813 when he encouraged the belief that he had discovered a cure for trachoma[+] and performed several operations – the controversy as to whether or not they were successful, and as to the originality of his treatment, lasted until he died. In 1825, he inherited a considerable sum of money from his wife's family and, in compliance with the terms of the will, changed his name to Rawson.

Banks, Sir Joseph, Bart (1743–1820) was a naturalist, botanist and patron of the natural sciences. He was the longest-serving president of the Royal Society, a founder-member of the Linnean Society, and a member of both the Royal Institution and the Royal Horticultural Society. He was admitted a Fellow of the Royal Society after returning from his first voyage of discovery with many species of plants and animals previously unknown to western science. In 1768 he joined

---

[1] G. Macilwain, *Memoirs of John Abernethy* (New York: Harper & Brothers, 1853), p. 146.

HMS *Endeavour*, accumulating yet more species previously unknown in Europe. He became a friend and adviser to George III and transformed the royal pleasure gardens at Kew into a major scientific centre. He was made a baronet in 1781 and a Knight Commander of the Order of the Bath in 1795.

Barclay, Dr John (1758–1826) was elected an Honorary Fellow of the Royal College of Physicians of Edinburgh in 1806. He was one of the city's most distinguished and respected teachers of anatomy.

Barnes, Samuel (1776–1858) was born in Devon and educated at Exeter Grammar School, after which he attended the Hunterian Medical School in London. He then went to St Bartholomew's for two years as house surgeon to John Abernethy (q.v.). He returned in 1813 to be surgeon at the Devon and Exeter Hospital, where he practised ophthalmic surgery and started a medical school. No more than five years later he was appointed surgeon to the Exeter Eye Infirmary.[2]

Beattie [Beatty], Sir William (1773–1842) qualified as a naval surgeon in 1795 and subsequently was appointed to HMS *Victory*. In 1806, he became physician of the fleet, based in Plymouth. He stood down at the end of the war and, after a short spell in Edinburgh, returned to Plymouth in 1818 to set up a medical practice. Four years later, he was appointed physician to Greenwich Hospital.

Beddoes, Thomas (1760–1808) was an English physician and scientific writer who took a particular interest in tuberculosis.

Bell, Sir Charles (1774–1842) was a physiologist and surgeon who attended Edinburgh University Medical School. While assisting his brother John, who was teaching anatomy and surgery at Edinburgh, Charles developed a talent for making wax models of anatomical and pathological specimens that were used for teaching purposes, some of which still survive in the museum of the Royal College of Surgeons in Edinburgh. He practised and taught medicine in London from 1804 to 1836, after which he returned to Edinburgh where he spent the remainder of his career.

Bidder, George Parker (1806–78) was born in Lime Street, Moretonhampstead, where a bust has been erected in his memory. As a child, he was exhibited by his father at fairs and shows as 'The Calculating Boy' – Butter saw him performing in Plymouth. A brilliant mathematician, Bidder later worked with Robert Stephenson on a number of projects including the London and Birmingham railway.[3]

Blicke, Sir Charles (1745–1815) trained at St Bartholomew's and became assistant surgeon in 1779, succeeding Percival Pott as surgeon in 1789. In 1803 he became Master of the Royal College of Surgeons in London and was knighted the same year.

Boyer, Alexis (1757–1833) was appointed second surgeon at Hôtel-Dieu in 1794. Subsequently he became consulting surgeon to Louis XVIII and Charles X. His final appointment was as surgeon-in-chief at the Hôpital de la Charité, Paris.

Brewster, David (1781–1868) was a renowned scientist, inventor, author and academic administrator who wrote numerous works of popular science. With Robert Jameson (q.v.) he edited the *Edinburgh Philosophical Journal*.

[2] livesonline.rcseng.ac.uk
[3] A. W. Skempton et al. (eds), *A Biographical Dictionary of Civil Engineers, Volume 1: 1500–1830* (London: Thomas Telford Publishing, 2002), p. 58.

Brockedon, William (1787–1854) was born in Totnes. He was an artist who exhibited at the Royal Academy and at the British Institution, a writer and an inventor – among his many inventions was a machine for shaping pills and lozenges.

Brodie, Captain Sir Benjamin Collins, Bart (1783–1862) was a physiologist and surgeon who pioneered research into joint diseases. He was made sergeant-surgeon to William IV and continued in office under Queen Victoria. He was made a baronet in 1834 and was President of the Royal Medical & Chirurgical Society in 1839.

Buller: *see* **Yarde-Buller**.

Burnett, Sir William (1779–1861) was born in Montrose and trained in Edinburgh. In 1810 he was appointed physician and inspector of hospitals to the Mediterranean fleet and was awarded his MD by St Andrew's University. During his long career he received several honours, including a knighthood in 1831. He introduced a number of reforms, including regular classified returns of diseases from every naval medical officer, and urged that a hospital should be built at Chatham to replace the hospital ship then in use.

Burrell, Sir Charles, Bart (1774–1862) was MP for New Shoreham from 1806 until his death, at which time he was Father of the House of Commons.

Chantrey, Sir Francis Leggatt (1781–1841) became the 'most outstanding sculptor of his generation'.[4] His best known pieces include a statue of James Watt, and busts of William Wordsworth and Sir Walter Scott. He left his £150,000 fortune to the Royal Academy.[5]

Cline, Henry (1750–1827) was a surgeon at St Thomas's Hospital and an examiner at the Royal College of Surgeons.

Cochrane, Sir Alexander Inglis (1758–1832) was MP for Stirling Burghs from 1800 to 1802 and 1803 to 1806. He was also a senior naval officer, reaching the rank of admiral. He served as commander-in-chief at Plymouth from 1821 to 1824 and as Admiral of the White from May 1825. He is buried in Paris, where he died suddenly in January 1832.

Cooper, Sir Astley Paston, Bart (1768–1841) was a renowned anatomist and surgeon at Guy's Hospital and was created a baronet in 1821, following his removal of a cyst from the head of George IV. He was a vice-president of the Royal Society and a leading figure in the Royal College of Surgeons. He once dissected an elephant in his front garden!

Cribb, Tom (1781–1848) was an English bare-knuckle boxer, nicknamed 'The Black Diamond'. He beat Bob Gregson in 1808 to became champion of England. He was most famous, however, for his victories in 1810 and 1811 against Tom Molineaux (q.v.), which were arguably the first significant international contests in sporting history.[6]

Cuvier, Georges (1769–1832) was a French naturalist and zoologist, sometimes referred to as the founding father of palaeontology. He also wrote and lectured on the history of science.[7]

---

[4] *The Iconographic Encyclopaedia of the Arts and Sciences* (Philadelphia: Iconographic Publishing Co., 1887), p. 158.

[5] https://www.nationalgallery.org.uk/artists/sir-francis-legatt-chantrey

[6] Henry Downes Miles, *Pugilistica* (Edinburgh: J. Grant, 1906), pp. 242–77.

[7] https://ucmp.berkeley.edu/history/cuvier.html

De La Garde, Philip Chilwell (1797–1871) worked as a surgeon at both the Devon and Exeter hospital and the West of England Eye Infirmary, although his bias was always towards ophthalmic work. He wrote several medical books, including *A Treatise on Cataracts*[8] and many papers on other subjects, including a 'History of the Exeter Canal' in the *Transactions of the Institution of Civil Engineers*. He was mayor of Exeter in 1834/5.

Dickson, Sir David James Hamilton (1780–1850) was a naval surgeon whose life-long interest in botany led to his being elected a Fellow of both the Linnean Society and the Royal Society of Edinburgh. He joined the navy in 1798 and served in a variety of roles, including as physician to the Royal Naval hospital at Plymouth from 1824. He was knighted in 1834, and in 1840 he was promoted to inspector of hospitals and fleets. He died at Stonehouse.[9]

Duncan, Dr Andrew senior (1744–1828) was a physician and professor at Edinburgh University, a position he held for thirty years. He was a joint founder of the Royal Society of Edinburgh, became President of the Edinburgh College of Physicians and delivered the first British lecture on forensic medicine. In 1773 he established the *Medical and Philosophical Commentaries* as the first medical review to be published in Great Britain.

Duncan, Dr Andrew junior (1773–1832) was a physician and an expert in forensic science. The oldest son of Andrew Duncan senior (q.v.), he was the only one of his twelve children to enter the medical profession. In 1805 he became chief editor of the newly founded *Edinburgh Medical and Surgical Journal* and he also wrote *The Edinburgh New Dispensatory*,[10] which became very popular and went into ten editions by 1822.

Dupuytren, Professor Guillaume (1777–1835) was regarded as the greatest surgeon of the early nineteenth century. He was one of the founders of the Société Médicale d'Émulation de Paris in 1796. In 1803 he founded the Société Anatomique de Paris and around 1813 was appointed chief surgeon of the Hôtel-Dieu hospital. He was elected a member of the Académie Nationale de Médecine in 1820 (becoming Chairman in 1824) and a member of the Académie des Sciences in 1825. Way ahead of his time, Dupuytren understood the risks of infection and imposed strict rules of hygiene.[11]

Eastlake, Sir Charles Lock (1793–1865) was born in Plymouth, the son of George Eastlake (q.v.). At the age of sixteen Charles was admitted to the Royal Academy, where he met a number of leading artists, including Turner, who became a close friend. His success derived from his painting of Napoleon when in captivity on the *Bellerophon* in Plymouth Sound. He moved to France and then to Rome in 1816 and was persuaded to reluctantly return to England in 1830. He was given the freedom of the city of Plymouth in 1832 and appointed by Prince Albert to serve on the Fine Arts Commission and to advise on the Great Exhibition of 1851.[12]

[8] Published in London in 1821 by Longman, Hurst, Rees, Orme & Brown.
[9] https://history.rcplondon.ac.uk/inspiring-physicians/sir-david-james-hamilton-dickson
[10] Published initially by William Creech, but most later editions were published by Bell and Bradfute of Edinburgh.
[11] Paul Wylock, *The Life and Times of Guillaume Dupuytren, 1777–1835* (Brussels: Brussels University Press, 2010).
[12] Jenny Pery, 'The Art of Devon Painters – "the Alpha and Omega of the Victorian Art World" – Focus on Sir Charles Lock Eastlake', *Transactions of the Devonshire Association*

Eastlake, George (c.1758–1820) was judge-advocate and solicitor to the Admiralty in Plymouth and was present at the Guildhall, supporting Butter, when the Eye Infirmary was established.

Eccles, John Henry (1817–1902) was a surgeon at the Eye Infirmary. He married Milly Soltau in 1839, the year in which her father was both mayor of Plymouth and a vice-president of the Infirmary.

Edye, John (1802–70) was a surgeon at the West of England Eye Infirmary and, from 1846 to 1865, surgeon to the Devon and Exeter Hospital. In 1867 he moved to Uruguay and worked in a hospital there. His son and grandson both practised as surgeons in Uruguay.[13]

Fanshawe, Robert (1740–1823) was MP for Plymouth from 1784 to 1790 and Commander of Plymouth dockyard from 1790 to 1815.[14]

Fauntleroy, Henry (1784–1824) was one of the last people to be executed for forgery before it ceased to be a capital crime in 1836.

Fisk, William Hawley (1799–1870) was born in Ipswich. Before becoming Adjutant of the SDM he was a captain in the 17th Regiment of Lancers. In 1851 he was living with his wife Mary and their daughter at 4 Athenaeum Street, Plymouth, which he had bought two years earlier.[15]

Granville, Augustus Bozzi (1783–1872) was born in Milan and graduated as a doctor of medicine from the University of Pavia in 1802. After travelling in Europe he joined the British navy in 1807, rising to the rank of surgeon, and retired on half pay in 1813. He settled in Saville Row, was admitted a Licentiate of the College of Physicians, and became a Fellow of the Royal Society in 1817. He twice visited Russia in a professional capacity, and whilst travelling in Germany was attracted to the benefits of the mineral waters and thereafter devoted himself to making them more widely known.[16]

Gregory, Dr James (1753–1821) was professor of the practice of physic at Edinburgh University and a superb lecturer. He wrote a leading textbook (in Latin) on the theory of medicine, and from 1799 he was first physician to the king in Scotland.

Hamilton, Dr James (1767–1839) was involved with his father in the foundation of the lying-in hospital in Edinburgh in 1793. He was one of the original Directors of the hospital and later succeeded his father as professor of midwifery at Edinburgh in 1800.[17]

Hey, William (1736–1819) trained at St George's hospital, London, and set up a practice in Leeds. He helped to establish the Leeds General Infirmary, which opened in 1767, and was senior surgeon there from 1773 until he retired in 1812. Hey was also a prominent figure in Leeds civic life – he was mayor twice – and founded the Leeds Medical Society. He became a Fellow of the Royal Society in 1775, published a number of medical pamphlets, and invented a number of medical tools, perhaps the most famous being Hey's saw, used for trepanning.[+]

151 (Exeter: D. A., 2019), p. 201.

[13] www.geni.com/people/john-edye-M-D

[14] Michael Duffy, *The Navy Miscellany, Vol. VI* (Farnham: Ashgate, 2003), p. 186.

[15] DHC: DEX/7/b/1/1826/270.

[16] William Munk, *Roll of the Royal College of Physicians, Vol. III* (London: The Royal College of Physicians, 1878), p. 174.

[17] *Laws, Orders and Regulations of the Edinburgh General Lying-In Hospital 1793* [US National Library of Medicine, Accession no. 2471O34R].

Hill, John (d. 1807). Not much is known about his personal life, except that he had a wife Anna and two children and owned a farm and other property in the Barnstaple area. In addition to his medical skills, his interest in geology led him to discover 'hydrargillite in north Devon where its extension was not previously known'.[18]

Holmes, Dr Andrew Fernando (1797–1860) was born in Cadiz, Spain, and became a physician in Canada. He received a diploma from the Royal College of Surgeons of Edinburgh in 1818 and a medical degree in 1819. In Canada, along with four others, he founded the Montreal Medical Institution, which in 1829 became the medical faculty of McGill University. Holmes was the first professor of botany in 1829 and the first dean of the medical faculty in 1854. He was an active member of the Montreal Natural History Society.[19]

Hope, Thomas Charles (1766–1843) was professor of chemistry at Edinburgh University and served as President of the Royal College of Physicians of Edinburgh from 1815 to 1819. Charles Darwin viewed Hope's lectures as highlights in an otherwise dull education at the University.

Horsfall, William (1770–1812) was a wool-textile manufacturer and owner of a factory in Marsden, West Yorkshire. He was a strong advocate of the use of machinery in the production of textiles, an outspoken opponent of the Luddites and one of several mill-owners targeted by them. He died of his wounds after being ambushed and shot on 28 April 1812.[20]

Jameson, Professor Robert (1774–1854) was professor of natural history at the University of Edinburgh for fifty years. He was the first eminent scholar of the Wernerian geological system,[21] which was the belief in an all-encompassing ocean that gradually receded to its present location whilst precipitating or depositing almost all the rocks and minerals in the Earth's crust.

Lacépède, Count Bernard-Germain-Élienne de la Ville-sur-Illon (1756–1825) was a French naturalist. He was appointed Grand Chancellor of the Legion of Honour in 1803 and created a Peer of France in 1819.

Laénnec, Professor René-Théophile-Hyacinthe (1781–1826) was the inventor of the stethoscope. In 1795, aged fourteen, Laénnec was helping the sick and wounded at the Hôtel Dieu, and by the time he was eighteen he was serving in the military hospital there. He studied dissection in Guillaume Dupuytren's (q.v.) laboratory at the École Pratique, where, within a year, he obtained first prize in both medicine and surgery. He became editor and a shareholder in the *Journal de Médicine*, and in 1808 he founded the Athénée Médical, which later merged with the Société Académique de Paris. Soon afterwards, he was appointed personal physician to Cardinal Joseph Fesch, the uncle of Napoleon, who was exiled after Napoleon's fall in 1814. In 1816, Laénnec took up a position as surgeon at the Necker hospital, now the Hôpital des Enfants Malades, the first paediatric hospital in the world.[22]

---

[18] Lieut-Col. Harding, 'A Paper on Morwenstowe Church', in *Transactions of the Exeter Diocesan Architectural & Archaeological Society* (Exeter: EDA&AS, 1867), p. 218.

[19] Frances G. Halfpenny (ed.), *Dictionary of Canadian Biography, Vol. 8 (1851–1860)* (Toronto: University of Toronto Press, 1985).

[20] Anon., *An Historical Account of the Luddites and Their Trials at York Castle* (Huddersfield: John Cowgill, 1862), pp. 17–80.

[21] *The Encyclopaedia Britannica*, vol. XIII (Edinburgh: Adam & Charles Black, 1880), p. 563.

[22] Ariel Roguin, 'René Théophile Hyacinthe Laénnec (1781–1826): The Man behind the Stethoscope', *Clinical Medicine & Research* 4, no. 3 (September 2006), pp. 230–5.

Larrey, Baron Dominique Jean (1766–1842) became chief surgeon of Napoleon's Grande Armée. He established new surgical guidelines for treating the wounded in the field, improved the organisation of field hospitals, and created a revolutionary system of flying ambulances. These were horse-drawn vehicles with a sprung lightweight chassis that could both deliver surgical staff and remove the wounded speedily and in relative comfort.[23]

Lawrence, Baron William (1783–1867) was apprenticed to John Abernethy (q.v.), whom he succeeded as lecturer in surgery, a position he held until 1862. A gifted surgeon, he specialised in ophthalmology, and worked at St Bartholomew's for sixty-five years. In addition to twice serving as President of the Royal College of Surgeons, he was President of the Medical and Chirurgical Society of London. He was appointed Surgeon Extraordinary, and then Sergeant-Surgeon to Queen Victoria, and was made a Baron in 1867.

Leach, Dr William Elford (1791–1836) was born in Plymouth and attended a school in Exeter attached to the Devon and Exeter hospital, where he learned anatomy and chemistry. He then studied medicine at St Bartholomew's and at the Edinburgh medical school, finally graduating from St Andrew's. Having been nurtured by his father George Leach, a solicitor and well-known naturalist, his interest in natural history took precedence over medicine, and in 1813 he was employed as an assistant at the British Museum. His interests ranged widely across all areas of zoology, and he became the world's leading expert on crustacea. He was elected a Fellow of the Royal Society in 1816.

Leslie, Sir John (1766–1832) was a Scottish mathematician and physicist who became professor of natural philosophy at Edinburgh. He was elected a Fellow of the Royal Society of Edinburgh in 1807, and a Corresponding Member of the Académie des Sciences in 1820. He was knighted in 1832.

Lister, Joseph (1827–1912) was born in Essex, became a student at University College London in 1844 and was present when Robert Liston (q.v.) first used ether in an operation. Following a move to Scotland in 1869, he was appointed to the chair of surgery at Glasgow University and became a Fellow of the Royal Society. He returned to London in 1877 as professor of surgery at King's College Hospital. A somewhat controversial figure, Lister's medical life centred on his experimental work, particularly with antiseptic surgery, and the resultant revolution in surgical procedures is his lasting legacy.

Liston, Robert (1794–1847) entered the University of Edinburgh in 1808 and in 1810 became assistant to John Barclay (q.v.), from whom he derived his love of anatomy. In 1814, he became surgeon clerk (houseman) at Edinburgh Royal Infirmary before going to London in 1816, where he attended John Abernethy's (q.v.) lectures. He returned to Edinburgh, gaining a reputation as a teacher in anatomy and as a surgeon. He quarrelled constantly with the infirmary authorities, which led to his expulsion from the Royal Infirmary in 1822, although he was reinstated in 1827. His career led him back to London, and in 1835 he was appointed professor of clinical surgery at London University.

Lockyer, Edmund (1750–1836) was a solicitor, a magistrate and a deputy-lieutenant of Devon. He was mayor of Plymouth in 1803–4, 1810–11, 1821–22 and 1824–25.

---

[23] Kate Kelly, *The History of Medicine, Old World and New* (New York: Infobase Publishing, 2010), p. 42.

Locock, Sir Charles, Bart (1799–1875) became a Fellow of the Royal College of Physicians in 1836 and was Queen Victoria's obstetrician, attending the birth of all her children. He was also a justice of the peace and a deputy-lieutenant for the county of Kent.

Lopes, Manasseh Masseh (1755–1831) was a politician and one of the largest land-owners in Devon, with holdings in the South Hams and around Plymouth. He was Sheriff of Devon in 1810–11, and in 1812 he was elected MP for Barnstaple, but after being re-elected in 1818 he was found guilty of bribery and unseated. On his release from prison, he was elected for the pocket borough of Westbury, which he owned. When he died his estates were valued at £800,000.

Lopes, Sir Ralph, Bart (1788–1854) was the nephew of Manasseh Masseh Lopes (q.v.), inheriting most of his uncle's fortune and his seat at Maristow. Ralph was MP for Westbury and in 1849 for South Devon. He was a captain in the North Devon Militia by 1808 and a major by 1821.

Lucas, John (1807–74) was a London-born artist, apprenticed to Samuel William Reynolds, a mezzotint engraver. Lucas exhibited his first portrait at the Royal Academy in 1828 and showed ninety-six more before his death. His sitters included Queen Adelaide, the Princess Royal, the Duke of Wellington, Lord and Lady Palmerston and William Gladstone.

Magrath, Sir George (c.1772–1857) was a surgeon on the *Victory* in 1803, was elected a Fellow of the Royal Society in 1819, and was knighted in 1831 by William IV, to whom he had been physician when William was Lord High Admiral. He obtained his doctorate of medicine from the University of St Andrews in 1822, was admitted a licentiate of the College of Physicians the same year and made a Fellow in 1847. He was surgeon at Dartmoor prison for nine years, before settling as a physician in Plymouth until he died.

Mare, Charles John (1814–98) initially trained as a lawyer but used his social connections to enter into a partnership with Thomas Ditchburn and establish the iron-shipbuilders, Ditchburn Mare & Co., in Blackwall. Like Bidder (q.v.), he was involved with Robert Stephenson in building the Britannia bridge over the Menai Straits, his company producing seven of the eight revolutionary wrought-iron tubes that carried the railway. His receipt of a government contract to supply eight ships for mail services from Plymouth to India, and his position as majority share-holder in the General Screw Steam Company, led to his candidacy at the Plymouth election in 1852.[24]

Molineaux, Thomas (1784–1818) allegedly gained his freedom from slavery in Virginia by winning a boxing match involving a $100,000 wager. He moved to New York and then to London to challenge Tom Crib (q.v.).[25]

Monro(e), Professor Alexander (1773–1859) was the son of Professor Alexander Monroe (1733–1817). Both taught anatomy at Edinburgh University, and both were Fellows of the Royal College of Physicians of Edinburgh: father was President from 1779 to 1782, and son from 1825 to 1827.

Morley, Earl of: John Parker (1772–1840) was the only son of the first Baron Boringdon, although the family seat was transferred from Boringdon to Saltram in the

---

[24] https://victoriancommons.wordpress.com/2018/12/13/innovation-corruption-and-bankruptcy-charles-john-mare-1814-1898/

[25] Miles, *Pugilistica*, pp. 278–88.

seventeenth century. In 1812 Parker tried, unsuccessfully, to persuade Parliament to provide for vaccination against smallpox. In 1815, he was created Earl of Morley. He had been made Colonel of the North Devon Militia in 1794.

Morley, 2nd Earl of: Edmund Parker (1810–64) was the son of John Parker (q.v.). He became Colonel of the South Devon Militia in 1845.

Paris, Dr John Ayrton (1785–1856) was a physician and author, mostly of medical books. He was elected physician at Westminster Hospital in 1808, where he lectured in pharmaceutical medicine. He moved to Penzance in 1813 as physician to the Penzance Dispensary and in 1814 played a leading role in founding the Royal Geological Society of Cornwall. He returned to London in 1817, became a member of the Linnean Society and of the Royal Institution, and was President of the Royal College of Physicians in 1844.

Pellew, Sir Israel (1758–1832) was a British naval officer who was promoted to rear-admiral in 1810 and made Captain of the Fleet in 1816, having been knighted in 1815.

Pipon, Captain Philip (1771–1829) had an interesting and varied naval career during which he found the survivors of the *Bounty* on Pitcairn island, served briefly on the *Victory*, did some very successful surveying in the South Seas and ended as Flag-Captain to Lord de Saumarez on the *Britannia* at Plymouth.[26]

Playfair, Professor John (1748–1819) was a Church of Scotland minister, a mathematician and geologist, and a professor of natural philosophy at the University of Edinburgh, where he started lecturing in 1785. He was a founding member of the Royal Society of Edinburgh.

Radcliffe, Sir Joseph, Bart (1744–1819) was a Huddersfield magistrate who was given his baronetcy in 1813 for his actions against the Luddite rioters. In 1812 he had begun a prolonged campaign against them that rapidly became a vendetta. He set up a system of spies and informers to help convict his suspects, three of whom were hanged.

Rae, Sir William (1786–1873) graduated from Edinburgh University in 1804 and after a long and distinguished career as a naval surgeon retired in 1855 to a country practice near Barnstaple. He was knighted that same year.

Rolle, Lord John, 1st Baron Rolle (1756–1842) was MP for Devon from 1780 to 1796 and owned large areas of land in the county. As well as becoming Colonel of the SDM, he was instrumental in forming the Royal 1st Devon Yeomanry and the North Devon Yeomanry. He is chiefly remembered as the inspiration and butt of a satirical poem called the 'Rolliad', after he shouted down Edmund Burke in the Houses of Parliament, and for his accident at Queen Victoria's coronation in 1838, when, at the age of eighty-two and 'dreadfully infirm', he fell and 'rolled quite down' the steps of the throne while paying homage.[27]

Saumarez, Lord James, 1st Baron de Saumarez (1757–1836) joined the navy in 1770 and had a distinguished career. He was given his first command in 1778, served for a while on the *Victory* and was made an admiral in 1814. From 1824 to 1827 he was Port Admiral at Plymouth.

[26] *The United Service Journal, Part I* (London: Henry Colburn, 1834), pp. 191–9.
[27] R. G. Thorne (ed.), *The History of Parliament: The House of Commons, 1790–1820* (Woodbridge: Boydell & Brewer, 1986).

Saunders, John Cunningham (1773–1810) was born in Huish, Devon, and went to school initially in Tavistock and then in South Molton. He was apprenticed to John Hill (q.v.) at the age of seventeen and stayed for five years before going to London to study at St Thomas's hospital and then at Guy's medical school under Astley Cooper (q.v.).

Savigny, Paul gave his name to the business of a cutler's widow, which he bought in 1720, and was the first cutler in England to become a specialist maker of surgical instruments. He 'custom-made the Wenzel knife' used to remove cataracts.[28]

Scarpa, Professor Antonio (1752–1832) was an acclaimed anatomist and neurologist. He graduated with honours from the University of Padua and became professor of anatomy and surgery at the University of Modena, after which he travelled to the Netherlands, France and England, before being appointed professor of anatomy at the University of Pavia in 1783. He became an honorary member of the Royal Society in 1791 and of the Royal Swedish Academy of Sciences in 1821.[29]

Seale, Sir John Henry, Bart (1780–1844) held extensive property and land in and around Dartmouth and served as its Whig MP from 1832 to 1844. He was created a baronet in 1838. Together with the Earl of Morley (q.v.), he arranged the building of several bridges in Dartmouth, most notably the Dart crossing.[30]

Sheldon, John (1752–1808) was an anatomist and surgeon whose pioneering study of the lymphatic system earned him a worldwide reputation and recognition as one of the founders of modern-day surgery. He was elected a Fellow of the Royal Society in 1784, the year in which he published *The History of the Absorbent System*.[31] He became surgeon to Westminster Hospital in 1786, although he had to resign two years later because of ill health. After recovering, he was appointed surgeon to the Devon and Exeter Hospital in 1797. He had a wide range of interests, including ballooning and the anatomy of whales.

Simpson, Professor Sir James Young (1811–70) was a Scottish obstetrician, credited with the discovery of the use of chloroform as an anaesthetic. Having previously experimented with minor procedures, he used it for the first time in obstetrics in 1847. He was elected President of the Royal Medical Society of Edinburgh in 1835 and President of the Royal College of Physicians of Edinburgh in 1850. A man of wide interests, he was honoured by the placing of his bust in Westminster Abbey, acknowledging the benefits to the world of his use of chloroform. He was the first man to be knighted for services to medicine and was given a state funeral.

Snow, Dr John (1813–58) changed the face of medical practice with his accomplishments in medicine, anaesthesia and epidemiology. He became a member of the Royal College of Surgeons in 1838 and was recognised as an astute diagnostician. He was not, however, recognised in his lifetime for his two greatest achievements. Thanks to his work, surgeons used a ling mask to measure chloroform doses with a specially designed 'drop bottle', which made the process controlled and safe – he anaesthetised more than four thousand people, only one of whom died. His second

[28] https://georgianpapers.com/2016/11/29/eye-surgery-georgian-age/
[29] Benjamin Ward Richardson, *The Asclepiad, Vol. 3* (London: Longmans Green & Co., 1886), pp. 128–48.
[30] www.bythedart.co.uk
[31] Self-published in London.

great achievement was to map the spread of cholera and develop a transmission theory based on his knowledge of respiratory physiology.[32]

Stewart, Dugald (1753–1828) was a Scottish philosopher and mathematician. He was joint founder of the Royal Society of Edinburgh in 1783.

Waller, Sir Jonathan Wathen (1769–1853) was oculist to George III and to William IV. Ironically, like Butter, he lost his sight before he died.

Wood, James (1756–1836) was the owner of Gloucester Old Bank, which he had inherited from the founder, his father. He was said to be the richest commoner in the British Empire and was known as 'The Gloucester Miser'.

Woollcombe, Dr William (d. 1822) was a Plymouth doctor who published several papers in the *Edinburgh Medical & Surgical Journal*. He was also interested in local antiquities.

Yarde-Buller, Captain John, 1st Baron Churston (1799–1871) became MP for Devon South in 1832, retaining the seat until his elevation to the peerage in 1858. He was a magistrate and a deputy-lieutenant of Devon, a special deputy warden of the Stannaries and Lieutenant-Colonel of the South Devon Militia from 1845 to 1863.[33]

Yonge, Dr James (1794–1870) was the fourth son of Duke Yonge, vicar of Cornwood, Devon, and was educated at Eton and Exeter College Oxford. He was elected a Fellow of the College of Physicians of London in 1822 and was physician to the Devonshire and Cornwall hospital for many years.

---

[32] Richard Hollingham, *Blood and Guts: A History of Surgery* (London: BBC Books, 2008), p. 76.

[33] *Debrett Peerage and Titles of Courtesy* (London: Dean & Son, 1879), p. 131.

APPENDIX 2: MEDICAL GLOSSARY

Abdominal viscera – a collective term for the solid and hollow organs within the abdominal cavity.

Accoucheur – midwife.

Adema – *see* **Oedema**.

Aesculapian staff – a symbol of the medical profession, consisting of a branched staff with a single snake twined around it.

Amoroses [Amaurosis] – partial or total blindness without visible change in the eye, typically due to disease of the optic nerve, spinal cord or brain.

Aneurysm – a swelling in a blood vessel.

Angina pectoris – severe pain in the lower part of the chest accompanied by a feeling of suffocation.

Apoplexy – used to describe what is now known as a stroke.

Aqueous humour – the clear liquid filling the space in the front of the eyeball between the lens and the cornea.

Ascites – a build-up of fluid in the abdomen.

Biciphidal [bicipital] – relating to the biceps.

Calculi – stones, concretions of material, usually mineral salts, that form in the body.

Capsular ligaments – play a key role in maintaining the mobility and stability of the hip joint.

Caries – decay of the bones or teeth.

Cataplasm – a poultice or a plaster.

Celiac Plexus – a complex network of nerves located in the abdomen, known also as the solar plexus.

Clerotic coat – *see* **sclerotic**.

Colchicum – a flowering plant used to reduce swelling, inflammation and pain.

Collyrium – eye wash.

Cornea – the transparent layer forming the front of the eye.

Corneitis – inflammation of the cornea.

Crepitus – a cracking or popping sound in a joint.

Cupping – the placing of a warm cup on an affected area of skin, thus creating a suction that was thought to increase the flow of blood.

Cutaneous – relating to the skin.

Dropsy – oedema (q.v.) most often associated with cardiac failure.

Dura mater – the outermost membranous envelope of the brain and spinal cord.

Ectropion – a condition where the eyelid turns outwards.

Elefantiasis [elephantiasis] – the gross enlargement of an area of the body, especially the limbs.

Emphysematous – relating to emphysema, a lung condition that causes shortness of breath.

Epistaxis – nosebleed.

Esipelaus, exsipelaus [erysipelas] – a feverish disease caused by bacterial infection and characterised by red patches on the skin.

Eversion – tilting of the foot so that the sole faces away from the line of the body.

External iliac artery – *see* **iliac**.

Extravasion – the leakage of blood, lymph or other fluid.

Febrifuge – a medicine to reduce fever.

Femoral artery – the main vessel supplying blood to the lower body.

Fistula – an abnormal connection or passageway linking two organs or vessels that do not usually connect.

Fundus – the base of an organ or the part furthest away from its opening – the interior surface of the eye, opposite the lens.

Gangrenous erysipelas – an infection of the upper layers of skin.

German Key – initially modelled on a door key. Its 'claw' was tightened over the tooth and the instrument rotated to effect extraction. Replaced by forceps only in the twentieth century.

Glyster – a tobacco enema.

Goulard's Extract/Liniment – a solution of sub-acetate of lead used to treat inflammation.

Granulation – *see* **corneitis**.

Grumous blood – thick or clotted.

Gutta Serena – *see* **Amaurosis**.

Halient – acceding to a patient's wishes.

Hernia – a tumour formed when an internal part of the body pushes through a weakness in the muscle or surrounding tissue wall.

Hydrastic purge – a herbal supplement used to treat a number of conditions.

Hydrocele – a swelling caused by an accumulation of fluids.

Hydrophobia – a fear of water, often induced by rabies.

Hydrophthalmia – enlargement of the eyeball as a result of congenital glaucoma.

Hydrothorax – an excess of fluid in the pleural cavity (i.e. the space between the two layers of the lungs).

Iliac arteries – provide blood to the legs and to various organs in the pelvic area.

Ilium – the uppermost and largest part of the hip bone.

Inguinal – relating to the groin.

Integument – a natural covering, skin.

Ipecacuanha – a small South American shrub whose root is used as an emetic and expectorant.

Iridectomy – surgical procedure to remove part of the iris.

Issue – an incision or artificial ulcer made for the purpose of causing a discharge of blood or diseased matter from the body.

Lacrimal [Lachrymal] sac – a dilated end of the lachrymal duct, adjacent to the nose, that fills with tears secreted by the lachrymal glands.

Lamine [lamina] – lamina fusca is the pigmentary layer of the sclera (*see* **sclerotic**).

Litholomy [lithotomy] – a surgical method for the removal of stones (calculi).

Lunar caustic – silver nitrate fused into sticks and used to cauterise tissue.

Materia medica – collected knowledge about the therapeutic properties of substances used for healing.

Medulla – the lowest part of the brain and of the brainstem. It plays a critical role in transmitting signals between the spinal cord and the higher parts of the brain, and in controlling activities such as heartbeat and respiration.

Mortification – gangrene.

Nasdom's splint – no record found.

Nates – buttocks.

Nephrotic [nephritic] – relating to pain or disease in the kidneys.

Oedema – a swelling of watery fluid collecting in the cavities or tissues of the body.

Omentum – a fold or duplication of the peritoneum (q.v.), connecting the stomach with the liver, spleen, colon, etc.

Opaque cornea – occurs when the cornea becomes scarred, thus stopping light from passing through to the retina.

Ophthalmy [ophthalmia] – inflammation of the eye, conjunctivitis.

Ossified – hardened like bone.

Oxymuriate of mercury – a very poisonous, white crystalline powder.

Par Vagum – a cranial nerve.

Paracentesis – the perforation of a body cavity, usually for the removal of a fluid or gas.

Parietal bone – part of the skull.

Paroxysm – a fit or convulsion.

Percarditas [pericarditis] – inflammation of the pericardium.

Pereicardium [pericardium] – a fibrous sac that encloses the heart.

Peritoneum – a membrane that lines the inside of the abdomen and pelvis.

Petechial fever – a fever characterised by a rash of tiny red, purple or brown spots.

Phagedenic ulcer – a fast-spreading ulcer.

Pleuritic – relating to the tissue between the lungs and the chest wall.

Plura [pleura] – a membrane enveloping the lungs.

Pneumo-gastric – relating to the lungs and the stomach or abdomen.

Pons varolii – a band of nerve fibres that connects the hemispheres of the brain.

Ptosis – drooping eyelid.

Pulmonary – pertaining to the lungs.

Punctum [lacrimal punctum] – a minute opening on the margins of the eyelids that collects tears produced by the lachrymal glands.

Purulent – containing or composed of pus.

Quinsy – inflammation of the throat.

St Vitus Dance – i.e. Sydenham's chorea, an auto-immune disease characterised by rapid, uncoordinated jerking movements primarily affecting the face, hands and feet.

Sarcocele – a swelling or tumour of the testes.

Sclerotic – relating to the sclera, part of the outer covering and protection for the eyeball.

Scrafolas [scrofulous] – relating to scrofula, a constitutional disease characterised mainly by chronic enlargement and degeneration of the lymphatic glands.

Seton – a thread drawn through a fold of skin, a sinus or a cavity so as to maintain an issue (q.v.).

Sicmoid flexure – the s-shaped curve of the colon immediately above the rectum.

Sloughing – the shedding of diseased tissue.

Staphyloma – a protrusion of the cornea or sclera (q.v.) resulting from inflammation.

Style – a blunt-pointed probe.

Suppurative – inducing the formation of pus.

Syphiloma – a tumour caused by syphilis.

Tertian Fever – a form of malaria recurring every other day.

Thalamus – the part of the brain responsible for relaying sensory signals and for the regulation of consciousness, sleep and alertness.

Tincea capita – ringworm.

Tobacco glyster – a tobacco-smoke enema.

Trachoma – the so-called Egyptian ophthalmia, a bacterial infection of the eye causing blindness.

Trepanning – a surgical intervention in which a hole is drilled into the skull.

Trichiasis – inward-turning eyelashes.

Trocanter – part of the hip.

Vascular – the vascular system is made up of the vessels that carry blood and lymph through the body.

Venesection – blood-letting.

Ventral hernia – a hernia (q.v.) in the abdominal wall.

Vertebrae – there are seven cervical vertebrae at the top of the spinal column, below which are twelve dorsal or thoracic vertebrae and five lumbar vertebrae.

Vitreous humour – the transparent gelatinous tissue filling the eyeball behind the lens.

Walcheren fever – a mixture of malaria, typhoid and typhus.

BIBLIOGRAPHY

Unpublished Sources

Lattimore, M. I., 'The History of Libraries in Plymouth to 1914' (Unpublished PhD thesis, University of Plymouth, 1982).

Palluault, F., 'Medical Students in England and France 1815–1858, a Comparative Study' (Unpublished DPhil thesis, University of Oxford, 2003).

'South Devon Militia Mess Minutes Book, 1853–1907' (DHC 6855L/1/6/5)

Stoneman, R. J., 'The Reformed British Militia, c.1852–1908' (Unpublished PhD thesis, University of Kentucky, 2014).

Newspapers

Exeter Flying Post
Exeter and Plymouth Gazette
Kentish Gazette
Kentish Weekly Post or Canterbury Journal
Morning Advertiser
Morning Post
North Devon Journal
Nottingham Mercury
Plymouth Herald
Plymouth and Plymouth Dock Weekly Journal
Royal Devonport Telegraph & Plymouth Chronicle
Sander's Newsletter
Star (London)
Western Courier, West of England Conservative, Plymouth and Devonport Advertiser
Western Daily Mercury
Western Morning News
Western Times

Published Sources

Adams, W., *Practical Observations on Ectropium or Eversion of the Eye-Lids* (London: J. Callow, 1812).

—— *A Reply to a Recent Publication against Him* (London: Baldwin, Craddock and Joy, 1818).

Anon., 'Boyer, Alexis', in *The Encyclopaedia Britannica: Vol. IV* (New York: Horace Everett Hooper, 1911).

Anon., *Case Notes on Frederick ..., Published as Centenary of the First Public Operation under an Anæsthetic in Europe, Carried Out at University College Hospital by Robert Liston on 21st December 1846* (London: University College Hospital, 1946).

Anon., *An Historical Account of the Luddites and Their Trials at York Castle* (Huddersfield: John Cowgill, 1862).

Anon., 'Jameson, Robert', in *The Encyclopaedia Britannica: Vol. XIII* (Edinburgh: Adam & Charles Black, 1880).

Anon., 'Lacépède, Bernard', in *The Encyclopaedia Britannica: Vol. XVI* (New York: Horace Everett Hooper, 1911).

Anon., Review of John Butter, *Remarks on Irritative Fever*, *The Lancet* 9, no. 120 (1825).

Billet, J., *Brief History of Ophthalmic Surgery in Great Britain during the Present Century* (Taunton: A. Pile, 1866).

Bishop, P. J., 'Reception of the Stethoscope and Laénnec's Book', *Thorax* 36 (1981).

Bond, A., 'Working Class Housing in Victorian Plymouth: From Slum to Council House, Part 1; Slums and Artisans' Dwellings', *The Devon Historian* 81 (Exeter: Devon History Society, 2012).

Bonner, T. N., *Becoming a Physician: Medical Education in Britain, France, Germany and the United States 1750–1945* (Baltimore and London: Johns Hopkins University Press, 1995).

Bracken, C. W., 'Historical Notes on the City of Plymouth', in *The Book of Plymouth* (Plymouth: British Medical Association, 1938).

Brayshay, M. and Pointon, V., 'Local Politics and Public Health in mid-Nineteenth-Century Plymouth', *Medical History* 27 (1983).

Brendon, F., *A Directory of Plymouth, Stonehouse, Devonport, Stoke and Moricetown* (Plymouth: F. Brendon, 1852).

Brown, M., *Performing Medicine: Medical Culture and Identity in Provincial England, c.1760–1850* (Manchester: Manchester University Press, 2014).

Buckland, W. and Conybeare, W., *Ten Plates Comprising a Plan, Sections and Views, Representing the Changes Produced on the Coast of East Devon, between Axmouth and Lyme Regis, by the Subsidence of the Land and Elevation of the Bottom of the Sea on 26 December 1838 and 3 February 1840* (London: John Murray, 1840).

Butter, J., *An Address Delivered in the Guildhall, at Plymouth, on the 6th Day of December, 1821: At the First General Meeting of the Subscribers to the Plymouth Eye Infirmary* (Plymouth: Rowes, 1821).

—— *Change of Plumage in Hen Birds* (extracted from the *Memoirs of the Wernerian Natural History Society*, vol. 3, for the years 1817–18–19–20) (Edinburgh: Archibald Constable & Co., 1821).

—— *Disputatio Medica inauguralis, quaedam de ophthalmia complectens* (Edinburgh: P. Neill, 1820).

—— 'General Observations on the Pathology and Cure of Squinting', reviewed in *Notices and Abstract of Communications to the British Association for the Advancement of Science to the Plymouth Meeting, August 1841, an Addendum to Report of the Eleventh Meeting of the British Association for the Advancement of Science; Held at Plymouth in July 1841* (London: John Murray, 1842).

—— 'Letter on Erysipelas', *The Lancet* 9, no. 224 (1827).

—— *Observations upon the Action of Mercury in the Cure of Venereal Diseases: Intended as a Reply to Those of Professor Thomson, Contained in the 53rd Number of the Edinburgh Medical & Surgical Journal* (Edinburgh: G. Ramsay and Co., 1820).

—— 'Remarks on the Faculty of Perceiving Colours', in *Transactions of the Phrenological Society* vol. 1 (1824).

—— 'Remarks on the Insensibility of the Eye to Certain Colours', in *Edinburgh Philosophical Journal* vol. 6 (1822).

—— *Remarks on Irritative Fever, Commonly Called the Plymouth Dockyard Disease, with Mr. Dryden's Detailed Account of the Fatal Cases, Including that of the Lamented Surgeon, Dr. Bell* (London: Underwoods; Edinburgh: Black; Dublin: MacArthur, 1825).

—— *Two Memoirs, On the Poisonous Effects of Nitre; and, Practical Observations on the Compression of Cancerous Breasts* (Edinburgh: G. Ramsay and Co., 1820).

Corvisart, J. N., *An Essay on the Organic Diseases and Lesions of the Heart* (Philadelphia: Anthony Finley, 1812).

Darwin, C. (ed. Barlow, N.), *The Autobiography of Charles Darwin, 1809–1882* (London: Collins, 1958).

Debrett Peerage and Titles of Courtesy (London: Dean & Son, 1879).

Digby, A., *Making a Medical Living: Doctors and Patients in the English Market for Medicine, 1720–1911* (Cambridge: Cambridge University Press, 2002).

Dingwall, R. et al., *An Introduction to the Social History of Nursing* (Abingdon: Routledge, 2002).

Doyle, D., 'Notable Fellows: William Porterfield (1696–1771)', *Journal of the Royal College of Physicians of Edinburgh* 40, no. 2 (2010).

Duffy, M., *The Navy Miscellany*, vol. VI (Farnham: Ashgate, 2003).

Eaton, M., *The Cook and Housekeeper's Universal Dictionary* (Bungay: I & R Chubb, 1822).

Ellis, H., 'John Abernethy, Surgeon: A Founder of the Medical School at St. Bartholomew's Hospital', *Hospital Medicine* 75, no. 3 (2014).

Farr, R., *The Distin Legacy: The Rise of the Brass Band in Nineteenth-Century Britain* (Cambridge: Cambridge Scholars Publishing, 2013).

Farre, J. R., *A Treatise on Some Practical Points Relating to the Diseases of the Eye by the Late John Cunningham Saunders* (London: Longman, Hurst, Rees, Orme and Brown, 1811).

Fisk, Colonel, *Annals of the Militia, Being the Records of the South Devon Regiment Prefaced by an Historical Account of Militia Organisation, from Memoranda Put Together by Col. Fisk* (Plymouth: Wm. Brendon & Son, 1875).

Fitzharris, L., *The Butchering Art* (London: Penguin Random House UK, 2017).

Flintoff, G., *Flintoff's Directory and Guide Book to Plymouth, Devonport, Stonehouse and Their Vicinities* (Plymouth: G. Flintoff, 1844).

Frank, J. B., 'Body Snatching: A Grave Medical Problem', *Yale Journal of Biology and Medicine* 49 (1976).

Gill, C., 'Ocean Liners at Plymouth', in Michael Duffy et al. (eds), *The New Maritime History of Devon*, vol. 2 (London: Conway Maritime Press, 1994).

—— *Plymouth: A New History* (Newton Abbot: David and Charles, 1979).

Goodall, F., *Lost Plymouth* (Edinburgh: Birlinn, 2009).

Gray, Mr., 'New French Mode of Discovering Ulcers in the Lungs', *London Medical Repository* 12 (1819).

Green, M., 'William Buckland's Model of Plymouth Breakwater', *Archives of Natural History* 23 (1996).

Halfpenny, F. G. (ed.), *Dictionary of Canadian Biography*, vol. 8 (1851–60) (Toronto: University of Toronto Press, 1985).

Harding, Lieut-Col., 'A Paper on Morwenstowe Church', in *Transactions of the Exeter Diocesan Architectural & Archaeological Society* (Exeter: EDA&AS, 1867).

Henkes, H. E., *History of Ophthalmology 5* (London: Kluwer Academic Publishers, 1993).

Hilditch, P., 'Devon and Naval Strategy since 1815', in Michael Duffy et al. (eds), *The New Maritime History of Devon*, vol. 2 (London: Conway Maritime Press, 1994).

Hill, C. P., *British Economic and Social History, 1700–1939* (London: Edward Arnold, 1967).

Hollingham, R., *Blood and Guts, a History of Surgery* (London: BBC Books, 2008).

Hoskins, W. G., *Devon* (Chichester: Phillimore & Co., 1954, re-published 2003).

—— *The Making of the English Landscape* (London: Penguin, 1985).

The Iconographic Encyclopaedia of the Arts and Sciences (Philadelphia: Iconographic Publishing Co., 1887).

Kelly, K., *The History of Medicine, Old World and New* (New York: Infobase Publishing, 2010).

Laénnec, R., *A Treatise on the Diseases of the Chest and on Mediate Auscultation – Translated, with Notes, Biography and Bibliography by Sir John Forbes* (New York: Samuel S. and William Wood, 1838).

Lawrence, W., *A Treatise on the Diseases of the Eye* (Washington: Duff Green, 1834).

Laws, Orders and Regulations of the Edinburgh Lying-in Hospital (Edinburgh: n.p., 1793).

List of Fellows of the Royal Society, 1660–2019 (London: The Royal Society, 2020).

The Literary Panorama and Annual Register, vol. 9 (Holborn: C. Taylor, 1811).

The London Medical Repository (London: Thomas & George Underwood, 1819 and 1825).

Loudon, I., *Medical Care and the General Practitioner, 1750–1850* (Oxford: Oxford University Press, 1986).

Macilwain, G., *Memoirs of John Abernethy* (New York: Harper & Brothers, 1853).

Mackenzie, W., *A Practical Treatise on the Diseases of the Eye* (London: Longmans, 1833).

Mathiasen, H., 'Mastectomy without Anaesthesia: The Case of Abigail Adams Smith and Fanny Burney', *American Journal of Medicine, Medical Humanities Perspective* 124 (May 2011).

Maton, W. G., 'Observations on the Western Counties of England', in R. Pearse Chope (ed.), *Early Tours in Devon and Cornwall* (Newton Abbot: David & Charles, 1967).

Medical Times & Gazette.

Miles, H. D., *Pugilistica* (Edinburgh: J. Grant, 1906).

Minchinton, W., *Devon's Industrial Past: A Guide* (Dartington: Dartington Centre for Education and Research, 1986).

Morris, C. (ed.), *The Illustrated Journeys of Celia Fiennes 1685–c.1712* (London: Macdonald & Co., 1982).

Mortimer, I., *The Time Traveller's Guide to Regency Britain* (London: The Bodley Head, 2020).

Munk, W., *Roll of the Royal College of Physicians*, vol. III (London: The Royal College of Physicians, 1878).

Northway, A., 'The Devon Fishing Industry in the Eighteenth and Nineteenth Centuries', in Michael Duffy et al. (eds), *The New Maritime History of Devon*, vol. 2 (London: Conway Maritime Press, 1994).

Peacock, G., *Miscellaneous Works of the Late Thomas Young*, vol. 1 (London: John Murray, 1855).

Pery, J., 'The Art of Devon Painters: The "Alpha and Omega of the Victorian Art World"; Focus on Sir Charles Lock Eastlake', in *The Devonshire Association Reports and Transactions* (Exeter: D. A., 2019).

Porter, R., *The Greatest Benefit to Mankind* (London: W. W. Norton & Co., 1997).

'Proceedings of Societies', *British Medical Journal* (Clinical Research Edition) (1848).

Richardson, B. W., *The Asclepiad*, vol. 3 (London: Longmans, Green & Co., 1886).

Risse, Guenter B., *Hospital Life in Enlightenment Scotland: Care and Teaching at the Royal Infirmary of Edinburgh* (Cambridge: Cambridge University Press, 2010).

Roguin, A., 'René Théophile Hyacinthe Laénnec (1781–1826): The Man behind the Stethoscope', *Clinical Medicine & Research* 4, no. 3 (September 2006).

Shapter, T., *The History of the Cholera in Exeter in 1832* (London/Exeter: John Churchill/Adam Holden, 1849).

The Shorter Oxford English Dictionary (Oxford University Press, 1973).

Skempton, A. W. et al. (eds), *A Biographical Dictionary of Civil Engineers*, vol. 1, 1500–

1830 (London: Thomas Telford Publishing, 2002).

Square, J. E., 'Medical History of Plymouth, with Anecdotes and Reminiscences', in *The Book of Plymouth* (Plymouth: British Medical Association, 1938).

Starkey, D. J., 'Devon's Shipbuilding Industry, 1786–1970', in Michael Duffy et al. (eds), *The New Maritime History of Devon*, vol. 2 (London: Conway Maritime Press, 1994).

—— 'The Ports, Seaborne Trade and Shipping Industry of South Devon, 1786–1914', in Michael Duffy et al. (eds), *The New Maritime History of Devon*, vol. 2 (London: Conway Maritime Press, 1994).

Thorne, R. G. (ed.), *The History of Parliament: The House of Commons, 1790–1820* (Woodbridge: Boydell & Brewer, 1986).

Thurston, L. and Williams, G., 'An Examination of John Fewster's Role in the Discovery of Smallpox Vaccination', *The Journal of the Royal College of Physicians of Edinburgh* 45, no. 2 (2015).

The United Service Journal, Part 1 (London: Henry Colburn, 1834).

Waddington, K., *Medical Education at St. Bartholomew's Hospital, 1123–1995* (Woodbridge: Boydell Press, 2003).

Ware, J. (ed.), *A Treatise on the Cataract; With Cases to Prove the Necessity of Dividing the Transparent Cornea.... By M. de Wenzel, jun. Baron of the Holy Roman Empire* (London: Dilly, 1791).

Wootton, D., *Bad Medicine: Doctors Doing Harm since Hippocrates* (Oxford: Oxford University Press, 2006).

Worth, R. N., *A History of Devonshire* (London: Elliot Stock, 1886).

—— *The History of Plymouth from the Earliest Period to the Present Time* (Plymouth: W. Brendon & Son, 1871).

Wyatt, M., 'The Quaker Contribution to Education in Plymouth', in *Transactions of the Devonshire Association* (Exeter: D. A., 2020).

Wylock, P., *The Life and Times of Guillaume Dupuytren, 1777–1835* (Brussels: Brussels University Press, 2010).

Wyman, A. L., 'Baron de Wenzel, Oculist to King George III: His Impact on British Ophthalmologists', *Medical History* 35 (1991).

Websites Consulted

Dartmouth: bythedart.co.uk

Devonport history: olddevonport.uk

Exeter School: exeterschool.co.uk

Genealogy: familysearch.org

geni.com

Georgian Papers Programme: georgianpapers.com

Luddites: ludditebicentenary.blogspot.com

Oxford Dictionary of National Biography: oxforddnb.com

Plymouth history: oldplymouth.uk

Plymouth Law Society: plymouthlawsociety.co.uk

Royal College of Physicians: rcplondon.ac.uk

Royal College of Surgeons of England: rcseng.ac.uk

The National Gallery: nationalgallery.org.uk

The Victorian House of Commons (History of Parliament): victoriancommons.wordpress.com

University of California Museum of Palaeontology: ucmp.berkeley.edu

University of Edinburgh: ourhistory.is.ed.ac.uk

INDEX

Note: French, Irish and Italian places and institutions have been indexed under the relevant country. Similar treatment has been applied to Devonport, Edinburgh, Exeter, London, Plymouth and Stonehouse. Banks, barracks, dispensaries, hospitals, infirmaries, militias and universities are all listed as such.

Abdominal viscera 179, 212
Abercrombie, Sir (Robert) Ralph 78, 201
Abernethie, Col. 143, 153, 175
  Mrs 143
Abernethy, John 21, 93–4, 118, 121, 124, 137–8, 201
  Surgical Technique 19–20, 65, 105
  Training of Butter 11, 50, 52–3
Abscess 18, 54, 87, 88, 105, 108, 139, 142, 155, 159, 174, 178, 197
Accoucheur see Midwifery
Ac(k)land, Lt General Wroth Palmer 71
Acland, Sir Thomas Dyke 39, 41, 198, 201
Adams, Andrew 185
Adams, Sir William 34, 36, 50, 69, 78, 79, 80, 195, 201
Adema see Oedema
Aesculapian staff 113, 212
Albert, Prince 41, 158, 178, 179, 191, 204
Amaurosis 76, 88, 128, 144, 145, 152, 156, 167, 212, 213
American War 26
Amputation 18, 19, 21, 61, 68, 158
Anaesthesia 18–19, 114, 210; see also Chloroform
Anatomy 7, 11, 14, 15, 50, 70, 78, 90, 95, 98, 109, 112, 114, 124, 201, 202, 207, 208, 210
Anatomy Act, 1832 14
Aneurysm 114, 180, 212
Angina pectoris 142, 148, 212
Anning, Mary 111
Apoplexy 36, 78, 119, 128, 129, 135, 138, 148, 162, 163, 175, 177, 182, 184, 193, 212
Apothecaries 41, 80, 87, 123, 166
Apothecaries Act, 1815 11
Apothecaries Company 144
Aqueous humour 44, 79, 144, 158, 212
Archer, Addis 89, 159
Ascites 57, 212
Ashburton 108, 121, 144–5, 154–5, 173, 194
Ashford, Catherine née Butter 1, 7, 8, 126, 150
  Charles Edwin 10
  James 1, 7, 9, 10, 144, 174

John Butter 7, 159, 178, 187, 188, 191
  Julia 174
  Louisa 174, 175
  William 10
Auscultation see Stethoscope
Axmouth 157

Bacot Mr 144–5
Baker, Josias 13, 14, 50, 51
Baldy, Dr W P 120, 140, 153
Banks 28, 85, 104, 134
  Childs 135
  Failure of in 1825 138–9
  Gibbs & Co 97
  Gloucester Old 211
  Herries, Farquhar & Co 93, 94, 97, 105, 107
  Marsh, Tracey & Fauntleroy 126
  Naval 24
  Shields & Johns 127, 139
  Sir W Elford & Co 127
Banks, Sir Joseph 118, 201
Barclay, Dr John 109, 202, 207
Barnes, Samuel 37, 74–5, 80, 146, 202
Barnstaple 23, 206, 208, 209
Barracks, Chatham 52, 55
  Dartmoor Prison 74
  Exeter 110
  Frankfort 26, 82
  Georges Square 26, 82, 83, 84, 85
  Horse (Exeter) 50
  Horse (Sheffield) 62
  Longroom, Stonehouse (Royal Marines) 23, 28, 124
  Mutley 26
  Ottery 73, 93
  Shorncliffe 24, 56, 59, 60, 85
Bartholomew, Rev. 7, 49
Bath 3, 88, 107, 126, 130, 131, 132, 138, 163
Bayntun, Eliza 41, 42, 181
  George 40, 41, 42, 45, 137, 181
Beattie, Sir William 89, 165, 202
Beddoes, Thomas 102, 202
Bell, Sir Charles 98, 202
Bell, John 99, 100, 102
Bell, Professor John 99, 202

Bellerophon   28, 204
Berkley Castle   136
Bewes, Cordelia   39, 131, 147, 156
Bicephaly   66, 212
Bicton   56, 68, 108, 151, 161, 163
Bidder, George Parker   115, 202, 208
Bideford   23, 116, 162
Bird, Mr   51, 90
Birkenhead   188
Black, Lt   55, 57, 60, 85
Blainville   14, 94, 105
Blicke, Sir Charles   53, 201, 202
Blood-letting see Venesection
Bodmin   91, 149
Body-snatching   14
Bonaparte, Lucien   139
   Napoleon   28, 57, 97, 99, 108, 201, 204,
      206
Bosgesmen   189
Boyer, Alexis   202
Boyer's splint   120
Braddon, Capt.   84, 91
Bray, Anna Elisa   145
Breast, compression of   13, 19, 111
Brent see South Brent
Brent, Dr   142, 174
Brent Fair   8, 196
Brent Moor   182
Brewster, David   202
Brewster's Philosophical Journal   77, 115
Brighton   106–7, 191
Bristol   73, 186
British Association for the Advancement of
      Science   43, 157, 160
Brockedon, William   157, 161, 203
Brodie, Captain Sir Benjamin Collins   103,
      155, 203
Buckland, Frank   111
Buckland, Rev. Dr William   111, 160
Buller, Sir Edward   132
Buller, John see Yarde-Buller
Burdett, Sir Francis   59, 71
Burnett, Sir William   195, 203
Burney, Fanny   19
Burrell, Sir Charles   106, 203
Butter, Agnes, née Langdon   4
   Aunt (Elizabeth of Bath)   4, 7, 93, 107,
      109, 115, 118, 121, 126, 128, 130, 131,
      132, 134, 135, 136
   Barnard (Bernard)   7, 93, 107, 109, 110,
      125–6, 163, 167
   Catherine see Ashford
   Catherine, née Farr   4, 5, 7, 49, 54,
      150–1, 153–4

Elizabeth White, née Veale   4, 8, 9, 19,
      135, 136, 137, 138, 145–6, 151, 155,
      160, 191, 196, 198
Jacob, junior   4, 5, 7, 8, 49, 105, 144, 150,
      151, 153, 154
Jacob, senior   4, 5
Jacobus   5, 7, 8, 10, 49, 54, 82, 85, 86,
      126, 127, 142, 150, 153, 167, 172, 174,
      175
James   4, 191
John, Blindness   1, 7, 44, 45, 99
   Death   1, 9–10
   Executorships   148–9, 161, 168, 193
   Freeman of City of Plymouth   7
   Landholdings
      Aishridge   184
      Axmouth   8
      Binnamoor Estate   184
      Broadamoor   184
      Broom Parks   139
      Butterford Estate   87, 179
      Colyton   8, 156
      Corringdon   139, 172
      Covingdon Estate   144, 175
      Glasscombe   159, 164
      Merrifield Estate   147
      Monksmoor Estate   167
      Musbury   8, 156
      Musbury Field   154
      Shillingham Barton   183
      South Brent   8, 155, 156
      Summers Wood Estate   173–4, 184
      Ugborough   8
      Whifferton Estate   167, 190
      Woodbury   8
      see also Owley
   Magistracy   7, 190
   Portrait of   197
   Publications   13, 21, 43, 110, 111, 112,
      115, 118, 134, 146
Mary née Langdon   4, 5, 191
Philip   4

Calculi   173, 127, 133, 159, 161, 196, 212,
      213; see also Lithotomy
Cambridge   11, 178, 179
Cambridge, Duke of   190
Cancer   13, 66, 111, 114, 122, 180
Canterbury   60
Capsular ligament   147, 212
Caries   88, 108, 212
Carne, Lt John   130
Cartwright, Major   59, 71
Cataplasm   191, 212

Cataract   34, 35, 36, 38, 42, 44, 62, 66, 69,
      74, 76, 77, 78, 79, 115, 123, 128, 156,
      190, 204, 210,
   Extracapsular extraction   34
   Intracapsular extraction   34
   Spontaneous dispersion of   77, 115
Caunter, Miss Mary Grace   184
   Mrs (Henry)   159
Celiac plexus   103, 212
Celsus   45, 145
Chantrey, Sir Francis Leggatt   124, 162,
      176, 203
Chapple, Adj.   148, 150
Chatham   24, 25, 52, 54, 55, 60, 70
Chatsworth   73, 189
Cheirosurgeon   5
Cheltenham   73, 135, 136
Chester   187
Chesterfield   63
Chloroform   15, 18, 19, 103, 114, 177, 210;
      see also Anaesthesia
Cholera   21–2, 54, 85, 101, 140, 141, 142, 143,
      149, 164, 185, 211
Churchill, John   80, 81
Churston, Col. Lord see Yarde-Buller
Clarence, Duchess of   25
Clarence, Duke of   41, 203, 208, 211; see
      also William IV
Clerotic see Sclerotic
Cline, Henry   53, 54, 78, 203
Cochrane, Sir Alexander Inglis   128–9, 203
Colby, James   24
Colchicum   140, 154, 212
Cole, Capt.   190
Collins, Rev. Dr   138
Collyrium   66, 212
Colyford   156
Colyton   8
Conan Doyle, Sir Arthur   15
Consumption see Pulmonary
Cooks Venmore see Higher Venmore
Cookworthy, Dr   91, 140, 159, 164, 165
Cookworthy, Miss   80
Cooper, Sir Astley Paston   21, 78, 86, 90,
      124, 203, 210
Coram, Mr   89
Cordoza, Antonio   51
Cornea   76, 78, 79, 84, 143–4, 148, 177,
      212, 214
   Opaque   76, 78, 79, 214
Corneitis   78, 212, 213
Cornish, James   151, 190
Cornwood   168, 211
Corunna, battle of   11, 50, 100, 110
Coryndon, Mr G   143

Couching   34, 77, 154
Cowes   161
Crepitus   196, 212
Cribb, Tom   58, 59, 203, 208
Cupping   87, 128, 152, 212
Cutaneous diseases   95, 178, 212
Cuvier, Georges   94, 203

Dangerfield, Mr   73
Dartmoor   28, 30, 75, 80, 82
Dartmoor Prison   26, 73, 74, 165, 208
   Governor Shortland   165
Dartmouth   32, 93, 210
Darwin, Charles   15, 206
Daviel, Jacques   34, 35
Davies, Dr   62
Davy, Humphrey   18, 103, 176
Dawe, Mr   85, 86
Deeble Boger   39
Defence Act, 1803   23
De la Beche, Sir Henry   111
De la Garde, Philip Chilwell   80, 204
Delirium   124, 146, 162, 176
Derby   189
Devonport   26, 30, 43, 129, 134, 142, 182,
      190, 195, 197
   Column   30
   Dock Public School   29
   Dockyard   27, 32, 195
   Guildhall   30
   Leat   28
   Local Board of Health   32
   Mount Wise   128, 192
Dickson, Sir David James Hamilton   167,
      186, 204
Dislocation   61, 69, 140–1, 154
Dispensaries, Devonport Public   33
   Dispensary for curing diseases of the eye
      and the ear see Hospitals, London,
      Moorfields
   Dock and Stonehouse   37
   Plymouth Eye   37, 38, 123, 129; see also
      Infirmaries, Plymouth Royal Eye
   Plymouth Public   33, 37, 80, 123, 125
   see also Hospitals and Infirmaries
Distin, John Henry   25
Dock Public School for boys   29
Dockyard Disease see Fever, Irritative
Dogs   180
   Juno   80, 82, 83, 84, 87, 89, 90, 122, 139
   Otho   82, 83, 84, 85, 89, 90
Donald murder trial   91–2
Doncaster   64
Droitwich   187
Dropsy   5, 55, 57, 114, 142, 172, 183, 197, 212

Dryden, Mr 21
Duncan, Dr Andrew junior 15, 17, 109, 110, 115, 204
Duncan, Dr Andrew senior 204
Dunning, Richard 190
Dupuytren, Professor Guillaume 14, 35, 86, 95, 204, 206
Dura mater 145, 183, 212
Dysentery 11

East Budleigh 4
Eastlake, Sir Charles Lock 28, 99, 204
Eastlake, George 94, 204, 205
Eccles, John Henry 40, 46, 205
Ectropion 43, 138, 143, 167, 212
Eddystone light 27
Edinburgh 1, 109–10, 111, 112–15, 118, 120
  Edinburgh Medical and Surgical Journal
    13, 15, 17, 110, 111, 112, 144, 204, 211
  Edinburgh New Dispensatory 204
  Edinburgh Philosophical Journal 202
  Royal College of Physicians 7, 20, 123, 202, 204, 206, 208, 210
  Royal College of Surgeons 202, 206
  Royal Medical Society 114, 115, 210
  Royal Society 77, 115, 204, 207, 209, 211
  Transactions of the Phrenological Society 171
Edsall, Rev. 152, 171, 175
Edye, John 80, 205
Egyptian Ophthalmy *see* Trachoma
Eldon, Lord 151
Elephantiasis 61, 212
Elgin, Lord 67, 68
Elliot, John 182
Elliott, Eliza 37, 41, 161
  Sgt Major John 37, 41, 141, 180, 181
Emphysematous 181, 212
English, Mrs Charles 196
Epistaxis 164, 212
Erysipelas 87, 146, 212, 213
Ether 18, 19, 103, 207
Eversion 196, 212
Exeter 51, 75, 127, 131, 142, 153, 168, 174, 175, 196, 201, 204
  Assizes 190
  Asylum 193
  Exeter Flying Post 22, 38
  Grammar School 7, 49, 106, 138, 202
  Medical Society 13
  Phillpotts, Bishop of 185
Exeter Province Medical & Surgical Association 164
Exmouth 49, 65, 175, 197
Extravasation 212

Falmouth 31, 91, 156
Fanshawe, Robert 99, 205
Faraday, Michael 18
Farr, Samuel 4
Farre, John Richard 35, 79, 80
Fauntleroy, Henry 126, 127, 205
Febrifuge 115, 213
Femoral artery 19, 54, 63, 213
Fever 100, 105, 112, 113, 124, 125, 140, 141, 142, 146, 150, 183, 184
  Gastric 180
  Irritative 21, 112, 134
  Malaria 100, 101, 214, 215
  Rheumatic 8, 157, 161, 162, 164, 166
  Scarlet/Scarlatina Maligna 146–7, 176
  Tertian 112, 214
  Typhus/Typhoid 11, 50, 100, 101, 124, 143, 154, 159, 176, 177, 180, 184, 215
  Walcheren 57, 100, 215
Fewster (Newster), John 136
Field Sports 1, 4, 7, 24, 25, 52, 56, 64, 72, 73, 74, 78, 83–5, 89, 90, 102, 104, 112, 119–20, 121, 127, 140, 143, 156, 160, 172, 175, 180, 183, 187, 197
Fish-hook extraction 1, 120–1
Fisk, Capt. William Hawley 25, 45, 150, 170, 205
Fistula 54, 88, 180, 213
Flip club 52
Forbes, John 17
Ford, Miss P 191
Forrest, Lady Mary 197
Foulston, John 8, 29, 30, 38, 108
Fowler's Solution 112
France 14, 15, 26, 57
  Boulogne, The Pillar 57
  Calais 94
  Dieppe 106
  Dijon 104
  Lyons 95–6, 103, 105
  Paris 14, 15, 16, 94–5, 105–6, 110, 120, 147
    Académie des Sciences 18, 204, 207
    École de Médecine 14, 147
    Institut de France 14, 94, 105
    Société Médicale d'Émulation 105, 204
  Rouen 106
Frederick, Prince Augustus *see* Duke of Sussex
French Revolutionary wars *see* Napoleonic wars
French, Tommy 156
Fuge, John Hele 37, 110, 123, 146, 161, 172, 186
Fulford, Col. 177

Fulford, Mr 159
Fundus 159, 213

Gall stones *see* Calculi
Gasking Mrs 133
Geneva 95, 96, 103, 104, 105
German key 10, 49, 119, 213
Gest, Mr 122, 142, 147, 155, 182
  Mrs 171
Gillies, Mrs 112, 115, 116, 120
Glasgow 110, 116, 118, 119, 144, 207
  Harley's Cow-houses 110
  Hunterian Museum 110
Glaucoma 44, 213
Gloucester 130, 131, 134, 136–7, 189, 211
  Guildhall 136–7
Glyster 54, 213
Goodman, James 153
Gosling, Mary 89, 159
  Thomas 158, 159
Goulard's Extract/Liniment 78, 153, 213
Gout 74, 115, 142, 194; *see also* Rheumatic
  gout
Graefe, Dr 44
Grant, Mrs 109, 110, 115
Granulation *see* Corneitis
Granville, Augustus Bozzi 16, 106, 205
Great Exhibition 3, 191, 204
Great Fulford Park 159
Great Western Railway 31
Gregory, Dr James 109, 113, 205
Grizel, Abbé 90
Grove, Capt. Thomas 39
Grumous Blood 181, 213
Guillotine 95–6
Gully, John 58, 59
Gunning, Mr 77, 83, 84
Guthrie, Professor 128, 154
Gutta Serena *see* Amaurosis

Haemorrhage 65, 82, 105, 112, 122, 153,
  158, 162, 164
Haigh, Mr & Mrs 72, 73, 74
Halient 113, 213
Hallett, Mrs 121
Hamilton, Dr James 114, 205
Hamlyn, Betty 168
Hammick, Mr 128–9
Harding, Sheila née Ashford 1
Harford 156, 159, 168
Harness, Dr 86
Harris, W Snow 157
Harrogate 73, 161
Hart, Samuel 28
Harvey, Joshua 112, 117

Hatchard, Rev. John 45
Hatchett, Charles & Mrs 124, 126, 162, 176
Hawkins, Capt. John 23, 56, 74, 80, 82, 183
Hawkins, Stuart 183
Heart disease 70, 72, 88, 103, 110, 142, 148,
  168, 172, 179, 182, 183, 193, 197
Heathfield, Lord 59
Hele's Charity 39
Helmholtz, Hermann von 44
Hemerdon 83, 84
Hernia 53, 54, 55, 79, 82, 86, 87, 95, 137,
  147–8, 213, 215
Hey, William 65, 69, 79, 205
Higher Venmore 4, 5, 7
Hill, John 34, 36, 201, 206, 210
Himalaya, SS 9, 198
Holmes, Dr Andrew Fernando 109, 206
Holmfirth 67, 69
Holwill, Mary *see* Langdon
Home, Professor 113, 115
Honiton 51
Hope, Professor Thomas Charles 113, 115,
  116, 206
Horsfall, William 65, 206
Hosking, Alice 156
Hospitals 13, 14, 16, 20, 22, 28, 77, 79, 165,
  169, 203, 204, 207
  Bath 163
  Bologna 104
  Devon and Exeter 10, 20, 36, 49, 50, 53,
    120, 161, 202, 204, 205, 207, 210
  Devonport, Royal Albert 33
  Devonshire and Cornwall 211
  Dublin 117
  Florence 99, 103
  Greenwich 202
  London 11, 78, 90, 120
    Guy's 11, 34, 53, 201, 203, 210
    Kings College 207
    Moorfields 35, 36, 62, 78, 80, 115, 201
    St Bartholomew's 11, 15, 50, 53, 54,
      98, 155, 161, 166, 201, 202, 207
    St George's 114, 205
    St Thomas' 11, 34, 201, 203, 210
    University 114
    Westminster 209, 210
  Lyons 96
  Milan 96
  Nottingham 61
  Ophthalmic Military 78, 195
  Paris 15, 95, 105, 120
    Hôtel Dieu 14, 95, 120, 202, 204, 206
    Military 14, 18, 94, 105
    Necker 16, 206
  Pavia 97

Plymouth   37, 110
   Derriford   46
      League of Friends   46
   Five Fields   22
   Military   28, 78
   Royal Naval   27, 28, 128, 129, 186,
      192, 204
   Regimental   61
      Chatham   70
      Citadel   76
      Frankfort   26, 82, 83, 84
      Huddersfield   13, 36, 65, 66, 68, 69
      Sheffield   24, 63, 65
      Shorncliffe   57
   Rome   99
   Ships   203
   South Devon and East Cornwall   33, 41
   Turin   96
   Uruguay   205
   Veterinarian   170
   Westminster   209, 210
   York   109
   see also Dispensaries and Infirmaries
Hôtel Dieu see Hospitals, Paris
Howard, Rev. Arscott   176
Howe, Baroness   79
Huddersfield   19, 21, 24, 36, 64–72, 73, 74,
   188–9, 209
Hull, Major   81, 82
Hunt, George   8, 18, 148–9
Hutchinson, Mr   144, 145
Hydrastic purge   57, 213
Hydrocele   114, 213
Hydrophobia   153, 155, 213
Hydrophthalmia   37, 76, 213
Hydrothorax   163, 182, 197, 213
Hythe   55, 56, 57, 58

Ichthyology   95
Ilbert, Peter   89, 90
Iliac arteries   65, 212, 213
Ilium   61, 140, 155, 213
Infection   19, 21, 22, 28, 101, 102, 204, 212,
   213, 215
Infirmaries, Edinburgh Eye   113, 115, 118
   Edinburgh, Royal   15, 207
   Exeter Eye see West of England Eye
   Leeds General   69, 205
   London Eye and London Ophthalmic see
      Hospitals, Moorfields
   Plymouth Royal Eye   1, 4, 7, 23, 34–46,
      122–3, 129, 141, 156, 158, 161, 169–70,
      172, 180, 181, 192, 196, 197, 205
   Sheffield   62

West of England Eye   36, 37, 50, 79, 80,
   201, 202, 204, 205
   see also Dispensaries and Hospitals
Influenza   101, 149
Inguinal   147, 213
Integument   155, 213
Ipecacuanha   16, 116, 213
Iredale, Mrs   147
Ireland   116–17
   Armagh   112, 116, 117
   Belfast   116, 117
   Dublin   117, 213
   Giant's Causeway   116
Iridectomy   44
Issue(s)   31, 40, 88, 152, 178, 213, 214
Italy, Bologna   104, 180
   Florence   98, 99, 103, 104, 127
      Albergo de York   98, 99, 103, 104; see
         also Sambolina, Mr & Mrs
      Waxworks   15, 98
   Genoa   97
   Milan   96, 106, 107, 205
   Naples   102, 103, 106
   Pavia   97, 205, 210
   Pisa   98
   Pontine Marshes   100, 102
   Rome   99, 100, 103, 133, 204
   Turin   4, 96
Ivybridge   75, 88, 143, 144, 155, 158, 168,
   172, 180

Jackman, Sgt   76
Jacobite rebellion   23
Jameson, Professor Robert   109, 111, 114,
   202, 206
Jenner, Edward   45, 136, 190
Jewell, Mr & Mrs   38
Johns, Mr   177–8, 180
Jones, Sgt   134

Kellock, Mr   171, 182
Kilpack, Rev.   182
King, Miss Ann   155
King, Thomas   142–3, 159, 167
   Mrs   142, 147
Kingsbridge   82, 89, 129, 153
Kinsman, Mr   157
Knaresborough Jack see Metcalfe, John

Lacépède, Count Bernard-Germain-Élienne
   de la Ville-sur-Illon   94, 206
Lachrymal passages   44
Lachrymal sac   54, 154, 213
Laénnec, Professor René-Théophile-
   Hyacinthe   16, 17, 110, 206

Laing, David 30
Lamina 78, 213
Lang, Lt Col. 57, 67
Langdon, Agnes *see* Butter
  Gilbert, junior 4, 5, 49
  Gilbert, senior 4, 5
  Gilbert, Rev. Dr 11
  Mary *see* Butter
  Mary née Holwill 5
Larrey, Baron Dominique Jean 14, 18, 94,
  105, 207
Laudanum *see* Opium
Launceston 60, 61, 91
Lawrence, Baron William 35, 50, 94, 124,
  161, 207
Leach, Col. 119
Leach family 75, 82, 87, 105, 109
Leach, Dr William Elford 75, 94, 109, 118,
  124, 142, 149, 157, 207
Leah, Miss 154
Leeches 40, 87, 128, 131, 141, 178, 183, 191
Leeds 65, 68, 73, 79, 205
Leicester 60, 61
Leigham 89, 159
Leslie, Professor Sir John 116, 207
Lew Down 85, 86
Lindsay, Admiral & Mrs 163
Linnean Society 7, 201, 204, 209
Lipson Farm 185
Lister, Joseph 15, 18, 207
Liston, Robert 18, 19, 114, 155, 180, 207
Lithotomy 82, 114, 161, 213; *see also*
  Calculi
Little, Mrs Henry 181
Liver disease 55, 57, 73, 142, 157, 159, 165,
  174, 179, 181, 193, 197
Liverpool 32, 68, 77, 110, 188
Lockyer, Edmund 37, 122, 147, 175, 207
Locock, Sir Charles 162, 208
London 50, 135, 161, 191
  Broad Street, Soho 22
  Cannon Coffee House 107
  Royal College of Physicians 123, 205,
    209, 211
  Royal College of Surgeons 7, 13, 53,
    202, 203, 207, 208, 210
  Royal Society 7, 35, 124, 126, 162, 176,
    201, 203, 205, 207, 208, 210
Lopes, Manasseh Masseh 37, 208
Lopes, Sir Ralph 41, 139, 148, 170, 196, 208
Lostwithiel 91, 149
Lucas, John 45, 197, 198, 208
Luddites 1, 22, 24, 25, 60, 61, 65, 67, 68,
  69, 206, 209
Lumber abscess 18, 105, 108

Lunar caustic 153, 213
Luscombe, John 37, 50, 91, 123, 141
Lyme Regis 52, 55, 93, 110–11, 125, 157
Lympstone 5, 59, 85, 142

Mackenzie, Miss 63
Magrath, Sir George 144, 145, 162, 164,
  165, 166, 208
Malaria *see* Fever
Mallack, Capt. 161, 168, 172
Malvern Wells 186
Manchester 32, 68, 77, 110, 171, 188
Mare, Charles John 8–9, 39, 194, 195, 196,
  197, 198–9, 208
Marshall, Dr 122, 191
Martello Towers 55, 57
Mastectomy 19, 66, 122, 135, 145; *see also*
  Breast, compression of
Materia medica 11, 109, 116, 213
Medulla 158, 213
Menai Straits Bridge 187–8, 208
Mengles, Mrs 196, 198
Mennie, Mr 40
Mercury 3, 13, 69, 78, 112, 214
  Oxymuriate of 69
Metcalfe, John 77, 188
Midwifery 11, 19, 114, 205, 212
Milford, Samuel 50, 79
Militia, Act of 1757 23
  Act of 1852 26, 27
  Bedford 61
  Defence Act of 1803 23
  Denbigh 52
  East Devon 177
  Monaghan 26
  North Devon, (2nd) 27, 90, 208, 209
  North Yorks 52
  South Devon (SDM) 1, 5, 14, 20, 22–7,
    51–2, 53, 55–76, 80, 82, 85, 92, 93,
    118, 123, 124, 139, 196, 197
    Band 25, 72, 108
    Medical/Surgical 4, 13, 19, 21, 36, 52,
      55, 57, 59, 61, 63, 66–7, 68–70, 72,
      74, 76, 123, 148
    Mess/Social 4, 24, 26, 52, 57–8, 61,
      67, 70, 73, 74
    Officers (inc. NCOs) 23, 26, 56, 80,
      125, 130, 134, 141, 150, 171, 172, 181,
      183, 185, 190, 193, 205, 209, 211
  Tipperary 57
Miller, Dr 50, 91
Mills Bridge 67, 68
Modbury 159, 171, 182
Mogridge, Mr 145, 154
Molineaux, Thomas 71, 203, 208

Monro(e), Professor Alexander   109, 113, 115, 208
Moore, Edward   37, 41, 45, 46, 123, 141, 146, 177
Moore, Sir John   50, 58, 100
Moreton (hampstead)   73, 115, 202
Morgan, Justice   84, 86
Morley   23, 93, 196
Morley, Countess   41
Morley, Earl of see John Parker
Morley, 2nd Earl of   23, 209
Mortification   95, 153, 154, 213
Mount Edgecumbe, Earl of   39, 41
Mount Wise see Devonport
Murray, Sir John   57

Napoleonic wars   24, 26, 28, 35, 57, 59
Nasdom's splint see Splint
Nates   150, 213
Neale, Patrick   115, 118
Nephritic   191, 213
Newton (Abbot)   50, 172, 174, 175, 192, 197
Norris, James   183
North Huish   142, 147, 159, 167, 179
Nottingham   61, 62, 63, 65

Oedema   197, 212, 214
Omentum   148, 214
Ommanney, Sir Francis   135
Ommanney, Sir John   191, 192, 195
Ophthalmia   34, 36, 37, 50, 66, 74, 76, 78, 79, 115, 123, 129, 138, 152, 167, 202, 204, 214, 215; see also Rheumatic Ophthalmia
Ophthalmology   34, 35, 66, 207
Ophthalmoscope   44
Opium   19, 57, 87, 157
Oreston quarry   29, 124
Ossification/Ossified   148, 167, 214
Ottery (St Mary)   51, 65, 148, 167
Ougier family   4, 193
Owley   8, 139, 144, 156, 158, 160, 162, 164, 167, 171, 172, 173, 174, 175
  Minerva Cottage   160
Oxenham, Rev. Mr   149, 168
Oxford   11, 109, 111, 135, 157, 211

Pack, Major General Sir D   23
Palmer, Roundell   194, 195
Palmerston, Lord   78, 195, 208
Par Vagum   103, 214
Parham   167, 175, 180
Parham, Fox   172, 180
Parham, Judge B   166, 177, 186, 187, 188
Palmerston, Lord   78, 195–6, 208

Paracentesis   197, 214
Parietal bone   144–5, 214
Paris, Dr John Ayrton   91, 209
Parker, John   108, 134, 156, 163, 208, 209, 210
Paroxysm   112, 214
Parry, Mr   184
Paxton, Joseph   3, 188, 189, 191
Peach, Mr   63, 72
Pellew, Sir Israel   76, 209
Pembroke, Earl of   132
Pendarves, Mr, MP   144, 184
Peninsular & Oriental Steam Navigation Company   195
Pennell, Dr   186
Penzance   91, 154, 162, 178, 209
Pericarditis   197, 214
Pericardium   167, 171, 214
Peritoneum   54, 155, 174, 214
Petechial fever   100, 214
Phagedenic ulcer   105, 214
Phrenological Transactions see Edinburgh
Pipon, Captain Philip   134, 209
Pitt, William   67, 98
Playfair, Professor John   109, 116, 209
Plesner's pill   49
Pleura   167, 171, 182, 197, 214
Pleuritic   191, 214
Plymouth   1, 8, 27–33, 80, 86–7, 111
  Athenaeum/Plymouth Institution   7, 28, 90, 176
  Breakwater   8, 29, 32, 109, 124, 134
  Buckland House   39, 43, 46, 170
  Cattewater wharves   31
  Chain bridge   163
  Chamber of Commerce   29
  Chelson Meadow   164
  Citadel   23, 75, 76, 88, 109, 148
  Commercial Port   31
  Cornwall Street   37, 38, 85, 129
  Custom House   30
  Dock/Dockyard   21, 27, 32, 39, 99, 133, 188, 192, 205
  Drake Circus   38
  Drake's Leat   28, 140
  Exchange   29
  Ford Park see Plymouth, Devonport and Stonehouse Cemetery
  Garrison   76, 158, 161
  George Street   8, 13, 20, 121, 127, 163, 165, 175, 177
  Great Western Docks   31
  Guildhall   37, 38, 81, 108, 115, 123, 205
  Hamoaze   26
  Hoe   8, 23, 39, 108, 109

Household of Faith 28
Keyham Steam Yard 32, 175, 195
Laira 25, 31, 134, 182, 194
Libraries, Medical Society 13
    Proprietary 28
    Public 38
Local Board of Health 32–3
Lockyer Street 8, 184
Marsh 30, 84, 85, 134
Medical Officer of Health 33
Medical Society 13, 33
Millbay 29, 30, 31, 140, 165, 195
Millbay Road 39, 43
Mount Wise 192
Mutley 26, 139, 175, 185
Mutley Station 46
Pannier Market 38
Plymouth and Dartmoor Railway 30
Plymouth Devonport and Stonehouse
    Cemetery (Ford Park) 9, 32, 33,
    139, 175, 176, 181, 185, 186; *see also*
    Plymouth, St Andrew's Church,
    Graveyard
Population 30, 32
Princes Square 169
Public Baths 30, 108–9
Public Free School 29
Railway Station 170
Royal Albert Bridge 31
Royal Hotel 29, 38, 87, 124, 179
Royal Union Baths 30
Royal William Victualling Yard 31
St Andrew's Church 9, 87, 125, 160,
    176, 192
    Graveyard 22, 176
Shipbuilding 31–2
Sound 195, 204
Sutton Harbour 29, 31
Theatre 28
Theatre Royal 29
Torpoint Passage 28, 31, 132, 145, 183
Union Road/Street 8, 30, 84, 121, 170
Vocal Association 40
West Hoe Baths 30
Westwell Street 39, 43, 129, 169
Windsor Villas 7, 8, 9, 164, 165, 166,
    167, 169, 175
Plympton 28, 39, 83, 89, 171, 192
Pneumo-gastric 103, 214
Pneumonia 163, 171
Polacca 97–8
Pompey's pillar 78
Pons varolii 158, 214
Porterfield, William 35
Portsmouth 31, 57, 192

Praede, Mr 190
Price, Dr 142, 172
Prideaux, Mrs 177
Priestley, Joseph 18
Prince Regent 30, 36, 106
Princetown 30
Proctor, Ambrose & Mrs 92, 93–6, 105
Prynn Sgt 185
Ptosis 43, 214
Pulmonary 55, 70, 102, 142, 143, 145, 148,
    149, 153, 171, 193, 214
Punctum 54, 214
Purging 49, 54, 140, 149
Purulent 78, 100, 142, 174, 193, 214

Quack 35, 69, 88
Quick Silver Mail 150
Quinine (incl. bark) 69, 88, 100
Quinsy 21, 70, 74, 214

Radcliffe, Miss 192
Radcliffe, Sir Joseph 67, 68, 70, 72, 209
Rae, Sir William 192, 209
Rape 3, 172
Rashleigh, Miss 152, 154, 159, 175
Rawfall's Mill 65
Rendel, James Meadows 31, 136
Rendle, Dr Edmund 40
Rennie, John (junior) 29, 31
Rennie, John (senior) 29, 31, 126
Repton, Mr 151
Restormel Castle 149
Reynolds, Sir Joshua 28, 45, 208
Rheumatic gout 99, 141
Rheumatic ophthalmia 154
Rheumatism 73, 115, 140
Richards, Mr 104–7
Rinderpest 100–1, 102
Ringworm 10, 215
Rochester 24, 52
Rolle, Lord John 5, 38, 41, 81, 82, 127, 209
    Birthdays 152, 157, 161
    Bicton 68, 151–2, 162, 163
    SDM 23, 24, 26, 51, 56, 62, 71, 93,
    107–8, 109, 116, 118, 124, 125
    Lady Louisa 41, 151, 162
Rolt, Peter 194, 198
Rosie, Mr & Mrs 121
Rowe, Carpenter 161
Rowe, Mr & Mrs 38, 85
Royal Academy 28, 99, 203, 204, 208
Royal College of Physicians *see* Edinburgh
    and London
Royal College of Surgeons *see* Edinburgh
    and London

Royal Hotel, Chester 187
Royal Hotel, Derby 189
Royal Marines 25, 28, 157
Royal Society *see* Edinburgh *and* London
Royal Western Yacht Club 7
Royse, Rev. N 197
Runell, Mr 136
Russia 16, 26, 101, 205

Sadler, Lt Benjamin 130, 131
St Germans, Earl of 41
St Vitus Dance 110, 122, 214
Saltram 134, 163, 208
Sambolina Mr & Mrs 98, 103, 104; *see
    also* Italy, Florence, Albergo de York
Sarcocele 114, 214
Sargent, Mr 144
Saumarez, Lord James 134, 209
Saunders, John Cunningham 34, 35, 36,
    62, 78, 79, 201, 210
Savage, Rev. 156, 159
Savigny, Paul 60, 210
Scarlatina maligna/scarlet fever *see* Fever
Scarpa, Professor Antonio 14, 35, 79, 97,
    118, 210
Sclerotic 79, 177, 212, 213, 214
Scotland 1, 15, 16, 110, 114, 205
Scott, Col. 68
Scott, Sir Walter 82, 109, 203
Scrofula 66, 69, 178, 214
Seale, Sir John Henry 13, 23, 56, 57, 93,
    118, 210
Seaton 156
Seccombe, Mr 76, 175
Seton 152, 214
Shapter, Dr 164
Sheffield 24, 25, 62, 63, 64, 65, 68, 71, 72,
    88, 189
  Festival Orchestra 25
Sheldon, John 34, 210
Shorncliffe 25, 55, 58, 59, 60; *see also*
    Hospitals, Regimental *and* Barracks
Shrewsbury 187
Sicmoid flexure 155, 214
Simmons, Henry 167
Simpson, Professor Sir James Young 15,
    18, 19, 114, 210
Sims, Mr 162
Sloughing 105, 150, 168, 169, 214
Smallpox 77, 101, 102, 136, 193, 209
Smerdon, Thomas 144
Smith, Jane/Jenny 87, 157
Snow, Dr John 18, 19, 22, 114, 210
Snow, Thomas 138

South Brent 22, 137, 140, 164, 172–3, 182,
    185, 194
South Devon Railway 30, 31, 32, 170, 171,
    174, 182, 185
Southampton 161
Speke, William 116, 118–19, 120
Splint 3, 147
  Boyer's 120
  Hagsdoris' 148
  Nasdom's 20, 120, 150, 213
Square, William Joseph 41, 45, 46, 148,
    152, 155, 172, 177
Square, William, junior 41
Squinting 43, 44, 125, 157
Squire, Miss Clarissa 178
Stafford, Mr 195
Stanford, Mr 112, 116
Staphyloma 171, 177, 214
Stephenson, George 77, 109, 188
Stephenson, Robert 115, 202, 208
Sterling, Mr 193
Stethoscope 1, 3, 15–18, 110, 206
Stewart, Dugald 109, 211
Stokes, Mr 124
Stonehouse 8, 27, 32, 37, 43, 128, 129, 130,
    132, 154, 157, 166, 204
  Bridge 28
  Creek 28, 31
  Dock 8, 121
  Lane 22, 85, 185
  Leat 28
  Pool 128
  Sanitary District 32–3
Style 54, 154, 214
Suppuration/Suppurative 178, 197, 214
Sussex, Duke of 41
Symons, Col. 171
  Miss Dorothea 76
  Mrs 37, 76
  Salton 171
Syphilis/Syphiloma 3, 43, 214

Talbot, Frances, Countess of Morley 41
Tally Ho coach 174
Tanner, Charles 152
Tapeworm 68
Tar Ointment 49
Tavistock 84, 85, 86, 91, 128, 142, 197, 210
  Turnpike Road 75
Taxidermy 88, 92
Teignmouth 21, 121, 132, 174, 175, 178, 190
Telford, Thomas 188
Templer, Major 172
Territorial and Reserve Forces Act, 1907
    27

Tewksbury   73
Thalamus   158, 214
Tincea capita   49, 214
Tithe Commutation Act   155–6
Tobacco glyster   54, 215
Todhunter, Mr   117
Toll, Capt.   58, 59, 63, 83
Tolpuddle   4
Tompson, Mr   179
Tonsil/tonsillectomy   14, 95, 140, 146
Toothache and extraction   10, 49, 119, 120,
   130–1, 164, 213
Totnes   92, 161, 171, 196
Tottan, Mr   4, 36–7, 76
Tozer, Solomon   168
Trachoma   35, 78, 201, 215
Travers, Benjamin   79, 128
Trelawny, Rev.   179
Trepanning   183, 205, 215
Trewman, Mrs   88
Trichiasis   43, 215
Trocanter   178, 215
Truro   91
Trustee see Butter, John, Executorship
Tuberculosis see pulmonary
Tucker, John, Assistant Surgeon   24, 55, 67
Tucker, John, Surgeon   24, 52, 54, 55, 56,
   93, 125
Tumour   19, 43, 66, 67, 114, 145, 146, 154,
   158, 159, 174, 213, 214
Turnock Joyce   4
Typhus/Typhoid see Fever
Tyrwhitt, Sir Thomas   30

Ugborough   8, 135, 137
Universities, Cambridge   178–9
   Edinburgh   109, 111, 115, 123, 204, 205,
      206, 207, 208, 209
      Medical School   15, 202, 207
   Glasgow   207
   Gottingen   35
   London   18, 114, 207
   McGill   206
   Modena   210
   Padua   210
   Pavia   205, 210
   St Andrews   203, 207, 208

Vaccination   101
Vascular   158, 215
Veale, Betty   8
   Elizabeth White see Butter
   John   8
Venesection   3, 21, 54, 55, 59, 63, 66, 78,
   92, 105, 112, 125, 126, 128, 135–6, 138,
   141, 143, 148, 149, 151, 152, 162, 163,
   164, 171, 182, 197, 215
Venmore   7; see also Higher Venmore
Ventral hernia   54, 55, 215
Vertebrae   88, 168–9, 182, 215
Vesuvius   102
Veterinary Medicine   50, 63, 72, 102, 149,
   150, 170
Victoria, Queen   19, 144, 157, 158, 179, 203,
   207, 208, 209
Vinnicombe, General   128, 161
   Mary Ann   168
   Mrs   168
Vitreous humour   77, 79, 158, 215

Waldegrove, Lord   62
Wales, Prince of   3, 41, 162
Waller, Sir Jonathan Wathen   79, 211
Ware, James   79
Warleigh Mansion   126
Webber, Barnard   126
Welsford, Louisa   75, 76, 87, 93, 152, 171
   Mr   74, 75, 76, 87, 115
   Mrs   76, 87, 105, 158
Wenzel, Baron de   34–5, 79, 210
Wernerian Society   7, 89, 111, 206
West of England Institution for the Deaf and
   Dumb   7
West of England Provincial Medical &
   Surgical Association   186
Westwood Park   186–7
Wheeler, Charles   166
Whewell, Rev. Dr   160
Whiddon, Mr/Mrs   124, 134, 179
Whiddon, Rev.   179
Whipple, Mr   159, 196
Whitaker, Miss & Mrs   73
White, James   50, 63
White, Robert   24, 52
Whitworth doctors   69
William IV   150; see also Duke of Clarence
Williams, Dr. (Quack)   88
Williams, John   157, 170
Williams Lt   175
Williams, Rev. Dr   192
Wilton House   131–2
Wise, Admiral   128, 170
Wise, George Furlong   153
Wishart, Mr   118
Wood, James   137, 211
Woodbury   4–5, 49, 51, 65, 81, 107, 137,
   150–1, 153, 154, 161–2, 172, 174, 175
   Camp/Castle   81, 153
   Common   51, 108
Woodovis   84

Woollcombe, Henry   136, 175, 176
Woollcombe, Dr William   76, 87, 125, 166,
     211
Wootton Courtney   4
Worcester   186
Wrangaton   8

Yarde-Buller, Col. John, Lord Churston
     26, 124–5, 150, 162, 196, 198, 203, 211
Yonge, Dr James   125, 211
York   70, 109, 147
Young, Thomas   35

Zumbo   98

DEVON AND CORNWALL
RECORD SOCIETY PUBLICATIONS

Previous volumes are available from Boydell & Brewer Ltd.

A Shelf List of the Society's Collections, ed. S. Stride, revised 1986

New Series

1 *Devon Monastic Lands: Calendar of Particulars for Grants 1536–1558*, ed. Joyce Youings, 1955

2 *Exeter in the Seventeenth Century: Tax and Rate Assessments 1602–1699*, ed. W. G. Hoskins, 1957

3 *The Diocese of Exeter in 1821: Bishop Carey's Replies to Queries before Visitation, Vol. I Cornwall*, ed. Michael Cook, 1958

4 *The Diocese of Exeter in 1821: Bishop Carey's Replies to Queries before Visitation, Vol. II Devon*, ed. Michael Cook, 1960

5 *The Cartulary of St Michael's Mount*, ed. P. L. Hull, 1962

6 *The Exeter Assembly: Minutes of the Assemblies of the United Brethren of Devon and Cornwall 1691–1717, as Transcribed by the Reverend Isaac Gilling*, ed. Allan Brockett, 1963

7 *The Register of Edmund Lacy, Bishop of Exeter 1420–1455, Vol. 1*, ed. G. R. Dunstan

8 *The Cartulary of Canonsleigh Abbey*, ed. C. M. Vera, 1965

9 *Benjamin Donn's Map of Devon 1765*, Introduction by W. L. D. Ravenhill, 1965

10 *The Register of Edmund Lacy, Bishop of Exeter 1420–1455, Vol. 2*, ed. G. R. Dunstan, 1966

11 *Devon Inventories of the 16th & 17th Centuries*, ed. Margaret Cash, 1966

12 *Plymouth Building Accounts of the 16th & 17th Centuries*, ed. Edwin Welch, 1967

13 *The Register of Edmund Lacy, Bishop of Exeter 1420–1455, Vol. 3*, ed. G. R. Dunstan, 1968

14 *The Devonshire Lay Subsidy of 1332*, ed. Audrey M. Erskine, 1969

15 *Churchwardens' Accounts of Ashburton 1479–1580*, ed. Alison Hanham, 1970

16 *The Register of Edmund Lacy, Bishop of Exeter 1420–1455, Vol. 4*, ed. G. R. Dunstan, 1971

17 *The Caption of Seisin of the Duchy of Cornwall 1337*, ed. P. L. Hull, 1971

18 *The Register of Edmund Lacy, Bishop of Exeter 1420–1455, Vol. 5*, ed. G. R. Dunstan, 1972

19 *A Calendar of Cornish Glebe Terriers 1673–1735*, ed. Richard Potts, 1974

20 *John Lydford's Book: The Fourteenth-Century Formulary of the Archdeacon of Totnes*, ed. Dorothy M. Owen, 1975 (with Historical Manuscripts Commission)

21 *A Calendar of Early Chancery Proceedings relating to West Country Shipping 1388–1493*, ed. Dorothy A. Gardiner, 1976

22 *Tudor Exeter: Tax Assessments 1489–1595*, ed. Margery M. Rowe, 1977

23 *The Devon Cloth Industry in the 18th Century*, ed. Stanley D. Chapman, 1978

24 *The Accounts of the Fabric of Exeter Cathedral 1279–1353, Part I*, ed. Audrey M. Erskine, 1981

25 *The Parliamentary Survey of the Duchy of Cornwall, Part I*, ed. Norman J. G. Pounds, 1982

26 *The Accounts of the Fabric of Exeter Cathedral 1279–1353, Part II*, ed. Audrey M. Erskine, 1983

27 *The Parliamentary Survey of the Duchy of Cornwall, Part II*, ed. Norman J. G. Pounds, 1984

28 *Crown Pleas of the Devon Eyre 1238*, ed. Henry Summerson, 1985

29 *Georgian Tiverton, The Political Memoranda of Beavis Wood 1768–98*, ed. John Bourne, 1986

30 *The Cartulary of Launceston Priory (Lambeth Palace MS.719): A Calendar*, ed. P. L. Hull, 1987

31 *Shipbuilding on the Exe: The Memoranda Book of Daniel Bishop Davy (1799–1874) of Topsham, Devon*, ed. Clive N. Ponsford, 1988

32 *The Receivers' Accounts of the City of Exeter 1304–1353*, ed. Margery Rowe and John M. Draisey, 1989

33 *Early-Stuart Mariners and Shipping: The Maritime Surveys of Devon and Cornwall 1619–35*, ed. Todd Gray, 1990

34 *Joel Gascoyne's Map of Cornwall 1699*, Introduction by W. L. D. Ravenhill and O. J. Padel, 1991

35 *Nicholas Roscarrock's 'Lives of the Saints': Cornwall and Devon*, ed. Nicholas Orme, 1992

36 *The Local Customs Accounts of the Port of Exeter 1266–1321*, ed. Maryanne Kowaleski, 1993

37 *Charters of the Redvers Family and the Earldom of Devon 1090–1217*, ed. Robert Bearman, 1994

38 *Devon Household Accounts, 1627–59, Part I: Sir Richard and Lady Lucy Reynell of Forde House, 1627–43, John Willoughby of Leyhill, 1644–6, and Sir Edward Wise of Sydenham, 1656–9*, ed. Todd Gray, 1995

39 *Devon Household Accounts 1627–59, Part II: Henry, Earl of Bath, and Rachel, Countess of Bath, of Tawstock and London, 1639–54*, ed. Todd Gray, 1996

40 *The Uffculme Wills and Inventories, 16th to 18th Centuries*, ed. Peter Wyatt, with Introduction by Robin Stanes, 1997

41 *The Cornish Lands of the Arundells of Lanherne, Fourteenth to Sixteenth Centuries*, ed. H. S. A. Fox and O. J. Padel, 1998

42 *Liberalism in West Cornwall: The 1868 Election Papers of A. Pendarves Vivian MP*, ed. Edwin Jaggard, 1999

43 *Devon Maps and Map-Makers: Manuscript Maps before 1840*, ed. with Introduction Mary R. Ravenhill and Margery M. Rowe, 2000

44 *The Havener's Accounts of the Earldom and Duchy of Cornwall, 1287–1356*, ed. Maryanne Kowaleski, 2001

45 *Devon Maps and Map-Makers: Manuscript Maps before 1840*, ed. with Introduction Mary R. Ravenhill and Margery M. Rowe, 2002

46 *Death and Memory in Medieval Exeter*, ed. David Lepine and Nicholas Orme, 2003

47 *The Survey of Cornwall by Richard Carew*, ed. John Chynoweth, Nicholas Orme and Alexandra Walsham, 2004

48 *Killerton, Camborne and Westminster: The Political Correspondence of Sir Francis and Lady Acland, 1910–1929*, ed. Garry Tregidga, 2006

49 *The Acland Family: Maps and Surveys 1720–1840*, ed. with Introduction Mary R. Ravenhill and Margery M. Rowe, 2006

50 *Cornish Wills 1342–1540*, ed. Nicholas Orme, 2007

51 *The Letter Book of Thomas Hill 1660–1661*, ed. June Palmer, 2008

52 *Collecting the New, Rare and Curious: Letters Selected from the Correspondence of the Cornish Mineralogists Philip Rashleigh, John Hawkins and William Gregor, 1755–1822*, ed. R. J. Cleevely, 2011

53 *Robert Furse: A Devon Family Memoir of 1593*, ed. Anita Travers, 2012

54 *The Minor Clergy of Exeter Cathedral: Biographies, 1250–1548*, Nicholas Orme, 2013

55 *The Chancery Case between Nicholas Radford and Thomas Tremayne: the Exeter Depositions of 1439*, ed. Hannes Kleineke, 2013

56 *Elizabethan Inventories and Wills of the Exeter Orphans' Court, Vol. 1*, ed. Jeanine Crocker, 2016

57 *Elizabethan Inventories and Wills of the Exeter Orphans' Court, Vol. 2*, ed. Jeanine Crocker, 2016

58 *Devon Parish Taxpayers, Vol. 1, Abbotskerswell to Beer & Seaton*, ed. Todd Gray, 2016

59 *Devon Parish Taxpayers, Vol. 2, Bere Ferrers to Chudleigh*, ed. Todd Gray, 2017

60 *Stratton Churchwardens' Accounts, 1512–1578*, ed. Joanna Mattingly, 2018

61 *A Lord Lieutenant in Wartime: The Experiences of the Fourth Earl Fortescue during the First World War*, Richard Batten, 2018

62 *Sir Francis Henry Drake (1723–1794): Letters from the Country, Letters from the City*, ed. Charity Scott-Stokes and Alan Lumb, 2019

63 *The Exeter Cloth Dispatch Book, 1763–1765*, ed. Todd Gray, 2021

64 *James Davidson's East Devon Church Notes*, ed. Jill Cobley, 2022

65 *Devon Parish Taxpayers, Vol. 3, Churchstow to Dunkeswell*, ed. Todd Gray, 2022

Devon Maps and Map-makers: Manuscript Maps before 1840. Supplement to Volumes 43 and 45, ed. Mary R. Ravenhill and Margery M. Rowe, 2010

Extra Series

1 *Exeter Freemen 1266–1967*, ed. Margery M. Rowe and Andrew M. Jackson, 1973

2 *Guide to the Parish and Non-Parochial Registers of Devon and Cornwall 1538–1837*, ed. Hugh Peskett, 1979, supplement 1983

3 *William Birchynshaw's Map of Exeter, 1743*, ed. Richard Oliver, Roger Kain and Todd Gray, 2019